The Nature of History

The Explosion of British Society 1914–1962 (1963)

Clifford Allen: The Open Conspirator (1964)

The Deluge: British Society and the First World War (1965)

Britain in the Century of Total War: War, Peace and Social Change, 1900–1967 (1968)

The Explosion of British Society 1914–1970 (1971)

War and Social Change in the Twentieth Century (1974)

The Home Front: The British and the Second World War (1976)

Women at War 1914–1918 (1977)

Class: Image and Reality in Britain, France and the USA since 1930 (1980)

(editor) *The Illustrated Dictionary of British History* (1980)

British Society since 1945 (Expanded edition 1989)

Beauty in History: Society, Politics and Personal Appearance c. 1500 to Present (1988)

(editor) *Total War and Social Change* (1988)

(editor) *The Arts, Literature and Society* (1989)

The Nature of History

Third Edition

ARTHUR MARWICK

LYCEUM
BOOKS INC

224 S. Michigan Ave.
Chicago, IL 60604

First published 1973. Third edition 1989

Published in Great Britain by
MACMILLAN EDUCATION LTD.
Houndmills, Basingstoke, Hampshire RG21 2XS
and London

This U.S. edition published by
LYCEUM BOOKS, INC.
224 S. Michigan Avenue
Chicago, Illinois 60604

Printed in the People's Republic of China

Library of Congress Cataloging-in-Publication Data

Marwick, Arthur, 1936–
  The nature of history.

  Bibliography: p
  Includes index.
  1. Historiography.   I. Title.
D13.M32 1989   907.2   89-2786

ISBN 0-925065-00-5

Contents

Preface

This has always been a simple, utilitarian book aimed at students and general readers looking for a straightforward guide to the methods and purposes of historical study. It seeks to explore the nature of historical evidence, to show how history comes to be written, and to offer a basis on which 'good' history can be distinguished from 'bad'. The original edition was published in 1970, with a partially revised second edition appearing in 1981. This edition retains the same basic objectives and much of the old structure. But I have written an entirely fresh typescript, leaving few passages unaltered in some way, deleting a fair amount, and introducing a good deal of new material. The new edition is markedly less Britannocentric than the old, though my knowledge and experience continue to be limited to historical studies in the West (Before I am castigated for cultural myopia, I would point out that while finishing this text I was also planning and organizing an International Symposium on 'Chinese Civilisation and European Civilisation: Separation and Contact').

Over the period of the life of the book, which coincides with my period of employment at the Open University, I have learned greatly from colleagues and students. It is only proper, however, that I should re-acknowledge, first of all, the two scholars who, with advice on and criticism of my entire text, contributed vitally to the successful completion of the initial enterprise – Lord Bullock and Mr Owen Dudley Edwards – and, second, others who gave critical help at that early stage – Professors Denys Hay, A. J. P. Taylor, Max Beloff, Harry Hanham, John Bromley, James Joll, Christopher Hill, Eric Hobsbawm, Raymond O. Rockwood, John T. Halstead, Tom Burns, Paul Smith, and Christopher Harvie, and Drs Henry Pelling, Eric Forbes, and Neil Wynn.

I now wish to thank my colleagues Clive Emsley, Tony Lentin and Bill Purdue who have commented most helpfully on the new text, and Gill Wood, who typed it.

Chapter 1 Justifications and Definitions

1. The Past, History, Sources and Myths

What happened in the past profoundly affects all aspects of our lives in the present and will, indeed, affect what happens in the future. In almost every city, town, village or country throughout the world the overwhelming majority of buildings currently in existence was built in past times to meet the needs and aspirations of human beings now dead and societies now in greater or lesser degree changed, or even defunct. This is most obviously so with respect to great temples and cathedrals, fine palaces and manor houses and castles, city halls, houses of parliament and other public buildings; but it is also true of the most humdrum streets and the meanest housing. Look around at the areas of conflict across the globe which every second experience death and destruction, in the Indian sub-continent and Sri Lanka, in the Persian Gulf, in Palestine and the Lebanon, in the Republic of South Africa and neighbouring territories, in Central America, in Northern Ireland, in the Basque regions of Spain. Past movements of population, past oppression by the then-mighty of the then-weak, religious faiths and communal identities established in the past, often the very distant past, everywhere are the fundamental sources of tension and conflict. Systems of government (as well as the buildings which embody them), political ideas (radical as well as conservative), beliefs about art and culture, educational practices, customs and behaviour are all products of the past, recent and remote.

Put this way the case that the past is important, the past is all-pervasive, that, indeed, we can't escape from the past, is persuasive. But what exactly is 'the past'? From the examples given, clearly it signifies 'what actually happened' – events (battles, assassinations, invasions, general elections) which have

taken place, societies which have risen and fallen, ideas and institutions, eating habits, marital customs, all aspects of human
behaviour in the past, matters large and small. All that is clear
enough; but the big difficulty with the past is that though most of
us find no difficulty in believing in a past that actually happened,
by definition it does not actually exist now, it is 'past', it has gone
for good. This is related both to that elusive but all-absorbing
concept, 'time', and to the fact of human mortality. What I have
been speaking of is the past of human activities, of human
societies, of, in fact, 'the human past' (no doubt the cosmic past
has affected human evolution, but that is another subject). Human
beings die, human families, human communities, sometimes
whole nations die out. More important is the phenomenon of the
passing of time, fascinating – as is shown by all the literature,
weighty and trivial, about defying time, about time capsules and
travel in time – but ineluctable, as we all in the very depths of
our fibre appreciate.

The past, then, no longer exists, it has gone for good. It has
left relics and traces – most obviously, the buildings, the cities,
the streets which are open to every gaze; less obviously, the
billions upon billions of sources of all types which have to be
sought out in libraries, and archives and in archaeological digs.
Traces of the past exist too in the memories, traditions and
ceremonies which are relayed on from generation to generation.
All human societies betray a preoccupation with their own past,
whether through ancestor worship, the invocation of past triumphs
by 'witch doctors' or 'medicine men', the scriptures and chronicles
of holy men and monks, or the regular mounting of national
parades and ceremonies. Much, of course, of what is preserved,
celebrated, and passed on from age to age may have only a
tenuous relationship to the past as it really happened; much of it
may well be 'myth' or 'fable'. But then myth believed by one
generation and passed on to the next also becomes a part of this
awesomely large and complex cluster of events and ideas, great
systems and trivial pursuits, 'the past'.

The two-fold point, at once so simple and so fraught with
devilish implications which this opening disquisition seeks to drive
home, is that while the past is manifestly important it is also
impossible to apprehend *directly* (as one might apprehend the
mountain and river system of Europe, the production and collec-

tion in a laboratory of H₂S gas, or the functions of the heart in pumping blood round the human body): it can only be apprehended through memories, myths, and, most important, through the relics and 'sources', archaeological, written, printed, painted, etc., etc., – which it leaves.

Thus far – have you noticed? – I have not used the words 'history', 'historian', or 'historical'. I have done this deliberately in order to demonstrate that, even though at any given point in time, the past no longer exists (an issue which tends to bother philosophers), the phrase itself (or, more exactly, the phrase 'the human past') is meaningful and viable, with a legitimate usage signifying 'that which actually happened' (and, by extension, that which has entailed the pre-conditions for so many bloody problems in the world of the present, as well as the political systems, cultural standards and modern conveniences which today we – according to taste, and of course geographical location – enjoy or don't enjoy); and further to demonstrate that in this usage 'the past' (or 'the human past') is a clearer and more precise locution than 'history.' True, in the rather loose usage of everyday speech we do sometimes use the word 'history' when what is really meant is 'the human past.' There is nothing we can do about ordinary usage, but in serious discussion and in serious study it is best always to use words in the most rigorous way possible.

Actually, it is that very two-fold character of the past I have just identified which accounts for the coming into existence of 'history', in the rough and ready sense of 'the attempt by human beings to give a continuing, present existence to what no longer actually exists, the past' (I'll offer sharper definitions later). Because the past is important to the present most societies have felt a need to produce some sort of account or *interpretation* of their past, usually, because of the impossibility of directly apprehending the past, rather unsatisfactory ones. Because of this very impossibility the profession, or discipline of history arose, using the special skills of analysing and interpreting sources as the only possible means of getting to grips with the past. The Greek word from which our 'history' is derived meant 'enquiry', in the sense both of the processes of enquiry and of the report resulting from this enquiry. History, then, is an interpretation of the past, one in which a serious effort has been made to filter out myth and fable. As interpretations of the past multiplied down the ages, something like a body of knowledge about the past began to accumulate (since it derived from the interpretations of different individual historians it was never completely consistent, in places it could be downright contradictory – a matter upon which those who are sceptical about the value of history are apt to seize). But what is the purpose of this body of knowledge? Surely (I say 'surely' because I know I am on contentious ground here) it is to, as it were, open up the past, to make the past, or rather those parts of the past thought to be of interest or significance, known and comprehensible. Thus, the meaning of 'history' is often extended, even in serious discourse, beyond 'interpretation' and 'body of knowledge' to signify 'that which this body of knowledge relates to,' that is to say 'those parts of what actually happened (the past) which have been described and explained, and whose significance has been expounded, by historians.' Maybe this is a dubious, perhaps merely rhetorical, usage, but usage it certainly is.

Consider these statements:

(1) 'People, not the environment, make History; yet the conditions under which history is made are circumscribed by the physical environment . . .' (a genuine quotation from the opening sentence of Edward Royle's excellent textbook *Modern Britain: A Social History 1750–1985* (1987));

(2) 'Ideas are a more powerful force in history than economics' (I've just made this one up);

(3) 'Everything has a history, including underwear and alcoholic drinks' (and this one);

(4) 'Celebrating the 70th anniversary of the Revolution, the Soviet leader has exhorted his fellow citizens to face their history: but the legacy of the past may yet defeat him' (a genuine sub-heading which appeared in a British newspaper – *The Independent*, 6 November 1987 – while I was writing this chapter).

(1) It would be possible (just!) to rewrite the statement, 'People, not the environment, make the human past; yet the conditions under which the human past is made are circumscribed by the physical environment', or, even more pedantically, 'People, not the environment, make what actually happened in the past; yet the conditions under which what actually happened in the past is made are circumscribed by the physical environment', but it is practically impossible to imagine any user of standard English

actually doing so. The notions of 'making' and 'being made' are rhetorical and metaphorical, and, sitting uneasily with the human past or 'what actually happened', call for the word 'history'. If the first clause were rephrased, 'People, not the environment, make interpretations of, or the body of knowledge about, the past', it would have a kind of banal truth, but the meaning would have been totally altered; the second clause certainly could not be rephrased, 'yet the conditions under which interpretations of, or the body of knowledge about, the past are made are circumscribed by the physical environment.' What Royle wished to convey is that people themselves have been the most important element in those aspects of the past he considers to be significant, but that these aspects have also been affected by the physical environment. The phrase could, of course, be totally rewritten to read: 'According to my [Royle's] interpretation of the past (or according to the established body of knowledge about the past), people determine what actually happens, but (still according to that interpretation or that body of knowledge) the physical environment imposes certain constraints.' This sounds not merely pedantic but otiose. Evidently in using 'history' as he does, Royle intends that word (both times) to mean something like 'those significant aspects of the past which are suitable for, and worthy of, study in a book such as the one he is writing'.

(2) Well, try substituting all the other possible definitions of 'history' and there is an imperfect fit each time. The meaning is something like: 'In those parts of the past which I (or historians in general) have examined, ideas can be shown to be a more powerful force than economics.'

(3) 'Everything has a past . . .' would sound banal and general and without any positive meaning. What is meant is that in those parts of the past investigated by historians there are important and illuminating things to be said about the development of the way in which individuals and societies have used and reacted to underwear and alcoholic drinks.

Statement (4) makes a clear distinction between the past which leaves a legacy, and the history, now being more fully explored than before, which can be 'faced'.

As used today, then, 'history' can mean one, several or all of the following:

(1) What actually happened in the past: better, in my view, described as 'the (human) past.'

(2) The activity of enquiry into that past, based on the rigorous study of sources, and striving conscientiously to challenge myth and legend (not always easy: the twentieth century has its own myths).

(3) The interpretation or interpretations produced by this activity.

(4) The accumulated body of knowledge about the past: being based on the interpretations of fallible human beings (historians), using often fragmentary and imperfect source materials, this knowledge may often be provisional in nature, and sometimes even contradictory.

(5) Those aspects of the past, felt to be significant or interesting, which have been made accessible by historical enquiry and the accumulating body of historical knowledge; those parts of the past which are known and documented; the actuality to which the body of knowledge refers. It may be that this usage of the word 'history' is metaphorical and rhetorical, and that a more rigorous (and long-winded) re-writing could always be found; I am uncertain on this point because, in common with most other historians, I have never been able to forswear using the word 'history' in this way. Words mean what they are used to mean; thus by that token we have here a fifth meaning of the word 'history'.

In my view these five points summarise clearly and sensibly the different ways in which the word 'history' is used: on this basis, a historian today is someone who, essentially through the analysis of sources, produces interpretations of the past, which are contributions to the accumulating body of knowledge about the past, and which together, it may be held, permit aspects of the past and interrelationships between aspects of the past to be viewed as coherent 'history' (in the fifth sense of the term). Some philosophers, however, would remain unhappy about the distinction between, on the one hand, 'the past', and on the other 'the interpretation of, and body of knowledge about, the past', and would be quite outraged at the notion of history as aspects of the actual past. Their argument is that since we can't actually know the past directly our only knowledge of it in fact coincides with what the historians tell us. In our minds, which is what we use as soon as we start talking or arguing about what we may think of as the past or aspects of it, the past can have no existence independent of the history created by historians. The past, what actually happened, even if we could apprehend it directly, is in any case uncomprehendable in its vastness, comprising as it does *all* actions, *all* thoughts, *all* products of *all* human beings who have ever lived. The past we think we are talking about, this line of argument continues, is really a past upon which order has been imposed, sequences have been organised, the *significant* has been highlighted; there is no 'real' past, independent of the activities of historians; thus *a fortiori* the idea of 'history' as 'aspects of the past in which relationships and sequences have been revealed' is absurd.

Personally, as already indicated, I reject the contention that it is not meaningful to speak of a past independent of the activities of historians. Just because one can only comprehend a tiny part of the past, that does not mean that one cannot believe in the existence of the past in all its vastness (one can only have knowledge of a small part of the history produced by historians but that need not prevent us from believing in the existence of the history written by historians). The 'real' existence of the past, as I have said, manifests itself in the relics and traces it leaves. It is possible in standard English to say either 'Parliamentary government is a product of the past' or 'Parliamentary government is a product of history', but it would be manifest nonsense to say 'Parliamentary government is a legacy of the interpretations of historians, or of the body of knowledge produced by historians'. There *is* a difference between 'the past', or 'history used to mean the past', and history as interpretation or body of knowledge. Whether the distinction between history as 'the past' (definition 1) and history as 'significant aspects of the past' (definition 5), and between that and definitions 3 and 4 (interpretation and body of knowledge, respectively) are philosophically fully sustainable, I am less certain: they are, for sure, sanctioned by usage.

However the discussion is a salutary one in reminding us always to be asking ourselves 'how do we know what we know?' or, more relevantly perhaps, 'how do we know what we think we know?' What we know, or think we know, about the past is very thoroughly coloured by what historians have said about the past. Historians don't aim, even if it were possible, to give a breathless narrative of every single thing which happened in the past.

Secondly, whether they are aware of it or not, historians will pick out, from the opening into the past offered them by the sources, what they find interesting, important, or *significant*. Historians impose order, possibly pattern, define relationships and interactions; they decide what to put in and what to leave out; even if aiming at no more than coherent narrative, they are still contributing form or shape to that narrative. In all this, many historians (including myself) would say, there is still a real past which is being engaged with, and that what historians are trying to do is to explain how and why what actually happened did happen. Sharing in the widespread perception that what happens earlier in time plays a part in determining what happens later, historians naturally look for what is significant in this process. But because historians *identify* what, to the best of their abilities, they believe to be significant in the past, that does not mean that they *put* it there, that they invent it, that the significant has no independent existence outside the activities of historians. By that argument, history as 'significant aspects of the past' or 'those parts of the past to which the interpretation of historians, or the body of historical knowledge relates' (the fifth definition) could be held to have a 'real' existence.

But we move into further complexities which we must wrestle through if we are to have a feel for the nature of history in all its aspects. Some philosophers of a slightly different cast, and some historians, would argue that there is another meaning of 'history' which I have not fully allowed for in my five-part definition (though it could be seen as a more thoroughgoing and comprehensive version of definition 5). This sixth definition springs from a conviction that in 'what actually happened' can be discerned not only significant events, developments, patterns, and interrelationships, but indeed one overarching significance or 'meaning', one particular unfolding pattern or purpose. Within this type of conception the phrase 'the past' becomes inadequate, for the meaning, purpose, or pattern is taken to govern not just the past, but the present, and above all, the future as well. Thus for some historians there is inherent in the word 'history' a particularly rich and vibrant level of meaning: history as 'process', linking past, present and future, unfolding in response to certain imperatives, usually (it is held) in a definite direction or series of stages, perhaps in a series of cycles (two classic instances are those of

traditional Marxism and Arnold Toynbee's *A Study of History*).
Readers may well disagree with me (and I shall try to be as fair
as I can), but to me such a conception, and definition, of history
reeks of the nineteenth century. In the late twentieth century –
time of sophisticated methodologies and much scepticism – few
historians can really expect to establish (as distinct, perhaps, from
asserting as an article of faith) the existence of such overarching
patterns. Even when the level-headed and pragmatic historiographer Ernst Breisach defines historical writing ('historiography', he
calls it; why he can't just say 'history', I don't know) as 'reconcili-
ations between past, present, and future'[1] that seems to me viable
more as a rhetorical justification for the study of history than a
serious definition of what history is (I call him a 'historiographer',
incidentally, because what he has written is not history – an
interpretation of, or body of knowledge about, the past – but a
history of such interpretations, a 'history of history' in short,
though he persists in seeing his book as a 'history of historiography', which, correctly, would be a history of all the Breisachs
and their ilk).

There are minor uses of the word 'history' which we can quickly
dismiss before spending some moments on the adjective
'historical'. In medicine, or psychology, or social work it is
customary to speak of a patient's or client's 'case history'. This is
history in its most preliminary sense of a present record of what
actually belongs to the past – in this case the relevant (or what
are thought to be relevant) parts of the past experiences of the
particular patient or client. 'Historical' is often used in this general
way, to mean 'pertaining to a present record of the past', but it
often has to do duty as well for 'pertaining to the past'; indeed,
as we shall see in a moment, it is the way 'historical' is used which
often betrays a belief in history as aspects of the 'real past' or as
'process'. When a journalist writes that the British T.V. series
Yes, Prime Minister (a comedy based on the premise that civil
servants dominate ministers rather than vice versa) 'is now based
on historical rather than contemporary truth'[2] what is meant is
that the premise, now no longer true (no one, but no one, could
dominate Margaret Thatcher), was true in the past (in this case
the very recent past). The meaning is perfectly clear, and probably
as efficiently expressed as language allows, though it would have
been possible to say 'based on past rather than present truth'.

'Historical', equally, can mean 'to do with the study of (or an interest in) history as a discipline and as a body of knowledge': many universities have student 'historical societies', though some (the meaning here is the same) are called 'history societies'.

If this seems a little tiresome, my madness is provoked by concern over certain phrases, frequently encountered in academic writing, particularly egregious examples being 'historical factors', 'historical forces', and 'historical context' (or, 'historical background'). The problem we run into immediately is that every past 'age' or 'period' (problematic words, too, but I'll leave them for a later chapter) was once a present 'age' or 'period' (it was, that is, to the people who lived in it). Every past society has its own particular past. The 'historical factors' or 'historical forces' alleged by a historian to be affecting a particular society are the 'factors' or 'forces' which have their origins in that society's own past. It is a matter of philosophical taste whether these 'factors' or 'forces' belong to a 'real' past or a real 'history' (fifth definition), or simply to an interpretation or body of knowledge. The historian (unless he or she too is troubled by deep philosophical doubt; most historians are not) will believe that he or she is being as true as is humanly possible to the past as it actually happened; the 'factors' or 'forces' are 'real' in that they are based on 'real' evidence. But these 'factors' or 'forces' (metaphors both, but historians have to use such language as comes to hand) may well be estimated differently as the body of knowledge changes. 'Historical background' is not in my view an overly felicitous phrase (how do we determine what is background and what foreground?) but it does instantly indicate that 'historical' here is referring to a different sort of time-scale. The 'historical background', or, more exact phrase, the 'historical context', for the novels of Charles Dickens refers not to what happened in the past prior to the age and society in which Dickens lived, roughly definable as 'Victorian Britain', but to that society itself (though, undoubtedly, many facets of that society were determined by its past). 'Historical context' usually means the 'social, political, economic and cultural circumstances prevailing in the particular society being studied', it being a prime contention of both historians and sociologists that these circumstances will *in some way or another* affect every novel, painting or other cultural artefact produced in that society. It might be clearer to say 'social, cultural, etc., context' ('of the time, or age,' being understood): some writers do say this.

As with the noun 'history', so with the adjective 'historical': some thought, some self-consciousness, is needed when we encounter, and above all, when we *use* it. Historians in their everyday activities, unlike most scientists in their everyday activities, still live in a world where rhetoric and elegance of expression are highly valued: it is important that fine phrasing should not obscure meaning. Thus I propose now to list a number of sentences involving some of the problems of meaning I have been discussing. As you go through the list, you, my reader, are invited to make your own comments on each phrase and the meaning which seems to be intended (perhaps even writing them down); my own comments follow immediately.

(1) War is the locomotive of history.
(2) The past is a fertile source of myth.
(3) Geography is an important influence on history.
(4) We have had too much drum-and-trumpet history.
(5) Ideology plays a crucial role in history.
(6) That T.V. programme was very good as history.
(7) The Gulf War has its roots in history.

My comments:

(1) Obviously, 'history' is seen here as 'what actually happened' but, 'war is the locomotive of the past' would sound rather odd. The phrase is Trotsky's, and as a Marxist he would have meant history as 'process', the sixth meaning I have identified; but taken at face value it could equally well refer to the fifth meaning, 'those aspects of the past explored and explained by historians'. It may be noted once again that it is in metaphorical and rhetorical statements that one most usually encounters the more debatable usages of 'history'.

(2) There is no unambiguous way of re-phrasing this statement. If one substituted 'history' it would not be completely clear whether one did indeed mean history as the past, or whether one were claiming that history as a body of knowledge was a fertile source of myth, a totally different matter.

(3) I have already discussed a not dissimilar (though more complex) sentence. This one (I claim no great originality for it) forms the opening sentence of one of my own books, published in 1968. I do not myself believe in history as process, but

'Geography is an important influence on the past' would not be quite right. What I *was* trying to say is, I think, perfectly clear. A proper gloss would have to take something like the following cumbersome form: 'Geography is an influence on what, according to the interpretations of historians (including myself), actually happens'. Was my usage purely rhetorical, and metaphorical? Or does it not, in fact, *combine* all the main elements of definitions 2 to 5? I think we are making progress, and shall, in a moment, suggest one single all-embracing definition.

(4) Here the reference can only be to the history written by historians: that is to say to history as interpretation or body of (unsatisfactory) knowledge. The view was that of the nineteenth century English historian J. R. Green, who was criticising his colleagues for neglecting social history.

(5) This must either be history as 'process', or history as 'the significant aspects of the past'; or maybe a more inclusive meaning is intended, as in statement 3.

(6) Meanings 3 and 4 are subsumed here, and possibly also meaning 2. In its fullest gloss the sentence would read: 'That T.V. programme was very good as an interpretation of the past conforming to the body of knowledge accumulated by historians and showing elements of the historian's own methods of enquiry.' Perhaps again we are moving towards one single, sensible, all-embracing definition of history.

(7) The clearest and most unambiguous way of expressing this would be: 'The Gulf War has its roots in the past.' The original rendering, however, may be intended to stress that it will take the labours of historians to trace out these roots – once more we are being pushed towards a central definition of history, something like 'the past as we know it through the work of historians.'

In later chapters we shall come to the various sub-histories, 'constitutional history', 'economic history', 'social history', etc. In each case there are all the complexities and nuances of meaning I have just been discussing.

In that long, and perhaps irksome, exposition I have tried to set out the many ways in which the word 'history' is in fact used. For myself, as a result of that last little discussion, I am now happy to commend to readers one simple, central, definition (all the others, it begins to become clear, being corollaries or extensions of this, with some, perhaps, being metaphorical, rhetorical, or even ideological in character). By this definition, History is:

> the past as we know it [or, if a more cautious phrasing is preferred, 'what we know of the past'] from the interpretations of historians based on the critical study of the widest possible range of relevant sources, every effort having been made to challenge, and avoid the perpetuation of, myth.

Sources (to be discussed in detail in a later chapter), as we know, are those traces of all types left by the past. Let us look more closely at myth. The characteristic of myth is that while containing some element, often highly attenuated, of faithfulness to what actually happened in the past, it is also highly distorted or exaggerated, almost invariably with a view to glorifying or asserting the special powers of one particular individual, or family, or community, or nation, or religious faith, or to blackening the character of some perceived enemy. Myths exploit the past in order to serve some current national, political or religious purpose

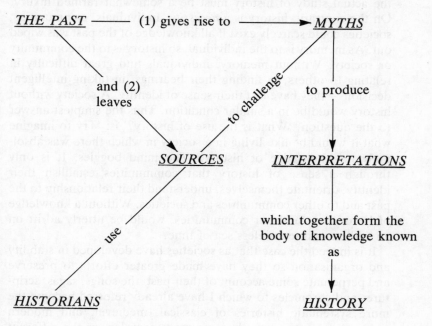

THE PAST —— (1) gives rise to ——▶ *MYTHS*

and (2) leaves

to challenge

to produce

SOURCES　　*INTERPRETATIONS*

use

which together form the
body of knowledge known
as

HISTORIANS　　　　　　*HISTORY*

(See Appendix C). In earlier eras it was often genuinely impossible for chroniclers and 'historians' to distinguish between what
was reasonably accurate and what was entirely mythical. But one
of the purposes of serious historical study is, in advancing understanding of the past, to challenge and deflate myths, while at the
same time, perhaps, explaining their origins and significance.
After my exploration of all the complicated shades of meaning it
may be of value to set out, in very simple schematic fashion, the
relationship between history, as I have just defined it, and the
past, sources, and myths.

2. The Necessity for History

Given the contortions I have had to go through in pinning down
the different ways in which the word 'history' is used, and in
establishing one viable definition, it might well be thought that
the actual study of history must be a somewhat rarified luxury.
On the contrary, history is a *necessity*. Individuals, communities,
societies could scarcely exist if all knowledge of the past was wiped
out. As memory is to the individual, so history is to the community
or society. Without memory, individuals find great difficulty in
relating to others, in finding their bearings, in taking intelligent
decisions – they have lost their sense of identity. A society without
history would be in a similar condition. Thus the simplest answer
to the question, 'What is the use of history?' is: 'Try to imagine
what it would be like living in a society in which there was absolutely no knowledge of history.' The mind boggles. It is only
through a sense of history that communities establish their
identity, orientate themselves, understand their relationship to the
past and to other communities and societies. Without a knowledge
of history we, and our communities, would be utterly adrift on
an endless and featureless sea of time.

It is indeed the case that as societies have developed in stability
and organisation so they have made greater efforts to preserve
and perpetuate some account of their past: the songs, sagas, scriptures and chronicles to which I have already referred become the
more systematic histories of classical, medieval, and modern
times. As societies have become more complex, as the different
areas of the world have become more closely interconnected, so

more rigorous interpretations of the past have become necessary. Every advanced nation has (apart from its historical professions with their own institutes and associations) museums and archives and libraries devoted to the preservation of these sources and relics from the past out of which history is written. Cut into the neo-classical architecture of the National Archives in Washington are the following inscriptions: 'What is Past is Prologue'; 'Study the Past'; 'The glory and romance of our history are here preserved in the chronicles of those who conceived and builded the structure of our nation'; 'The ties which bind the lives of our people in one indissoluble union are perpetuated in the archives of our government and to their custody this building is dedicated'; 'This building holds in trust the records of our national life and symbolises our faith in the permanency of our national institutions'. The tone may be excessively nationalistic (but then, as I have said, all nations are deeply preoccupied with their own past); it is also one of participation and sharing – history, the inscriptions suggest, is important to the whole nation, not just to a handful of scholars or the ruling élite. This is an important element in the argument that history is a necessity. In the past, history was often thought of in a functional way as a necessary education for princes and rulers. In a world of, if not democracy, mass society, an awareness of history must be diffused as widely as possible; the closer the contact between the history of the historians and the history that is widely diffused, the greater the awareness of how history actually comes to be written, the better. It is necessary that new research should be constantly undertaken; it is also necessary that what is already known should be widely known.

The case that history is a necessity has two aspects, the functional, and the 'instinctive' or 'poetic'. The functional case is based on the importance and all-pervasiveness of the past to which I have already alluded. We cannot, as I put it, escape from the past; wherever we go we keep stubbing our toes on the past. The human past has determined much of the built environment, the political boundaries which divide country from country, their forms of government, the precise character of social and economic distinctions, the sources of tension within and between nations: deep in the past lie beliefs and prejudices, modes of thought, the rise, spread and fission of religious faiths, conquests and atrocities, all still exercising potent sway today. To understand the religious and communal structure of Northern Ireland, for instance, one must go back at least to the seventeenth-century settlement on the lands of the indigenous Irish Catholic population, of Protestants from mainland Britain. All over the world population movements of this sort have left bitter and intractable legacies.

It is a commonplace that we live in a time of rapid and far-reaching cultural change. If we are to make a rational assessment of the extent and significance of this change we have no other recourse than to look to the past: how does present change compare with previous periods of change? If we wish to discuss contemporary morality, we can only effectively do so by making comparisons with past moralities. The very stuff of so many pub conversations is in fact drawn from the past. The functional argument, then, is that to understand contemporary problems, to take part in contemporary debate, we *need* history.

The 'instinctive' or 'poetic' aspect of this case is first of all demonstrated by the enormous appeal that physical manifestations of the past have for so many ordinary people. Consider some of the most famous tourist traps: the Tower of London, the Conciergerie in Paris, the gold-rush towns of California, the late-medieval village of San Gimignano in Tuscany (to choose but four from the thousands recorded on picture postcards around the world). There does seem, in most people, to be an instinctive curiosity about the past, a sense of wonder, a poetic desire to be somehow in contact with that past. One English historian, G. M. Trevelyan, spoke of the sensations aroused by 'the quasi-miraculous fact that once, on this earth . . . walked other men and women, as actual as we are today, thinking their own thoughts, swayed by their own passions, but now all gone, one generation vanishing after another, gone as utterly as we ourselves shall shortly be gone like ghosts at cock-crow';[3] another, May MacKisack declared that there exists in the human imagination, 'an instinctive wish to break down the barriers of time and mortality and so to extend the limits of human consciousness beyond the span of a single life'.[4] The Dutch historian Gustav Renier believed that feelings for the past were akin to instincts aroused on those autumnal days when there is woodsmoke on the air and a strange disordered nostalgia pervades the mind;[5] Denys Hay has referred to the emotions inspired by distant church bells on a calm Sunday morning.[6] It may be, of course, that the rigorous enquiries of the historian destroy the poetry and emotionalism, though what the historians just quoted are in fact saying is that the poetic instinct provides the motivation for research into the past. The overall contention, at any rate, is that since the past has such a powerful influence on all of us, and on the problems which affect the world, as well as having such a deep instinctive appeal, then it really is essential that it should be studied as systematically and thoroughly as possible: that is, that history is indeed a necessity.

There is a further, supplementary, justification for historical study. The world in which we live is one dominated by information and communication systems. We have newspapers, magazines, television, advertisements, political statements, expert announcements, graphs, histograms, graphic visual imagery: in short a torrent of persuasion, propaganda and pap; information, disinformation and misinformation. Fundamental to historical study, of course, is the analysis and interpretation of intractable sources, too profuse in some areas, gravely inadequate in others, frequently confusing and contradictory, often obscure. The skills required of the historian, and the skills, and, more important, the attitude of mind transmitted in the teaching of history, are of vital importance in assessing and filtering the messages constantly battering against us.

Other justifications for the study of history are sometimes advanced: that history familiarises us with customs, thought processes, and standards different from our own, tells us about humanity and its various activities and environments and then helps us to know and understand our fellow human beings; that knowledge of our past gives us greater freedom in the control of our present; that history is a valuable training of the mind, assisting critical judgement and the orderly presentation of arguments. But these are secondary to, or corollaries of, the central argument: the past determines and pervades the present – we'd better understand it. The argument is not, it should be stressed, that history enables us to solve the problems of the present, still less to predict the future. The argument is simply that without history we shall not begin to understand the problems of the present and will be without the basic knowledge essential for grappling intelligently with the future.

One other familiar justification for the study of history merits attention. History, C. N. L. Brooke has said, unfolds not one but many different forms of thought. At one extreme historians amass and analyse evidence, very much like a descriptive science – and so gain an uneasy respectability from the kindlier logical positivists; at the other extreme we analyse the play of human personality and all the subtleties of the human mind, and so mingle with literary criticism. History is not a separate mode of thought, but the common home of many interests and techniques and traditions, devised by those who have dedicated their best energies to the study of the past.[7]

More succinctly, history, in the words of Stuart Hughes, has always thought of itself as 'an inclusive, a mediating discipline'. Having formerly linked philosophy with poetry, he claims, it now links literature with social science.[8] Historians do not always serve their subject well by making over-large claims for it. However there are good grounds for claiming this central synthesising role. Because everything has a history, history as a body of knowledge and as a discipline covers everything. The young clerk studying the principles of insurance will in part be studying the history of insurance; part of the work of the literary critic, part of the work of the scientist who studies the development of his subject, must be historical. History therefore does become a meeting ground for different disciplines. Yet all of this is merely elaboration upon the fundamental justification for history as a necessity: human beings must know their past, and so they must know its infinite richness and variety – in art and science as well as social organisation and politics. That richness and variety is the subject matter of history.

However, there is a more conclusive way of rounding out the argument, one derived from Marc Ferro's studies of the way in which history is taught around the world, published in English as *The Use and Abuse of History: or how the past is taught* (the French title, less clamorously, *Comment on raconte l'histoire aux enfants*, has 'history' not 'the past'). Such is the necessity for history that all societies do indeed teach a form of history. But the 'history' taught in very many countries is in fact a 'history' designed to meet national needs, or serve the interests of the ruling regime: history is liberally mixed with myth. The history taught in white South Africa glamorises the struggles, and sufferings of the Dutch settlers, attributes great qualities of tolerance to them while insisting on the primitive nature of Black Africans, and claims that as the settlers moved north the land they occupied was empty and ownerless.[9] But de-colonised Black Africa has its own self-serving history. As Ferro points out, to take one example, the long record of the Arab slave trade and the appalling atrocities it involved is practically excised while all attention is focussed on the evils of the subsequent European slave trade.[10] Ferro shows how in the West Indies the myth is propagated of a long established, naturally cohesive, multi-racial society.[11] Indian history underplays the extent of hostility and conflict between the different nationalities, and overplays the extent of a persistent national resistance to British rule.[12] Thus, Ferro concludes,

> history in India, through its desire to legitimise the country's unity and – as we know – the dream of re-unification, finally deprives history of much of its substance. India and its people lose, thereby, a part of their identity.[13]

In Islamic countries, history subserves theology: the history of Islam which is taught depends upon which branch of that faith is espoused by the country's rulers.[14] How, in general, history is written and re-written in the Soviet Union is well-known. Of incidental significance is the actual recognition of the potency of proper history and proper historical method. Not only is Trotsky eliminated from historical accounts, but the very document of October 1917 in which Lenin praised Trotsky has been removed from the archives.[15] As Kruschev said in 1956: 'historians are dangerous, and capable of turning everything topsy-turvy. They have to be watched.'[16] Ferro does not ignore the fact that much European history has been written to serve the interest of the dominant classes, and to perpetuate national myths.[17] However, there can be no doubt that in open, pluralist societies, one can on the whole see the practice of history being conducted as the challenge to, rather than the perpetuation of, myths. Ferro gives particular praise to the work of contemporary Japanese historians.[18]

So, have we here a justification for history or simply confirmation of what critics have long suspected: that much history is no better than self-serving myth? Two points emerge from Ferro's discoveries. First of all, it would not be possible for Ferro to expose the mythical quality of the history he discusses, nor to explain why particular societies foster the myths they do, if there was not already in existence a body of historical knowledge which gives us a more accurate picture of those societies against which to assess what is currently taught there. That this body of knowledge exists is a tribute to generations of professional historians. Its value is immediately clear: if it did not exist, it would not be possible to expose and explain the versions of history taught in so many countries. More than this, though: as long as countries go on teaching their biased versions of history, so long will conflicts and tensions exist between different countries. Accurate, professional history is a *necessity* if tensions and suspicions are ever to be removed. And the nations themselves, as Ferro puts it, are denied their true identities.

3. Stories and Dialogues

In many European languages the word for history is the same as the word for story. Though the view I have just presented is of history as a body of knowledge against which inadequate or mythical history can be tested, there are those in the scholarly community who see history as essentially a literary activity, whose value is not so much that it casts systematic light on the past but that it gives insights, rather as novels do, into the preoccupations of the age in which it was actually written, and, perhaps, invites admiration for the author's very virtuosity. That is to say a history of the middle ages written in the nineteenth century is of more value for what it tells us about the assumptions of the nineteenth century than for what it tells us about the Middle Ages; similarly with works written in the nineteen-twenties, or nineteen-fifties, or nineteen-eighties; works by 'great' historians are valued for the talents they display in the composition of historical narrative. History, by this token, is little more than an elegant read, offering some bright but highly subjective thoughts on aspects of the past, no doubt, but essentially illuminating of the prejudices, preoccupations and style of the author and his times, and of little more. If my contention that an essential characteristic of a true work of history is that it contributes, however patchily and inadequately, to the body of historical knowledge were shown to be false, if it were established that a piece of historical writing is no more than a well-told story, then I would recommend the abandonment of the study of history for the reading of novels. That any work of history will be affected by the preconceptions of the age and society in which it is written is not in contention. What is in contention is the emphasis to be placed upon this consideration.

It is part of the conventional wisdom of our own day that all facets of human experience and activity are socially constructed, that is to say that there can be no totally objective science, history, literary scholarship, etc., all being influenced by the society in which they are created. That preoccupations, topics felt suitable for inquiry, 'paradigms' change as society changes is not to be doubted. But that is not the same as saying that scientific knowledge is without objective value; that it is not subject to continual development and refinement. Broadly the same, I believe is true of historical knowledge. History, certainly, in that it deals with human behaviour, human institutions, and human values, is no doubt more prone to the influences of the ideological environment in which it is created (and we have just seen how in some countries history is dominated by that environment). But that does not mean that history *must* be so dominated. After all, it is the task of historians to study past societies, to analyse the context in which artefacts and written works of all sorts are produced; thus, historians above all are aware that they are subject to the influences of the particular social context in which they are writing. In common with scientists they cannot totally escape from this, but all their training and experience teaches them to be on their guard against it. Those who take a total 'sociology of knowledge', or 'discourse theory' view, who argue that the accounts of historians are socially constructed, are determined by the era and society in which the historians are living, do tend to claim for themselves the ability to penetrate through the sham facade of objectivity and to be able themselves to present something approaching objective accounts. If they claim this for their particular application of theory, I don't see why historians shouldn't be able to make the same claim for their application of their intensive methodology.

In delivering to his Cambridge audience of the early 1960s the series of sparkling and urbane lectures to which he gave the title 'What is History?', E. H. Carr usually managed to end each lecture with the sort of phrase which sticks. History, he said, concluding lecture one, 'is an unending dialogue between past and present.'[19] The historian's 'facts' (those I shall explore in Chapter 5), he had explained, belong to the past, but the historian is situated in the present, subject to the influences of the present. More directly, it is often said that 'each age writes its own history', or that 'each age must reinterpret the past in the light of its own preoccupations.' Though belonging to the genre of rhetorical overstatement or simplistic generalisation, such sayings contain important truth: when picking up a book it is always worthwhile to consider *who* wrote it, and *when*.

Nineteenth-century historians (in Western Europe and North America) dealt largely with governments and great men, and with the development of national consciousness and the growth of political liberalism; twentieth-century historians, more interested in economic and social democracy, have turned towards economic and social history, towards peoples and away from individuals. Traditionally, historians in the western countries were interested only in their own civilisation, seeing the rest of the world, if at all, in terms of interaction with western culture. Now that many new nationalities compete for attention on the world stage there has been a boom in African history, in Latin American history, and, above all, in Chinese, Japanese and East Asian history. In these days when colonisation is in disrepute the attempt is made to study the various civilisations involved from the standpoint of their indigenous development, rather than from that of their contact and conflict with the west. The shape and content of history, too, vary according to the methods and materials available to different generations. The explosion of historical studies at the beginning of the nineteenth century was in part touched off by the opening at that time of the major European archives. Heavy emphasis today is placed on those problems, such as population growth or the social stratification of small communities, which are amenable to today's sophisticated techniques of quantification. The entire spirit in which history is written varies according to the prevailing beliefs at the time of writing. Lord Acton, at the end of the nineteenth century, believed it his duty to make overt moral judgements; later twentieth-century historians are less sure. Nineteenth-century historians tended to believe that facts could be established 'as they really were' and to present the past as an unfolding process, implying a faith in progress from age to age; there was a considerable vogue for envisaging the unfolding of the past as subject to a series of general laws. Historians of the earlier twentieth century, working in the shade of Freud and

Einstein, developed, as a riposte to the earlier belief in objectivity, an attitude described by its leading exponents in the United States as 'historical relativism'. Historians more recent yet, having lived through great wars and social upheavals, have tended to discount the notion of 'continuity' in history, and to examine closely the tensions between individuals and groups which so often issue in violence and bloodshed. Recent developments in the feminist movement and current preoccupations with women's rights have been paralleled by the production of 'feminist history'.

Since, as I have already suggested, historians are themselves concerned with understanding how one age differs from another, they should above all be aware of these problems, though in fact this awareness is a relatively recent development. Ranke, one of the German pioneers of the history which aimed to establish the facts as they really were, was largely unaware of the way in which his own work was coloured by his ultra-conservative sentiments. Bishop Stubbs, Ranke's foremost disciple in England, was so dedicated to, and blinded by, his painstaking search for documentary materials that he did not realise how far his study of medieval England was governed by a basic Victorian faith in evolutionary liberalism and parliamentary institutions. However, T. H. Buckle, who aspired to the formulation of general laws of historical development, was sharp enough to express awareness in the first volume of his *History of Civilization in England*, published between 1856 and 1861, that 'there will always be a connection between the way in which men contemplate the past and the way in which they contemplate the present'.[20] Today all historians would accept that they are in some sense prisoners of the age and society in which they live. But, to repeat, this very self-awareness is the saving grace of the historians of our own time. As servants of human society they must write history in a manner which has meaning and significance for their readers. But since history is so important to society, it must be the best possible history – it must be as 'true' as possible. Historians who are aware of the limitations imposed upon them by their stance in space and time can strive more successfully to counteract distortions caused by these limitations.

In the 1920s and 1930s the American 'historical relativists' were claiming that there were no objective standards, that one historian was as good as another, and that older historians, as they fell out

of fashion, should be scrapped; they move, Conyers Read, a
leading historical relativist, said wittily, if not wisely 'in a never-
ending march from our studies to our attics and from our attics
to our dustbins'.[21] Actually one historian is not as good as another;
and a good historian writing in the nineteenth century is still far
more worthy of the attention of today's reader than a bad historian
writing in the twentieth century. If history is a constant re-writing
and re-interpretation, it is also a cumulative development. Seeing
where our predecessors were entrapped by the fallacies of their
age, we are that little bit better equipped to avert the fallacies of
our own age. There is truth in the notion of history as dialogue
between present and past, in the notion that each age must reinterpret its own past; nonetheless with advances in technique,
with advances in self-awareness, and with the powerful shoulders
of our illustrious predecessors bowed for us to stand on, there
is also an absolute advance in the quality, the 'truthfulness' of
history.

A less familiar notion than that history is a dialogue between
present and past, and one that I personally would like to advocate
strenuously, is that history, being a participatory activity, being a
necessity to everyone, should also be a dialogue between
historians and their readers. To advocate this, of course, is
perhaps to ask even more of readers than of historians. Often
readers, very properly, simply wish the historian, in an authoritative manner, to 'give them the facts', to tell them how it was.
But the most fruitful encounter between historian and reader will
take place in the realisation that the historian is always offering
an interpretation, some parts of which will be more substantiable
than others, some parts more open to challenge than others. The
totally definitive historical work on any topic has not been written
and never will be. The reader may accept four-fifths of a book
and reject the other fifth as inconsistent with the rest, clearly
reflective of personal or national bias, or perhaps as sheer
rhetorical fancy. The reader may, while finding a book stimulating, reject its overall conclusions. He or she may derive glim-
merings of perception which the historian, too immersed perhaps
in the documentation, had not overtly intended. Readers certainly
should neither be battered by methodology, nor seduced by style,
into complete acquiescence. The more readers know of the fundamental nature and methods of history (which it is the purpose of

this book to explain), the better will they be able to perform this critical function. Historians will try to present their interpretations in as persuasive a fashion as possible; but they must also play fair with readers. Correctly used, the critical apparatus of bibliography and references is intended, not as an overweening demonstration of the historian's self-important pedantry, but as an aid to readers in playing their part in the dialogue.

History as a social activity is as old as human society. History as a scholarly discipline *and* a social activity is still quite young. It is easy to condemn the discipline through reference to writers who make little pretence at scholarship. Furthermore, some of the statements of scholars, over eager to present a personal point of view, have not always done just justice to the study of history as a whole. It may sometimes seem that different historians or different schools of history have held views about the nature of history, about the tasks of historians, which flatly contradict each other. In recent years one of the most prestigious schools of historical study has been that, based on Paris, known as the *Annales* school; some members of this school write as if their approach is the only acceptable one, and all other approaches have been superseded.[22] Other historians have responded by parodying the *Annales* approach, or, perhaps, asserting the primacy of traditional narrative in historical writing. To me it is very much a question of what sorts of problems the historian is trying to solve: one approach will be suitable for one type of problem, another for a different type of problem. One can recognise the achievements of the *Annales* school, as one can recognise the achievements of Marx and many Marxists, without giving exclusive privileges to any one approach.

Some writers on historiography and the nature and methods of historical study exult in the variousness of approach of different historians, perhaps even in the particular manifestations of their 'genius' (to me historians are no more than skilled artisans, history a profession in which one should look neither for geniuses nor great men). Others tend to impose one standard ('relevance' is a favourite) against which all historians are judged. In recent years historiographers, following Thomas H. Kühn, who suggested that scientific study moves from one paradigm to another,[23] have applied the notion of the paradigm and 'paradigm shifts' to the development of historical writing. But nothing remotely like consensus exists: indeed different writers offer vastly different time-scales. Traian Stoianovich, in his study of the *Annales* school envisages the whole history of historical study as being covered by three paradigms, culminating (of course) in the *Annales* or 'functional-structural' paradigm: the other two are 'exemplar history' (whose object was training for public service) and 'evolutionary history' (history with a clear sense of change through time).[24] John Higham, however, confining himself to not much more than a hundred years of the writing of American history finds at least half a dozen different paradigms ('Scientific History', 'New History', 'Relativism', 'Conservative Evolutionism', 'Progressive History', 'New Left History').[25]

In the next two chapters I do no more than offer a simple account of the manner in which the modern practice of history, as a discipline which has to meet social as well as intellectual demands, has developed. Undoubtedly, as has already been stressed, the fashion and style of history change as styles of life, politics and economic organisation change. Yet the history of historical writing cannot be chopped up into neat compartments: on the one hand there is a continuity of purpose which it will be a main task of the next chapter to identify: on the other there has often been a vociferous opposition to whatever orthodoxy has in conventional historiography been regarded as the prevailing one of the time. My contention will be that whatever self aggrandising utterances historians may sometimes be betrayed into uttering, the exploration of the past, while inevitably generating much controversy, is a unifying rather than a divisive enterprise.

Notes

1. Ernst Breisach, *Historiography: Ancient, Medieval and Modern* (Chicago, 1983), p. 404.
2. In a review of *The Media in British Politics* (1987), edited by Jean Seaton and Ben Pimlott, *New Society*, 6 November 1987.
3. G. M. Trevelyan, *An Autobiography and Other Essays* (1949), p. 13.
4. May MacKisack, *History as Education* (1956), p. 10.
5. G. J. Renier, *History: Its Purpose and Method* (1950), p. 29.
6. In an annotation on the original typescript of this book, 1968.
7. G. N. L. Brooke, *The Dullness of the Past* (1957), p. 3.

8. H. Stuart Hughes, 'The Historian and the Social Scientist', *American Historical Review* LXVI (1960).

9. Marc Ferro, *The Use and Abuse of History: or how the past is taught* (1984), pp. 5–11.

10. Ibid., p. 27.

11. Ibid., p. 28.

12. Ibid., pp. 37, 45, 51–2.

13. Ibid., p. 52.

14. Ibid., pp. 50, 79–88.

15. Ibid., p. 117.

16. Ibid., p. 114.

17. This comes out most strongly in his subsequent book *L'histoire sous surveillance* (Paris, 1985).

18. *Use and Abuse of History*, p. 205.

19. E. H. Carr, *What is History?* (1961, paperback 1964), p. 30.

20. T. H. Buckle, *History of Civilization in England*, 1 (1856), p. 266.

21. Quoted by Westfall Thompson, p. 410.

22. See in particular, Francois Furet, *In the Workshop of History* (Chicago, 1984), chapter 1; and Marc Ferro, *L'histoire sous surveillance* (Paris, 1985).

23. Thomas H. Kühn, *The Structure of Scientific Revolutions* (New York, 1962).

24. Traian Stoianovich, *French Historical Method: The Annales Paradigm*, (Ithaca, N.Y., 1976), pp. 25–36.

25. John Higham, *History: Professional Scholarship in America* (Baltimore, 1983), *passim*.

Chapter 2 The Development of Historical Studies to the End of the Nineteenth Century

1. From the Beginnings to the Enlightenment

The governing influences upon our life today, and therefore upon the writing and study of history today, are the continuing scientific and technological revolutions of the seventeenth century and onwards, and the continuing national and democratic revolutions of the late eighteenth century and onwards. Historians of historical writing disagree over which age should be credited with producing the first recognisably modern historian. The first era in which the influence of the scientific revolution fully permeated the arts, industry and letters was named at the time, and may be so named by us now, the Enlightenment: Voltaire, the greatest ornament of eighteenth-century intellectual life, is often identified as the first modern historian. Other commentators have preferred to lay emphasis on the great transformation in historical scholarship carried through by German historians at the beginning of the nineteenth century, while others have written about the 'historical revolution' of the seventeenth century.[1] History as a functional social activity stretches back to the beginning of human society; it took a relatively sophisticated shape in the period of classical antiquity, lapsed somewhat after the fall of the Roman Empire into that older condition in which myth and attempt to establish what actually happened were inextricably bound together, then, under the stimulus of Renaissance learning in the sixteenth and seventeenth centuries, achieved a higher level of rational perception and a more advanced methodology than ever before. Many crudities remained, however, and it was the achievement of the Enlightenment to sweep these away. Voltaire and his contemporaries, therefore, might best be regarded as standing, not so much at the beginning of a new historical tradition, but at the highest point of an old one. For history, as a disciplined academic activity and body of knowledge, begins only with Ranke and his German compatriots at the beginning of the nineteenth century. This does not mean that we single out great historical writers of the period before the nineteenth century (and perhaps several since) and say that they are 'not historians'. 'History', as we have seen, has a number of interrelated levels of meaning, and we cannot blame Voltaire, Tacitus or anyone else for not having a conception of history which did not come into being till a later age. What is of interest is to note the fundamentals to which all historians of all ages have subscribed, and to assess the contributions to modern historical study which various writers have made down the ages.

The Western historical tradition in the broad sense goes back to Herodotus (*c.* 484 B.C.–*c.* 425 B.C.) and Thucydides (*c.* 455 B.C.–*c.* 400 B.C.), writing towards the end of the great classical age in Ancient Greece, Polybius (*c.* 198 B.C.–117 B.C.) writing when Greece was falling under the dominion of Rome; and to Livy (59 B.C.–A.D. 17), Tacitus (*c.* A.D. 55–120) and Plutarch (A.D. 50–120), the great historians of Imperial Rome (Plutarch was himself actually a Greek). It is no disparagement of the much-praised powerful style and unitary content of the *History of the Peloponnesian War* by Thucydides, to suggest that perhaps his most significant contribution to the development of historical studies was his sense of precise chronology, essential to historical writing if it is to be more than vague celebration of past cultures and past achievements. For the Greek and Roman writers history was quite unabashedly 'exemplar history', a preparation for life, especially political and military life. Essentially it was a narration of memorable events designed to preserve the memory and propagate the knowledge of glorious deeds, or of events which were important to a man, a family, or a people. As Ernst Breisach has pointed out both the achievements and limitations (though the point here is to stress the achievements) of contemporary Greek chronology can be seen in the manner in which Thucydides dates the beginning of the Peloponnesian War:

> For fourteen years, the thirty years peace which was concluded after the recovery of Euboea remained unbroken. But in the fifteenth year, when Chrysis the High Priestess of Argos was in the forty-eighth year

of her priesthood, Zenesias was Ephor of Sparta, and Pythodorus had four months of his Archonship to run at Athens, in the tenth month after the engagement at Potideaea at the beginning of Spring, about the first watch of the night, an armed force of somewhat more than three hundred Thebans entered Plataea, a city of Boeotia, which was an ally of Athens.[2]

Political incidents, wars and revolutions, predominated. But there was, and this is important, a positive attempt to identify and evaluate sources.

In the post-classical period the tradition was left almost exclusively in the hands of monkish chroniclers, whose annalistic accounts lack the elements of reflection or analysis which would make them history. Occasionally a chronicler would pause in his headlong flight through the years for a judgement such as this by the Anglo-Saxon Chronicler on William the Conqueror (d. 1087):

> King William, of whom we speak, was a man of great wisdom and power, and surpassed in honour and in strength all those who had gone before him. Though stern beyond measure to those who opposed his will, he was kind to those good men who loved God . . . Such was the state of religion in his time that every man who wished to, whatever considerations there might be with regard to his rank, could follow the profession of a monk . . . Among other things we must not forget the good order he kept in the land, so that a man of any substance could travel unmolested throughout the country with his bosom full of gold. No man dare to slay another, no matter what evil the other might have done him. If a man lay with a woman against her will, he was forthwith condemned to forfeit those members with which he disported himself . . . He ruled over England and by his foresight it was surveyed so carefully that there was not a 'hide' of land in England of which he did not know who held it and how much it was worth . . . Assuredly in his time men suffered grievous oppression and manifold injuries.[3]

The Venerable Bede (d. 735) showed more of the qualities of true historical scholarship. He paid special attention to chronology; he enumerated his written sources and he made some effort to test and evaluate oral traditions. His premises and assumptions are vastly different from ours, yet at times it is possible to feel a real contact with what is continous in human experience. Bede quotes in full the reply of Pope Gregory to the questionings of Augustine who has newly established the see of Canterbury. Gregory comes through as a man of intense humanity and warm common sense, as for instance in his reply to Augustine's anxieties regarding the variations in religious practice to be found in Britain:

My brother, you are familiar with the usage of the Roman Church, in which you were brought up. But if you have found customs, whether in the Roman, Gallican, or any other Churches that may be more acceptable to God, I wish you to make a careful selection of them, and teach the Church of the English, which is still young in the Faith, whatever you can profitably learn from the various Churches. For things should not be loved for the sake of places, but places for the sake of good things.[4]

Medieval historians often found it difficult to distinguish clearly between sacred and profane matters: events, from time to time, are expressed as judgements of God, and miracles are accepted. Such writers as Otto of Freising (1111/1115–58) a member of the German Imperial Hohenstaufen family, Matthew Paris (d. *c.* 1259), a monastic chronicler based at St Albans, and the Burgundian historian of the Hundred Years War, Jean Froissart (*c.* 1337–*c.* 1410), provided fairly reliable accounts of their own times, but none found it easy to shake off the all-pervasive influence of St Augustine's *City of God* (426), a work of Christian apologetics portraying the history of the world as the long unfolding of God's will. Though often themselves expert forgers, medieval chroniclers were quite uncritical in their treatment of documentary evidence. They accepted in full the sanctions of tradition, and, since they believed in divine intervention were inhibited in their analysis of historical causation.

Renaissance writers turned again to the example of the classical historians. Their great achievements were the rational, secular approach which they brought to bear on matters formerly held to be part of the divine mystery, and their development of a form of critical scholarship. The latter, however, owed a great deal to medieval scholars who had developed the technique of the 'gloss' or explanatory note: Valla (*c.* 1407–57) had used critical techniques to expose the forged Donation of Constantine, upon which many of the claims of the medieval Church were based.

The real goad to historical study in the Renaissance was external circumstance. Geographical exploration created a demand for exact information, historical as well as geographical. The invention of printing created a new emphasis on communication – and history, as historical writing and as social necessity, is, of course, nothing if not communication. In the scientific and intellectual revolution which culminates in the work of Sir Isaac Newton

(1642–1727) history, along with all other scholarly pursuits, took its share. Everywhere among the intelligent and articulate there was an awareness of, and interest in, the processes of change. The battles of the Reformation and Counter-Reformation provided further stimulus to historical study, as each side endeavoured to demonstrate the historical validity of its position: Luther's associate Melanchthon (1497–1560) brought to the German universities at which he taught an enthusiasm for the academic study of history, and Flacius Illyricus (1520–75) directed the publication of the 'Magdeburg Centuries', an ecclesiastical history (to 1200 or thereabouts), which, though strongly biased in the Lutheran cause, did contain masses of source material.

The first great vernacular writers were Niccolò Machiavelli (1469–1527) and Francesco Guicciardini (1483–1540), though the way had already been lit by Leonardo Bruni (1374?–1444), whose *Florentine History* (1415–29) serves today's historians as a central text in the study of Renaissance civic humanism. To Machiavelli and Guicciardini more than any other writers belongs the credit for bringing to history a genuine inductive method – arguing from the evidence rather than 'deducing' from some a priori theory. Apart from his famous work, *The Prince* (completed in 1513, published in 1532), Machiavelli, significantly enough, also published a series of *Discourses* (1516) on the classical historian Livy; his *History of Florence* was published in 1522. *The Prince* is a work of political philosophy as well as history, for there is no sense of the complete autonomy of history till the nineteenth century (and even in the twentieth century it was common for political science and history to be taught in the same university department); yet essentially *The Prince* is a realistic presentation of the nature of Italian Government, politics and diplomacy at the beginning of the sixteenth century, rather than, as often popularly thought, a guide to the worst techniques of *Realpolitik*. Guicciardini's *History of Italy* (uncompleted on his death in 1540) offers a highly skilled analysis of political motivation; its purpose, in keeping with a long tradition, was to give the reader 'wholesome instructions'.[5]

The great Italians had no immediate disciples. In England Sir Walter Raleigh's *History of the World* (1614) is very much a mixture of medieval and modern elements. William Camden's *Britannia* (six editions, 1586–1607), however, was based on deep learning and extensive research: in his preface Camden (1551–1623) touched again on the fundamental justification for the study of history: 'If there are any who desire to be strangers in their own country, foreigners in their own cities and always children in knowledge, let them please themselves: I write not for such humours.'[6] Camden's essay in contemporary history, his *History of Elizabeth* (1615) was based on the great mass of records made available to him. In writing his *Survey of London* (1598), John Stow took it for granted that his historical treatment would be of intrinsic interest to his readers. The scientific method, detailed examination of evidence and vigorous enquiry into causal relationships, was best represented in the work of Sir Francis Bacon (1561–1626), for whom history – his only complete work was the *History of Henry VII* – was but one of many interests. Most noteworthy of all English historians before the Enlightenment was Edward Hyde, Earl of Clarendon, a statesman who played a leading part in the Royalist cause during the revolutionary period in English history. Accordingly his *History of the Rebellion and Civil Wars in England begun in the year 1641* is far from being a piece of detailed scholarship, though, dealing as it does with matters of great complexity, it is a masterpiece of organisation: the nearest parallels in modern times are Winston Churchill's histories of the two World Wars.

Throughout Europe in the sixteenth and seventeenth centuries major scholarly enterprises were undertaken to bring together precious collections of original documents. In part these were responses to the unhappy dispersal of valuable materials during the periods of religious strife: after the dissolution of the monasteries in sixteenth-century England, complained a contemporary with pardonable exaggeration, the new owners used the contents of their libraries for profitable sale overseas, 'to rub their boots', or to 'serve their jakes'.[7] The positive interest of Elizabeth's Privy Council can be seen in a letter of 1568 when holders of records are instructed to make them available to the deputies of Archbishop Parker, 'so as both when any need shall require, resort may be made for the testimony that may be found in them, and also by conference of them, the antiquity of the state of these countries may be restored to the knowledge of the world'.[8] The most significant advances in historical scholarship were made in seventeenth-century France, where such scholars as Duchesne, Baluze,

Mabillon and Montfaucon created 'the science of history and placed new tools such as palaeography, archaeology, and diplomatics in the historian's hands'.[9] The greatest work in the scholarly compilation of collected texts was carried through by the French Benedictines at St Maur. Among other large enterprises were those of certain Belgian Jesuits, followers of John Bolland (1596–1665), who initiated the *Acta Sanctorum*, and the collection of German documents *Monarchia romani imperii*, associated with Melchior Goldast (d. 1635). The leading theorist of historical study was Jean Bodin (*c.* 1530–96), French author of *Method for the Easy Understanding of History*, who declared the subject to be both of intellectual interest and of pragmatic value for morals and politics: if studied carefully, he maintained, history did manifest certain orderly principles.[10]

In historiography emphasis is naturally placed on the striking achievements of such men of genius as Voltaire and Gibbon. Yet contemporaneously with these famous writers of great interpretative works, those who laboured in the school of 'erudition' continued the vital work of collecting and criticising historical records. However it was undoubtedly the public successes of the literary figures which prepared the way for the nineteenth-century establishment of disciplined historical study: while the *érudits* advanced the cause of scholarship, the interpreters created the first weighty narrative histories of high literary and artistic quality, and, more critically, made the first serious attempts to analyse the development of human civilisation. Recent historiographical writing has drawn attention to the important work carried out at the University of Göttingen (founded 1737), where, in addition to the collection of economic, demographic, and geographic 'statistics' (data relating to States), attempts were made to write histories bringing together narrative and analysis: Johann Christoph Gatterer (1727–99), in particular, has been seen as an eighteenth-century precursor of Ranke.[11]

The French Enlightenment historians carried through the final destruction of the theological base of historical writing which had persisted through the Renaissance and had, in some ways, been revivified by the Reformation and Counter-Reformation, when it was most brilliantly presented by Jacques Bénigne Bossuet (1627–1704), Bishop of Meaux in France, whose *Discourse on Universal History* was written for the education of the Dauphin.

Both Montesquieu (1689–1755) and Voltaire (1694–1778) wrote in a fashion directly antithetical to that of Bossuet. Montesquieu's *The Spirit of the Laws* (1748) stresses the importance of physical environment and of tradition, but is lacking in any real sense of historical change through time. Save for the efficiency and elegance of the narrative there was nothing outstandingly original about Voltaire's *History of Charles XII* (1731): it was while working on *The Century of Louis XIV* (published in 1751) that he began to develop the broader cultural and social approach which characterised his *Essay on the Manners and Character of the Nations* (first complete edition published in 1756). In eloquent testimony to the principle that no new method is ever as new as its eager sponsors believe, or, if you like, to the principle that each age must rediscover old truths for itself, Voltaire now insisted that the historian must give due attention to the civilisations of India and China, that religions should be treated comparatively, with no suggestion that any automatic primacy was inherent in Judaeo-Christianity, and that economic, social and cultural matters were as much the concern of the historian as the doings of popes and kings.[12]

This broad view of history was a characteristic of the eighteenth-century Scottish school of historical writing. That the two most celebrated figures in the Scottish eighteenth-century Enlightenment, one a philosopher, the other an economist, should both also in some sense be historians, is further demonstration of the central importance of history in human activity. David Hume (1711–76) is best known as a philosopher – though the lines delimiting history were still not firmly drawn; writing rather as Tory historian than general philosopher, he demonstrated the absurdity of the idea that human society had originated in a 'social contract'. His *History of England* was published in six volumes between 1754 and 1762. Largely a work of synthesis rather than exhaustive original scholarship (Hume once referred to research as the 'dark industry'), the *History* had a tremendous popular success; the first volume brought the author £2000, the others a good deal more. The main text was essentially straight political narrative but Hume did include, in the form of appendices, details of wages, prices, dress and other matters now conventionally referred to as social history. The rationalist element in Hume's thinking is very clear in his *Natural History of Religion* (1759). In an essay called 'On the

Study of History' Hume referred to the subject as an 'agreeable entertainment' more interesting than fiction. In history, Hume said, one observes 'the rise, progress, declensions and final extinction of the most flourishing empires; the virtues which contributed to their greatness and the vices which drew on their ruin'. Most important of all with regard to the central argument of this book, Hume declared that 'a man acquainted with history may, in some respect, be said to have lived from the beginning of the world'.[13]

Adam Smith (1723–90) is renowned as the founder of the classical school of political economy, but his *The Wealth of Nations* (1776) is essentially historical in its approach to the study of man's economic activities. Smith, perhaps more than any of his contemporaries, was aware of the economic imperatives underpinning human society, and he had already, in the *Theory of Moral Sentiments* (1759) made the point that man can 'subsist only in society'. Although a minister of the Scottish Presbyterian Church, William Robertson (1721–93) was the complete Enlightenment historian. Dividing his *History of Scotland* (1759) into four periods, he remarked of the first that it 'is the region of pure fable and conjecture, and ought to be totally neglected, or abandoned to the industry and credulity of antiquarians'. His *The History of the Reign of the Emperor Charles V* (1769) was important both for its attempt to deal with social as well as political matters, and for the extensive scholarly apparatus: Robertson provided bare references in the text, then an appendix of 'Proofs and Illustrations' as long as the text itself. That there was nothing parochial about Robertson's approach to history was shown by his *The History of America* (1777–94) which again demonstrated his concept of history as the development of human society and civilisation.

Most interesting of all the Scottish historians was John Millar (1735–1801), Professor of Civil law at the University of Glasgow from 1761 to his death in the second year of the nineteenth century. Millar, as his fellow Scot, Francis Jeffrey, pointed out in 1806, sought 'to trace back the history of society to its most simple and universal elements – to resolve almost all that has been ascribed to positive institution into the spontaneous and irresistible development of certain obvious principles – and to show with how little contrivance or political wisdom the most complicated and apparently artificial schemes of policy might have been erected'. In *The Origin of the Distinction of Ranks* (1771) Millar endeavours to explain changes in the power-structure of society and of groups within society: in a manner which subsequently influenced Marx, he associated these with changes in property relations. His *An Historical View of the English Government* (1787) divided English history into three periods, each based on the predominant system of property-holding obtaining at the time: the 'feudal aristocracy' to 1066, the 'feudal monarchy' to 1603, and 'the commercial government' thereafter.[14]

Frequently careless in detail, the Scottish writers did have a broad, sociological conception of historical study. It was their famous English contemporary who, in enunciating an important but partial truth, helped to set history in English upon the narrow path that it was for too long to follow in both Britain and the U.S.A.: 'Wars, and the administration of public affairs', wrote Edward Gibbon (1737–94) in the preface to his *Decline and Fall of the Roman Empire* (1776–88), 'are the principal subjects of history'. Nonetheless Gibbon's monumental work was a masterpiece of organisation and of sustained narrative. It brought him the fame and fortune he had sought from the moment he realised that history was the most popular of all forms of literature (that is, before the novel established its ascendancy). Gibbon announced himself a man of the Enlightenment in his empirical treatment of the development of Christianity: 'The theologian', as he remarked in a famous sentence, 'may indulge in the pleasing task of describing Religion as she descended from Heaven arrayed in her native purity'; he, as a historian, was happy to explain the successes of early Christianity in terms of 'exclusive zeal, the immediate expectation of another world, the claim of miracles, the practice of rigid virtue, and the constitution of the primitive church'. Gibbon's view of history was a disenchanted one: he accepted, in another famous phrase, the 'melancholy truth . . . that the Christians in the course of their intestine dissensions have inflicted far greater severities on each other than they experienced from the zeal of the infidels'. Indeed he came closer to the world-view of the disillusioned twentieth century than to the nineteenth-century belief in the progress of human history: every page, Gibbon wrote, 'has been stained with civil blood . . . from the ardour of contention, the pride of victory, the despair of success, the memory of past injustice and the fear of future dangers . . .

[which] . . . all contribute to inflame the mind and silence the voice of pity'.

Historians in the eighteenth century did make an attempt at the cultural and sociological approach, though not always a very powerful one. There were still plenty of critics then, as now, to join in the lament (1789) of the agricultural journalist and pioneer social researcher, Arthur Young, that

> to a mind that has the least turn after philosophical inquiry, reading modern history is generally the most tormenting employment that a man can have: one is plagued with the actions of a detestable set of men called conquerors, heroes, and great generals; and we wade through pages loaded with military details; but when you want to know the progress of agriculture, of commerce, and industry, their effect in different ages and nations on each other – the wealth that resulted – the division of that wealth – its employment – and the manners it produced – all is a blank. Voltaire set an example, but how has it been followed?[15]

But the history (i.e. historical writing – see why I spent so much time on definitions?!) of the age of Gibbon and Voltaire had three more fundamental weaknesses. First, and most important, being concerned with universal principles of human behaviour, it was remarkably innocent of any sense of human development and change; thus both Gibbon and Voltaire could exercise their magnificent wit upon the obvious fact that men in past ages had not always disported themselves in a fashion considered suitable in the eighteenth-century 'Age of Reason'. The medieval period was usually treated scrappily and with little respect; Gibbon was seriously in error in depreciating the achievements of the Byzantine Empire. Secondly, although important scholarly work continued side-by-side with the great interpretative works, there was little contact between the two. 'Confound details', exclaimed Voltaire, with some reason: 'they are a vermin which destroy books.'[16] Yet in their contempt for basic scholarship and research the eighteenth-century historians sometimes showed an unjustifiable carelessness. The charge cannot with great justice be laid upon Gibbon, who was scrupulous in his search of the available evidence; but that evidence was essentially the product of the labours of seventeenth-century erudition. One problem, certainly, was that many important archives kept their doors closed to scholars. History at its highest must be interpretation, not fact-grubbing. But without a continued sponsorship of detailed research, conducted with the widest available collection of mechanical and conceptual aids, and, more important, a constant intercourse between interpretative history and primary research, history must quickly wither.

The third great weakness still attending upon history in the eighteenth century was that nowhere was it efficiently taught as an intellectual discipline, save in the palaces of princes and statesmen. True, the Camden chair had been established at Oxford in the Elizabethan period: but Camden professors confined themselves to Roman history. In the 1720s George I instituted Regius Chairs of Modern History at Oxford and Cambridge, but this was essentially a political rather than an educational move, designed to bring Whig nominees into these centres of Toryism. The early incumbents of the chairs were completely without distinction in historical studies. The second Oxford Professor, his recent successor, Hugh Trevor-Roper, tells us, was remembered only for bringing 'one Handel, a foreigner, who they say was born in Hanover' with his 'lousy crew' of 'fiddlers' to play in the Sheldonian Theatre.[17] From 1757 history was taught on a more serious basis at the University of Göttingen in Germany; and in 1769 a Chair of History and Morals was established at the Collège de France. But till history was admitted to all the main centres of learning, it could not hope to develop as a true intellectual discipline.

2. Ranke: his Disciples and his Critics

It was from the simultaneous attack on these three weaknesses that history as an academic discipline was born. After the great revolutionary upheavals at the end of the eighteenth century it was no longer possible to believe in the unchanging character of human behaviour, nor in the immutable nature of social institutions; as never before, thinking men became preoccupied with the carefully documented study of historical origins and historical change. 'It was a time when we were experiencing the most incredible and exceptional events, when we were reminded of many forgotten and decayed institutions by the sound of their downfall,' explained Barthold Georg Niebuhr (1776–1831), the pioneer of the new school of text-based historical study.[18] The hitherto neglected ideas of Vico (whose *New Science* had been published in 1725) and Herder (whose short *Philosophy of History* of 1774 was followed by a four-volume *Philosophy of History*, published between 1784 and 1791) now came into fashion.

Giambattista Vico (1668–1744) presented a scheme of the development of human civilisation in three stages, 'divine', 'heroic' and 'human': such a scheme was new to Europeans, though not unusual in Chinese and Muslim historical writing. Vico's real contribution, however, was his appreciation of the cultural differences between different ages and different nations: in contrast to the main Enlightenment historians he was aware of the danger of importing ideas, or judgements, from a later age into an earlier one. Johann Gottfried von Herder (1744–1803) presented similar ideas in much more sophisticated and coherent form: he conceived of history as an onward march; he stressed (as Montesquieu had done) the importance of geography, and developed for the first time the concept of 'national character' which he believed greatly influenced the history of any nation. Herder coined the verb *einfühlen*, as used in his injunction to historians: 'First sympathise with the nation, go into the era, into the geography, into the entire history, *feel* yourself into it.' Herder was the first to oppose to the confident contempt of the Enlightenment historians the notion that everything, *relatively*, is right *in its own historical context*.

The desire to see the past from the inside, 'as it really was', in the celebrated (and notorious) words of Ranke, was one aspect of the aspirations of the romantic imagination, typified at this time in the novels of Sir Walter Scott, who had himself set out with the fixed purpose of portraying the manners and morals of past ages, and whose novels had a profound direct influence on Ranke and other historians. Overstatement is the venial sin of all mighty innovators, and Ranke was undoubtedly guilty of it when, in the modest and self-deprecating preface to his first book, *Histories of the Latin and Teutonic Nations 1494–1514* (1824), he permitted himself the following much-quoted, and much-traduced, pontification:

> To history has been assigned the office of judging the past, of instructing the present for the benefit of future ages. To such high offices this work does not aspire: it wants only to show how it actually was (*wie es eigentlich gewesen*).[19]

Yet the issue is crucial: historians may judge, must, if only implicitly, instruct – but before all else it is important that they *understand*. The interest in historical origins and development, in understanding the past 'on its own terms', was combined with a new precision of documentation (which may be seen as a facet of the romantic emphasis on the particular at the expense of the classical emphasis on the general). At the head of this new tradition of critical method stands Niebuhr, a native of Denmark, who from 1806 worked in the service of the Prussian Government, and was closely associated with the Prussian reform movement, itself a response to the challenge of Napoleon. In 1810 he was appointed to give lectures at the newly founded university of Berlin, a product of the reform movement. The lectures, published in two volumes in 1811–12 as the *History of Rome* (with a completely revised three-volume edition in 1827–32), were a reconstruction of the historical origins of the Roman state, employing the most advanced methods of philology and textual criticism. This application of 'scientific' methods revealed grave weaknesses in Livy, and discredited those authors whose own accounts were simply repetitions of Livy. Clumsily written – Niebuhr himself believed that you couldn't have both historical accuracy and persuasive style (a doctrine endorsed by many historians since) – the *History of Rome* can nonetheless be said without exaggeration to inaugurate modern historical methodology. Ranke was explicitly following this methodology when he described the sources for his *Histories of the Latin and Teutonic Nations* as 'memoirs, diaries, letters, diplomatic reports, and original narratives of eye-witnesses; other writings were used only if they were immediately derived from the above-mentioned or seemed to equal them because of some original information.'[20] Ranke added that these sources would be identified on every page, and, in the form first used by Robertson, 'a second volume, to be published concurrently, will present the method of investigation and the critical conclusions.'[21] The new methodology in its most austere form was seen in the inauguration of the collection of German historical texts, the *Monumenta Germaniae Historica*, initiated by the nationalist politician Karl Freiherr von Stein and edited (from 1823) by the Hanoverian scholar Georg Heinrich Pertz. Other countries followed: nationalism was a major impulse, but scholarship was a main outcome.

In France, under the direction of the historian-statesman François Guizot, author of *History of Civilization in Europe* (1828) and *History of Civilization in France* (1829–32), and dominant minister during the constitutional (though far from democratic) monarchy, 1830–48, committees were established for the publication in hundreds of volumes of thousands of manuscripts, charts, memoirs and correspondence. Augustin Thierry (1795–1856) explained how in writing his *History of the Norman Conquest of England* (1825) he had to 'devour long folio pages, in order to extract a single sentence, or even word, among a thousand'.[22] In 1821 the École des Chartes was founded for the purpose of providing a training in the handling of historical sources. A new historical methodology was being created. Not, I have indicated, out of a purely abstract notion of making history a scientific discipline; recent political and social upheavals, the forces of nationalism and romanticism played an important part. But because developments are stimulated by the immediate historical and social context, that does not mean that they cannot also be advances in knowledge more abstractly conceived: the notion of the primacy of the 'original source' could become an excuse for pedantry and even blindness, but on the whole it does act as a control upon mere speculation or mythologising. Ranke was no cold, unemotional scholar. So much is he a man of his time, that his strongest motives were in fact religious: he sought to show that behind human history lay God's plan, above human activities 'God's hand'; states he called 'thoughts of God'.[23] And it is not enough to have a methodology if that methodology produces no results. In fact Ranke produced well over a dozen substantial (usually multi-volume) works, including *The Ottoman and the Spanish Empires in the Sixteenth and Seventeenth Centuries* (1827), using an invaluable source, the reports of the Venetian ambassadors, *The Popes of Rome, their Church and State, in the Sixteenth and Seventeenth Centuries* (1834–6), and *History of the Reformation in Germany* (1845–7), both of which remain starting-points for scholars today. No single individual created the modern discipline of history, but if a founder has to be sought the title need not be denied to Ranke – though we shall have to give careful consideration to those who were provoked into strong criticism of Ranke and to a rather different tradition, whose prime proponent is Karl Marx. Two rather pompous words (much misused by later polemicists, as is the way with pompous words – and with polemicists) define the historical discipline associated with Ranke and his followers: it is *hermeneutic* in its insistence on the over-riding importance of primary texts (hermeneutics being the science of correctly understanding texts, or rather, of *endeavouring* to correctly understand texts – like all historians Ranke sometimes got things wrong); and it is *historicist* in the insistence both that the past is different from the present, and that there is a process of change linking past with present.

Ranke, in fact, played a central part in a third important development; the establishment of the teaching of history at university level. At Berlin he instituted seminars on research techniques. Other countries lagged far behind: France, where the universities had been abolished in the Revolution, lacked system and standards, there being various chairs of history in different institutions of different types, such as the Collège de France, the Faculties of Letters, and in some of the great *écoles* (schools of advanced study), notably the École Normale Supérieure and the École des Chartes. Largely owing to the efforts of Frenchmen impressed by their experiences in Germany, instruction in research techniques was provided at the new École Pratique des Hautes Études established at the Sorbonne in 1868. As a consequence there was a general improvement in the teaching of history, though universities were not re-established before 1896. As we shall see later in this chapter, the German example spread also to Britain and the United States, though progress was slow; but by the second half of the nineteenth century history was beginning to establish itself throughout the Western world as an autonomous academic discipline, with much of the paraphernalia which is today associated with that elevated status. In 1859 the first of the professional historical journals, the *Historische Zeitschrift* was launched. It would, its founders declared, be above all else a 'scientific' periodical: 'Its first task, therefore, should be to represent the true method of historical research and to point out the deviations therefrom.'[24]

Ranke did little to cast off the prejudices and assumptions of his nation and class. With the influential German Idealist philosopher of the early nineteenth century, Georg Wilhelm Friedrich Hegel (1770–1831), author, *inter alia*, of *The Philosophy of World History* (1825), he shared in the belief that the national political state was vital to the progress of human society. Religious and political fervour came together in Ranke's conviction that nation states were 'thoughts of God', and, partly because the newly opened archives in which he was particularly interested were necessarily the archives of princes and prelates (the poor do not leave much in the way of primary sources), he gave history a firm orientation towards 'past politics' and the relations between states ('diplomatic history'), together known as *Staatengeschichte* or political history. He was an extreme conservative, supporting the repressive Press Law passed in the German Confederation after the 1830 upheavals, and rejoicing in the events of 1870–1 'as the victory of Conservative Europe over the revolution'. Yet Ranke's final work was a massive *Universal History*, completed after his death by his students. Already he had written: 'Universal history comprehends the past life of mankind, not in its particular relations and trends, but in its fullness and totality.' Although absolutely dedicated to the necessity for specialised research, Ranke was aware of 'the danger of losing sight of the universal, of the type of knowledge everyone desires':

> For history is not simply an academic subject: the knowledge of the history of mankind should be a common property of humanity and should above all benefit our nation, without which our work could not have been accomplished.[25]

Here Ranke the rather strident conservative nationalist owns that history is indeed a social necessity, the property of all humanity. But the line between use and abuse of history can be easily transgressed. In the works of Ranke's young compatriot, Heinrich von Treitschke (1834–96), for example *German History in the Nineteenth Century* (1877), history became the servant of militant chauvinism: the German state was glorified, and so was war.

While the methodological innovations of Niebuhr and Ranke had powerful and salutary effects throughout the world of historical studies, that world by no means succumbed to the over-lordship of Ranke. Theodor Mommsen (1817–1903), in his multi-volume *Roman History* was in his meticulous scholarship almost more Rankean than Ranke, but his instincts, revealed in his studies of numismatics, classical philology, and Roman epigraphy, were towards a history that was more widely cultural than that favoured by Ranke. Mommsen, too, was caught up in politics (as a nationalist he at first supported Bismarck, but as a liberal he opposed *Realpolitik*). History can never escape its social applications, yet it must be rigorous in its scholarship: Mommsen was aware of the dilemma, but, it is, he said, 'the worst of all mistakes to suspend being a citizen, so as not to compromise one's scholarly work.'[26] Johan Gustav Droysen (1808–84), Professor of History at Berlin from 1859 to 1884, author of the highly pro-Prussian *History of Prussian Politics* and of a *Methodology of History* (see below) was responsible for the famous remark that the objectivity of Ranke was 'the objectivity of a eunuch'.[27] The most powerful alternative to Rankean approaches was the work of Jacob Burckhardt (1818–97), Professor of History at Basle from 1845. Burckhardt, descendant of a patrician Swiss family, studied under Ranke at Berlin and from him derived his basic understanding of historical method; but Burckhardt reacted against what he believed to be Ranke's suppression of the poetry in history, and he later showed his hostility to the Rankean tradition by refusing to become Ranke's successor in the Berlin chair in 1872. Burckhardt established his reputation with *The Era of Constantine the Great* (1853), and, above all, *The Civilisation of the Renaissance in Italy* (1860), and the *History of the Renaissance in Italy* (1867), works which played an impressive part in furthering the concept, in whose interest Voltaire had laboured, of history as the history of culture and civilisation in all its manifold aspects; his vision of, and pronouncements upon, the Renaissance still have to be grappled with today by students of that topic. Burckhardt, incidentally, was even more conservative in general political outlook than Ranke: where Ranke could retain a proud nineteenth-century optimism about the development of human society, Burckhardt was deeply pessimistic.

Burckhardt's approach to history owed much to the French contemporaries of Ranke, Augustin Thierry and Jules Michelet (1798–1874). Thierry said that the essential object of his *History of the Norman Conquest of England* (1825) was to 'envisage the destiny of peoples and not of certain famous men, to present the adventures of social life and not those of the individual': attacking 'writers without imagination who have not known how to paint', he expressed the hope, which many later historians have heartily echoed, that he might produce 'art at the same time as science'.[28] Thierry was a romantic, and his work suffered excessively from the faults of romanticism: over-dramatisation and luxuriance in emotionalism. Michelet, also a romantic and a political partisan, nonetheless played an important role in the three key advances by which history became modern academic discipline. First, he did much for the teaching of history in France, publishing two useful little textbooks, the *Précis of Modern History* (1827) and *An Introduction to Universal History* (1831), as well as lecturing at the École Normale, the Sorbonne and the Collège de France (where he received the history chair in 1838). Secondly, Michelet was at one with the school of historical writing which saw the need to see history from the inside, to 'resurrect' the past as Michelet himself put it; it was indeed Michelet who brought the neglected work of Vico to the attention of other scholars. Finally Michelet shared the passion of his contemporaries for primary source materials: in 1831 he was appointed Chief of the Historical Section of the National Archives. Michelet is seen at his best in the first six volumes of his seventeen-volume *History of France* (1833–67) – the later volumes are spoiled by his growing anti-clericalism – and in his *History of the French Revolution* (1846–53). Often marked by romantic exaggeration, this work is characterised by that sympathy with an era and its people which is the first requirement in a modern historian. Still more, Michelet showed that, in this age of the professionalisation of the discipline, history should be concerned not just with politics and diplomacy, but with all facets of human societies.

Best known today of the French writers of the mid-nineteenth century is Alexis de Tocqueville (1805–59). De Tocqueville was an aristocrat, a practising politician, and a political thinker deeply concerned with the problems of liberty and democracy. His *Democracy in America* (whose two volumes appeared in 1835 and 1840), product of his visit to that country in 1831, is still cited today for its grasp of some of the essential features of American society. His reputation as a historian depends upon his *The Ancien Régime and the Revolution* (1856), part only of what was projected as a much larger work covering the whole course of the revolution. In no way a political narrative of the events leading to the revolution, de Tocqueville's study is a thorough analysis of the nature of the *ancien régime*. He searched diligently for his documents and brought new sorts of sources into play: he consulted land registers, deeds of sale, grievance-lists, and a great range of administrative documents both national and local. Set within its larger European, rather than a purely French, context, and illumined by brilliant aphorisms, *The Ancien Régime and the Revolution* remains an authoritative work in its field; as a landowner de Tocqueville understood well the enduring preoccupations of aristocracy and peasants, but was perhaps less comprehending of the strength of the newer commercial interests.

All the writers of this era, then, had their weaknesses and their blind spots; while Ranke set his close followers off on a too narrow study of diplomacy and politics, those historians who aimed rather at the study of human civilisation were still often guilty of imprecision and romantic overstatement. Ranke and his followers saw their kind of history as 'scientific', in the sense of being systematic and based on critical techniques. There were others who wished to make history 'scientific' in the sense of having general laws.

3. Positivism and Marxism

The objective of Auguste Comte (1798–1857) was to study society in the same way that the natural world was studied by, as he put it, the 'positive' sciences. Comte impinged, as all social scientists must, on the study of history through his acceptance that history provided the raw material for the understanding of society (and he was the man most responsible for securing the establishment of a Chair of History in the Collège de France in 1831). Comte, in effect, was seeking the laws governing history conceived of as *process*, laws which would, he believed, enable man to predict the future course of events; among these was the 'law of the three states' which stated that the history of all societies and all branches of experience must pass through three stages, which he called the Theological, the Metaphysical and the Scientific. Comte's two major works, *Course of Positivist Philosophy* (1830–42) and *System of Positivist Politics* (1851–4), are ponderous, convoluted, ill-written studies which certainly did not justify the claims he made for his 'positivism'; nonetheless they are of outstanding importance as an unequivocal statement that human society is amenable to scientific study.

Much greater importance attaches to the theory of history which originated with Karl Marx. Marx was born in 1818, son of a lawyer in the German Rhineland, but he lived much of his writing life in England, where he died in 1883. He never presented a full and rounded account of his theory, elements of which can be found in writings spread over the period from the 1840s to the 1880s. The fullest early statement is to be found in the *German Ideology*, written in collaboration with Friedrich Engels and completed in 1846, though only a part was published during Marx's lifetime; no complete edition appeared till 1932. There is a lively sketch in the rousing *Communist Manifesto* (1848), in which Engels again collaborated, and a brief summary in the preface (first published posthumously in 1897) which Marx wrote for his *A Contribution to the Critique of Political Economy* (first published in 1859). His major work, *Capital* (1867–94), which like Adam Smith's *Wealth of Nations* is historical in approach, concentrates on the development of the capitalist economy, which Marx saw as the dynamic factor in modern history. Other writings by Marx, and by his close associate Friedrich Engels, add various glosses; to this have been added the explanations and extrapolations of admirers and disciples, both scholarly and polemical. Here I briefly set out the basic tenets of the Marxist view of history.

First, a fundamental distinction is made between the basic economic structure of any society, determined by the conditions under which wealth is produced in that society, and the 'super-structure', by which Marx meant the laws, institutions, ideas, literature, art, and so on. Secondly, history (in the sense of what has actually happened, the human past, or, if preferred, history as *process*), has unfolded through a series of stages, Asiatic, antique, feudal, and modern bourgeois, each of these stages being determined by the prevailing conditions under which wealth is produced (for example, in the feudal stage wealth is derived from ownership of land, in the bourgeois period it is derived from the ownership of capital, particularly capital which is used for the setting up of factories). Thirdly, the motor for this development from stage to stage is provided by the 'class struggle', classes themselves being determined by the relationship of particular groups to the specific conditions under which wealth is produced: the bourgeoisie, for example, own the means of capitalist production. Previously, according to Marx, the bourgeoisie had led the class struggle against the dominant class in the feudal stage, the aristocracy. Now, in the modern bourgeois, or capitalist period, the period in which Marx himself was writing, it finds itself engaged in a struggle with the class below, the proletariat or working class. The first section of the *Communist Manifesto* begins with the challenging statement: 'The history of all hitherto existing society is the history of class struggles.' Fourthly, Marx argued, the ending of each stage is signalled as new productive forces come into conflict with existing relations of production thus inaugurating 'an epoch of social revolution'. There was 'social revolution' when feudalism was overthrown by capitalism; there will be further 'social revolution' when capitalism, as its own inherent contradictions become apparent, begins to collapse and the proletariat are successful in their struggle against it.

Behind this view of the unfolding of history (which, of course, has some similarities with the ideas of Vico and Comte) is the philosophical notion of the dialectic, originally put forward by the Idealist philosopher Hegel (Hegel was an Idealist in that he saw ideas as the prime factors in historical change; Marx, of course, with his emphasis on the basic economic structure, was a Materialist). In essence the notion is the simple one that each age contains a dominant Idea, the *thesis*, but also holds within it an oppositional Idea, the *antithesis*: out of the clash of these two (hence *dialectic*) is produced a synthesis, the dominant idea of the new age. (It may be noted that this apparently impressive theory derived from the method of Plato's Dialogues, is simply conjured out of thin air, there being absolutely no empirical evidence to support it.) Marx, as he put it himself, 'stood Hegel on his head', applying the dialectic to material developments, not ideas: each historical stage, according to Marx, though based on one economic system, contains within itself the elements of a new economic system. Eventually, as noted above, there is a clash, 'an epoch of social revolution'. The theory of the dialectic can be used to explain the English Revolution of the seventeenth century which

> . . . occurred because the forces of production characteristic of capitalism had reached the point where their further development was held back by the feudal property relations sanctioned by the early Stuart monarchy; the outcome of the revolution was a re-modelling of the relations of production which cleared the way for the Industrial Revolution a hundred years later.[29]

It is important to note here that while this view still holds sway in Russia and China it gets little support from the empirical evidence thrown up by present-day experts in the field. However, given the period in which Marx was writing, one of harsh conditions and frequent economic crises, his overall analysis had much to recommend it; his also was a period in which grand-scale 'philosophy of history' in the manner of Hegel, the search for patterns in history, was in fashion. But, the fact is, the immediate influence of Marxism on historical studies was not great. In world history, of course, Marxism is of the utmost importance as a revolutionary doctrine which has taken hold of many parts of the world and which was at the heart of two of the most profound twentieth-century revolutions (though not all revolutions are Marxist – those of Kemal Ataturk and of the Ayatollahs are cases in point). Many of Marx's ideas were taken up (and transformed) by Max Weber (1864–1920), Professor of Economics at Freiburg in the 1890s. The influence of sociological approaches deriving from Marx and from Weber will be discussed in Chapter 4. Marxist ideas did influence a number of historians in the early twentieth century, who gave a strong emphasis to economic factors. After the Russian Revolution there were historians around the world who accepted Lenin's claim that Marxism had discovered 'the objective law behind social relations.' More recently there has grown up a much more subtle and sophisticated school of Marxism which I shall discuss later. But in my view the greatest importance of Marx in the development of historical studies, which I would put on a par with that of Ranke, is that while much of his theory has simply been falsified by subsequent developments, many of his most important insights have, though often slowly and against much resistance, been absorbed into the mainstream of the academic discipline. Marxism has been important for revealing the importance of economic history, of social classes, of technology, and of work and the workplace. It has had the further importance, through its postulation of the relationship between structure and super-structure, of directing attention towards a wider cultural history, towards interdisciplinary study, in which the interrelationship between art, literature, ideas, and politics and economics are studied. I shall want in particular, in Chapter 7, to discuss the Marxist, and Marxist-derived notions of cultural production and consumption, of dominant and alternative ideologies, of cultural hegemony, and of discourses as reflecting relations of dominance. Some historians argue that Marxism offers useful hypotheses, which can clarify arguments, demonstrate what can and cannot be proved by the evidence. That also is an issue to be taken up later.

Approaches derived from Marx (though not necessarily from Marx alone), finally, can act as a useful corrective to the nominalism which sometimes results from the unimaginative application of the Rankean mode ('nominalism' is that view which holds that universals or abstractions are simply names without corresponding realities, a view, in effect, which shuns all generalisations or explanatory interconnections). Not that it really needs Marxism to make the point, as is suggested by some wise words from Thomas Henry Buckle (1821–62), the self-taught English historian who, without knowing anything of Marx, sought to follow the positivists in their search for the general laws of human development. One can reject the system he adopted for his *History of Civilization in England* (the two volumes published in 1856 and 1861 in fact covered European as well as English history), but sympathise with his observation that among historians

> a strange idea prevails, that their business is merely to relate events, which they may occasionally enliven by such moral and political reflections as seem likely to be useful. According to this scheme, any author who from indolence of thought, or from natural incapacity, is unfit to deal with the highest branches of knowledge, has only to pass some years in reading a certain number of books, and then he is qualified to be an historian; he is able to write the history of a great people, and his work becomes an authority on the subject which it professes to treat.

'The establishment of this narrow standard,' said Buckle, 'has led to results very prejudicial to the progress of our knowledge.'[30]

'Positivism' is an awkward word. The French scholar Numa Denis Fustel de Coulanges (1830–89) presented a 'positivism of the document', which in effect was an extreme statement of the Rankean position. He declared (in his *History of the Political Institutions of Ancient France*) that what was not in the documents did not exist:

> success in reconstruction of the past could only be achieved by a patient study of the writings and documents that each age has left of itself. No other means exists which allows our spirit to detach itself sufficiently from present preoccupations and to escape sufficiently from every kind

of predilection or prejudice in order to be able to imagine with some
exactness the life of men of former times.[31]

When Marxists today criticise non-Marxist historians as 'positivist', it is Fustel they have in mind rather than Comte or Buckle
(the better word would be 'hermeneutic', but then certain Marxists
of today, led by Jürgen Habermas (b. 1929) have developed a
'hermeneutics' of their own on the basis that only they know the
correct method of interpreting texts – readers may well feel that
such elaborate words are best avoided if at all possible). However,
if we can stomach further elaborate language, we may define those
who look for general laws (like Marx and Buckle) as *nomothetic*
in their approach and those who seek the detailed and the unique
(like Ranke or Fustel) as *idiographic* in theirs (the distinction
originates with the German philosopher Wilhelm Windelband
(1848–1915) who in his *German History* (1891–98) insisted that
there were general laws in history, which he took to be based on
what he saw as the collective psychologies of different nations).
In what is sometimes known as 'the Lamprecht controversy' the
German historical profession made it clear that it was totally
behind the Rankean tradition and totally opposed to the search
for general laws.

4. Anglo-Saxon Attitudes

The new techniques of historical study pioneered in Berlin were
slow to affect history in Britain and America. Indeed in Britain
the main thrust of Ranke's immediate contemporaries was to re-
emphasise history as a literary art rather than as a science in either
of the two senses mentioned in the previous section. Foremost
among these was Thomas Babington Macaulay (1800–59), whose
approach to history, in some measure at least, is illumined by the
much-quoted sentence he penned in 1841: 'I shall not be satisfied
unless I produce something which shall for a few days supersede
the last fashionable novel on the tables of the young ladies.' His
History of England (four volumes, 1848–55, the fifth volume being
incomplete at his death) enjoyed an unrivalled success in both
Britain and America: according to the American historiographer
Westfall Thompson, sales in the U.S.A. exceeded those of any
book ever printed, save the Bible and some school texts; in the

U.K. 140,000 copies had been sold by 1875. He was enough a man of the romantic revival to state that 'the perfect historian is he in whose work the character and spirit of an age is exhibited in miniature'; but his work was characterised by 'the constant avowed or unavowed comparison . . . with the present' which S. R. Gardiner, a later English disciple of Ranke, declared to be 'altogether destructive of historical knowledge'.[32] Macaulay did some services to history as a discipline in providing so magnificent a demonstration of the literary effect to be achieved through the exercise of the highest powers of selection and organisation, and through his pioneering attempt at social history in the famous Chapter 3. It must also be recorded that he showed immense energy in seeking out primary sources of many kinds: broadsheets and songs, as well as maps, political documents, ambassadors' dispatches, and private papers. But in his search after effect, and in his political partisanship, he sometimes cheated, so that his rendering of the past was less 'truthful' than, given the resources available to him, it could have been. One notorious example of this is the passage in the first volume of the *History* describing the speech in which William III bade farewell to the States of Holland before setting out for Britain. Macaulay writes:

> In all that grave senate there was none who could refrain from shedding tears. But the iron stoicism of William never gave way; and he stood among his weeping friends calm and austere, as if he had been about to leave them only for a short visit to his hunting-grounds at Loo.

Macaulay had no reliable source for this fanciful description. In fact it is a direct plagiarism (conscious or unconscious) from the *Odes* of Horace, the description of Regulus making his farewell to the Senate.[33]

Macaulay's other great failing is of interest in connection with the point about history being a 'dialogue between present and past'. Macaulay was, in a precise, party-political sense, a 'Whig historian' who brought to his historical work the bias of a practising Whig politician and whose writings, in an obvious way, were an example of history as party propaganda. More significant is Macaulay's contribution to what has become famous and notorious as the 'Whig interpretation of history', conceived in the broader, non-party sense as a product of the intellectual and material developments of the time and the reaction of liberal upper-class intellectuals to these developments. Macaulay was actually born in the first year of the nineteenth century; with the ruling class of his time he could confidently state (in the first chapter of his *History*): 'The history of our country during the last hundred and sixty years is eminently the history of physical, of moral and of intellectual improvement.' The first Whig historian (in both narrow and broad senses) was Henry Hallam (1777–1859), whose *Constitutional History of England from the Accession of Henry VII to the Death of George II* was published in 1827, and the tradition was continued throughout the nineteenth century by historians who would have repudiated the overt party bias which attached to Macaulay. All shared with Hallam a spoken or unspoken assumption that the central theme in English history was the development of liberal institutions: thus in the study of remote ages they greatly exaggerated the importance of 'parliaments' or of bodies, real or imagined, that they thought were parliaments; and they tended to interpret all political struggles in terms of the parliamentary situation in Britain in the nineteenth century, in terms that is of Whig reformers fighting the good fight against Tory defenders of the *status quo*.

Thomas Carlyle (1795–1881) really stands quite outside the accepted canons of historical scholarship. His works are literature, poetry, prophecy. In that they are full of lessons and morals for his times, in that they were very widely read, they demonstrate clearly the social affiliations of historical writing. They had a considerable effect on the attitudes of the wider public towards the problems of history, and upon the teaching of history at the lower levels. On the whole the influence was an unfortunate one, for Carlyle, who often seemed to regard 'history' as synonymous with 'biography', greatly exaggerated the importance of 'great men', as in his *Frederick the Great* (1858–65) which in turn served to foster at lower educational levels the most naïve forms of historical analysis. At the same time it should be noted that Carlyle's *Letters and Speeches of Oliver Cromwell* (1845) made an important contribution to historical interpretation: for two centuries the Puritan dictator had been described as one of the most evil villains of English history; thanks to Carlyle he now began to take his place as one of the 'great men' of English history.

The attitudes of the great English historical writers of the early nineteenth century were amply reflected in the absence of any efficient provision for the systematic teaching of history at university level. History in Britain, much later than history in Germany and France, remained a branch of literature, or a study to be pursued purely for its more obvious utility to soldiers, statesmen and lawyers. Only against strong resistance was history established as an autonomous academic discipline, and even then the literary and the utilitarian traditions proved very enduring. In fact the first big changes in the ancient Universities of Oxford and Cambridge came about as a by-product of the utilitarian concept of history, for the men who wished to reform the slumbering condition of the universities were strong believers in history as a 'useful' subject for study. Thus in 1850 when history was first given status as a subject suitable for academic study at Oxford, it was as part of a combined school of Law and History. In attacking even this project, a contemporary broadsheet raised a number of questions which, in the continuing debate over the nature of history, have not always been satisfactorily answered:

> Is the subject suitable for Education? Is it an exercise of the mind? Is it not better left till Education is completed? Is it not sufficiently attractive to ensure a voluntary attention to it? Is it a convenient subject for Examination? Where is the standard author like Thucydides, etc.? If there is not a standard author, how are the comparative merits of the candidates to be judged?[34]

'Will it not', queried the anonymous author, putting a point over which somebody, some of the time, has worried ever since, 'supersede those subjects where a severer discipline is required?'

There had been a Regius Professor of History since the early eighteenth century: from the deliberations of the Royal Commission on Oxford University there followed a Professorship of International Law and Diplomacy and the Chichele Professorship of Modern History ('Modern' as distinct from 'Ancient'). Yet in the new history school standards remained far from rigorous: history's purpose, the Regius Professor openly boasted, was 'the better education of the gentry', so that they could, in these changing times, continue to run the country. Instruction took the very rudimentary form of commentary on a textbook: examination papers were provided with a small space into which the student could insert his answers. Only with the appointment in 1866 of William Stubbs (1825–1901) to the Regius Chair, was the basis

laid for the serious study of history at Oxford. Much later than
in the leading European countries the British Government had
initiated a redirection of energies towards the publication of basic
source materials in British history; Stubbs had for many years
been working on editions of the twelfth-century chroniclers for the
Rolls Series, begun in 1857. Stubbs had produced nearly twenty
volumes of texts, all magnificent works of critical scholarship,
when in 1870 he produced his volume of *Select Charters* which
long remained a basic source book in constitutional history classes.
Between 1874 and 1878 he published his *Constitutional History of
England*, based as no other work of an English historian had
been, on meticulous scholarship and exhaustive study of all available sources. For all that, Stubbs could not, any more than Ranke,
escape the prejudices and received attitudes of his times. As Sir
Ernest Barker once remarked, 'he wrote his *Constitutional History
of England* in spectacles – the spectacles of Victorian Liberalism,
which are all the more curious on his nose when one remembers
that he was a natural Tory'[35] – the Whig interpretation of history,
we have noted, was no narrow party matter. Stubbs began with
high hopes of teaching history based 'not upon Hallam and
Palgrave and Kemble and Froude and Macaulay, but on the abundant collected and arranged materials now in course of publication'. While Ranke had stressed diplomatic history, Stubbs, a
child of an era when British parliamentary institutions still stood
forth in men's eyes as one of humanity's great inventions, saw in
constitutional history the sturdy discipline upon which to base his
teaching.

Stubbs retired from his chair in 1884 (to become Bishop of
Chester and, later, Oxford), a disappointed man. Despite the
founding of the Historical Manuscripts Commission in 1870, publication of source materials in Britain was lagging far behind the
achievements in this respect of Germany. And although in the
long term Stubbs had as profound an effect on historical scholarship and teaching in Britain as Ranke had in Germany, resistance
at Oxford to any complete adoption of German methods was too
strong for Stubbs to overcome. 'Research! Research! A mere
excuse for idleness; it has never achieved, and never will achieve,
any results of the slightest value!' Such was the conviction of
Benjamin Jowett, Master of Balliol, and promoter of the famous
Oxford tutorial system.

Stubbs' successor in the Regius Chair, Edward Augustus Freeman (1823–92), expressed many of the basic features of the Oxford attitude in his brief but memorable aphorism: 'History is past politics, and politics is present history.'[36] To John Richard Green (1837–83) is often given the credit for mounting the challenge to the assumptions behind the first part of this aphorism. In his *Short History of the English People* (1874) Green deliberately turned away from what in a fine phrase he called 'drum and trumpet history': 'I have devoted more space', he declared, 'to Chaucer than to Cressy, to Caxton than to the petty strife of Yorkist and Lancastrian, to the poor law of Elizabeth than to her victory at Cadiz, to the Methodist revival than to the escape of the Young Pretender.'[37] It may be, though, that Green contributed to the idea of social history as an inferior kind of history because the records available to him were still of the type upon which a political or constitutional narrative could most easily and reliably be constructed. He was in fact very much in the Whig tradition, entertaining quaint notions about the essentially democratic character of the English 'people': in his history the men of the Middle Ages speak with the accents of Victorian reformers. The most persuasive investigations into life as it really was in the distant past were carried out by F. W. Maitland (1850–96) who, 'working backwards from the known to the unknown, from the certain to the uncertain' (as he himself put it), and (as G. M. Trevelyan put it) using medieval law 'as the tool to prise open the mind of medieval men' produced a work of social and legal history which can still speak to today's reader, *Domesday Book and Beyond* (1897).[38]

The best rejoinder to the implications of the second part of Freeman's aphorism was that of Samuel Rawson Gardiner (1829–1902), an Oxford historian in the style of Ranke and Stubbs, who was for a time Professor of History at King's College, London. Gardiner declared: 'He who studies the society of the past will be of the greater service to the society of the present in proportion as he leaves it out of account.'[39] Here we are back to the central point in regard to history considered as a social necessity: Gardiner is recognising the necessary service to present society of history, but stresses that the quality of the history, that is to say the value of that service, will be higher the more the historian disabuses his mind of the preoccupations and values of present society. The 'past-minded' historian renders the truer service to the present than does the 'present-minded' historian. Gardiner's sixteen-volume *History of England from 1603–1660*, based on the highest canons of scientific scholarship, still forms an initial resource for all students of seventeenth-century English history.

At Cambridge historical study began to glimmer into life after the appointment (in 1869) of Sir John Seeley (1834–95) to the Regius Chair in immediate succession to Charles Kingsley, who as a novelist and Christian socialist has some claims to historical eminence, though none to eminence as a historian. The real founder of the Cambridge school of history was Lord Acton (1834–1902), of whom more in the next section. Seeley was an active politician, and one of the group of intellectuals who played a part in the development of the ideals of British imperialism at the end of the century: his most important book, *The Expansion of England* (1883), one of the earliest ventures into the realm of imperial history, is remembered for the classic remark about the British Empire being acquired (in the seventeenth and eighteenth centuries) 'in a fit of absence of mind'.[40] In 1890 Thomas Frederick Tout (1855–1929), a pupil of Stubbs, became Professor at Manchester University, building it into one of the best history schools in the United Kingdom. The Scottish historians of the eighteenth century, unlike their English counterparts, had been university teachers, but in the intervening years historical studies had sunk low in the Scottish universities: in the 1880s R. L. Stevenson, the novelist, was seriously considered for the History Chair at Edinburgh. At the beginning of the new century the Edinburgh history school, followed by those of the other Scottish universities, was remodelled on the Oxford pattern, that is, the hard core was provided by constitutional history, involving some study of documents; the softer outer flesh was a combination of history as a literary, and history as a useful 'liberal' subject.

As has been the case in other spheres, the United States of America proved more receptive to the best European ideas about the study of history than did Britain, though for much of the nineteenth century the literary approach to history, informed by noble liberal sentiments, predominated. George Bancroft (1800–91) was as much a nationalist as a democrat: his ten-volume *History of the United States from the Discovery of America*

(1834–87) established the legend of the glories of the American Revolution carried through entirely by disinterested patriots on behalf of the liberties of mankind. But American literary historians were not parochial: while John Motley (1814–77) turned to the study of the Dutch Republic, William H. Prescott (1796–1859) wrote his impressive and colourful pioneering studies of the Spanish expansion in South America. As American historical study on a formal basis was developed in the last quarter of the nineteenth century the influence of Ranke was undoubtedly very strong, though it would be wrong to suggest that American scholarship succumbed entirely to the great German and his less great apostles. At the other extreme positivism, at least in the somewhat reduced and common-sense form of a desire for synthesis and a search for patterns and tendencies, was accorded more respect by some American professionals than was the case in Britain. Among leading scholars in both countries, however, there was to be found in abundant degree a stress on the usefulness of history. The Rankean seminar method was imported into America in the 1870s by Herbert Baxter Adams of Johns Hopkins University; and Ranke himself was made first and only honorary member of the American Historical Association (A.H.A.) on its foundation in 1884. Justin Winsor, President in 1887, was a strong Rankean, and the German 'scientific' approach was developed by Henry Adams (1838–1918), who inaugurated graduate studies in history at Harvard. First President of the A.H.A. was Andrew D. White, who as Professor of History at the University of Michigan had endeavoured to establish contact with European standards. But on the whole White, an influential educator (he became President of Cornell University), concentrated on the exemplar function of history and was rather impatient of detailed research. He did do something to combat the view, sponsored by Bancroft, and fostered by the disciples of Ranke, that the main concern of history was politics. Alfred T. Mahan (1840–1914), like White, was interested in the 'lessons' afforded by history, rather than in deep primary research: he was thus led to his important and creative idea of the vital importance in warfare of control of the sea (expressed in two books, *The Influence of Sea Power on History, 1660–1783* and *The Influence of Sea Power on the French Revolution and Empire, 1793–1812*). On the whole it can be said that American historical study only began its phenomenal expansion in the twentieth century.

5. The End of the Century

No sooner, indeed, was history established as a discipline than quarrels broke out as to the nature of that discipline – though as I have said before public debate can mask a substantial amount of essential agreement. Indeed public debate may be a demonstration that there *is* essential agreement; that the limits within which, and the common ground over which, differences may be voiced, are widely recognised. From the end of the nineteenth century there were known standards against which professional historical work could be judged, and professional history, in the last analysis, provided a standard against which all forms of amateur and popular history could be judged. Like all professionals historians have a vested interest in proclaiming the novelty, the uniqueness, the correctness of their own particular approaches, and in declaring the approaches of others redundant, trivial, or wrong. Some historians like to insist that only certain questions should be asked, only certain methods used. In fact the history that we know is the cumulative result of different historians asking different questions and using different methods. The wider the subject tackled, of course, the wider must be the range of methods deployed. But with regard to the limited, manageable tasks that most historians undertake, some methods will be more appropriate than others, *depending on the topic studied and the questions asked*. That is the critical point so often ignored by those who indulge in polemics on behalf of one historical school or another. In fact, by 1900, the basic principles of the nature of historical evidence had been settled.

However that is not to deny that there were big issues to be discussed. I shall need another long chapter to take the development of historical studies up to date, but shall hazard the proposition here that the central issues in that development can be reduced to five.

1. Is the central concern of history the political state and relationships between states, as Ranke thought? Or are there other particular 'sub-histories' which ought to be given primacy:

economic history (this was the strongest candidate at the beginning of the new century, supported by those who, whether they knew it or not, shared with Marx a belief in the determining influence of economic factors); intellectual history (reasserting the supremacy of 'ideal' factors over 'material' ones)? Or should not the 'sub-histories' be reintegrated together into a 'total history', a cultural history as aspired to by Voltaire or Burckhardt, but based on the most rigorous new methods?

2. Should history seek to emulate the sciences, or should it retain its affiliations (and the readership that went with them) with literature? An important figure here, as we shall see in a moment, was the German philosopher, Wilhelm Dilthey (1833–1911) who suggested that history, having modes of thought of its own, should not seek to be a science (though it is probable that working historians, as is their way, were unaware of his agonisings on their behalf).

3. Could history be 'objective', or was it always subject to the assumptions and prejudices of the historian? Could knowledge of universal validity be established, or was it always socially constructed? Rankeans believed that the rigorous use of primary sources would entail objectivity; Marx in effect argued that such methods merely revealed the outer husk, the bourgeois view of society – what was thought of as knowledge in bourgeois society was merely part of the superstructure, it was 'constructed' in order to preserve bourgeois dominance (and thus, of course, only those possessed of the 'scientific' insights of Marxism could penetrate through to the reality). In fact it was again Dilthey who made the important contribution (for those who were actually bothered one way or another) that historians are inevitably part of their own researches, inevitably shaping their results one way or another, but that this was no totally disabling condition.

4. As new techniques were developed (psychological, statistical, etc.) were they to be: (a) treated with suspicion; (b) embraced, and trumpeted as superseding all older techniques; or (c) considered as merely a further addition to the historian's constantly growing armoury?

5. How legitimate, and how important, were the new areas for study which from time to time were proposed – such as the masses, economic motives and interests, religious superstition, urbanisation, demography, women? Did such new areas simply extend

the scope of existing history or did they turn history into something different? (for example did the study of the masses and of economic interests entail the creation of a 'New History'; or, much later, did the study of urbanisation, or of women, replace old history by, respectively, 'urban history' or 'feminist history'?).

The leading figures in non-Marxist German economic history were Wilhelm Roscher (1817–94), Karl Wilhelm Nitzsch (1818–80), Gustav Schmoller (1838–1917), and, when young, Karl Lamprecht. The intensity of feeling they aroused among those who held to Rankean *Staatensgeschichte* can be seen in the riposte of one Rankean, Dietrich Schäfer: 'History is not a feeding trough.'[41] This school then came to a somewhat sudden end as its protagonists became involved either in controversies over contemporary German social policy, or in the debate over nomothetic approaches to history. The scholar who bridged the gulf between this group, and later economic historians was Werner Sombart (1863–1941), author of many important works, including *War and Capitalism* (1913) which laid emphasis on the part played by war in stimulating eighteenth-century industrialisation. In Britain there was no intellectual battle, and indeed there was only one real piece of solid economic history, though a massive one at that: between 1866 and 1902 there appeared seven volumes of *A History of Agriculture and Prices in England* by J. E. Thorold Rogers (1823–90). On the fringes Arnold Toynbee the elder had begun the debate on what was then as much a current social and political, as historical, topic, *The Industrial Revolution in England* (1884). More of that later.

The big issue of whether or not history was a science was addressed by the philosopher Dilthey in his *Introduction to Historical Knowledge* (1883) and subsequent essays. Dilthey maintained that there was a fundamental distinction between scientific knowledge and cultural knowledge, and that, as part of the latter, history had no need to attempt to conform to the norm of scientific knowledge. Dilthey and his followers also observed that historians did not stand apart from, and observe, an objective reality; they observe a reality at least partially constructed in the process of observing. Now, whether or not the historian can remain sufficiently self-aware to counteract this tendency, or whether in fact all historical knowledge is 'constructed' eventually became a matter of serious contention. For the moment the lesson that most working historians were content to draw was that history need not ape the natural sciences and need not feel ashamed for not doing so. This was the essential message contained in Droysen's *Encyclopaedia and Methodology of History* (1868), a reassertion of the validity of the methodology developed by (if not necessarily the narrow range of interests of) Ranke.

A very influential textbook of methodology at the turn of the century was *Introduction to the Study of History* (Paris and London, 1898) by C. V. Langlois (1863–1929) and Charles Seignobos (1854–1942). There was a no-nonsense, practical, dismissive quality about the general approach, much in tune with that generally adopted by most of the historical profession for the next fifty years. Langlois and Seignobos dismissed as 'idle questions' unworthy of consideration: 'whether history is a science or an art; what are the duties of history; what is the use of history'. The aim of history they declared: 'is not to please, nor to give practical maxims of conduct, nor to arouse the emotions, but knowledge pure and simple.' In fact, Langlois and Seignobos did regard history as a science, save that it is a science whose methods differ from those of all other sciences! Of all branches of study, they say, history most requires a consciousness of method:

> The reason is, that in history instinctive methods are, as we cannot too often repeat, irrational methods; some preparation is therefore required to counteract the first impulse. Besides, the rational methods of obtaining historical knowledge differ so widely from the methods of all other sciences, that some perception of their distinctive features is necessary to avoid the temptation of applying to history the methods of those sciences which have already been systematised.[42]

Langlois and Seignobos are clear that from around 1850, history had ceased, both for the historians and the public, to be a branch of literature. Previously, they remark, historians republished their works from time to time without feeling any necessity to make any changes in them:

> Now every scientific work needs to be continually recast, revised, brought up to date. Scientific workers do not claim to give their work an immutable form, they do not expect to be read by posterity or to achieve personal immortality; it is enough for them if the results of their researches, corrected, it may be, and possibly transformed by subsequent researches, should be incorporated in the fund of knowledge which forms the scientific heritage of mankind. No one reads Newton or Lavoisier; it is enough for their glory that their labours

should have contributed to the production of works by which their own have been superseded, and which will be, sooner or later, superseded in their turn.[43]

Only works of art, Langlois and Seignobos declare, 'enjoy perpetual youth'. This is the definitive rebuttal of the strange idea (which I mentioned in Chapter 1) that works of history can be equated with novels. No one would dream of 'up-dating' the novels of Henry Fielding; but one would get a very limited and inaccurate view of the decline and fall of the Roman Empire if one relied on Gibbon alone without recourse to the historical works which have been published since.

Most famous of all turn-of-the-century pronouncements was that of J. B. Bury in his inaugural address (1902) as successor to Lord Acton in the Regius Chair at Cambridge.

> If, year by year, history is to become a more and more powerful force for stripping the bandages of error from the eyes of men, for shaping public opinion and advancing the cause of intellectual and political liberty, she will best prepare her disciples for the performance of that task, not by considering the immediate utility of next week or next year or next century, not by accommodating her ideal or limiting her range, but by remembering always that, though she may supply material for literary art or philosophical speculation, she is herself simply a science, no less and no more.[44]

The last phrase has been much quoted, not always in a manner favourable to Bury or to the state of historical studies at the turn of the century (Bury clearly, was not aware of the arguments of Dilthey). In general historians of the twentieth century have been less certain (and Bury, too, in common with all men of intelligence, changed his views, as we shall see in the next chapter) that the painstaking accumulation by empirical means of 'fact' would ultimately produce a scientifically accurate representation of the past. Yet, whatever reservations they may have about the universal validity of their findings, all reputable historians of today still have as the core of their activities the 'scientific' study of evidence as understood by Ranke, Langlois and Seignobos and Bury. Concepts of science have changed since the turn of the century when the absolutes of Newtonian physics still held sway: certainties have given way to probabilities, the absolute to the relative. In fact the whole concept of the nature of human understanding and knowledge has become more complex and more subtle. When Bury said 'history is a science, no less and no more', science to him meant something concrete and ultimately knowable. Science has changed, and so has history: they have indeed, in a sense, changed in parallel, though that does not mean that there is no longer validity in the differences detected by Dilthey and Langlois and Seignobos (my subject for Chapter 4).

Bury was a man of wide culture and a writer of great literary grace. He believed that history had developed in scope since the time of Ranke:

> The exclusive idea of political history, *Staatengeschichte*, to which Ranke held so firmly has been gradually yielding to a more comprehensive definition which embraces as its material all records, whatever their nature may be, of the material and spiritual development, of the culture and the works, of man in society, from the stone age onwards.[45]

This had come about, Bury believed, because of the rise of nationalism with its emphasis on peoples rather than states; but, he argued, it owed most to the application of 'the historical method' to all the manifestations of human activity – social institutions, law, trade, the industrial and the fine arts, religion, philosophy, folklore, literature.

History then, said Bury, was concerned with 'the constant interaction and reciprocity among all the various manifestations of human brain power and human emotion'. It is important to note this broad conception of the nature of history, for the broadening of historical concerns is too often represented as a development only of the very recent past. The trouble, of course, is that although in inaugural addresses leading historians might preach the ideal of total history, in practice most of Bury's contemporaries did relapse into a concentration on political and constitutional history. There was a justification for this: sources existed in greater abundance for political and constitutional history, and, in lesser degree for economic history; however desirable the study of folklore or the conditions of the poor, the evidence was much more fragmentary. There remains today a fundamental divide between historians who believe that one should first decide what questions require answers, then wring answers out of whatever material is available, however unsatisfactory, and historians who prefer to be guided by the available material and to ask only those questions to which the material provides well-substantiated answers.

Among the most impressive memorials to the 'scientific' concept of history to which Bury subscribed, are the multi-volume *History of France* (1900–11) edited by Ernest Lavisse (1842–1922), and the *Cambridge Modern History*, launched by Bury's predecessor in the Regius Chair at Cambridge, Lord Acton (1834–1902). Aiming to 'meet the scientific demand for completeness and certainty' the *Cambridge Modern History* was to be, as are most important advances in natural science, the work of many hands. 'Contributors will understand', Lord Acton wrote,

> that our Waterloo must be one that satisfies French and English, German and Dutch alike; that nobody can tell, without examining the list of authors, where the Bishop of Oxford laid down the pen, and whether Fairbairn or Gasquet, Liebermann or Harrison took it up.[46]

Although there would be extensive bibliographies, there were to be no footnotes. As historians have lost confidence in the possibility of the complete and certain history which the *Cambridge Modern* was supposed to provide, footnotes have crept back in: they are not, as readers and publishers often think, the last words in complacent pedantry; they imply in fact an admission of fallibility on the part of historians, who are indicating their premises to their readers so that their readers may, if they wish, work out different conclusions of their own; they are, indeed, a sign of that dialogue between historians and readers of which I have already spoken, and which 'scientific history' in Acton's sense sought, in authoritarian fashion, to deny.

In the Anglo-Saxon world attempts continued to be made to appeal to the older literary tradition whose supersession by the disciples of Ranke had been so thoroughly welcomed by Langlois and Seignobos. In the December 1903 edition of the *Independent Review* George Macaulay Trevelyan (1876–1962), grand-nephew of Macaulay, published the celebrated essay 'Clio, a Muse', which was republished in 1913 in slightly less polemical form. History, Trevelyan argued, could perform neither of the functions properly expected of a physical science which he defined as 'direct utility in practical fields'; and, 'in more intellectual fields the deduction of laws of cause and effect'. The only fashion in which Trevelyan would allow that history could be scientific was in 'the collection of facts, the weighing of evidence as to what events happened'. Trevelyan then continued:

In dealing even with an affair of which the facts are so comparatively well known as those of the French Revolution, it is impossible accurately to examine the psychology of twenty-five million different persons, of whom – except a few hundreds of thousands – the lives and motives are buried in the black night of the utterly forgotten. No one, therefore, can ever give a completely or wholly true account of the French Revolution. But several imperfect readings of history are better than none at all; and he will give the best interpretation who, having discovered and weighed all the important evidence obtainable, has the largest grasp of intellect, the warmest human sympathy, the highest imaginative powers.[47]

Carlyle, Trevelyan claimed, had fulfilled these last two conditions in his *French Revolution*, so that his 'psychology of the mob' and his 'portraits of individual characters'

are in the most important sense more true than the cold analysis of the same events and the conventional summings up of the same person by scientific historians who, with more knowledge of facts, have less understanding of Man.

The development of modern psychology, which was not very far advanced when Trevelyan penned his reply to Bury, has rendered a substantial part of his argument invalid. 'You cannot', said Trevelyan, 'dissect a mind; and if you could, you could not argue thence about other minds. You can know nothing scientifically of the twenty million minds of a nation.' Therefore Trevelyan concluded,

in the most important part of its business, history is not a scientific deduction, but an imaginative guess at the most likely generalisations.

There is a pleasing honesty about this, though Trevelyan was unwise to state so categorically the limits of what is scientifically knowable. History today still employs 'imaginative guesses' – so indeed do all intellectual pursuits – but historians today would be unlikely to discuss the French Revolution, or any similar topic without acquainting themselves with the discoveries of the sciences of individual and social psychology.

Concluding then that history had no 'scientific value' (by this somewhat dubious phrase Trevelyan meant that history yielded neither useful inventions, nor causal laws of human behaviour in the mass), Trevelyan declared, as many in the opposition camp – including, as it happens, Langlois and Seignobos – had long agreed, that history's purpose is educative. The justification for the pursuit of historical studies which Trevelyan now developed is the one which, among teachers of history, most successfully held the field for the next fifty years, although, as I argued in the opening chapter, it both involves rather specious claims on behalf of history, and skirts the central point that history is a social necessity. History, said Trevelyan, provides a basic training in citizenship. The value, for example, of Lecky's Irish history is not that Lecky proves Irish Home Rule to be 'right or wrong, but he trains the mind of Unionists and Home Rulers to think sensibly about that and other problems'. History should not only remove prejudice, it should provide the ideals which inspire the life of the ordinary citizen. A knowledge of history enhances the understanding of literature, and doubles the pleasures of travel.

Returning again to the question of whether history is an art or a science, Trevelyan concluded, rather as Thierry had done before him, and as contemporaries like Stuart Hughes have agreed since, in this fashion: 'Let us call it both or call it neither. For it has an element of both.' Trevelyan distinguished between three distinct functions of history: the *scientific* (collecting and weighing evidence as to facts), the *imaginative* or *speculative* (selection and classification, interpretation and generalisation) and the *literary*. This last function, whose importance Trevelyan deliberately stressed, he defined as 'the exposition of the results of science and imagination in a form that will attract and educate our fellow-countrymen'. The remainder of 'Clio a Muse' took the form of a lament that since the 'scientists' had taken over, the intelligent layman had ceased to read history:

> The *Cambridge Modern History* is indeed bought by the yard to decorate bookshelves, but it is regarded like the *Encyclopaedia Britannica* as a work of reference; its mere presence in the library is enough.

Trevelyan's cry found its strongest responses among those with an amateur interest in history (a great many, given the nature of history). Theodore Roosevelt was one of the 'amateurs', who expressed his views in a letter to Trevelyan's father, George Otto Trevelyan:

> I am sorry to say that I think the Burys are doing much damage to the cause of historic writing . . . We have a preposterous organisation called I think the American Historical Association . . . They represent what is in itself the excellent revolt against superficiality and lack of research, but they have grown into the opposite and equally noxious

belief that research is all, that accumulation of facts is everything, and the ideal history of the future will consist not even of the work of one huge pedant but of a multitude of small pedants. They are honestly unconscious that all they are doing is to gather bricks and stones, and that whether their work will or will not amount to anything really worthy depends upon whether or not some great master builder hereafter arrives who will be able to go over their material, to reject the immense majority of it, and out of what is left to fashion some edifice of majesty and beauty instinct with the truth that both charms and teaches. A thousand Burys, and two thousand of the corresponding Germans whom he reverentially admires, would not in the aggregate begin to add to the wisdom of mankind what another Macaulay, should one arise, would add. The great historian must of course have scientific spirit which gives the power of research, which enables one to marshal and weigh the facts; but unless his finished work is literature of a very high type small will be his claim to greatness.[48]

The day of 'preposterous organisations' had dawned, essential if the historical profession was to be sufficiently well organised to fulfil its social function properly. 'Great historians' were less needed than honest ones. Truthfulness to what actually happened (as far as that is possible) was more important than literary quality, though the two were not inherently incompatible.

Notes

1. See F. Smith Fussner, *The Historical Revolution* (1962).
2. Breisach, p. 11, quoting Thucydides, *The Peloponnesian Wars* 2.2.
3. *The Anglo-Saxon Chronicle*, ed. G. N. Garmonsway (1953), pp. 219–20.
4. Bede, *A History of the English Church and People*, ed. Leo Sherley-Price (1955) pp. 72–3.
5. Francesco Guicciardini, *L'Historia d' Italia* (Florence, 1561), p. 1.
6. William Camden, *Britain, Written first in Latin by William Camden Translated newly into English by Philémon Holland* (London, 1610), fol. 2.
7. Quoted by Fussner, p. 23.
8. Ibid.
9. J. H. Brumfitt, *Voltaire: Historian* (1958), p. 2.
10. See Breisach, pp. 180–3.
11. Breisach, pp. 203, 219–20, 233; Georg G. Iggers, *New Directions in European Historiography* (1985), pp. 12, 14, 18, 22.
12. Voltaire, *Essay sur l'Histoire générale, et sur les moeurs et l'esprit des nations depuis Charlemagne jusqu'à nos jours*, vol. I (Paris 1756), pp. 1–9.

13. David Hume, *Two Short Essays, On the Study of History, and On General Reading* (Edinburgh, 1836) pp. 13–15.

14. For Millar, see S. W. F. Holloway, 'Sociology and history' in *History*, XLVIII (1963), 157–61.

15. Arthur Young, *Travels during the years 1787, 1788, 1789* (Bury St Edmunds, 1792), entry for 27 Nov. 1789, p. 242.

16. Voltaire to l'abbé Dubos, Feb., 1738, quoted by J. B. Black, *The Art of History* (1926), p. 55, and (in a slightly different translation) by Fritz Stern, *The Varieties of History* (New York, 1956, 1972) 1973 edn, p. 39.

17. H. R. Trevor-Roper, *History, Professional and Lay* (Oxford, 1957), p. 5.

18. Quoted by Stern, p. 51.

19. Translation in G. P. Gooch, *History and Historians in the Nineteenth Century* (1952), p. 74.

20. Translation in Stern, p. 57.

21. Ibid.

22. Quoted in J. Westfall Thompson, *History of Historical Writing*, vol. 2 (New York, 1942), p. 231.

23. Breisach, p. 233; Gooch, p. 80.

24. Quoted in Stern, p. 171.

25. Quoted in Stern, pp. 61, 62.

26. Cited by Breisach, p. 237.

27. J. G. Droysen, *Historik* (1858), 1937 edn, p. 287.

28. Augustin Thierry, *Histoire de la conquête de l'Angleterre par les Normands* (Paris, 1925), Introduction.

29. John Tosh, *The Pursuit of History* (1984), pp. 139–40.

30. Quoted in Stern, p. 124.

31. Quoted in Stern, p. 180.

32. See J. Westfall Thompson, pp. 297, 298.

33. See C. G. Crump, *History and Historical Research* (1928), pp. 151–2.

34. Quoted in R. W. Southern, *The Shape and Substance of Academic History* (1961), p. 9.

35. Quoted by J. Westfall Thompson, p. 300.

36. See J. Westfall Thompson, p. 317.

37. J. R. Green, *Short History of the English People* (1874), p. v.

38. Trevelyan, *Autobiography*, p. 7; H. E. Ball, *Maitland: A Critical Examination and Assessment* (1965); Robert L. Schuyler, *Frederick William Maitland, Historian* (Berkeley, Ca., 1960).

39. Quoted by Westfall Thompson, p. 322.

40. Sir John Seeley, *The Expansion of England* (1883).

41. Cited in Westfall Thompson, p. 423.

42. C. V. Langlois and Charles Seignobos, *Introduction to the Study of History* (1898), p. 7.

43. Ibid., pp. 302–3.

44. Quoted in Stern, p. 223.

45. Ibid., p. 221.

46. Quoted in Stern, p. 249.
47. Quoted in Stern, p. 231.
48. Letter of 25 January 1904, quoted by Howard K. Beale in *Pacific History Review*, XXII (1953), p. 228.

Chapter 3 The Development of Historical Studies: The Twentieth Century

1. New History and Total History

Sometimes different schools of historical writing or different paradigms of subject matter and method are presented as being of inherent interest in themselves, one school or one paradigm, perhaps, being advanced as having superseded all others. Actually historians, or groups of historians, are only of importance insofar as they actually add to our knowledge of the past. The significance of new schools, of course, is that they may produce better methods or, at least, different approaches, without which certain advances in knowledge would not be made. But much of the research which has ensured that we do have some tolerably exact accounts of the past, and makes possible judgements, such as Marc Ferro's, on the dangerous myth-making which is still so widely prevalent, has been carried out by historians working in a mainstream tradition, essentially based on Rankean methods. To have a proper understanding of where history stands today, it is necessary to appreciate the labours of the traditionalists as well as the vital advances made by the innovators. The 'traditionalist' who fails to take account, as appropriate to his or her particular enquiry, of such advances, is a bad historian. But there is no perfect approach, no perfect paradigm.

A substantial part of this chapter deals with historians alive and active today, not so much because what they do is up-to-the-minute and therefore 'good', but because they (unless they are woefully arrogant and short-sighted) are in the best position to have profited from the discoveries and the mistakes of their predecessors. There is a cruel truth in the words of Langlois and Seignobos on the impermanence of historical writings, so, while it is important to see broadly what happened between the last decades of the nineteenth and the last decades of the twentieth centuries, my account will be bare and, necessarily, a trifle arbitrary. My hope, in what I fully recognise as a most presumptuous exercise, is to say something interesting on some of the historians whose names are known to students and lay readers, and to bring out the variety of subjects addressed, and range of methods employed, at any point in time. I start, in this section, with two schools (or paradigms) which, prior to the Second World War, were, overtly, challenging the Rankean tradition. Then I move to a variety of traditionalists, all of whom brought in something new (a special emphasis on economic history, or on intellectual history, say), but whose importance lies in what they said about particular topics in the past, rather than in what they said about how it was that they were in a position to say what they said. Of course they had theories about the particular periods and countries they studied, about how the age of imperial Rome gave way to the Middle Ages, about the character of early English parliaments, about the causes of the French Revolution, about the nature of the American Republic (great experiment in democracy, say, or arena for the hegemony of powerful economic interests?): sometimes the concrete discoveries remain while the theories have to be discarded. Thirdly, I look at the continuing preoccupation with traditional areas of study after 1945, and at some of the new approaches brought to bear on them. Fourthly I look at the Marxist tradition, and at some of the problems that tradition has had to face in the light of research (some of it by Marxists) carried out since 1945. Fifthly I take, in its post-World War II form, the school of which everyone has heard, the *Annales* school; and finally I look at the very diverse range of activities going on today, arguing that what historians, in common with all other academics, do is solve problems, and repeating my contention that the approaches and techniques used will depend on the problems selected for solution. Throughout we shall see that, as always, historians are affected by the attitudes and political concerns of their time. We shall see that, like all thinking beings, they are affected by the theories of the subconscious and the irrational associated with Sigmund Freud, and by the dislocations and upheavals of the two world wars.

During the Depression in Britain in the 1930s Britain's *führer manqué* Sir Oswald Mosley set up what he called the 'New Party';

it was a feeble title for a feeble party. [Personally I always think
there is also something feeble about such titles as 'New History',
'New Economic History'. 'New Social History' – however, my task
is not to judge, but to understand.] One who strove consciously
(and legitimately, I intend no criticism) to be new was the American, Frederick Jackson Turner (1861–1932) whose essay on 'The
Significance of the Frontier in American History', was presented
to a meeting of the American Historical Association in 1893. In one
form or another the thesis (not completely unique to Turner, but
he was the one who expressed it most vividly) has affected American historical thinking ever since, soon provoking a violent reaction. Turner was a dedicated teacher and a profound influence;
but he did not himself publish a great deal. In 1906 there appeared
his *The Rise of the New West*, covering American history in the
years 1820–30. The continuation, *The United States 1830–1850*,
never completed, was published after his death in a version edited
by his students. The most important of only thirty or so articles
were grouped in two volumes, *The Frontier in American History*
(1920) and *The Significance of Sections in American History*
(1932). It has been argued that he never gave any valid demonstration of his thesis, but simply reiterated it over and over again.
    The thesis, as Turner put it to the American Historical Associ-
ation, was that

> Behind institutions, behind constitutional forms and modifications, lie
> the vital forces that call these organs into life and shape them to meet
> changing conditions. The peculiarity of American institutions is the
> fact that they have been compelled to adapt themselves to the changes
> of an expanding people – to the changes involved in crossing a conti-
> nent, in winning a wilderness, and in developing at each area of this
> progress out of the primitive economic and political conditions of the
> frontier into the complexity of city life.

The frontier to the Americans, said Turner, was what the Mediterranean had been to the Greeks. The second Turner thesis concerned the significance, once the frontier had disappeared, of a
geographically determined 'sectionalism' in the American nation:
the 'physical map' of America, he argued, 'may be regarded as
a map of potential nations and empires'. Turner was attacked,
particularly in regard to 'the significance of sections' for ignoring
economic imperatives, the growth of capitalism, the nature of
class antagonism; for ignoring technology and the true inspiration

behind cultural and artistic endeavour; above all Turner was attacked for fostering isolationism and nationalism, and denying the European roots of American civilisation. Isolationism, indeed, was an important part of the American political scene in the interwar years, as Prussian nationalism formed the context for so many German historians in the nineteenth century. On Turner's behalf, his pupil, Avery Craven, argued that prior to Turner's bold revisions: (a) the 'germ' theory of the European origins of American institutions remained unquestioned; and (b) economic, social and geographical factors had been neglected. 'Against such attitudes', Craven wrote, 'Turner revolted':

> A Wisconsin background enabled him to take a more penetrating view. He could enter by the back door. Because he had been part of a rapidly changing order, he saw American history as a huge stage on which men, in close contact with raw nature, were ever engaged in the evolution of society from simple beginnings to complex ends. Historians had answered 'what' long enough; it was time to inquire as to 'how' things came about. America, as it then existed, was the product of the interaction of 'economic, political and social forces in contact with peculiar geographic factors'. Such an understanding would give a new American history.[1]

The 'New History', in fact, was the label consciously adopted by James Harvey Robinson (1863–1936), borrowing it, apparently, from Edward Eggleston (1837–1902) whose *Transit of Civilization* (1901), ironically, presented that very view of ideas flowing from Europe to America against which Turner was protesting. The general tenor of the attack on the 'old history', was that it was pedantic, lacking relevance, neglectful of vast territories of the human experience. The New History was deliberately 'present-minded' in that it sought to use history to help in dealing with the social problems of the present; in fact it merged into that widely based school of historical writing which held sway in America till after the Second World War, always known as 'Progressive history', that is a history informed by liberal-reformist sentiments.[2] The New History claimed that it would give special attention to economic forces, as to intellectual and any other forces relevant to social problems; in so doing it would make use of the discoveries of the social scientists. The programme has been repeated often since; virtue, we are coming to realise, lies not in programmes, but in the manner in which and the extent to which they are carried out. Robinson himself was not much given to scholarly research and the best practical example of the New History is the work produced in collaboration with Charles A. Beard, *The Development of Modern Europe* (1907–8). Beard (1874–1948) was a tough-minded scholar. His *An Economic Interpretation of the Constitution* (1913) presents the framers of the American constitution as realistic appraisers of man's economic instincts, rather than as liberal-minded idealists. At the time Beard probably believed that he was offering *the* key to the American constitution, though later he was to contend that he had only offered *one* key among many, that, as his title had stated, this was merely *an* interpretation. The book at any rate was a stimulating one, and a valuable corrective both to the predominantly political orientation of American historical writing at that time and to the myth-making of Bancroft. Two years later there followed the detailed and penetrating study, the *Economic Origins of Jeffersonian Democracy* (1915).

One of the earliest American historians showing a special interest in economic history was Edward P. Cheyney, who published his *Introduction to the Industrial and Social History of England* in 1901. Later Cheyney went on to formulate a series of six general historical laws, which in fact were no more than a mix of traditional assumptions with a rather extreme expression of the attitudes of New and Progressive historians. The six laws were: first, the Law of Continuity, which states that 'all events, conditions, institutions, personalities come from immediately preceding events, conditions, institutions, personalities' and, further, that 'the immediate, sudden appearance of something, its creation by an individual or a group at some one moment of time, is unknown in history'. This is simply a re-statement of the main tenets of historicism. Second, the Law of Impermanence, which states that institutions must adapt or perish. Third, the Law of Interdependence: by this Cheyney held that no nation could make permanent gains at the expense of another, and he cited the case of the French occupation of the Ruhr (1923) which had not greatly benefited France. This one sounds suspiciously like liberal propaganda, as do the fourth, fifth and sixth laws, the Law of Democracy (proven only by demonstration of the 'failure' of all other systems), the Law of Necessity for Free Consent (coercion, being 'against human nature', would necessarily produce resistance) and the Law of Moral Progress: in support of the last Cheyney advanced the highly dubious proposition that 'the people, always more moral than their rulers, would not at any time within the last four centuries have supported their governments in wars merely of plunder, aggression or revenge.'[3]

The most important second-generation product of the New History movement was Arthur M. Schlesinger Sr (1888–1965).[4] As a graduate student at Columbia, Schlesinger was formally under the supervision of the Rankean traditionalist Herbert L. Osgood, from whom he derived an enduring respect for thorough and scholarly study of the sources. But the men who most influenced the thrust of his work were Robinson and Beard. His dissertation, finally published in 1918 under the title *The Colonial Merchants and the American Revolution, 1763–1776*, gave him, he wrote, 'an opportunity to examine the interrelation of economics and politics, something which Beard had so deeply interested me in'. The result, he believed, combined 'the research methods of Osgood with the insights of Beard'. While teaching at the State University of Iowa, Schlesinger in 1922 instituted a course on the 'Social and Cultural History of the United States', the first of its kind. This led naturally to his sponsorship of a multi-volume, co-operative *History of American Life* (first four volumes 1927). However, his famous dictum that Great Men are 'merely the mechanism through which the Great Many have spoken', now seems little more than a trite metaphor, an affirmation of personal bent, but no real explanation of historical processes. The continuance of the Progressive tradition after the Second World War was represented by Arthur Schlesinger Jr's *The Age of Jackson* (1945). However, the central notion of conflict between big business and an allegedly noncapitalistic common people was beginning, as many critics pointed out, to seem rather too simplistic.

It was in France that the more substantial advances in developing a genuinely new and wider approach to history took place. The guiding influence was that of Henri Berr (1863–1954), who sought through the journal he founded in 1900, the *Revue de Synthèse historique*, and through his projected one-hundred-volume *L'Évolution de L'Humanité*, to bring together in one great synthesis all the activities of man in society, calling to his aid the methods and insights of sociology and the other social sciences. But the two men who more than any others demonstrated how the perennial but vague aspirations after a history more truly

representative of the richness of man's life in society could be
turned into reality were Lucien Febvre (1878–1956) and Marc
Bloch (1886–1944).

   Lucien Febvre, born into a cultivated upper-middle-class family,
received a traditional historical training. At the same time he
found himself greatly attracted by the ideas and objectives of
Henri Berr, whom he affectionately described as the 'Trojan horse
in the territory of traditional scholarship'.[5] A stress on the importance of geography had been part of French historical scholarship
since the time of Michelet, and Febvre's first book was in fact
predominantly geographical: *The Regions of France: Franche-
Comté* (Paris, 1905). His long apprenticeship was completed with
the publication in 1911 of his dissertation *Philippe II and the
Franche-Comté*. Based on thorough research among extensive
archival materials, the book was strong in knowledge both of
geography and of economics. Already profoundly dissatisfied with
the simple monocausal explanations of earlier political historians,
Febvre was concerned to demonstrate what he called 'the multiple
action of profound causes'.[6] This work was followed immediately
by a *History of Franche-Comté*, then, after an interval spent in
the French Army during the First World War, Febvre swung to
something much more general, a volume on *The Earth and Human
Evolution* for Henri Berr's multi-volume series: among the large
number of points which Febvre made which have now become
platitudes was the rebuttal of the idea that rivers make 'natural
frontiers' – in fact they serve to link human groups together in
common activities. From a special interest in geography, Febvre,
in a manner typical of many twentieth-century intellectuals,
moved to an interest in group psychology. The new interest was
revealed first in a study of *Martin Luther un destin*, published in
1928; but his most impressive venture into what he himself called
'historical psychology' was his *Le problème de l'incroyance au XVI
siècle: la religion de Rabelais*, published just after the Second
World War (1947). This is a highly significant work in relation to
developments which were to come later in the realm of the study
of 'mentalities'. Febvre sought to illuminate the mental attitudes
of the age showing that it was quite impossible for Rabelais to be
an atheist or unbeliever in any modern sense, and that to regard
him as such was utterly unhistorical: in a most original way, and
addressing a most original topic, Febvre was endeavouring to

show the complex web of belief 'as it really was.' *Le Problème de l'incroyance au XVI siècle: la religion de Rabelais* was volume 53 in the projected *Library of Historical Synthesis: the evolution of humanity*, directed by Henri Berr, which envisaged a total of 96 volumes organised in 4 sections: 1. 'pre-history, proto-history, antiquity'; 2. 'origins of Christianity and the Middle Ages'; 3. 'the modern world' (in which Febvre's contribution was included); 4. 'towards the present'. The power of established professors in France, and the custom of publishing books as part of a prestigiously led joint project, can be a stimulus to highly original work; it can also impose the dead hand of fading orthodoxy. Febvre's book carried a foreword by Berr entitled 'Collective Psychology and Individual Reason' which (rather patronisingly it would seem to a British individualist) summarised Febvre's main conclusions.

Marc Bloch also came from a comfortable family: since his father was a Professor of Ancient History at the Sorbonne it has been said of him that he was 'by birthright a member of the intellectual élite of the Third Republic'. Significantly he graduated in both history and geography, and his earliest publication, paralleling that of Febvre, was a geographical study of *L'Île de France*. His historical apprenticeship was served in searching the archives of northern France for materials for a study of medieval society in the Île de France. At the end of the First World War (through which he served with distinction) he was appointed to a chair at Strasbourg, to which university Febvre had already been summoned. With Febvre, Bloch shared an interest both in geography and in collective psychology. Beyond that he sought to borrow from sociology an exactness of method and a precision of language which, as he lamented, was too often lacking in traditional historical writing, and he studied archaeology, agronomy, cartography, folklore and linguistics – the last subject with particular reference to place names and the genealogy of language. Bloch was an early believer in both the *comparative* and the *regressive* methods. Comparative study involving comparisons within a single country or between different countries, is of immense value, since in highlighting both similarities and differences it can be a source of new syntheses, new questions and, sometimes, convincing answers. The regressive method (previously most successfully used by Maitland) involves using evidence drawn from a later age of, say, customs, traditions, place names, field patterns, which may well have endured from an earlier age, in order to illuminate that earlier age. In a manner which in some ways echoes the early approach of Frederick Jackson Turner, and more obviously that of Michelet, Bloch himself tramped around the French countryside talking to the men who in the twentieth century still tilled the soil in a manner not too far different from that of their medieval predecessors.

Bloch's interest in collective psychology, in, above all, the manner in which the irrational imposes patterns on human behaviour, was seen most strongly in his book on *Les Rois Thaumaturges* (1924): in this Bloch showed that although the belief that both French and English kings were endowed with healing powers grew up almost by accident, that belief became a fundamental part of the concept of royalty and an important element in maintaining its strength. But Bloch's main contributions to historical study were his investigations into the nature of feudal society. *Rois et Serfs: un chapitre d'histoire capétienne* (1920) is a rather brief work, but it shows clearly the manner in which Bloch viewed feudal society from the standpoint of the peasants rather than that of the lords and kings. *Les Caractères originaux de l'histoire rurale française* (1931) turned firmly away from the historian's traditional preoccupation with legal and administrative institutions: Bloch endeavoured to show that the forms of French agricultural life depended less on such matters than upon the persistence of the forms of tenure and organisation established in the early Middle Ages. Through his refusal to examine only institutions and communities for which traditional primary materials existed, Bloch helped to rescue from oblivion the medieval village community, hitherto largely ignored by medieval historians who preferred to follow where the documents took them, that is to the seignorial manor and its legal apparatus. Bloch struck bold and powerful blows on behalf of the kind of history which questions first, then seeks around for any scrap of evidence of any kind which may provide answers; too many historians shoot first and ask questions later. *Feudal Society* (1940), though a sketch rather than a fully rounded work, drew upon the many types of source and the many methodologies with which he had familiarised himself.

The great vehicle for the broader history desired by Bloch and Febvre was the famous journal which they jointly launched in January 1929, *Annales d'Histoire Économique et Sociale*, widely known thereafter as *Annales*. The first editorial committee consisted of Albert Demangeon, Professor of Human Geography at the Sorbonne, G. Espinas, Archivist of the French Foreign Ministry, Maurice Halbwachs, Professor of Sociology at the University of Strasbourg, Henri Hauser, Professor of Economic History at the Sorbonne, A. Piganiol, Professor of Roman History at Strasbourg, Charles Rist, Professor of Political Economy at the Faculty of Law, Paris, André Siegfried, Professor at the School of Political Science, Paris, the Deputy Governor of the Bank of France and the distinguished Belgian historian, Henri Pirenne (see next section). In their introductory address to their readers, Bloch and Febvre referred to the gulf which had developed in historical and social studies:

> While historians apply their good old hallowed methods to the documents of the past, more and more people are devoting their activity to the study of contemporary societies and economies . . . Among the historians themselves, as among the students of contemporary problems, there are plenty of other lines of demarcation: ancient historians, medievalists and modernists; students dedicated to the description of societies terms 'civilised' . . . or, on the contrary, drawn to those which for lack of better terms, can be called 'primitive' or exotic. Nothing would be better, we absolutely agree than for each person, concentrating on a legitimate specialisation, laboriously cultivating his own back yard, nonetheless to force himself to follow his neighbour's work. But the walls are so high that, very often, they hide the view . . . It is against these deep schisms that we intend to raise our standards. Not by means of articles on method or theoretical dissertations, but by example and accomplishment. Brought together here, scholars in different disciplines and different specialities, all motivated by the same spirit of exact objectivity, will present the results of their researches in subjects which they have chosen and in which they are expert . . . Our enterprise is an act of faith in the exemplary virtue of honest labour, backed by solid and conscientious research.[7]

What *Annales* stated really was that there could be no short cut to a more interesting, a more *'intégrale'* (Febvre's word), a more 'human' (Bloch's word) history. If the older school of political and constitutional history was unsatisfactory, it was not necessarily because it was laborious and painstaking, but often because it was lacking in these qualities, was too prone to easy remedies and oversimplified conclusions. The lay reader, then, will find *Annales* a rather forbidding journal: like any other learned journal, it does not try to fulfil the necessary historical role of communication

with the wider audience, society as a whole. But the example of
Annales, as well as the direct teaching of Bloch and Febvre, gave
rise to a whole tradition of better historical writing. Febvre was the
more rounded historian; much of Bloch's writing has a provisional
character, and he is not always easy to read. Both made some of
their most stimulating contributions to our deeper knowledge of
the nature of history in the pages of *Annales*, often in the form
of short reviews. However, Bloch left behind after his death the
unfinished manuscript published in English as *The Historian's
Craft*. In this work there are obvious and understandable imperfections, but overall it succeeds marvellously in being a very
human testimony to a personal faith in history, and a manifesto
on behalf of the most advanced school of historical writing of the
interwar years. Bloch begins with the question: 'What is the use
of history?' First he dwells on the poetry of history, on its 'unques-
tionable fascination'. However, to entertain is not enough: the
use of history is that it aids understanding: 'to act reasonably, it
is first necessary to understand'. Recognising the human and social
need for history, Bloch remarks that 'we become indignant if . . .
it seems incapable of giving us guidance'. History, of course, is
'but a fragment of the universal march towards 'knowledge', and
it is only 'a science [Bloch used the word in the Continental sense,
as discussed in the next chapter] in infancy . . . it is still very
young as a rational attempt at analysis'. Bloch is proud of the
soul-searching, the hesitancies of his craft, but he hopes to see
ever-increasing numbers of historians 'arrive at that broadened
and deepened history which some of us – more every day – have
begun to conceive' – that is, the history of the *Annales* school.

After this introduction, Bloch attempts a definition of 'history':
history is 'the science of men in time'; the critical element is the
human one. Dismissing the debate over history as art or science,
Bloch nonetheless makes a fine personal statement on behalf of
the aesthetic and humane quality of history:

> Between the expression of physical and of human realities there is as
> much difference as between the task of a drill operator and that of a
> lutemaker: both work down to the last millimetre, but the driller uses
> precision tools, while the lutemaker is guided primarily by his sensitivity
> to sound and touch. It would be unwise either for the driller to adopt
> the empirical methods of the lutemaker or the lutemaker to imitate
> the driller.

In a section entitled 'Understanding the Present by the Past', Bloch elaborates one of his simplest but most compelling ideas, and one which is incidentally a perfect ancillary justification for the study of history: 'Man spends his time devising techniques of which he afterwards remains a more or less willing prisoner.' Although admitting the great technological transformation which has set the present apart from even the immediate past, Bloch singles out the 'understanding of the Protestant or the Catholic Reformation' as most important 'for a proper grasp of the world today'. In the section 'Understanding the Past by the Present', Bloch defends his famous regressive technique of historical research, then comes to the heart of his own humane affirmation: the 'faculty of understanding the living is, in very truth, the master quality of the historian'.

With the chapter on 'Historical Observation' Bloch moves into the realm of the historian's methods. Here he admits that not all historians in the past have made the best use of the wide variety of source materials open to them. He looks forward to the time when historians will be better equipped with linguistic and social science techniques, and hopes to see much more in the way of co-operative research. The manifesto-writer is very apparent in his plea that 'history as it can be' should not be made 'the scape-goat for the sins which belong to bad history alone.' Chapter Three, on 'Historical Criticism', deals with the problems of forgery, reliability of records and the like. Bloch makes a strong claim on behalf both of the difficulties of the historian's tasks and of his success in overcoming them, and, as one would expect from the editor of a scholarly journal, he looks for the highest standards in the use of references and other scholarly apparatus. In the next chapter Bloch goes on to affirm his abiding interest in group psychology as a basic study in history. His faith is in a total, integrated history, but since the individual cannot grasp history in its wholeness, he believes that each historian must be content with analysing one particular aspect of society. Bloch's treatment of the historian's use of words like 'serfs', 'bourgeoisie', 'Middle Ages' is so important that we must leave it for separate discussion in chapter six. The book concludes with an unfinished fragment on historical causation, where there is a clear echo from Lucien Febvre: 'History seeks for causal wave-trains and is not afraid, since life shows them to be so, to find them multiple.'

2. The Mainstream and its Many Tributaries (to 1945)

Two of the most distinguished continental European historians of
the earlier part of the twentieth century were both born in the
same year: Friedrich Meinecke (1862–1954) gave a special
emphasis to ideas, Henri Pirenne (1862–1935) gave a special
emphasis to economics. Meinecke sought in a kind of 'intellectual
history' to fuse the teachings of the two German masters who had
seemed to stand at opposite poles in historical study: Ranke, who
had glorified the might of the political state, and Burckhardt,
who contemplated (somewhat pessimistically) the development of
human civilisation and its creative artefacts. Clearly the stronger
pull was that of Ranke, and Meinecke's essential interest proved
to be the history of *political* ideas. After taking his Berlin
doctorate in 1886, he worked for fourteen years in the Prussian
state archives. His first book (two volumes, 1895 and 1899) was
a biography of General Hermann von Boyen, an activist in the
early nineteenth-century Prussian reform movement. In 1906 and
1907 there followed two further studies of Prussian liberalism; and
in 1908 he published a book on the origins of the German nation
state. His most famous work was *The Doctrine of Raison d'État
and its Place in Modern History* (Munich and Berlin, 1924).

Henri Pirenne is Belgium's best-known historian. After a long
and thorough training in what had become the established European manner, during which he developed a deep and abiding
interest in 'scientific' historical methodology in the Rankean sense,
he taught throughout his life at the University of Ghent save for
the untoward interruption while he was the defiant prisoner of
the Germans during the First World War. The contextual influences on Pirenne are clear. He belonged to a country which had
had an independent political existence only since the 1830s; it is
not therefore surprising that he should have turned so readily to
a study of economic and cultural forces in early Belgian, and, by
extension, European history (since there were no early *Belgian*
political institutions). Pirenne's contemporaries in the later nineteenth century were very conscious of the fact that urbanisation
was one of the major features which distinguished their culture
from that of earlier ages: hence, among historians, there was a
lively controversy over the origins of medieval towns. Belgium
itself, at the end of the nineteenth century, was an urban society:

and in the length of their continuous history, the towns of Belgium rivalled those of Italy.

From 1893 onwards Pirenne began publishing articles, based mainly on Belgian evidence, presenting his views on the origins of medieval towns, which, briefly, he associated with a revival of trade in the eleventh and twelfth centuries: the final statement appeared in *Medieval Cities: their origins and the revival of trade* (Princeton, N.J., 1925). Meantime Pirenne became involved in the bigger controversy of how and why the classical ages gave way to what, since the Renaissance, had been dubbed 'the Middle Ages'. Pirenne's famous thesis on the issue probably emerged first in his lectures at Ghent in 1910, though it appeared in print only in 1922 and 1923, and then in the form of two learned articles in the professional journals. A brief statement followed in the opening pages of *Medieval Cities*; the full statement was published posthumously in *Mohammed and Charlemagne* (1937). Through a study of economic rather than political institutions, Pirenne reached the conclusion that a Roman civilisation, based on the Mediterranean, survived the Barbarian invasions, and did not collapse till the Muslim expansion of the seventh century. Medieval civilisation began only with the Carolingians: 'Without Mohammed, Charlemagne would have been inconceivable.'

Though his two major theses have both been subject to damaging attack by subsequent researchers, Pirenne's other achievements, his seven-volume *History of Belgium* (1899–1932) and his works of popularisation, such as his *Economic and Social History of Europe*, still carry authority, a good example of the point I have several times made that it is often the more solid research which has the lasting value, theories being dispensable. To get the balance right, though, I must add that it is the theories which provoke thought and stimulate further research. As Pirenne himself put it: 'Every effort at synthesis, however premature it may seem, cannot fail to react usefully on investigations, provided one offers it in all frankness for what it is.'[8]

Pirenne and his co-workers permanently broadened the channels of medieval history, which, despite the best efforts of some of the 'constitutional' historians, did more and more become a true 'social history'. In this respect, indeed, medieval history outstripped modern history, as a glance at that major enterprise of the 1930s, *The Oxford History of England*, will confirm: the

medieval volumes are 'social history', the modern ones very
largely political and institutional. To the last Pirenne kept himself
within the accepted tradition of historical professionalism: as he
explained at the beginning of the final volume of the *History of
Belgium*: 'My sole end has been to seek to understand and to
explain.'

Still more austere was Georges Lefebvre (1874–1959), who
from the severe disciplines of Langlois and Seignobos evolved a
quantitative and finally a quasi-psychological approach to history.
Echoing Langlois and Seignobos ('No documents, no history'), he
said 'Without scholarship there can be no history.' Later he added
what was to become the password of our own age: 'Il faut compter'
('one must count') His 'mainstream' beginnings could hardly be
demonstrated more conclusively than by pointing out that his first
major labour (while a teacher at the Lycée of Lille) was to trans-
late for his patron, Charles Petit-Dutaillis, disciple of Stubbs, the
famous constitutional history by the Victorian bishop. Volumes I
and II of *Histoire Constitutionelle de l'Angleterre: son origine et
son développement par William Stubbs* appeared in 1907 and 1913
respectively; volume III in 1927, by which time 'G. Lefebvre',
now a professor at Clermont-Ferrand, had become 'Georges
Lefebvre' and was ranked above Dutaillis on the title page.
Lefebvre published his own first book (two volumes, of course)
in 1924, *Les Paysans du Nord pendant la Révolution française*,
which established his primary interest and his primary virtue:
studies in depth of the French peasantry during the Revolution,
a meticulous attempt to establish the concrete realities of the
social structure. Lefebvre was never a member of the French
Communist Party, but like most French intellectuals of the left
(and even centre) he believed in the reality of the class struggle,
as defined by Marx; to the end he vehemently insisted, in classical
Marxist fashion, that the Revolution was caused by the rise of the
bourgeoisie. In 1932 there followed a study of the peasant hysteria
of 1789 in face of an imagined aristocratic conspiracy, *La Grande
Peur de 1789*, the work which took him into the realms of social
psychology. However it was just at this time that there appeared
the most fundamental economic analysis yet of the preconditions
for revolution and one which set the scene for many post-war
studies. *Esquisse des mouvements des prix et des revenus en France
au XVIII siècle*, by the young C. Ernest Labrousse, appeared in

1933; it was followed in 1944 by the first volume of *La crise de l'économie française à la fin de l' Ancien Régime et au début de la Révolution.*

Lefebvre was leftist and working-class in his political associations, and doubtless this helped to guide the direction of his researches, though, as he believed, it would not affect his conclusions. A growing interest among the intellectual classes in the working-class movement and in socialism generally was undoubtedly a motive in spreading an interest in economic history. Particularly was this true in Great Britain. Arnold Toynbee the elder was an upper-class pioneer of the university settlement movement who is generally given the credit for popularising the concept of an Industrial Revolution: his major theme was the harsh effects industrialisation had had on the lower classes. A similar interest lay at the heart of the pioneering studies by J. L. and Barbara Hammond: *The Village Labourer* (1911), *The Town Labourer* (1917) and *The Skilled Labourer* (1919). The primary concern of the two great Fabian intellectuals Sidney (1859–1947) and Beatrice (1858–1943) Webb was to establish the social facts upon which to predicate social reform: they were thus led into producing a number of historical works, which for many years remained as standard authorities: *History of Trade Unionism* (1894) and *English Local Government* (nine volumes, 1906–29). R. H. Tawney (1880–1962), an Oxford graduate who later became a teacher at the London School of Economics, was also directly involved with the working-class movement through his activities in adult education and in the Labour Party. His first book, *The Agrarian Problem in the Sixteenth Century* (1912), was concerned with the decline of the English peasantry – the former 'yeomen of England' – in face of what he saw as the unscrupulous 'rise of the gentry'. Following a path which has proved to be not unusual among historians, Tawney began to reach from economic history into the realm of intellectual and sociological history. Much influenced by two famous articles on 'The Protestant Ethic and the Rise of Capitalism' published in 1904 and 1905 by the German sociologist Max Weber, Tawney in 1926 published his own best-known work; *Religion and the Rise of Capitalism.*

The major figure among early twentieth-century economic historians, certainly in Britain, perhaps in the whole English-speaking world, is J. H. Clapham (1873–1946). At Cambridge

Clapham came in contact with the economist Alfred Marshall, who in 1897 sent the following important and revealing letter to Acton:

> I feel that the absence of any tolerable account of the economic devel-
> opment of England in the last century and a half is a disgrace to the
> land, and a grievous hindrance to the right understanding of the econ-
> omic problems of our time. London and Cambridge are the only places
> where the work is likely to be done well; but till recently the man for
> the work had not appeared. But now I think the man is in sight.
> Clapham has more analytic faculty than any thorough historian whom
> I have ever taught; his future work is I think still uncertain; a little
> force would I think turn him this way or that. If you could turn him
> towards XVIII or XIX century economic history economists would
> ever be grateful to you . . .[9]

In those days, when economics was still essentially political economy, a change in direction was not difficult. In 1902 Clapham accepted appointment as Professor of Economics at the college which was shortly to become the University of Leeds. While based in this centre of the textile trade, he seized the opportunity to make full acquaintance with the world of business: in 1907 he published his first book, *The Woollen and Worsted Industries*. It was not until after the First World War that Clapham revealed his talent for sustained economic narrative in areas formerly illumined only by the occasional monograph: *The Economic Development of France and Germany 1815–1914* was published in 1921. Clapham now devoted himself to his major life's work, *An Economic History of Modern Britain*, published in three massive volumes between 1926 and 1938.

In the original preface to the first volume Clapham offered three justifications for his labours. First, that the story had never previously been handled on this scale. Clapham's second justification was that he intended to challenge certain widely accepted 'legends':

> Until very recently, historians' accounts of the dominant element of
> the nineteenth century, the great and rapid growth of population, were
> nearly all semi-legendary; sometimes they still are. Statisticians had
> always known the approximate truth; but historians had often followed
> a familiar literary tradition.

Actually Clapham's explanation of population increase as due to a falling death rate would now be rejected by historians employing today's sophisticated statistical techniques, so that there is a slightly hollow ring about Clapham's complacent reference to 'historians who neglect quantities'. In his preface Clapham cited also 'the legend that everything was getting worse for the working man, down to some unspecified date between the drafting of the People's Charter and the Great Exhibition'. This 'legend' – which had appeared most forcefully in the work of the Hammonds – he attributed to the way in which 'the work of statisticians on wages and prices' had been 'constantly ignored by social historians'. Against the psychological intuitions and emotional sympathies of the Hammonds, Clapham placed the quantities of the economist and the characteristic modern faith in the virtues of economic growth. The 'standard of living controversy' had begun. 'Thirdly', claimed Clapham in his preface:

> it is possible, all along the line, to make the story more nearly quanti-tative than it has yet been made. Dropped here and there in the sources – in the blue books above all – lie all kinds of exact information, not only about wages and prices, but about the sizes of businesses and farms and steam-engines and social groups . . . Much approximation must be tolerated, and some guessing; but if the dimensions of things are not always clear, at least an attempt has been made to offer dimensions, in place of blurred masses of unspecified size.

The information was often less exact than Clapham thought: more because of temperament than because of the technical point that he worked exclusively in printed sources, Clapham was probably further from the real stuff of history than Lefebvre. But together they enunciated the thesis which was to dominate economic sub-history, and later was increasingly to influence general history (and which was already being fully practised by Labrousse): one must count.

Most professional historians, however, throughout Europe and North America continued to be preoccupied with constitutional and political history. One central problem which the traditionalists attacked with vigour was that of the origins of the English parlia-ment, pride of the Whig historians. While New historians sought to stress the importance of the present in the study of the past, the traditionalists were able to show how deep misconceptions about the medieval 'parliament' had grown up because of the present-minded character of Stubbs and his like. Some of the most important work in this area was done by American scholars,

traditionally attracted either to medieval institutions as the fore-
bears of American concepts of law, or to the late-colonial origins
of American independence. Quoting with approval Tout's dictum,
'We investigate the past not to deduce practical political lessons,
but to find out what really happened', the Harvard historian
C. H. McIlwain explained in his 1936 presidential address to the
American Historical Association how professional revisions of
standard myths come about:

> They have usually come piecemeal because someone has been steeping
> himself in the thought and motives of some past epoch by extensive
> and careful reading of the records or writings of the time, and one day
> wakes up to find – usually to his utter amazement – that this thought
> or these motives and institutions are not at all the ones he has been
> reading about all these years in the standard modern books. Then he
> gets to work.

McIlwain described his own personal feeling of shock when he
'suddenly realised that men like Lambarde or Fitzherbert in Elizabeth's time, when they spoke of a parliament, were thinking of
something in many ways very different from what I had learned'.
That McIlwain was personally a man of strong commitment to
progressive politics was apparent in his reflection on the manner
in which the over-extension of checks and balances in American
constitutional theory tends to violate liberty, 'making government
innocuous only by making it ineffective, and by splitting it up
[rendering it] irresponsible'. In the end he did believe in the social
function of history, while asserting that the basic task of the
historian was to understand the past on its own terms:

> As historians, our real task is with history, not with its application; but
> when troubles come upon us, the question will always emerge – it will
> not down – whether it belongs to the historian, even if not strictly *as*
> historian, to find in all these facts and developments, assuming them
> to be accurate, any lessons of value that may be practically useful. I
> sincerely believe that it does . . .[10]

The distinction between the historian *as* historian, concerned with
accuracy in understanding the past, and, as it were, the *applied*
historian, drawing out present uses of history, is a valuable one
to which we shall return.

Perhaps the name of Lewis Namier (1888–1960) does not quite
have the resonance today it had when A. J. P. Taylor likened the
publication of *The Structure of Politics at the Accession of George*

III (two volumes, 1929) to the publication of Darwin's *The Origin of Species*.[11] Nonetheless the story of how (sideways on, as it were) he came to tackle the problems he did, and the approaches and results he came up with, are still of general interest. Lewis Namier was a Polish Jew, born near the town of Lukow which was then in the Austro-Hungarian Empire, who read history at Balliol in the years before the First World War. He originally planned to research into the British Empire at the time of the American Revolution. An American historian gently guided him away from the over-crowded American end to the British. Soon after he started on this assignment Namier became aware of how little was really known of the nature of English politics in the later eighteenth century: under the all-pervading influence of the Whig school it had been too readily accepted that eighteenth-century political assumptions were the same as those of the nineteenth century: the works of contemporary polemicists, like Edmund Burke, were taken at their face value. What was really intended by Namier as a preliminary clearing-up operation became the major part of his life's work. The fashionable Whig view of eight-eenth-century political history postulated that the Glorious Revolution of 1688 had created a constitutional monarchy, to which the Hanoverian accession in 1714 added cabinet government; however, in 1760, the misguided George III so the story went, had attempted, through a vast central machinery of corruption, and in face of the heroic resistance of the Whigs, to put the clock back and restore a personal monarchy. The essential basis of Namier's approach was the carrying out of a huge series of detailed studies of individual personages which could then be welded together into a composite portrayal of the age (*prosopography* is the elaborate name for this methodology): instead of generalis-ations (that is, guesses) about what 'people', parties or groups did or thought, Namier got down to the individual person and worked up from there. In *The Structure of Politics at the Accession of George III* he studied the separate members of parliament and the motives for their being there, showing how small was the part played by the lofty political ideals on which Whig historians loved to expatiate. Above all Namier brought out the extent of local political influence, and showed how insignificant in fact was the reputed power of corruption held by the central government. Namier's credo was essentially that of the Rankean professional:

'One has to steep oneself in the political life of a period before one can safely speak, or be sure of understanding, its language.' His materials were traditional: in fact he was the first researcher in the field to work through the five hundred volumes of the Newcastle papers in the British Museum.

England in the Age of the American Revolution (1930) was only the first volume of a projected multi-volume series under this general title. However, it contained enough meat in itself to force a revision of accepted views of the eighteenth century. Namier had already shown the limits to eighteenth-century corruption; now, seeing the system not in terms of latter-day moralising but as men saw it at the time, he justified such corruption as did exist as necessary to the smooth running of government. More than this he demonstrated how unreal it was to see eighteenth-century Whigs and Tories as analogous to nineteenth-century Conservatives and Liberals. At the national level much of the meaning had gone out of the terms 'Whig' and 'Tory' though at the local level it was still possible to distinguish between a Whig and a Tory 'mentality'. National politics were the politics of faction and connection rather than of party in any nineteenth-century sense. Finally Namier showed that the powers of George I and II were much greater than the Whig historians had allowed for: correspondingly there was a good deal less in the contemporary and later accusations that George III was in some way 'unconstitutional' in his actions. Ministers under the first two Georges, as Richard Pares, the most brilliant of the Namierites put it, were the King's servants: but they were servants who had had 'the run of the place'.[12]

Apart from his eighteenth-century interest, Namier wrote on the diplomatic origins of the Second World War (permitting his work here to be marked by some of the passion which he strove to exclude from the eighteenth-century books) and on the 1848 revolutions. But it is the books discussed here, along with the massive *History of Parliament* (on which many pairs of hands were set to work), which exemplify the Namierite approach. These are works of analysis, in which the narrative element, of which Macaulay was such a great master, is completely swamped. From outside the profession one of the great criticisms of twentieth-century professional history was to be centred on this very loss of narrative impetus. Namier, further, was a 'Tory' historian in that he appraised the individual, selfish motivations of human beings eschewing the abstract ideals of the political philosophers. Here consciously or unconsciously, he was implicated in the Freudian revolution, which had done so much to destroy the old high-blown theorising about human motivation. In a later work, to be discussed in the next chapter, Namier consciously adopted the concepts of modern psychology. There is another point about Namier which we shall also take up then: in a rudimentary way, his work was at bottom quantitative; instead of talking of 'the' Whigs and 'the' Tories, he was asking 'how many' Whigs?, 'how many' Tories? In this he was in parallel with Sir John Clapham; but Namier was arguably the better historian, for he went on asking questions while Clapham was too often content simply to print the answers he found in his Blue Books.

One other aspect of traditional history was much developed in the early part of the present century: diplomatic history. In most of the main Western universities where the study of history had been formalised, history was held to end some time in the nineteenth century, or even earlier, and there was no study of contemporary history. However, the preoccupation in the interwar years with the origins of the First World War gave a tremendous stimulus to the study of recent diplomatic history. Before the war Bernadotte Schmitt was being highly adventurous when he prepared a doctoral dissertation on Franco-German relations in the period after 1870. An American, Schmitt took the Honours History School at Oxford, where the tuition in 1906 (as indeed now) consisted in the writing and discussing of a weekly essay on such topics (they haven't changed much either) as 'Was Magna Carta a Feudal Document?', 'Was the Foreign Policy of Queen Elizabeth Vacillating?' and 'Did the Stamp Act cause the Loss of America?' Schmitt reckoned that the essay-writing discipline served him well when it came to presenting the results of his own historical researches. He also remarked that the examinations for his Oxford B.A. were harder than those subsequently taken for his doctorate at the University of Wisconsin.[13] In the years after the First World War the various nations published volume upon volume of their diplomatic correspondence, providing a plentiful supply of source material for this particular historical specialisation. In many British universities the curious tradition developed that it was all right to study diplomatic history for the recent period, though the ancient embargo still rested upon the study of recent domestic history. Although diplomatic history was soon to gain the reputation of being the most arid and sterile of all the sub-histories, much of the diplomatic history of this time was very definitely present-orientated. The works of G. P. Gooch and S. B. Fay were very much congruent with Western liberal opinion which sought to exonerate Germany from the extreme charges of war-guilt which had been laid upon her at the time of Versailles. (Schmitt, it may be said, consistently followed a line much less favourable to Germany, and, it may be said also, more in keeping with the documentary evidence; his general line was also taken by Pierre Renouvin, the distinguished French diplomatic historian, and, after the Second World War, by the equally distinguished Italian scholar Luigi Albertini.) A whole generation of students were conditioned to feel that if history was not constitutional charters, then it must be diplomatic correspondence: a piece of historical popularisation published as late as 1964 actually began with a dismissal of 'that tortuous train of Reinsurance treaties, Dual and Triple Alliances, Moroccan crises and Balkan imbroglios which historians have painstakingly followed in their search for origins'.[14] The author was somewhat out-of-date in her historiographical knowledge but the comment would certainly have been good for a quarter of a century earlier.

Among American traditionalists in the 1930s, one of the most noteworthy was Samuel Eliot Morison (1887–1976), a determined upholder of hermeneutic historicism. His studies of seventeenth-century American Puritanism both stressed the elements of continuity in American intellectual life and, by setting it firmly in the context of its own time, refurbished the image of Puritanism which had been somewhat tarnished by the interpretations of the New historians. Another traditionalist, R. L. Schuyler, had, in a number of scholarly monographs, played an important part in challenging the myths which, since Bancroft, had encrusted American accounts of the American Revolution. In Schuyler's own words:

It is only within the last generation that the Revolution has come to be studied in a more scientific spirit, with the desire to find out what happened, rather than to justify. The revolt from England, we now know, was no spontaneous uprising of a whole people in behalf of human rights. It was, on the contrary, the work of an aggressive minority, capable in leadership and strong in organisation, who managed to carry with them a more numerous body of less active persons. A large minority of the colonists, probably about one-third, detested the Revolution, remained loyal to King and Empire, and suffered loss of property and every species of indignity at the hands of their exasperated and often envious neighbours. No account of the Revolution which does not represent it as a civil war, involving confiscation of property and social upheaval, is even measurably true to facts. The nationalistic school of American history disregarded what did not suit their patriotic purposes. They slighted the arguments of the Loyalists, ignored the British official side of the case, and exalted the Revolutionary cause. In short, they gave a warped and biased interpretation of the Revolution.[15]

Schuyler's language, it may be noted, is almost as emotive as that of any 'patriotic' historian, for in fact Schuyler was strongly Tory in political outlook. Although determined in the hunt of those he described as 'present-minded' in their historical writing, he was not much more successful than Ranke in keeping his prejudices out of his writing. This does not necessarily reflect on Schuyler's scholarship, though, as always, it was useful to the reader wishing to play a part in the dialogue, to know of Schuyler's conservatism.

3. The Mainstream and Some New Approaches after 1945

By the outbreak of the Second World War the solid line of historical endeavour running back to early nineteenth-century Berlin had not been broken. Of the new approaches the most fruitful were also the ones which were, in the traditional sense, the most scholarly: Arthur Schlesinger was a pupil of Osgood as well as of Beard; *Annales*, above all, was a learned journal. Many of the new approaches anyway had broken down into rather sterile sub-histories: economic history, intellectual history, diplomatic history. After the Second World War there was a rebirth and re-orientation of the *Annales* tradition; in America the Progressives were superseded by what have been termed the Consensus historians (it has been pointed out that during the war America was a relatively unified nation[16]); in Germany historians were shaken out of a traditionalism which had endured through Weimar and National Socialism. The more radical departures I deal with in later sections. Here I look at the reaction of two German traditionalists to catastrophic military defeat, then at developments in first Britain, then the U.S.A.

Friedrich Meinecke's *German Catastrophe* (1946) voiced a repentance for his own concentration on political ideas; he argued that Germany had taken a wrong road in the nineteenth century when, instead of developing and extending her justly celebrated cultural tradition, she had turned towards the glorification of the political state. Having formerly kept up something of the bold self-confidence of Ranke, Meinecke now fell under the shadow of Burckhardt's deep pessimism. A younger compatriot of Meinecke's, an authority on the German Reformation and the author of an astonishingly wide range of books, Gerhard Ritter, commented on the imprint left by events in the later editions of his short biography, *Luther: His Life and Work*. In the preface to the 1959 edition he remarked that although the central sections of the book had not been much altered since the first editions of 1928–9, the introduction and conclusion had to be more extensively rewritten:

> The original plan of this book, made shortly after the end of the First World War, emphasised Luther's importance as a national hero, as the central figure of German culture, with vigour which I today feel to have been exaggerated. The catchword which was coined at that time – 'the Eternal German' – has been cut from this edition . . .

Ritter then explained how his theological understanding of Luther had been deepened by his participation in the struggle of the German Lutheran Church against the Nazi regime in the thirties:

> In retrospect I feel that my book reached full maturity in the third and extensively revised edition which appeared in 1943. The world catastrophe which we had already sensed then and which broke on us in 1945 brought Luther's ideas of the hidden God and the twilight of world history home to us Germans with remarkable actuality. This led me to rewrite the introduction almost completely in the fourth edition (1947).

Whether or not the war directly affected the best-known Italian historian of the age (after Benedetto Croce – see Chapter 5), Federico Chabod (1902–60) is hard to say. Chabod had studied at Berlin under Friedrich Meinecke, and his early work on Machiavelli and the Renaissance, published in the 1920s, reveals clearly the interest in intellectual history which was developing at that time. He did strive for a cultural dimension, his aim in regard to Machiavelli being, as he put it, to present him 'as the expression, almost the synthesis of Italian life throughout the fourteenth and

fifteenth centuries; and see reflected and clarified in his thought, as
it were in its essential outline, the age-long process of development
which leads from the downfall of the old, Communal freedom, to
the triumph of the princely, the absolute State'.[17] Otherwise much
of his writing was of the conventional type, concentrating on
political, diplomatic and sometimes religious themes. His aim was
the highly professional one: to elucidate obscure points, to banish
myths, rather than to open new approaches or new areas of study.
In the postwar period, however, Chabod received a special
acclaim for his *Storia della politica estera italiana dal 1870 al 1896*
(1951). This is diplomatic history of a broad, almost sociological
character, with a mass of intricate detail on the social and political
'background' (*pace* Kitson Clark – see next paragraphs), and a
depth analysis of the psychology of those who formulated Italian
foreign policy.

There are definitely no cataclysmic changes in the writings of
the more traditional British historians. George Kitson Clark
(1900–79) and Geoffrey Elton (b. 1921) present important points
of contrast. Elton, though he has written on European as well as
on British history, is unmistakably identified with a thesis, the
'Elton thesis' on the 'Tudor Revolution in Government'. Kitson
Clark, though a profound influence on the study of many aspects
of British nineteenth-century history, is not associated with any
one important thesis. His earlier researches were concentrated on
Britain in the period following upon the Great Reform Act of
1832, a period long bedevilled by the notion of the rise to power
of the 'middle class', a rise assumed to have been consummated
by the 1832 Act. The great vehicle of middle-class influence in
the 1830s and 1840s was the Anti-Corn Law League: historians
had tended to take at face value the assertions of the League that
the main opposition to repeal of the protectionist Corn Laws
came from the great landed interests, the aristocracy and the
squirearchy; and further that the landowners exerted undue influence upon the tenant farmers in persuading them to vote for
protectionist candidates. Going behind the polemical statements
of the League to the contemporary documents, Kitson Clark
showed that it was the tenant farmers, operating on a tiny economic margin, who were most strongly in favour of protection,
and that some of the violent agitation of the period sprang from
suspicion on the part of the tenants that the candidates supported

by the landowners were not sufficiently committed to the principle
of protection. In the wider context of the power structure of
British society after 1832, Kitson Clark's discoveries suggested
that real power in fact still rested with the landowners, and that,
as he put it in a later summary, 'the actual repeal was carried
through by the head of one aristocratic party because he believed
it to be desirable, with the assent of the other because, at least,
he believed it to be expedient'.[18] Kitson Clark was the relentless
enemy of that bland generalisation into which historical writing
can always so easily degenerate:

> The old bland confident general statements about whole groups of men,
> or classes or nations ought to disappear from history; or if something of
> their sort must remain, and it is difficult to say anything about history
> or politics or society without making use of general statements, they
> must remain under suspicion, as expedients which are convenient,
> possibly necessary, for use at the moment, but are not the best that
> we shall be able to do in the way of truth.[19]

History 'described entirely in terms of the relationships between
important individuals at the centre of politics' is history 'without
background, and therefore obviously questionable'; but, he says,
history without background is 'better than history with a false
background provided by well-worn general phrases about whose
general accuracy no one has ever bothered to think'. The point
here is particularly relevant to some of the history written in the
twenties and thirties when it was too often believed that the wish
to write cultural and social history would father that very history,
without the necessary recourse to hard labour in intractable source
materials. Picking up the threads from Élie Halévy (1870–1937),
famous French authority on Great Britain, Kitson Clark himself
stressed the importance of Christian religion in stimulating men
to undertake reform in early nineteenth-century Britain: he
explained, in the post-Freudian mode, that 'in order to understand
the springs of action it is important to try to understand the
emotions, the irrational feelings, the prejudices, the experiences
which form men's minds'.

The emphasis placed by G. R. Elton, upon the *discontinuous*
character of Tudor administrative history may possibly be related
to the sense of discontinuity created by modern total war. The
'Elton thesis' was first adumbrated in the late forties in the pages
of the learned journals; the fullest statement appeared in *The*

Tudor Revolution in Government (1953), and further refinements have appeared in a steady flood of learned articles and in *The Tudor Constitution and Commentary* (1960). According to a tradition established by Victorian historians, 1485 was a key date in English history when, following upon a century of civil war and social disintegration, Henry VII, succeeding to the throne by the right of conquest, proceeded to establish what J. R. Green called the 'new monarchy', developing quickly into the 'Tudor despotism' of Henry VIII. The traditionalist professional historians of the early twentieth century, led by A. F. Pollard (1869–1948) – founder of both the [English] Historical Association (1906) and the Institute of Historical Research – had endeavoured to replace this by a more evolutionary view, stressing on the one side that many of the characteristics of the 'new monarchy' were in fact inherited from Henry VII's immediate predecessors, Edward IV and Richard III, and on the other that medieval methods persisted far into the Tudor period. For this perhaps rather bland interpretation, Elton substituted a version which accepted continuity as between Henry VII and his predecessors, but postulated a 'Tudor revolution in government' in the 1530s; a revolution which equipped England with a modern, national bureaucracy which could function, and provide political stability, irrespective of the personal qualities of the king or his deputies – medieval government, of course, was subject to breakdown whenever a weak king succeeded to the throne. Although the particular thesis relating to administrative developments in the reign of Henry VIII is clear, coherent and consistent, Elton is a complete empiricist in his insistence that the motor of historical change is 'individuals working in a somewhat unorganised and haphazard manner'.[20] Elton in fact gives tremendous weight to the actions of one particular individual, Henry VIII's Secretary, Thomas Cromwell, whom he describes as 'the most remarkable revolutionary in English history'. The Elton thesis is a monument of constructive scholarship: as with all such theses it has been subjected to intensive attack.[21]

Though deeply versed in economic, social, literary and military matters – what Kitson Clark, misguidedly in my view, called the 'background' – Elton is clear that what counts for most is 'the condition, reconstruction, and gradual moulding of a state – the history of a nation and its leaders in political action and therefore

the history of government in the widest sense'; the words are
taken from the preface to his textbook *England Under the Tudors*
(1955). It should be noted that Elton is a brilliant and vivid stylist,
obviously concerned with the communication element in historical
writing. With Macaulay he shares a concern for keeping up the
narrative flow of his historical writing and in his own *Reformation
Europe* (1963) he has presented, as he puts it himself, a form of
historical narrative 'thickened by the results of analysis': that is
to say, instead of the conventional interlarding of bouts of narrative and bouts of analysis, there is continuous narrative with
analysis incorporated where internal logic demands it; for
instance, the point when Charles V becomes involved in war with
the Turks is the point where a brief analysis of Turkish despotism
is introduced. Elton, like Namier, is a Tory historian, only more
so: he is tough, unsentimental, interested in actions rather than
thoughts and ideals; while he clearly demonstrates that there was
no 'Tudor despotism', he defends the authoritarian nature of
Tudor government much as Namier defended the jobbery of eighteenth-century politics; there is an over-readiness, perhaps, to
come down on the side of the winners in history (fifth sense of
the term, of course; as occupant of the Cambridge Regius chair
– he has now retired – Elton could himself be considered a winner
in history, using the word in another of its senses).

Best-known, most admired, most criticised, most controversial,
most universally read of twentieth-century British historians is A.
J. P. Taylor (b. 1906). A first-year student of mine at Edinburgh
University many years ago who not only knew the names of no
other historians, but was scarcely aware that the writers of history
have names, was conscious of having seen Mr Taylor perform on
television. These performances on serious historical topics,
without notes and without visual aids, were indeed unique.
Taylor's own first interest was in that nineteenth-century working-
class movement, Chartism, but as a routine part of an Oxford
historian's apprenticeship he went to Vienna to learn German.
His first idea for research there was to study the relationship
between the 1848 upheavals in the Austrian Empire and British
radicalism, but it was soon apparent that this was much too
ambitious a project. In any case the notable Austrian scholar
A. F. Pribram, whose *The Secret Treaties of Austria–Hungary
1879–1914* had been published at the end of the war, and who

subsequently produced the classic (if dull) diplomatic history *England and the International Policy of the Great Powers 1871–1914* (1931), was keen that he should take on some diplomatic topic. Eventually Taylor lighted on the idea of a study of *The Italian Problem in European Diplomacy*, which called for research in the Paris and London archives as well as in those of Vienna. In all respects this is a model scholarly monograph: the period studied is short, the topic clearly delimited and studied in great depth from an impressive array of primary materials; the presentation is detached, almost antiseptic. Only in the annotations to the bibliography did the scathing Taylor wit come properly into play. Taylor's first university appointment was at the University of Manchester, where Namier held the Chair of Modern History; his monograph was published by the University Press in 1934. Four years later there followed a further monograph, *Germany's First Bid for Colonies, 1884–1885*: again there was the same impressive mastery of extensive source materials, principally the German, French and British diplomatic documents, along with the Granville Papers; now, however, Taylor had a novel and stimulating thesis to advance – that Bismarck's bid for colonies was designed to provoke a quarrel with Britain in order that he could draw closer to France. The thesis, though not universally accepted in all its implications, still stands today as a significant contribution to the understanding of late nineteenth-century imperialism, which is increasingly understood by historians as the outward projection of European conflicts rather than as a purely economic phenomenon. The argument is presented with great verve and cogency; and the book ends in what was soon to be recognised as characteristic style: Bismarck, said Taylor,

> left an unfortunate example to his successors, who imitated his unscrupulousness without possessing his genius. Short of a run of Bismarcks, there is perhaps something to be said for government by gentlemen, even when they are such incompetent muddlers as Lord Granville and Lord Derby.

Taylor was later to write a biography of *Bismarck* (1955) which took to its furthest length Taylor's own belief in the importance of the unexpected. and the fortuitous in history: Bismarck was presented not as a statesman with a fully worked-out policy for the creation of a German Empire, but as a brilliant opportunist with a remarkable facility for turning events to account. In shattering the familiar textbook stereotype Taylor again did a genuine service to historical study, though on balance recent evidence suggests that there was a greater element of forethought and planning in Bismarck's policies than Taylor allowed for. In between Taylor published three important textbooks, *The Habsburg Monarchy, 1815–1918* (1941), *The Course of German History* (1945) – characterised by a strong anti-German colouring verging on war propaganda, yet again a useful corrective to the liberal diplomatic histories of the interwar years – and the famous *The Struggle for the Mastery in Europe, 1848–1918* (1954); and a number of thoroughly professional learned articles mainly related to the 'special subject' which he taught at Manchester on diplomacy at the beginning of the twentieth century when the 'Mediterranean problem' was a matter of particular concern.

There could then be no question about Taylor's qualifications as a complete professional historian. To his thorough technical grounding he has added the personal quality of 'feel', 'intuition', or – as Namier said of his younger colleague – 'green fingers'. This quality is apparent and successfully vindicated, in Taylor's *English History 1914–1945* (1965); but it can be a dangerous quality too. Indeed Taylor is the greatest twentieth-century exponent of the history once defined by Richard Pares – history as a series of bright ideas.[22] The trouble is that history, as the past, does not always unfold as a series of breathtaking paradoxes: the uncomprehending ambitions of men and societies, which Taylor understands only too well, do not always conform to neat literary formulations. Taylor has not in fact shown great originality in his choice of topics for study: the early preoccupation with diplomatic history, fashionable in Europe in the thirties, has given way to a broadened approach in which, as with Elton, the political theme remains central. As an Englishman first, then as a European, Taylor has shown no interest in other parts of the world. But he has brought to his historical writing a style and manner of presentation unequalled in his own time, but very much of his own time. There are no long, orotund periods: the sentences are short, and hard and bright as diamonds, admirably fitted, despite the qualifications made above, to the tragic comedy of human frustration which Taylor relates. No one has resolved the problem of integrating analysis into narrative more successfully. Finally Taylor, in common with Shakespeare, Burns, Dickens and most other great literary practitioners, is an immensely witty writer: unhappily to many mean spirits it is incomprehensible that history seriously studied can be fun: Taylor shows that it *is* fun.

The most controversial of all Taylor's books is *The Origins of the Second World War* (1961, reprinted with a new introduction, 'Second Thoughts', in 1963). Since I propose to discuss the controversies over the origins of the Second World War in Chapter 8, it is only necessary here to make a few points relevant to Taylor's place in the development of historical studies. *The Origins of the Second World War* is in many ways a throw-back to the style of diplomatic history with which Taylor began his career; it is not as copiously supplied with references as the complete scholarly monograph should be, but essentially it is a work built up from documentary sources. Should a new edition of Fritz Stern's excellent *Varieties of History*, or a similar work, be planned, there could be no stronger candidate for inclusion than the foreword, 'Second Thoughts', added to the 1963 edition. The canons appealed to throughout are those of Ranke and Maitland. The achievement Taylor claims is that of the traditionalist professionals of the thirties, the destruction of legends, performed not as 'a vindication of Hitler', but as 'a service to truth': 'My book should be judged only on this basis, not for the political morals which people choose to draw from it.' Furthermore, says Taylor, 'it is no part of the historian's duty to say what ought to have been done. His whole duty is to find out what was done and why.' Taylor emerges very clearly as, in the non-party sense of course, a Tory historian. He is concerned as ever to stress the significance of contingency and accident as against advance planning – Hitler 'exploited events far more than he followed precise coherent plans' – and this theme is reiterated (to my mind rather tiresomely) throughout the text of the book. Early in Chapter 10 there is a revealing passage where Taylor refers to the widely held view that 'Hitler was a modern Attila, loving destruction for its own sake', but, says Taylor, with an interesting swing towards historical Whiggism, 'his policy is capable of rational explanation; and it is on these that history is built'. 'Human blunders', he continues, 'usually do more to shape history than human wickedness. At any rate this is a rival dogma which is worth developing, *if only as an*

academic exercise' (my italics). The book is indeed a most stimulating 'academic exercise', forcing a reappraisal of previously held
convictions by all students in the field. But it is not a complete
study of its topic: in particular, the 'Tory' emphasis on diplomatic
sources means that the extremely important social, cultural and
economic developments of Nazi Germany have been completely
left out of account. Taylor's short, neat reply to his most profound
critic on this score, Dr Tim Mason, is well worth extensive
quotation:

> Of course historians must explore the profound forces. But I am some-
> times tempted to think that they talk so much about these profound
> forces in order to avoid doing the detailed work. I prefer detail to
> generalisations: a grave fault no doubt, but at least it helps to redress
> the balance . . .

After suggesting that perhaps he should have called the book 'The
Origins of the Outbreak of War in 1939', Taylor admitted that
this might seem a trivial topic. However,

> historians spend much of their time on trivialities, and some of them
> believe that only by adding up trivialities can they safely arrive at
> generalisations. Take care of the pence and the pounds will look after
> themselves. This is an old-fashioned view. But I am an old-fashioned,
> hack historian.[23]

The first sentence recalls Bury; the last recalls that a younger
contemporary once referred to him as 'the last of the prima
donnas'.[24]

Hugh Trevor-Roper (now Lord Dacre, born 1914) began his
professional life as a student of seventeenth-century England, and
he has had a special mastery of that century ever since, spreading
his empire far beyond the confines of the British Isles. In
September 1945 Trevor-Roper, as an Intelligence officer with the
victorious Allies, was given the task of quashing the various
dangerous rumours which were circulating about the fate of Hitler
by tracking down the exact circumstances of his death. It was
a unique opportunity for a historian, whose work is sometimes
somewhat idly likened to detection; here the trail was hot, but
incredibly convoluted. Trevor-Roper's brilliant reconstruction,
The Last Days of Hitler (1947, and many subsequent editions),
was a classic; and it remains a standard authority unshaken by the
fragments of evidence that have since come to light. Subsequently

Trevor-Roper was responsible for scholarly editions of various important Nazi documents – for example, *Hitler's Table Talk* (1953) and the *Bormann Letters* (1954). He thus developed a reputation in a second field of study: Nazi Germany. Throughout, Trevor-Roper has shown an interest, unusual among British historians, in historiography. He is general editor of the New English Library series, *The Great Historians*, and is himself editor of the volume containing the abridgement of Gibbon's *Decline and Fall*; he has also edited Macaulay's *Essays* and he is the author of one of the very rare significant discussions of Ibn Khaldoun, the fourteenth-century Muslim historian, and his *Muqaddimah*.

Trevor-Roper was twenty-six when he published his biography of *Archbishop Laud* (1940), a sympathetic but far from uncritical study of the conservative High Churchman, set firmly in the context of the complicated social and religious circumstances of the time. The book has remained the standard work on its topic and upon attaining a majority was in fact republished. The first controversy in which Trevor-Roper became deeply involved, and with which he is still inextricably associated, was with R. H. Tawney: Tawney, in a kind of Marxian analysis, had sought to explain the conflicts of the seventeenth century in terms of a 'rising gentry'. Trevor-Roper postulated a 'falling gentry'; much of what Tawney had written was indeed open to criticism, but Trevor-Roper's counter-arguments did not command widespread acceptance.[25] However, he did put forward one fertile idea which was much argued over in subsequent studies of the Civil War: that the social and economic conflicts which finally issued in the Civil War can best be seen as a polarisation between a corrupt, high-living 'Court' at one end and the 'Country' at the other, peers and gentry who had not obtained the spoils of office, men of Puritan outlook, censorious of the standards of the court. One of the many merits of this typology is that it uses the very language of the seventeenth century instead of introducing entirely anachronistic concepts of class. Historians, Trevor-Roper declared, 'should recognise the limits of sociological or theoretical interpretations and admit that there are times when political parties and political attitudes are not the direct expression of social or political theories or interests, but are polarised round political events'.[26] From his investigations of English society in the seventeenth century he turned to Scotland and the Continent, developing a comparative study of Weber's dynamic duo, Calvinism and capitalism. Two relatively short papers heralded his new discovery, a 'general crisis' throughout Europe in the middle decades of the seventeenth century (the discovery, in fact, was not entirely new: the distinguished French historian Roland Mousnier had already written of much the same phenomenon, though the two historians differed greatly on certain points of detail, and E. J. Hobsbawm had written of a 'general economic crisis'). Trevor-Roper did not develop his thesis into a full-length study but it formed the central theme of a collection of essays (the essay is perhaps the typical Trevor-Roper format) published under the title *Religion, the Reformation and Social Change* (1967). Among the various aspects of the general problem studied is 'the European Witchcraze of the Sixteenth and Seventeenth Centuries' – very much a fit subject for a historian beglonging to the age of Freud and Hitler, Durkheim and Febvre. Trevor-Roper noted that persecution of 'witches' was more prevalent in Scotland and on the Continent than in England, and he endeavoured to show the manner in which the craze related to the rise and decline of the main intellectual and social movements of the time. Likening the craze to twentieth-century antisemitism he has, as most historians of his generation would be inclined to do, warned against any facile belief in a steady human progress towards greater rationality.

If it is true, as usually said, that American historians in the post-war years tended to stress the absence of social conflict in previous American history, they arrived at this so-called 'consensus' by some quite interestingly different routes. Most traditional in approach were Richard J. Hofstadter (1916–70), with his *Age of Reform* (1955) on the progressive era, Louis Hartz (born 1919), with his *The Liberal Tradition in America* (1955), and Daniel J. Boorstin, with his *The Genius of American Politics* (1953) and *The Americans: The Colonial Experience* (1958). Greater interest, perhaps, attaches to the work of Merle Curti and David M. Potter, both of whom applied the methods of social science and the techniques of statistics. Assisted by Robert Daniel, Shaw Livermore Jr., Joseph van Hise and Margaret W. Curti, as also by the Numerical Analysis Laboratory at Wisconsin, Curti undertook a historical study in depth of Trempealeau County, Wisconsin, with a view, as he saw it, to testing the possibility of complete objectivity in history, and to exploring the validity of Turner's proposition that the open frontier had promoted democracy in America. The resulting volume, *The Making of an American Commmunity: A Case Study of Democracy in a Frontier County* (1959), was, Curti explained, genuinely a collaborative work though it was in no way a collection of discrete essays: 'Each chapter, whether the first draft was written by me or by a collaborator, was prepared as part of a general scheme of treatment and directed by me.' He could not in the end claim that the work was 'completely objective', nor, of course, that Trempealeau was necessarily typical of all frontier counties, but he could very reasonably state that

> our operational approach to specific testable units of larger problems, combining as it has the traditional historical approach with certain social science methods, has yielded a higher degree of objectivity than we could have otherwise attained.

Among the points illumined by the study were, first, that despite traditional views as to the extreme poverty of Polish immigrant groups (a view which the authors were at first prepared, on the basis of their traditional researches in the literary sources, to accept), calculation of the median values of real and personal property showed that the Poles in fact were 'nowhere near the bottom of the economic scale'; second, that the common impression that the foreign-born, once settled on American land, were more likely to stay put than the native-born was without foundation; and, third, that the assertion that increasing concentration of capital and increasing misery went hand-in-hand was unsustainable – the rich in fact become 'somewhat richer' while the poor 'became a good deal less poor'. Conceiving of democracy as involving such processes as 'Americanisation' and 'multiple leadership' (and here obviously a subjective element comes in), Curti believed that the investigation did support the main implications of the Turner thesis: 'The story of the making of this American community is the story of progress towards democracy.' The first appendix to the book is a lucid guide to the methodology employed by Curti and his associates, and in its day a godsend to innumerate colleagues and those who were mystified by the use of machines in the study of history. But the book is very much that of a historian: the quantitative methods are seen as having 'very usefully supplemented the traditional historical methods'.

Quantification is not the only supplemental benefit which can be derived from social science; David M. Potter has explained how in preparing the series of lectures delivered at the University of Chicago in 1950, and subsequently published as *People of Plenty: Economic Abundance and the American Character* (1954), he was 'assailed by misgivings as to the validity of the whole concept of "national character" '. As a historian, he tells us, he became 'embarrassed' to discover 'that the most telling contributions . . . came from cultural anthropologists and social psychologists rather than from my fellow historians'. The notion of economic abundance as a central influence on American character is one which has commanded the attention of all subsequent writers. One other important example of the innovativeness of certain postwar American historians may be cited – Boyd C. Shafer's *Nationalism: Myth and Reality* (1955). His study of nationalism made it 'not only enlightening but imperative to draw upon the findings of other social sciences' – which he lists as psychology, anthropology and biology. Shafer confesses to his amateur status outside history, but states his belief that 'historical work may be enriched by the findings of other disciplines'. Sometimes, of course, social scientists object to this amateurishness: historians should either become social scientists through and through or not trespass at all, is the argument. Actually Shafer's work is authoritative precisely because of his twenty-year immersion in the historical literature of nationalism: had he used the time instead to study psychology, anthropology and biology he would presumably not have been able to develop his encyclopaedic understanding of nationalism as a historical phenomenon.

4. Marxist Approaches

I am not myself a Marxist (and in some of my writings, particularly on class, I have taken an explicitly non-Marxist approach), though some of the historians I most admire (for example, Christopher Hill, Eric Hobsbawm, E. P. Thompson) are Marxists, and some of the most important advances in fields which particularly interest me, such as élite and popular culture, have, I cheerfully recognise, been made by Marxists. The purpose of this section is simply to note the main changes in Marxist historical thinking which have affected the ways in which some of today's history is written, and to note those areas of study which Marxist historians have been particularly active in opening up. I confine myself to those who would explicitly wish to be considered Marxists; as already remarked, most historians have in some way or another been affected by some aspect of Marxist thinking. Many of the leading figures in the present-day *Annales* school went through, in common with most French intellectuals of advanced views, a Marxist phase, though *Annales* spokesmen now tend to be distinctly hostile towards Marxism.

In general, historical writers in the interwar years who took a more open and polemical Marxist stand than Georges Lefebvre (see section 2 above) are not highly regarded today: within the Marxist canon they are often referred to as 'vulgar Marxists', those who simply repeated the tenets of Marx (and, often, of Lenin) by rote, in a naïve and simplistic way. Here, it will be more profitable to move immediately to developments which took place after the Second World War, though much of the theory went back as far as the nineteen-twenties. The major stumbling block for Marxist thinkers was the notion of a superstructure determined by the economic structure. There was a widespread sentiment that greater autonomy must be accorded to laws, ideas, modes of cultural expression. There was also uneasiness with the rigid Marxian pattern of the unfolding of historical stages, though a fundamental preoccupation with systems of dominance, and a fundamental faith in the existence of potentially liberating alternatives (perhaps the two salient characteristics of Marxism in its modern form) remained. Since it also remained an accepted truism that what one directly perceived was merely the false bourgeois facade there was also a preoccupation with elaborating the positions from which objective insight into historical processes could (allegedly) be achieved. The major intellectual movements which affected the development of Marxist historical thinking were Freudian psychology, existentialism, and structuralism and post-structuralism. Reference should first of all be made to the Frankfurt school – the Institute for Social Theory was founded in Frankfurt in 1923 – whose most notable figures are Max Hork-heimer (1895–1973), Theodor W. Adorno (1903–69), and Herbert

Marcuse (1898–1979), whose main work, after the advent of Hitler, was accomplished in the United States. Their aim was to establish a flexible dynamic Marxism in place of 'vulgar Marxism' (they were the originators of the phrase). In the 1930s, the Frankfurt scholars sought inspiration from Freudian psychology; it is from this connection that there has arisen much contemporary writing about the family, and bourgeois sexual practices in general, as instruments of domination.

New ideas about how patterns of cultural domination are established derived from the writings of the Italian Antonio Gramsci (1891–1937) and the Hungarian Georg Lukacs (1885–1971). Gramsci, turning away from the simple notion of superstructure, sponsored the notion of the cultural 'hegemony' established by the dominant class, and unwittingly consented to by the working class. Lukacs put forward the idea of Marxism as a methodology, rather than a series of theses:

> Let us assume for the sake of argument that recent research had disproved once for all every one of Marx's individual theses. Even if this were to be proved, every serious 'orthodox' Marxist would still be able to accept all such modern findings without reservation and hence dismiss all of Marx's theses in total, without having to renounce his orthodoxy for a single moment. Orthodox Marxism therefore does not imply uncritical acceptance of the results of Marx's investigations. It is not the 'belief' in this or that thesis, nor the exegesis of a 'sacred' book. On the contrary, orthodoxy refers exclusively to method.[27]

The method, one would have to note, does, of course, continue to involve a number of assumptions about class and class struggle, dominance, the potential for an alternative 'liberated' society, and so on, which are not necessarily unproblematic.

What exact contribution, if any, was made by the 'existentialist Marxism' of Jean Paul Sartre, I am unable to say. Sartre's concept of 'totalisation' stressed the relative autonomy of different forms of domination and thus was consistent with the general move away from notions of the superstructure and economic determinism. Far more obviously influential, however, have been the assumptions and methodologies of structural linguistics and semiology, which seemed particularly useful in analysing that advanced capitalism which had assumed a shape Marx could scarcely have dreamed of:

> The predominant linguistic form in advanced capitalism is not the

symbol but the signal. Since the linguistic elements are fragmented, signifiers are able to 'float' as it were in the space of social practice and be combined with signifieds and referents at will. In fact, the process of production has been transformed by these floating signifiers. Capitalists no longer rely on 'use value', the imagined or real utility of a commodity, to sell their products. Instead, in the process of advertising, signifiers are attached to commodities seemingly at random. Qualities that are desired by the population (sexiness, self-confidence) are attributed to commodities irrespective of their functionality or material utility. Thus shaving creams promise sex appeal; deodorants guarantee self-confidence, automobiles are a means to an active social life; soft drinks are the key to community, love, popularity; and so forth. The process has advanced to such a degree that the mode of signification is central to the capitalist mode of production.[28]

Some of the concepts of structural linguistics have been taken over by Jürgen Habermas (b. 1929), the leading contemporary figure in the Frankfurt school, who has developed his own branch of 'hermeneutics'. We can probably forget Louis Althusser (1918–86), the French Marxist philosopher, vigorously attacked by E. P. Thompson, whose claim it was that historical approaches were inevitably so sloppy that they ought to be excluded from Marxism. A few words, however, are required for Michel Foucault (1926–85) who was the leading practitioner in recent years in unmasking patterns of domination (a consistent Marxist preoccupation) in areas which vulgar Marxists would have ignored as minor elements of superstructure, particularly the treatment of criminals, madness, medicine, and sexuality (against traditional Marxists, Foucault insisted that new modes of belief were not linked to economic development). Foucault's concept of the particular languages, or 'discourses' (a term, once more, taken from linguistics), associated with particular institutions of dominance, and designed to maintain that dominance, has become commonplace and, no doubt, widely abused; his *Madness and Civilization, Discipline and Punishment,* and *History of Sexuality,* which personally I find philosophical, intuitive, and imaginative, and lacking in effective historical underpinning, have had a great influence on younger historical writers striving to operate within a broadly Marxist tradition.

The more flexible, open, Marxism which developed after the Second World War is sometimes referred to as 'Western Marxism'. Its course was fostered by disillusionment with

Stalinism and hastened by revulsion against the post-Stalinist repression (1956) of the Hungarian attempt to establish a more liberal regime; among serious professional historians respect for evidence and for the need, wherever possible, to quantify, also played a part in drastically qualifying traditional Marxist assumptions. Lefebvre's contributions to historical study in general, and to understanding of the French Revolution in particular, were enormous, but as a Marxist, for all the complexity and detail of his arguments, he continued to insist that the ultimate cause of the revolution was the rise of the bourgeoisie, 1789 being the moment when it took power after several centuries of growing in numbers and wealth. In 1939 Lefebvre published a general synthesis, *Quatre-vingt-neuf*, which appeared in English translation after the war as *The Coming of the French Revolution* (1947). The challenges to Marxist orthodoxy mounted by Anglo-Saxon pragmatists (for example Alfred Cobban in his 1955 lecture 'The Myth of the French Revolution') were ignored in France; only in 1965 did a substantial indigenous challenge come from François Furet and Denis Richet. In 1971 Furet was able to use the prestige of *Annales* to publish in its pages a devastating attack on what he called the 'revolutionary catechism'. It is now clearly perceived that there was not in eighteenth-century France, on the one side, a distinctive aristocracy, and on the other a distinctive bourgeoisie. The upper bourgeoisie was to a considerable extent intermingled with the aristocracy; within both there were squabbles over status. The immediate circumstances leading to crisis were the financial needs of the crown; that the crisis became intense was due to the incompetence of the crown, and the manoeuvrings within the élite groups; that the crisis became revolutionary, was due to the pressure of the enormous and scarcely suppressed grievances of the ordinary people (particularly in Paris), suffering from a long trend of declining real incomes and, in short, frequently near starvation. Lefebvre's great achievements stand, and much of the detail which undermined the old Marxist certainty was provided by two avowed Marxists, the British historian George Rudé with his *The Crowd in the French Revolution*, and the French scholar Albert Soboul with his *Les sans-culottes parisiens en l'an II* (1958) and his *Paysans, Sans-culottes et Jacobins* (1966). The historiography of the French Revolution is but one example among many in which modern scholarship has shown Marxist theory, though by no means the professionalism and discoveries of Marxist scholars, to be seriously deficient.[29] Soboul was forced to reject any simple explanation of the Revolution as a legitimation of the maturing power of the bourgeoisie, but he continued to insist on the reality of 'the dialectic movement of history', endeavouring to relate aspects of the Revolution to it.

There is a very clear development in the writings of the British Marxist historian Christopher Hill (b. 1912). His long-term interest has been seventeenth century England, for he perceives this 'century of revolution' as crucial to the modern development of·society. His earliest writings betray a somewhat crude Marxism, but from the time of his major publications of the 1950s, *Economic Problems of the Church* (1956) and *Puritanism and Revolution* (1958), he moved steadily towards the study of ideas. At the heart of *Intellectual Origins of the English Revolution* (1965) is a positive conception of the place of ideas in the historical process, set out in the Introduction:

> Ideas were all-important for the individuals whom they impelled into action; but the historian must attach equal importance to the circumstances which gave these ideas their chance. Revolutions are not made without ideas, but they are not made by intellectuals. Steam is essential to driving a railway engine; but neither a locomotive nor a permanent way can be built out of steam. In this book I shall be dealing with the steam . . .
>
> It seems to me that any body of thought which plays a major part in history – Luther's, Rousseau's, Marx's own – 'takes on' because it meets the needs of significant groups in the society in which it comes into prominence . . .
>
> Men . . . do not break lightly with the past: if they are to challenge conventionally accepted standards they must have an alternative body of ideas to support them.

Hill has shared in what is the main distinguishing characteristic of the contemporary British school of Marxist historians, an interest in ordinary people as such, rather than just in their political organisations or roles as revolutionary agents. *The World Turned Up-Side-Down* (1972) is an exhilarating examination of the less well-known, 'unsuccessful', movements and experiments of the 'century of revolution'. There have followed major biographies of Cromwell (1970) and of Milton (1977) – interdisciplinarity being another welcome characteristic of Marxist approaches.

The interest in 'ordinary people as such' is very evident in the work of E. J. Hobsbawm (b. 1917): hence *Primitive Rebels: Studies of Archaic Forms of Social Movement in the 19th and 20th Centuries* (1959), *Labouring Men* (1964), and *Captain Swing* (1969), written in collaboration with George Rudé, which rescues the moving story of England's last agrarian rising, that of 1830, from the oblivion to which an exclusive interest in the development of the state, and an exclusive preoccupation with the winners in history, had consigned it. Over a period of almost thirty years, Hobsbawm has produced three complex, superior and well illustrated textbooks of total history covering the origins of the contemporary world: *The Age of Revolution 1789–1848* (1962), *The Age of Capital 1848–1875* (1975) and *The Age of Empire 1875–1914* (1987). The first of these kicks off with a fine piece of socio-historical scene-setting. 'The first thing to observe about the world of the 1780s', writes Hobsbawm,

is that it was at once much smaller and much larger than ours. It was smaller geographically, because even the best-educated and best-informed men then living . . . knew only patches of the inhabited globe . . .

Humanity was smaller . . . To take one illustration from the abundance of statistics about the physique of conscripts upon which this generalisation is based: in one canton on the Ligurian coast 72 per cent of recruits in 1792–9 were less than 1.50 metres (4ft 11in) tall. That did not mean that the men of the later eighteenth century were more fragile than we are. The scrawny, stunted, undrilled soldiers of the French Revolution were capable of a physical endurance equalled today only by the undersized guerillas in colonial mountains . . .

Yet if the world was in many respects smaller, the sheer difficulty or uncertainty of communications made it in practice much vaster than it is today . . . To be within reach of a port was to be within reach of the world: in a real sense London was closer to Plymouth or Leith than to villages in the Breckland of Norfolk; Seville was more accessible from Veracruz than from Valladolid, Hamburg from Bahia than from the Pomeranian hinterland . . .

The world of 1789 was therefore, for most of its inhabitants, incalculably vast. Most of them, unless snatched away by some awful hazard, such as military recruitment, lived and died in the county, and often in the parish, of their birth: as late as 1861 more than nine out of ten in seventy of the ninety French departments lived in the department of their birth. The rest of the globe was a matter of government agents and rumour . . .

E. P. Thompson. (b. 1924), the major figure in 'the New Left' in the late fifties and Britain's leading Marxist and *engagé* historian in the postwar era, achieved world fame with his *The Making of the English Working Class* (1963). Non-Marxist academics criticised Thompson's handling of his central thesis, the growth of a specifically 'working-class consciousness'. It is possible to be an admirer of the book, to agree that Thompson does triumphantly demonstrate the formation of a distinctive working class, and yet to feel that what he shows is rather 'working-class awareness' rather than 'working-class consciousness', in the technical Marxist sense which entails a sense of class conflict. Thompson argued that class is a 'historical phenomenon' not a 'structure' nor a 'category', 'something which in fact happens (and can be shown to have happened) in human relationships'; class is a 'historical relationship' with a fluency which 'evades analysis if we attempt to stop it dead at any given moment and anatomise its structure', a relationship which 'must always be embodied in real people and in a real context'. Class happens 'when some men, as a result of common experiences (inherited or shared), feel and articulate the identity of their interests as between themselves, and as against other men whose interests are different from (and usually opposed to) theirs'. The book, eight hundred pages long, is a treasure-house of fascinating information and deep historical insight, informed by Thompson's immense erudition in all aspects of the creative literature of this period (and indeed of many others) and his profound understanding of the current preoccupations of psychologists, social psychologists, and other social scientists. Where economic historians were content to assess the quantitative gains of the Industrial Revolution, Thompson sensitively explores the qualitative losses, an exploration which he has subsequently taken further in some sparkling studies of the effects of factory discipline. Violence, he says, was done to '*human* nature'; for there was 'a violent technological differentiation between work and life'. It is 'neither poverty nor disease but work itself which casts the blackest shadow over the years of the Industrial Revolution'. Implicitly Thompson alludes in an earlier chapter to the celebrated thesis of the great French historian Élie Halévy that the spread of Methodism had saved England from revolution in the early nineteenth century. Thompson's analysis is a good deal more subtle than that of Halévy, showing how Methodism could act both as an agent of the *status quo*, and as an agent of inspired political protest. Typical of a particular style of historical writing of which Thompson is a master is the fascinating but deeply serious passage in which he illustrates the 'obsessional Methodist concern with sexuality', which reveals itself in 'the perverted eroticism of Methodist imagery'. *The Making of the English Working Class* brings into perspective the aspirations and conscious efforts of working people, too often treated by other historians as an inert and faceless mass, passive to the central forces in history.

By launching the Centre for the Study of Social History at the University of Warwick, Thompson sponsored a whole new approach to the study 'from below' of the hidden complexities of earlier British society, particularly in the realm of 'crime' and law enforcement, seen at its best in his own *Whigs and Hunters: The Origin of the Black Act* (1975], which with patience, skill and flair recreated the world of the foresters of Windsor and East Hampshire in the early eighteenth century, and expounds the significance of the Black Act and the way it was used in eighteenth-century England. Thompson has emerged as the leading spokesman for a pragmatic and humane Marxism against the highly theoretical combination of Marxism and Structuralism of such continental figures as Althusser (*The Poverty of Theory* (1978) – see next chapter). In the 1970s Thompson returned to direct political activism in the cause of nuclear disarmament; most recently he has written a novel.

Eugene Genovese (b. 1930) was a leading figure in the American New Left of the 1960s and, like Thompson, an indefatigable essayist. His major collections of essays, published in the 1960s, *The Political Economy of Slavery: Studies in the Economy of the Society of the Slave South* and *In Red and Black: Marxian Explorations in Southern and Afro-American History* mix sharp polemics with learned professional studies. The preface to *In Red and Black* affords a nice example of Genovese's agreeably disrespectful style:

> Ironically, it was only a few years ago that a distinguished clown, who happened to be delivering the presidential address to the American Historical Association, bemoaned the influx of the non-WASP into the historical profession. After all, how could Jews, Italians, and Irishmen possibly understand an American culture that was so profoundly Anglo-Saxon and Teutonic? Putting the two arguments together, I have

concluded that I am qualified only on the history of Italian immigration
– a subject I know nothing about.

The book is divided into four parts. Part One, entitled 'A Point
of View', consists of two chapters, one on 'On Being a Socialist
and a Historian', and the other on 'Materialism and Idealism in
the History of Negro Slavery in the Americas'. Parts Two and
Three contain the main body of the book, Part Two commencing
with a chapter on 'Class and Nationality in Black America'. Part
Four is 'The Point of View Restated', and consists of one chapter
'On Antonio Gramsci'.

Genovese's words on being a socialist and a historian are worth
quoting fully: they bring out the commitment to the most rigorous
professional standards, but also the belief that this most
professional activity is also unavoidably political; the faith that
the socialist movement represents 'the hope of humanity' and the
conviction that historical truth can only serve the cause of that
movement.

> . . . what we stand for is the realisation that all historical writing and
> teaching – all cultural work – is unavoidably political intervention,
> but that ideologically motivated history is bad history and ultimately
> reactionary politics. The most technical essay in this book is neither
> more nor less political than the most directly partisan essay. But this
> assertion of political content has nothing in common with those
> demands for a political (a 'relevant') approach to history which ring
> across our campuses today. The assertion, in effect, rests on the belief
> that every contribution to history and the humanities, to the extent to
> which it takes a critical stance, helps to defend humanity against the
> barbarism of our age; and that it therefore constitutes as important a
> task for socialist intellectuals as opposition to the war in Vietnam.
> Holding this viewpoint, as we do, we do not find it surprising that
> nihilists and utopians accuse us of deserting the cause and embracing
> pure scholarship and value-free social science.
>
> Socialists do not advocate pure scholarship and value-free social
> science because we do not advocate the impossible. But we do insist
> that the inevitability of ideological bias does not free us from the
> responsibility to struggle for maximum objectivity . . . We are terribly
> smug people: we really do believe that our political movement
> represents the hope of humanity and the cause of the exploited and
> oppressed of the world. And we are terribly conceited: we are so
> convinced we are right that we believe we have nothing whatever to
> fear from the truth about anything. It is our contention, on the
> contrary, that only ruling classes and the waves of nihilists who regu-
> larly arise to entertain these same ruling classes have anything to gain

from the ideological approach to history. Our pretensions, therefore,
lead us to the fantastic idea that all good (true, valid, competent)
history serves our interest and that all poor (false, invalid, incompetent)
history serves the interest of our enemies – or at least of someone
other than ourselves. So, when we write a methodological essay on the
treatment of slaves, or an interpretative essay on Dante's religious
views, or a descriptive essay on the organization of the shipbuilding
industry in Bordeaux, or an informative essay on anything else of which
men and women have ever been a part – when, in other words, we
follow our calling or, as it were, do our thing – we think we are meeting
at least part of our political responsibility. We hold the strange notion
that socialists (and all decent human beings) have a duty to contribute
through their particular callings to the dignity of human life, a part
of which is necessarily the preservation of the record of all human
experience.[30]

In his final chapter Genovese comments: 'That the work and
indeed the name of Antonio Gramsci remain virtually unknown
to the American Left provides the fullest, if saddest proof of the
intellectual bankruptcy of "official" Marxism and its parties, old
and new.' Genovese's impressive *magnum opus* (all 800 pages of
it) is *Roll Jordan Roll: The World the Slaves Made* (New York,
1974). Just as E. P. Thompson was arguing that the British working-class were not simply inert mass, but active human beings
reacting to their situation and their experiences, so Genovese was
portraying the world of the slaves in all its fullness. Genovese was
able to reject both the view (that of many Black activists) that
the Black world was an entirely separate one from the rest of
American society, and the view (that of American liberals) that
Blacks were destined for steady integration into multi-racial
American society. Genovese was clear that the Black experience
was distinctively American: 'In this book I refer to the "black
nation" and argue that the slaves, as an objective social class,
laid the foundations for a separate black national culture while
enormously enriching American culture as a whole.' Throughout,
Genovese uses broadly Marxist categories, implicitly arguing with
the crudities of vulgar Marxism, but accepting the notions of
bourgeoisie, class rule, etc.; central to his writing is the Gramscian
concept of hegemony.

Genovese's compatriot Herbert Gutmann (1928–85) has owned
to learning from a range of British social historians not exclusively
Marxist.[31] On Marxism, he has written:

What is left when you clear away the determinist and teleological elements are good questions that direct your attention to critical ways of looking at on-going historical processes. A fundamental contribution of nineteenth- and twentieth-century Marxist thinking is a set of questions having to do with the way in which one examines class relations and how they change, the way in which one examines the institutionalization of power, the way in which one examines popular oppositional movements, the way in which one examines the integration of subordinate or exploited groups into a social system.[32]

Gutmann's major work is his massive *The Black Family in Slavery and Freedom, 1750–1825* (New York, 1976), stimulated Gutmann said, by the bitter public and academic controversy touched off by Daniel P. Moynihan's *The Negro Family in America* (1965) which claimed that life in white America had destroyed the Negro family, and created a 'tangle of pathology'. Gutmann's work, in fact, persuasively demonstrates the stability of Black families. Black history is now a major research area.

A slightly different strand of Marxism is represented in the writings of Gabriel Kolko (b. 1932) which, in a much more rounded and much more quantitatively substantiated way, reveal elements of the progressive tradition. *The Triumph of Conservatism: A Re-interpretation of American History, 1900–1916* (1963) debunks the notion of the high ideals and working-class sympathies of the progressive politicians of the so-called progressive era, but states explicitly that Marxism is inadequate as an explanation of developments in America. However, the book is informed by a general Marxist frame of reference, as was a most important book which appeared the previous year *Wealth and Power in America*. Kolko, at a time when there was still much faith in the classlessness of American society, brought out clearly that, just like unregenerate Europe, America did have classes, and indeed a ruling class. Most recently, studies along these lines have been pursued, in proto-Marxist manner, by W. William Domhoff.

Generally Marxist writers (in the West) have strong political commitments (in the manner of Thompson or Genovese), and a belief in the broad philosophy of history and social development associated with Marxism. However, the German historian, Jurgen Kocka, an authority on the white-collar lower middle class in both Germany and the United States in the late nineteenth and early twentieth century, avowedly distanced himself from Marxist philosophy of history while adopting a Marxist model of class for the

study published in English as *Facing Total War* (Göttingen, 1973
– English translation, 1984). Kocka uses a strictly Marxist definition of 'objective class position', that is to say class position as
defined by relationship to the dominant mode of production. He
writes:

> . . . their objective class position was not the defining condition for
> the life-styles, expectations, organisation and political behaviour of
> either white-collar employees or of handwerker [craftsmen] and klein-
> händler [small tradesmen]. Both groups organised themselves predomi-
> nantly against those whose class position they shared; the kleinhändler
> disassociated themselves from large-scale capital and industry, white-
> collar employees from the working class. Together they formed a
> significant factor by which Wilhelmine society was distinguished from
> a clearly marked, dichotomous class society. Encouraged by the State,
> they acted as a sort of padding, which somewhat muffled the growing
> class conflict. During the War, this padding was ripped apart.

Kocka sets up his classical Marxist dichotomous model, showing
how it diverged from reality in 1914, then arguing that the effect
of the war was to bring Germany much closer to the classical
dichotomous model. Kocka argues that the Marxist model is the
most effective one available for his purposes, that the model
'served as an instrument for historical understanding by permitting
the description and explanation of the variable "distance"
between model and reality.' Kocka's experiment in the use of
theory has been much praised, and also much criticised. In the
'Afterword' to the English translation, Kocka deals very fairly
with some of the main criticisms.

Finally, two direct disciples of Foucault. Michael Ignatieff's *A
Just Measure of Pain* (1978), overtly taking off from Foucault's
*Discipline and Punish: The Penitentiary in the Industrial Revol-
ution* set out to discover how, between 1770 and 1840, incarcer-
ation came to be accepted as the proper mode of punishment.
Ignatieff's conclusion, as summarised by Mark Poster, is that 'the
continued legitimacy afforded the prison system derived not from
its inherently humane qualities, but from the imperatives of domination in bourgeois society.'[33] Patricia O'Brien's *The Promise of
Punishment* (1982), dealing with prisons in nineteenth-century
France, brings out how prisoners were not simply passive recipients of prison discipline, but, as with E. P. Thompson's working
class, developed a distinctive culture of their own.

5. *Annales* since 1945

Societies need history. In modern societies the historical profession is highly organised and institutionalised. Bloch and Febvre believed profoundly in the need to understand the past; as profoundly, they believed that narrative political and constitutional history, mainstream history in France in the interwar years, provided a woefully inadequate and incomplete understanding of the past. They sought an understanding of humanity and human society in all its aspects, believing that this was to be achieved through co-operation with geography, psychology, anthropology, economics, sociology, with, indeed, all of the social sciences. Fernand Braudel, leading figure in the *Annales* school in the postwar years, has declared this openness to other disciplines to be the irreducible essence of the *Annales* approach. Other writers have concentrated on the new eminence and new influence attained by *Annales* after 1945. There can be no doubt that there was in France at the end of the Second World War a determination to break with many aspects of the old France. The history of Bloch and Febvre now had a special appeal, an appeal recognised in the creation of a new institutional framework. *Annales*, the journal, was revived in 1946 as *Annales, Économies, Societés, Civilisations* (usually abbreviated to *Annales, E.S.C.*); a new Sixth Section of the École Pratique des hautes Études was founded as an institute where research of the sort favoured by *Annales* could be carried out. Febvre became the first president of this new institution, being succeeded in 1957 by Braudel. The protagonists of the approaches advocated in *Annales*, thus, had gained the prestige, and more material assets, of an institutional base. From the outset, as François Furet current president of what since 1975 has been the École des hautes Études en Sciences Sociales, has commented, there was both a 'petty institutional war' and a 'great symbolic clash' with the degree-giving universities, and the Sorbonne in particular. 'Institutions,' Furet notes, 'have their own logic; there is nothing like their rivalries to confer an imaginary degree of intellectual coherence to political, collective, professional, or personal differences.'[34] Thus what is usually referred to as the *Annales* school, that is to say a group of scholars associated with the journal *Annales* and with the Sixth Section, came to be represented as having more of a unified and universally shared approach to historical study than was in fact the case. The three basic points I wish to stress about the *Annales* 'school' are, then, the legacy from Febvre and Bloch (openness to other disciplines and the striving for total history), the important institutional base, and the absence of a single unified approach. To these I shall here add three further points which will emerge in the next few paragraphs: a hostility to, and neglect of, political history; a concentration on medieval and early modern history, with a general avoidance of industrial and contemporary societies; and an attempt, not always completely comprehensible to the uninitiated, to annex structuralism to history. Finally, it is worth noting that the *Annales* writers disavowed an interest in 'events', the definition of 'events' here, however, being perhaps a rather narrow one. Braudel saw events as surface phenomena, misleadingly interesting, though he was very aware of the importance of wars. Some *Annalistes* believed in the study of 'significant events' (the phrase was Febvre's) for what they could reveal about deeper and more enduring structures.

The Sixth Section could sponsor research of particular types into particular areas, and could ensure publication. *Annales* could contrive debates in certain fields and could commission special issues on topics it considered important. Many of the areas of research which loom large today on the programmes of historical scholars were in fact initiated independently of the *Annales* school; but such was the importance of *Annales* and its institutions as sponsor and clearing house, that it did in practice become associated with practically all of the newest developments, particularly in social history. The *Annales* school, then, has pioneered approaches of its own (which do not in themselves necessarily form a conceptual unity) and has taken over approaches pioneered elsewhere. At the same time, approaches similar to those used by *Annales* historians have developed quite independently in other countries and other institutions. Generally, though, historians working in a manner similar to that of one or more historians within *Annales* have been happy to acknowledge a direct association; on the whole *Annales* connoted prestige. Often the direct influence outwards from *Annales* has been perfectly clear. Yet to speak of *Annales* having established 'a hegemony of influence and reputation', as Furet does[35] is, to me, to overstate. The fact is that reputable and useful historical writing, of a type which does not match with any of the many approaches identifiable within the *Annales* school, still goes on. I think in particular of political history in its various varieties. For, whatever the range of approaches espoused within the *Annales* school, that school can indisputably be characterised by its eschewal of anything resembling traditional political history. Noting that the older history was concerned with the study of politics, of human choices, Furet continues:

> . . . the price paid by history for remodelling itself on the pattern of the social sciences is that it focusses primarily on what underlies those choices, on what determines them and makes them inevitable despite the appearance of freedom. It prefers to analyse deeper trends rather than superficial changes, to study collective behaviour rather than individual choices, to examine economic and social determinants rather than institutions or government decisions. Thus, demography, economics, and sociology have taken over a field increasingly deserted by its traditonal inhabitants – kings, notables, nations, and the theatre of power around which they never ceased to gravitate.[36]

Bloch was a medievalist, Febvre a specialist in the seventeenth century. It does so happen that most of the major figures in the *Annales* school have been primarily students of the early modern or medieval periods. It may just be, as some critics have suggested, that 'deeper trends', 'collective behaviour', 'economic and social determinants' are more easily studied in pre-industrial times than they are in more recent periods of apparently hectic change. Be that as it may, there has been a disposition among many *Annales* historians to study the apparently inexorable forces of physical geography, the influences of the seasons, and of climate. There was a fascination with what a leading *Annaliste*, Pierre Chaunu, referred to as the 'long slow, immobile, hard, dense, geological rhythm of traditional society'[37], which could then be set against *conjonctures* (a favourite *Annales* word which usually turned out to refer to cyclical patterns, or trends, in prices, landholdings, or population movements).

Because French intellectual life at the top is highly centralised (the squabbles identified by Furet notwithstanding), and thus intimately interdisciplinary, it was inevitable that *Annales* historians should be strongly affected by structuralist linguistics and, even more critically, by structuralist anthropology; this despite the essentially anti-historical nature of structuralism, whose codes, allegedly, are independent of past development. Thus *structures* is another word much used in *Annaliste* discourse. The search for meaningful interrelationships is of course a very laudable one. From the semiologists there came a fascination with communication, so that, according to Ernst Breisach, *Annalistes* tended to see all human relationships as forms of communication: 'people communicated with their land by mastering it, family communicated with family by dowries and other exchanges, and merchant communicated with merchant by exchanging gold.'[38]

Bloch and Febvre had spoken of *histoire intégrale*: more recent figures have spoken of *histoire totale* or *histoire globale* (the phrase generally favoured by Braudel). Another type of *Annales* history was *histoire sériale*, based on the premise that the compiling of long statistical series (of birth and fertility rates, exports, agricultural prices, etc.) would provide rock-solid, authentically validated, structures around which to discuss other societal phenomena. Few *Annales* historians went as far in quantitative studies as the American practitioners of the New Economic History (see next section) or such contemporary French quantitative historians as Jean Marcewski; but a recognition of the need to quantify wherever conceivably possible, must be accounted another salient characteristic of the *Annales* school (though, of course, by no means a characteristic of them alone). Historical demography (see next section) was not pioneered by the *Annales* school but has certainly been absorbed into the heart of much of its writings. The use of psychology goes back to Bloch and Febvre in the interwar period, and has been allied to a preoccupation, shared by many of the Marxists I have already discussed, with the ordinary, relatively inarticulate, masses of the people. The interest in 'mentalities' forms a link between the original *Annales*, and the *Annales* of the Sixth Section.

Sometimes it seems that anything new under the sun must automatically be the prerogative of *Annales*. Highly prestigious and institutionally secure, it has continued to recruit new generations of original thinkers, who have steadily focussed attention on hitherto neglected communities and subjects. In the words of an American admirer:

> The object of *Annales* work is to construct a history of every group and subject whose investigation has been suppressed or neglected. It thus aspires to bring ancient, contemporary, and future history (but a

prospective future, not a projective or futurological history deprived of foundations in the past or with a basis in the recent past only) into its focus of concern instead of limiting itself to the years 1000 to 1800. It aims similarly at the 'demasculinisation of history' and at the development of a history of women, of youth, of childhood, of oral cultures, of voluntary associations, of non-Western civilizations, of nonconsensual cultures, of Lévi-Strauss's 'cold societies,' which are made to last, and Braudel's 'inert' societies, which offer constant resistance to the triumph of change and progress but ultimately lose.[39]

Again, the *Annales* historians have not been the only, or necessarily the first, into these fields: they were not the pioneers of either childhood or family history. But they have played an honourable part in the general movement towards the use of a much wider range of source materials including, in particular, visual sources and the artefacts of popular culture. One of the most distinguished contemporary figures, Mark Ferro, turning his back on the general preoccupations with pre-industrial society, has been a pioneer in the analysis of film and television (picking up, of course, from the concern with *communications*).

The interests of *Annales* seem enormous and coruscating. Yet in detail, much of its work is at least as tedious, in its earnest endeavours to avoid surface excitements and present instead the accoutrements of a serious scientific search for meaningful *conjonctures*, as the most traditional offerings of the *American Historical Review* or *English Historical Review*. Some of the debates, and a few of the articles, in *Annales* itself raise issues of considerable significance; but a large number of the articles, as with other learned journals, simply serve legitimate professional interests. Many of the monographs published from the Sixth Section (another sign of its power) are worthy rather than exciting. In *Annales* discourse statistical tables abound, their precise significance not always being made very clear (save that, allegedly, they demonstrate a solid structural base); flow charts and diagrams, too, sometimes seem designed more to impress than to illuminate; visual sources are sometimes reproduced as if they spoke for themselves (which, of course, they never do). Apart from the general commitments outlined above, the *Annales* school has no overarching philosophy (and is none the worse for that, in my view): what it has produced is inspiration, ideas, and – in book form – a number of truly distinguished examples of historical writing.

Fernand Braudel (1902–83) underwent the extended apprenticeship, traditionally demanded in the French academic world, protracted by the disruptions of the Second World War, most of which he spent as a prisoner of war in Germany: his massive thesis on *The Mediterranean and the Mediterranean World in the Age of Philip II* was almost finished in 1939, was successfully defended before his examiners in 1947, and published in 1949. In the light of what I have already said, it is obvious that this book cannot be taken as any kind of 'bible' of *Annales* methodology, though of course it shows many of the preoccupations already discussed. Braudel ignored political boundaries and sought to create a total history of a whole region centring on the Mediterranean. The spirit of the man, a spirit apparent in different ways in all the outstanding *Annales* writers, comes through in the opening words of the preface:

> I have loved the Mediterranean with passion, no doubt because I am a northerner like so many others in whose footsteps I have followed. I have joyfully dedicated long years of study to it – much more than all my youth. In return, I hope that a little of this joy and a great deal of Mediterranean sunlight will shine from the pages of this book.

The preface also sets out how the three parts of the book coincide with three different kinds of time:

> The first part is devoted to a history whose passage is almost imperceptible, that of man in his relationship to the environment, a history in which all change is slow, a history of constant repetition, ever-recurring cycles. I could not neglect this almost timeless history, the story of man's contact with the inanimate, neither could I be satisfied with the traditional geographical introduction to history that often figures to little purpose at the beginning of so many books, with the descriptions of the mineral deposits, types of agriculture, and typical flora, briefly listed and never mentioned again, as if the flowers did not come back every spring, the flocks of sheep migrate every year, or the ships sail on a real sea that changes with the seasons.
>
> On a different level from the first there can be distinguished another history, this time with slow but perceptible rhythms. If the expression had not been diverted from its full meaning, one could call it *social history*, the history of groups and groupings. How did these swelling currents affect Mediterranean life in general – this was the question I asked myself in the second part of the book, studying in turn economic systems, states, societies, civilizations and finally, in order to convey more clearly my conception of history, attempting to show how all these deep-seated forces were at work in the complex arena of warfare. For war, as we know, is not an arena governed purely by individual responsibilities.

Lastly, the third part gives a hearing to traditional history – history, one might say, on the scale not of man, but of individual men, what Paul Lacombe and François Simiand called '*l'histoire événementielle*', that is, the history of events: surface disturbances, crests of foam that the tides of history carry on their strong backs. A history of brief, rapid, nervous fluctuations, by definition ultra-sensitive; the least tremor sets all its antennae quivering. But as such it is the most exciting of all, the richest in human interest, and also the most dangerous. We must learn to distrust this history with its still burning passions, as it was felt, described, and lived by contemporaries whose lives were as short and as short-sighted as ours.

The first type of time became known to Braudel and the *Annales* school as *la longue durée*. Two other famous concepts lie at the heart of the kind of time dealt with in part two which, as Braudel explained, had 'to meet two contradictory purposes':

It is concerned with social structures, that is with mechanisms that withstand the march of time; it is also concerned with the development of those structures. It combines, therefore, what have come to be known as *structure* and *conjuncture* the permanent and the ephemeral, the slow-moving and the fast.

In 1966 a second edition was published in France. There were many revisions and extensions, including new material on the rural sector, and a discussion, under the heading 'Can a Model be Made of the Mediterranean Economy?' of the relationships between production, consumption, exchange and distribution. The new edition was published in English in 1972, followed a year later by *Capitalism and Material Life 1400–1800* which had been published in France in 1967, the first part of what was projected as a much larger work: these translations helped to bring Braudel a deserved reputation as the foremost historian of the age.

The new book addressed itself to that crucial period in which the world moved from bare subsistence and constant economic insecurity to a time when the way was clear for industrialisation and economic progress. At times Braudel had seemed over obsessed with the way in which permanent structures imposed themselves on human freedom: central to this work was man's growing mastery of his environment. The chapter headings are a roll-call of the areas of study which Braudel and the *Annales* school sponsored. First, of course, is 'The Weight of Numbers'. Topics then covered are 'Daily Bread', 'Food and Drink', 'Houses, Clothes and Fashion', 'The Spread of Technology',

'Money', 'Towns'. Characteristically, Braudel makes a brave, if possibly over-imaginative, effort to exactly quantify the sources of power available in Europe at the end of the eighteenth century. There are diagrams, tables, maps, and flow charts. The original French edition contains some interesting reproductions of visual material. There is little in the way of scholarly apparatus. The words knowledgeable reviewers used were 'unbearably exciting' (Max Beloff in the *Daily Telegraph*) and 'intoxicating' (C. S. L. Davies in *The Times Higher Education Supplement*). The complete work, with the first volume in revised version, was finally published in three volumes in Paris in 1979 (and in English in 1983–4). The riches are immense, but the conclusion to it all that three conditions were necessary for the successful development of capitalism, is clear and succinct:

(1) A developing market economy (a necessary, but not sufficient condition);
(2) The development over a long period of societies favourable to continuous wealth accumulation and to some social mobility within secure hierarchies;
(3) The impetus of world trade (the subject of volume three).[40]

In concluding the foreword to Book II, Braudel had quoted from Maitland (*Domesday Book and Beyond*): 'simplicity is the outcome of technical subtlety; it is the goal, not starting point'.

Two different features characteristic of *Annales* writing are readily apparent in two of the major works by François Furet (b. 1927). In *La Révolution* (Paris, 1965–6), written in collaboration with Denis Richet, the emphasis is on the analysis of social structure throughout the eighteenth century, this longer-term view being seen as necessary for an understanding of the actual events of the revolution (and, incidentally, as we saw, delivering a body blow to Marxist analysis). *Book and Society in Eighteenth-Century France* (Paris, 1965–70) was the product of a research team (a not untypical *Annales* phenomenon) headed by Furet. This was a vigorously quantitative study, 'for only quantity allows an appreciation of the whole weight of the social ingredient and of the past in the reading and writing of a society.'[41] Two classic studies using the quantitative disciplines of demography to develop a kind of total history examining material culture and the everyday life of the masses are *Beauvais et les Beauvaisis de 1600 à 1730* (Paris,

1960) by Pierre Goubert and *The Peasants of Languedoc* (Paris, 1966) by Emmanuel Leroy Ladurie (b. 1929). The work of Leroy Ladurie showed strongly a return to the earlier *Annales* concern with psychology and mentalities. It was Ladurie's *Montaillou: Cathars and Catholics in a French Village 1294–1324* (1978), a vivid recreation of the manners, morals, life-styles, and habits of thought of a medieval community, built up from the Inquisition Register of Jacques Fournière, Bishop of Pamiers which, totally unexpectedly, achieved international 'best-sellerdom.' Two years later there followed *Carnaval: A People's Uprising at Romans 1579–1580* which, though less enthusiastically received, certainly revealed to the full Ladurie's mastery of the disciplines of anthropology and social psychology, as well as that of history.

As already noted, Marc Ferro is rather unusual in the *Annales* school for his interest in twentieth-century history. In *The Russian Revolution of February 1917* (Paris, 1967) Ferro devised a skilful analysis of public opinion (mentalities again) through sampling letters and telegrams addressed to newspapers; he also used film in a highly original way to bring out the material reality of the truly degrading conditions against which, in one aspect, revolution was directed. In *The Great War 1914–1918* (Paris, 1969), there is again a sensitive analysis of mentalities, with a highly original deployment of non-traditional sources, posters, patriotic songs, films. Public opinion was formed also, Ferro notes, by 'official ceremonies, the commemoration of victories, the cult of the dead, the roar and tinkle of brasses and drums, and the jingle of medals.' Ferro is strongly concerned with the masses, with the forgotten, and the sacrificed. But precise quantities are there too in assessing the material resources available to the combatants. Ferro's seminal article 'Le film, une contra-analyse de la société?' was published in *Annales* in January 1973. Finally, the *Annales* aspiration towards a world view is most fruitfully revealed in the work referred to in Chapter 1, *The Use and Abuse of History: Or How the Past is Taught* (first published in Paris in 1981).

6. The Ruling Passion: Solving Problems

History, like other academic disciplines, is about solving problems. The problems need not be those defined by *Annales* historians, by Marxist historians, or by traditional political historians. They *may* be those defined by two further schools which we must discuss briefly, the New Economic Historians, and the New Social Historians, or they may be more traditional ones, like 'What caused the First World War?' or 'How did Europe recover from the Second World War?'

In the postwar years two new forms of economic history, deeply rooted in the methodology of economic science, developed. First, a form which had already gained wide acceptance and which was concerned with concepts of economic growth and the study of national economic statistics in the aggregate. This kind of economic history was pioneered in the United States by Simon Kuznets: it was due to his initiative that in 1950 the International Association for Research in Income and Wealth decided to embark on a series of analyses of the evolutions in national income, national wealth, and their components, for various countries, and that in 1956 the Social Science Research Council (of the U.S.A.) created a fund to finance research on economic growth in various countries, in the nineteenth and twentieth centuries. These initiatives have been developed in France by Jean Marczewski, who has coined the not altogether satisfactory description 'quantitative history', by Phyllis Deane in Britain, and by W. G. Hoffmann and J. H. Muller in Germany. This history, Marczewski has told us, 'differs from traditional history in using a model consisting of quantified and interdependent magnitudes, the definition of which has its origin in national accounting'; it not only ascertains 'the past evolution of the various aggregates, it also seeks to explain it'.[42] Marczewski finds the justification for the resort to national accounts in 'the growing interdependence of economic phenomena which is characteristic of the evolution of modern society'.

More controversial, and in some respects more stimulating, is the form of economic history called, boringly, the 'new economic history', or, pretentiously, 'cliometrics', or, least offensively, 'econometric history'. Econometric history, E. H. Hunt has written, can be considered to have three aspects.[43] The first actually differs only in degree from the approach long pursued by most economic historians: much greater emphasis is placed on statistical method and upon precision of definition and categorisation, and computers are enlisted to carry out calculations which formerly would have been impossible. As an example of this aspect, Hunt cites some work of R. P. Swierenga on land speculation in nineteenth-century Iowa:

> Earlier attempts to assess land speculator profits were characterised by a reliance on non-mathematical techniques, the omission of certain key elements, vague definitions of what constituted 'profits', and the sheer impossibility of undertaking sufficiently large studies without the mechanical aids now available. Swierenga defined each term carefully, chose a sample area and prepared a data card for each parcel of land sold. Chronological details, prices, agents' fees and other data were punched onto the cards. After processing he was able to give precise figures of rates of return, broken down into year of entry, size of holding, and other categories.

The second aspect of econometric history, the enlistment of economic and statistical theory in order to reconstruct 'measurements which might have existed in the past but are no longer extant' – to use the words of a leading econometric historian, R. W. Fogel (b. 1926) – is again a matter of degree rather than a complete break with older methods. Indirect quantification of a rather unsophisticated sort had been used, for example, in the standard-of-living controversy in the historiography of the British Industrial Revolution, or in tracing the expansion of a money economy in nineteenth-century Ireland through sales of Guinness beer. The indirect quantification of the econometric historians draws upon a much more sophisticated armoury: regression analysis, rent, input–output and location theory, hypergeometric distribution, and the von Neumann–Morgenstern utility index.

> The third aspect of econometric history, the most distinctive and ambitious is the use of the counterfactual conditional concept, starting with the premiss that we can understand the significance of what did happen only if we contrast it with what might have happened, and going on to quantify 'what might have happened'.[44]

The most famous exponent of the counterfactual conditional concept is R. W. Fogel, who, in challenging the long-standing theory about the central importance of American railroads in the expansion of the American economy, constructed a model of the American economy as it would have been *without* railroads: the American gross national product in 1890 would, he reckoned, have been only 6.3 per cent lower than it actually was. The other outstanding piece of work in this canon is that of John R. Meyer and Alfred H. Conrad on 'The Economics of Slavery in the Ante-Bellum South', which effectively challenged some old theories about the uneconomic nature of slavery. Wild claims therefore have been made on behalf of the achievements, real and potential, of econometric history, often by those who have least direct knowledge of its operation. When Keith Thomas, of *Past and Present* and a distinguished student of the English Revolution, declared in the *Times Literary Supplement* that econometric history was sweeping all before it and would soon provide 'definitive solutions' to various historical problems, he was answered by Peter Temin of the Massachusetts Institute of Technology, himself one of the most able of the econometric historians, who indicated the various limitations of this type of historical inquiry.[45]

Probably the single most important development in the postwar years came in the sphere of historical demography (in the widest sense, covering births, deaths, fertility rates, family composition, population growth and movements). The critical advance was the development in the mid-nineteen-fifties of the technique known as family reconstitution. Instead of using the aggregate figures of the census reports, which only exist for the modern era, information was built up from sources, such as parish registers, in which individuals are named. The first study was carried through by Louis Henry, of the French Institut National d'Études Démographiques into the bourgeois families of Geneva, and published in 1956 as *Anciennes Familles Genevoises*. To the French pioneers, were added a group of English historians E. A. Wrigley, D. E. C. Eversley, R. S. Schofield, and Peter Laslett, who in 1962 founded the Cambridge Group for the History of Population and Social Structure. The methods and operations involved in, and the fruitful possibilities of, family reconstitution using English parish registers were explained in the book edited by Wrigley, *An Introduction to English Historical Demography* (1966); some of the more dramatic aspects of the work, including the discovery that despite 'evidence' drawn, say, from the plays of Shakespeare, marriage ages for ordinary people in the pre-industrial world were very high (late twenties), were publicised in *The World We Have Lost* (1965) by Laslett.

Historical demography was central to many important areas of historical study, some only just coming to be fully recognised, such as the family, some long a matter of contention, such as the 'population explosion' of the late eighteenth century. On the latter topic work by K. H. Connell, J. T. Krause and many others threw into disrepute the thesis which associated rising population with a falling death rate which in turn was associated with improved medicine, environment, etc. It is now as well established as such matters can be that whatever was happening to the death rate, there was in the middle and later eighteenth century a very definite rise in the birth rate; not to put too fine a point upon it, people were copulating earlier and oftener. Developments in historical demography made possible a new 'urban history', fulfilling what Asa Briggs, a pioneer urban historian in Britain, called 'the need to examine in detail social structure and change in the most meaningful units that historians can discover', and providing 'knowledge of local relationships and pressures.'[46] In France the demographic stimulus to the study of urban history came from the Institut National d'Études Démographiques, while important contributions were also made by the long-established interest of French scholars in historical geography and by the *Annales* school. Numbered among the most influential French contributors to the study of urban history are Adeline Daumard, Pierre Goubert and Louis Chevalier. In America and, subsequently, in Europe, the Chicago school of urban sociology has been a strong influence. From his work on immigrant groups (*Boston's Immigrants* (1941); *The Uprooted* (1951)) Oscar Handlin moved into the main stream of urban history, and in 1963 he, with John Burchard, edited the important collection of studies *The Historian and the City* (1963). The critical work in showing how the extent of, and limitations upon, social mobility could be accurately traced was *Poverty and Progress: Social Mobility in a Nineteenth-Century City* (1964) by Stephen Thernstrom, in which ordinary families in Newburyport, Massachusetts, were followed across three generations.

The New Social History also places strong emphasis on quantities; and, like *Annales* history, seeks to enlist the help of the social sciences, demography, perhaps, being given the privileged position. It also tends to be articulate on the role of theory and the value of models, and to advocate the clear enunciation of hypotheses; it favours such concepts as 'ideology', 'hegemony', and 'social control', and likes to talk of individuals, groups, or even ideas, 'finding space'. I'm a trifle agnostic myself about the material existence of this New Social History, not nearly as well defined as the New Economic History, and lacking in any kind of institutional basis such as that of *Annales*. Perhaps it is more accurate to speak of a new *emphasis* on social history, character- ised by an insistence that social history should be rigorous in its application of quantities and relevant social science techniques, and not simply descriptive and impressionistic.[47] In the Anglo- Saxon countries the most obvious signs of the new emphasis were the founding, all in the 1970s, of the journals *Social History* (U.K.) and *Journal of Social History* (U.S.A.), of History Workshop and of the Social History Society (both U.K.). But some of the most original work was being carried out in West Germany. Werner Conze at Heidelberg set up a 'Working Circle for Modern Social History', and edited a series entitled 'The Industrial World'. Rein- hart Koselleck, whose *Prussia Between Reform and Revolution* was published in Stuttgart in 1967, shared with Conze a belief that social history must essentially be concerned with the concepts which, as they saw it, predominate in a particular epoch. Conze and his collaborators have organised a major dictionary of 'Basic Historical Concepts', as an aid to understanding the industrial world through its language. But social history since the 1960s has also, as relevant, made use of the oral testimony acquired through the systematic interviewing of survivors from a former era: Paul Thompson has been the celebrated pioneer in Britain, Lutz Niethammer, with his work on industrial workers in the Ruhr, has been a leading German figure.

As new works of social history have appeared in the seventies and eighties an ever-changing balance has been struck between quantitative elements and qualitative ones. There has been a desire to get as close as possible both to the material conditions of past peoples, and to the quality of life; interest in 'mentalities' and in the symbolism of ordinary life has advanced unabated; the movement (in the humanities as a whole) from a preoccupation with élite culture to one with popular culture has led on to a concern with the relations between the two. Certain books, all in some way representative of these trends, attracted particular attention: Carlo Ginzburg's *The Cheese and the Worms: The Cosmos of a Sixteenth-Century Miller* (Turin, 1976) took (rather as Febvre had taken Rabelais) one exceptional heretical figure, the miller Menochio, in order to illuminate the symbolic world of communication of the wider pre-industrial peasant culture to which Menochio belonged; *Man and the Natural World: Changing Attitudes in England 1500–1800* (1984), by Keith Thomas, author also of *Religion and the Decline of Magic* (1971), addressed a completely new area of human sensibility, in particular 'how to reconcile the physical requirements of civilization with the new feelings and values which that same civilization had generated' with regard to behaviour towards animal creation.

I have referred to the balance between quantity and quality: there is another balance, that between the general experience and the actual particular experiences of normal individuals. One British historian who has been obsessed with that problem is Richard Cobb. Cobb's *The Revolutionary Armies*, published in French in Paris in 1961 and 1963, formed a part of that new analysis of the French Revolution also being carried on by Soboul and Rudé, but already showed the fascination with the life of the individual which was to be carried further and culminated in *Death in Paris* which sought to recapture the world of Parisian suicides. Cobb, who dared to declare that for millions of Frenchmen the Revolution was a 'magnificent irrelevance',[48] has been engaged in some bitter exchanges with the *Annales* school; it throws further light on that school, though it in no way condemns Cobb, to note Furet's criticism that while Cobb takes on new subject matter ('he has swapped Dukes for tramps, respectable folk for the destitute, great men for small fry, deeds for daily life') his methods are the old ones.[49] The process of 'swapping Dukes for tramps' is, as has already become obvious, a widespread one.

One particular growth area which clearly shows the move towards incorporating the study of attitudes, sensitivities, and emotions with the more basic demographic information, is family history – an area of study, incidentally, brilliantly justified by the pioneer demographer E. A. Wrigley: 'If the criterion of the importance of a theme to history is the proportion of the population it involves, and its centrality to other historical themes, then the history of the family need fear few rivals.'[50] As so often, there was a great French precursor, Philippe Ariès, whose *L'Enfant et la vie familiale sous l'ancien régime* (see Chapter 8) was published in Paris in 1960, with an English translation (1972) under the vacuous title of *Centuries of Childhood*. The recent literature is enormous, but three books which have attracted attention for the width of their range are: Jean-Louis Flandrin, *Familles: parenté, maison, sexualité dans l'ancienne société* (Paris, 1976), Edward Shorter, *The Making of the Modern Family* (New York, 1976), and Lawrence Stone, *The Family, Sex and Marriage in England 1500–1800* (London, 1977).

Studies of women's role in past societies had not been completely absent from earlier historical writing, whether general overviews like Doris Stenton's *The English Woman in History* (1957), or thoroughly detailed studies such as Ivy Pinchbeck's study of *Women Workers and the Industrial Revolution* (1930), but without any doubt at all the movement for Women's Rights from the 1960s onwards has been accompanied by the opening up of a whole new area of the history of women, much of it dominated by writers taking an explicitly feminist stance. Characteristically, much of this work has appeared in the form of collaborative ventures, collections of essays, as with *Suffer and Be Still: Women in the Victorian Age* (Indiana, 1972), edited by Martha Vicinus, *Becoming Visible, Women in European History* (Boston, 1977), edited by Renata Bridenthal and Claudia Koonz – containing, among other things, the interesting question posed by Joan Kelly-Gadol 'Did Women have a Renaissance?', and *Women, War and Revolution* (New York, 1980), edited by Carol R. Birkin and Clara M. Lovett. Full-length general studies include Carroll Camden, *The Elizabethan Woman* (New York, 1975), A. M. Lucas, *Women in the Middle Ages* (1983), and Antonia Fraser, *The Weaker Vessel: Women's Lot in Seventeenth Century England* (1984), while Judith C. Brown, *Immodest Acts: The Life of a Lesbian Nun in Renaissance Italy* (New York, 1985) is a most original scholarly monograph and Jan Marsh, *The Pre-Raphaelite Sisterhood* (1985) a brilliant work of cultural history. The new interest in women's history has brought a new scholarship to an old subject of perennial fascination, as seen in: Lois W. Banner, *American Beauty* (New York, 1983), Valerie Steele, *Fashion and Eroticism: Ideals of Feminine Beauty from the Victorian Era to the Jazz Age* (New York, 1985), and Anne de Marnhac, *Femmes au bain: les métamorphoses de la beauté* (Paris, 1986).

I want now to move back towards the more traditional concerns of historians, concerns which throughout the entire postwar period still preoccupied large numbers of very able professional historians. But first I must pause over one branch of history which has undergone enormous changes since the Second World War but which seems not to have established as secure a place at the centre of historical studies as it ought to have: the history of science and technology. A generation or so ago science history was almost the exclusive monopoly of a few specialists who confined themselves to the internal development of science, paying little attention to social and cultural influences. Outside this specialist school there were only two other approaches: the economic histories, which presented somewhat bald catalogues of scientific and technological innovation without any very satisfactory explanation of how these came about or how they were related to the wider context; and the Marxist accounts, which had the great merit of stressing the social relations of science, but which were often rather facile in their insistence upon the dependence of scientific advance upon economic imperatives. Science history is now a much more sophisticated subject, involving on the part of the historian both an understanding of the scientific theories being discussed and of the processes of historical causation and change:[51] both of these qualities are to be found in high degree in the work of the dean of contemporary science historians, G. C. Gillispie.[52] Some of the most interesting work in the history of technology, however, has been done by researchers whose starting-point lies in the refined techniques of contemporary economic history. The progression of David Landes of Harvard University, from his *Bankers and Pashas: International Finance and Economic Imperialism in Egypt* (1960) to his present enviable position as an accepted authority on technological innovation and industrial change, based on his *The Unbound Prometheus* (1966), is instructive. A particular case in point is Margaret Gowing, historian of atomic energy in the United Kingdom, and a major figure in the history of science and technology. The current achievements and problems of the sub-discipline are effectively analysed by Arnold Thackray in his paper 'History of Science in the 1980s' in *The New History* (Princeton, N.J., 1982), edited by Theodore K. Rabb and Robert I. Rotberg.

Great events, the causes of wars, the lives and actions of politicians continued to preoccupy distinguished scholars, and rightly so: the understanding of the past needed by society is not confined to those aspects of the past which happen to be in high fashion. Always, new source materials are being discovered, or, with respect to the very recent period, being made available for the first time for examination by historians. Thus, for example, in Britain a group of historians associated with the Committee for Contemporary History (chaired by Donald Cameron Watt) has been working on various aspects of Britain's foreign policy in the 1950s, as the relevant official documents become available. The work is not necessarily particularly exciting, or imaginative, but it provides basic information which needs to be known. A major controversy of a rather conventional, but really quite exciting, type which has been occupying numbers of historians for a generation, is that over Germany's part in initiating the First World War, touched off by Fritz Fischer (b. 1908) whose *Grasp After World Power* first appeared in 1961. Fischer argued that even apparently moderate German leaders such as Bethmann-Hollweg nourished extensive annexionist war aims, and that there was a close relationship between economic interests within Germany and Germany's bellicose policies. The ideas opened up by Fischer were developed and refined by such writers as Hans-Ulrich Wehler, author of *Bismarck and Imperialism* (Göttingen, 1969), and *Crises in the Imperial Empire 1871–1918* (Göttingen, 1970), and Volker Berghahn, author of *Germany and the Approach of War in 1914* (1973). The personality and policies of Adolf Hitler, and the origins of the Second World War have also, very reasonably, continued to be matters of great interest (these are discussed briefly in Chapter 8). It is my personal prejudice that political biography is often the least demanding and the least illuminating of all branches of historical study. Yet the major political biographies now regularly being produced, where the authors have been assiduous in tracking down all relevant source materials (not simply confining themselves to the private papers of their subject – the easy way) and in explicating all relevant contextual issues, have clearly been invaluable in filling serious gaps in historical knowledge. I think, in particular, of one of the most massive of them all, Martin Gilbert's multi-volume biography of Winston Churchill – descendant of one Duke, and close relative of another.[53]

Has this chapter rushed too quickly from one historian, one type of history, to another? Have I left no clear impression of what is distinctive about the history of the late 1980s? The apparent shapelessness has been deliberate; there is no universal fashion, no accepted party line, no unbroken formation of 'New Social

Historians'. However if I have to single out one distinctive trend as we approach the 1990s, it would be the move from public history to private history (seen in many of the titles I have cited; seen in works by Peter Gay and Simon Schama to which I shall return later, seen in the major multi-volume collaborative enterprise – French of course, under the direction of Georges Duby on *The History of Private Life*[54]). A second, lesser, though important trend is the new insistence on the significance of contemporary history (*L'Institut d'Histoire du Temps Présent*, under François Bedarida in Paris, has been followed by the Institute of Contemporary British History under Anthony Seldon and Peter Hennessy, neither of whom are members of the academic establishment). As I have been making my own minuscule contributions to both private history and contemporary history since the early 1960s, I have no axe to grind in commenting that society will continue also to need public history (with, perhaps, a further exploration of the relations between public and private) and that, vitally important as is the study of contemporary history, history confined to the recent past would quickly fail to meet the demands which society, rightly, places upon it.

Notes

1. Turner and Craven are quoted in G. R. Taylor (ed.), *The Turner Thesis* (1956).
2. Breisach, p. 314. See John Higham, *History: Professional Scholarship in America* (1983), Chapters II (2), III (3), (4), and (5).
3. Edward P. Cheyney, *Law in History and Other Essays* (New York, 1927).
4. See A. M. Schlesinger Sr, *In Retrospect: The History of a Historian* (1963).
5. See chapter on Febvre by Palmer A. Throop in S. William Halperin (ed.), *Some 20th Century Historians* (Chicago, 1961).
6. Ibid.
7. *Annales d'Histoire Économique et Social*, II (Jan. 1929): my translation.
8. See chapter by James L. Cate in Halperin.
9. Quoted by G. N. Clark, *Sir John Harold Clapham* (1946), p. 6.
10. The address is printed in the *American Historical Review*, XLII (1937).
11. See Richard Pares and A. J. P. Taylor, *Essays Presented to Sir Lewis Namier* (1956).

12. Richard Pares, *George III and the Politicians* (paperback edn, 1968), p. 64.

13. Bernadotte Schmitt, *The Fashion and the Future of History* (1960), pp. 4ff.

14. Barbara Tuchman, *The Proud Tower* (1966), p. xiv.

15. R. L. Schuyler, 'Some Historical Idols' in *Political Science Quarterly*, XLVII (1932), pp. 5–6.

16. Breisach, p. 386.

17. Federico Chabod, *Machiavelli and the Renaissance* (New York, 1958), p. xiii.

18. See Kitson Clark, *The Making of Victorian England* (pb edn, 1965), p. 7.

19. Ibid., p. 4.

20. G. R. Elton, *The Tudor Revolution in Government* (Cambridge, 1953).

21. See the critical discussion of the Elton thesis by Penry Williams and G. L. Harris, in *Past and Present*, XXV (July 1963).

22. Richard Pares, *The Historian's Business* (Oxford, 1961), p. 14.

23. *Past and Present*, XXX (1965), p. 113.

24. The speaker was Keith Thomas, but I can't remember where he said it.

25. Tawney's article was originally published in the *Economic History Review* in 1941. All the main articles are reprinted in Laurence Stone, *Social Change and Revolution in England* (1965).

26. H. R. Trevor-Roper, *Religion, the Reformation and Social Change* (1967), p. xiii.

27. Quoted by Breisach, pp. 354–5.

28. Mark Poster, *Foucault, Marxism and History: Mode of Production Versus Mode of Information* (1984), p. 29.

29. The best recent guide is William Doyle, *Origins of the French Revolution* (Oxford, 1980).

30. *The Political Economy of Slavery: Studies in the Economy and Society of the Slave South* (New York, 1965), pp. 10–11.

31. Herbert G. Gutmann, *Work, Culture and Society in Industrialising America: Essays in American Working Class and Social History* (New York, 1976), pp. 10–11.

32. In *Visions of History* (Manchester, 1983), eds. Henry Ableove, Betsy Blackmar, Peter Dimock, and Jonathan Schneer, p. 2.

33. Poster, p. 109.

34. François Furet, *In the Workshop of History* (Paris, 1982; Chicago, 1984), p. 2.

35. Ibid., p. 3.

36. Ibid., p. 10.

37. Quoted Breisach, p. 373.

38. Breisach, p. 375.

39. Traian Stoianovich, *French Historical Method: The Annales Paradigm* (Ithaca, N.Y., 1976), pp. 158–9.

40. Fernand Braudel, *Civilisation matérielle, économie et capitalisme, XV–XVIII siècle*, vol. II, *Les jeux de l'échange*, pp. 535–6.

41. Quoted Stoianovich, p. 190.

42. Jean Marczewski, 'Quantitative History' in *Journal of Contemporary History*, III 2 (1968), p. 179–91.

43. E. H. Hunt, 'The New Economic History' in *History*, LIII 177 (1968) 3–13. What follows draws heavily on Hunt's model exposition.

44. Hunt, in *History*, LIII, 5.

45. *Times Literary Supplement*, 7 April and 28 July 1966.

46. Asa Briggs, in H. J. Dyos (ed.), *The Study of Urban History* (1968) pp. v–xi.

47. See the editors' Introduction to Pat Thane and Anthony Sutcliffe (eds), *Essays in Social History*, 2 (1986).

48. Richard Cobb, *Reactions to the French Revolution* (Oxford, 1972), p. 125.

49. Furet, p. 19.

50. E. A. Wrigley, 'Population, Family and Household' in Martin Ballard (ed.) *New Movements in the Study and Teaching of History* (1971), p. 93.

51. See A. C. Crombie and M. A. Hoskin, 'A Note on History of Science as an Academic Discipline', and Henry Guerlac, 'Some Historical Assumptions of the History of Science' in A. C. Crombie (ed.), *Scientific Change* (1963).

52. See G. C. Gillispie, *Genesis and Geology* (1951) and *The Edge of Objectivity* (1960).

53. The first two volumes were written by Churchill's son, Randolph. To great acclaim Martin Gilbert published the eighth and final volume in the spring of 1988.

54. Philippe Ariès and Georges Duby (eds.), *Histoire de la vie privée* (Paris, 1985–   ).

Chapter 4 The Place of Theory: History, Science and Social Science

1. Theory in History

Subjected to a violent attack for his attempts to bring a Marxist analysis to bear upon developments in seventeenth-century English society, Christopher Hill (discussed in the previous chapter) responded by referring to what he saw as the fundamental distinction 'between those who try to make sense of history and those who see nothing in it but the play of the contingent and the unforeseen, who think everything is so complicated that no general statements can safely be made, who are so busy making qualifications that they forget that anything actually happened.'[1] The desire to 'make sense of history', that is to uncover deeper principles which explain the relationships between the different phenomena of the past, and how one past age is transformed into another, is a powerful one, felt by many of the historians discussed in the previous two chapters. The desire to bring order to a subject which might otherwise be shapeless and meaningless is a highly reputable one. The notion of developing a science which might provide deep truths about the organisation and development of society is an exciting one. There are those, both inside and outside the historical profession, who feel that without a body of theory history cannot claim to be regarded as a respectable academic subject. There are those who find the highest intellectual challenge in the development and refinement of theory. Yet, the simple indisputable fact remains that practising historians as a profession are united neither in the acceptance of one body of theory, nor even in the view that theoretical approaches are helpful or desirable. Partly the divisions on this major issue are a matter of individual predilection or mental set, partly they may even be attributed to different educational traditions in different countries.

On the surface at least (and generalising rather wildly) greatest weight on theoretical approaches appears to be found in German and Italian writings, somewhat less in French and American writings, and least of all in British writings. However, many of the generation which came to the fore (in all countries) in the sixties and seventies felt the need to give history the shape and (as they saw it) the rigour of clearly stated theory.

What kinds of theories are there, and where do they come from? In all intellectual endeavour theory arises from a combination of observation and reflection, from research and from pondering the results of that research. But, as historians above all are trained to be aware, theory, and indeed the very processes of research, are likely to be governed by the assumptions and conventions of the age and society in which that research and reflection takes place. Indeed, sometimes when we speak of 'theories' it might be better to speak of 'assumptions'. Then again, one of the arguments for clearly stated theory, based it is to be hoped on serious empirical observation and rigorous analytical thought, is that such theory, boldly announced, is to be preferred to the unspoken, and often unrecognised assumptions which would otherwise be colouring historical interpretation. Ranke believed that he had developed methods of source criticism which would tell him 'how it really was', but his conclusions were coloured by his deeply held Protestant *faith* and his *assumption* that the growth of the nation state was part of God's plan for humanity. Generations of later historians have assumed that self-expression for the smaller nationalities, or the spread of democracy, or the growth of state-sponsored social welfare, or the maintenance of social stability were inevitable facets of social development. Some have assumed that the conclusions drawn from written documents override any drawn from other forms of evidence or analysis. I do not necessarily criticise these assumptions, indeed I may share some of them; I simply recognise the argument that since we all have assumptions it may be better to have a rigorously thought out theory. The theoretical approaches most widely deployed today depend, in essence, upon a contention that there are structural factors within society which, in the last analysis, determine the course of events within that society, or, more precisely, create the crises which greater or lesser political and managerial skills may avert or postpone. There are various forms, apparent among: members of the

Annales school; the West German social historians discussed in the previous chapter; and some American, and some British, historians. It would be fair to say, I think, that these forms mostly have their fundamental origins in the sociology of Max Weber, though Marxism of course, is another major source. Sometimes the distinction has little meaning, partly because of the many refinements to modern Marxist writing, partly also because, in the very last analysis, Weber himself was greatly influenced by Marx. There are other 'philosophical' positions, as we shall see in Chapter 7, but they are not important to this general discussion.

At the opposite extreme are those historians (a dwindling force though every now and then their case is re-made, though usually, one suspects, for provocative effect rather than constructive advance of knowledge), who claim that history is simply the unfolding of events, a narrative account of which will contain all the explanation which is possible, and that all attempts at abstraction or generalisation are futile. Actually, as has been pointed out over and over again, historians cannot begin to do their humblest chores without drawing upon generalising concepts such as war, revolution, class, peasantry, feudalism, the Renaissance. This mundane circumstance has provoked the argument that since historians can't avoid generalisations and concepts they should be firmly disciplined into a clearly articulated theory. That is an argument, self-evidently, that large numbers of historians have resisted. But while very many historians (a substantial majority, I would think) reject the notion of one over-arching theoretical approach, large numbers do make use of specific theories (plural) and some develop a theory of their own of the kind which is usually described as a 'thesis', as in Mahan's thesis about the influence of sea power, or Turner's frontier thesis, or the Pirenne thesis. In their everyday work historians may well wish to draw upon, say, models of urban development, location theory, the theory of the product cycle (and other concepts drawn from economics), principles of human behaviour drawn from psychoanalysis, notions of shared values, concepts such as modernisation and social control.[2] In some cases the usage is carefully delimited by the discipline from which the concept is drawn; but there are no effective general rules about the usage of such terms as 'social control' and 'modernisation'. Social control was a concept originally developed by conservative sociologists to explain the stability they saw as inherent in societies; it was then taken over by left-wing sociologists to explain how the inevitable forces of change, as they perceived them, were contained by society's rulers. Some historians adopt a theoretical stance which postulates social control as an actual given fact; others prefer to deploy the term more pragmatically and cautiously. Few historians now employ 'modernisation' (briefly, the whole complex of developments associated with industrialisation in the western countries) as a universal explanatory term, but many find it a most helpful generalising concept.

All historians, then, whether they admit it or not, employ concepts and generalisations. However, that is not the same as having one over-arching theory about how societies develop and change. Some of the most important contributions to historical knowledge have been made by historians adhering to such a theory. For myself, I have to confess to having difficulties with both Marxism and those 'structural' theories derived from Marx through Weber. The classic criticism of Marxism (and similar holistic approaches) is that it is not subject to empirical validation: it cannot be disproved, and therefore it cannot be proved. To that I feel bound to add that much which is contained in Marxist and related approaches simply defies actual observation. Marxist scholars have long appreciated this, and hence Marxist analysis in recent decades has gone off in different directions. On the one side there has been the production of ever more complex, more abstract, and more uncompromising theory in which anything so mundane as what actually happens in real human societies seems to become less and less relevant. I am thinking here of such scholars as Althusser and Habermas.[3] With someone like Foucault it is probably truer to say that he sought refuge in imaginative leaps of greater and greater incredibility, rather than in any coherent theory.[4] The other direction was that of such American New Left writers as Gutmann and Genovese and such British writers as E. P. Thompson. Thompson is the author of the magnificent 'The Poverty of Theory' a long essay which (in my view) totally destroys the pretensions of Althusser and his like, and which is also a fine statement of the historian's practices.[5] What, in the everyday workplace of ordinary historians, stands out as, in my view, a handicap to sound scholarship, is a complex of basic Marxist notions which have never really been abandoned, together with a whole elaborate vocabulary which perpetuates untested and often unsound assumptions. Marx performed a great service in pointing out in arresting fashion that social arrangements are not always what they seem, that, for instance, parliamentary institutions and 'the rule of law' could in fact mask the monopoly of power by one social group and the oppression of another. But in the hands of latter-day Marxists this perception often becomes a cliché, wrapped up in pretentious verbiage.

Nothing is more certain in the study of history than that as societies develop and alter over time values, attitudes, standards, notions of what is normal, change. Just what was meant in a particular society by, say, 'democracy', or 'emancipation', or 'socialism', or 'beauty' must always be a matter for very careful investigation: we can never afford to jump to the conclusion that the people of a past society used such words in exactly the same way as we do today. Much less certainty, however, attaches to two extensions of the simple and fundamental premise: first, the assertion that *everything* related to human activities is 'socially constructed', that nothing in human affairs has a 'real', 'essential', or 'universal' existence; thus, it is maintained, human sexuality, to take perhaps the most extreme instance, is not some biological fundamental, but in any particular period and society is determined by the forces dominant in that particular society; that, indeed, there is no such thing as essential 'humanness' but that 'humanness is socio-culturally variable';[6] second, the assumption (often taken as given rather than openly expressed) that the key to the way in which meanings change (here there is a link back to approaches we have already discussed) is to be found in the way in which at any particular stage in historical development one class dominates society, and in the dialectical process by which this class is challenged by an emergent class. The development and refinement of theory has involved the articulation of a more elaborate vocabulary. Now there is certainly a very sound argument that the precise use of technical terms is a great advance over the loose rhetoric of traditional historical writing. For example 'dominant ideology', related as it is to a clear theory about the relationship of class to social change, is certainly more satisfactory than those vague old stand-bys of the impressionistic historian 'spirit of the age' or 'climate of the times'; and the employment of the word 'gender' draws attention to the fact that just because women have fulfilled certain distinctive roles in certain societies that does not mean that these roles are related to inherent and unchanging sexual characteristics. The new vocabulary seeks to escape both from the errors of traditional history, and of traditional Marxism. Thus the 'hegemony' of the ideas and cultural practices of the dominant class are seen as coming about by quite complex processes of 'negotiation' rather than through the naked exercise of economic and political power (this is the approach associated with Gramsci, whom we have already encountered). There does exist, then, quite an elaborate body of theory employed by some historians, as well as by practitioners in other areas (for example, sociology, and cultural and literary studies): without doubt, much illuminating work has been done by those employing its concepts. But it is important to be clear that for all its sophistication of vocabulary this approach is ultimately dependent upon one or two basic tenets of Marxism (which, as I have already suggested, are a matter of faith rather than proof). Fundamental are the assumptions that classes are formed broadly in the way that Marx said they were, that ideology is related to class and serves as a mask for class interests, that the 'emergent class', the working class, is necessarily in conflict with the current dominant class (the bourgeoisie) and should, other things being equal, overthrow it in revolution. The stumbling block, of course, has been the manifest absence of, and (to say the least) decreasing likelihood of, proletarian revolution. The essence of all the elaborate theories about hegemony, negotiation, etc., is that they seek to explain why the dominant class, which *ought* to have been overthrown, has in fact continued to exercise its dominance. But if you remove the initial premise that it is the historical mission of the working class to overthrow the bourgeoisie, or (in more cautious formulation) that in keeping with the workings of the dialectic there is an alternative society waiting to emerge, there really is no need for the elaborate theory.

The appeal of the notion of the dialectic is a powerful one. How neat and clear it makes analysis if one can postulate that every society contains within it the seeds of a new society struggling to be born. How impressive it then becomes to contrast institutions and ideas which belong to the existing or dying society, with those alleged to belong to the emerging or alternative society. As a mode of analysis, or means of organising information, this approach may have its uses, though more often it is presented not so much as a method of analysis but as a profound underlying truth. As I have already stated there is actually no hard evidence that societies do in fact develop according to some dialectical process; alternative societies are certainly very hard to spot.

The weakness of 'social construction of reality' or 'sociology of knowledge' approaches is that they push sensible observations about the manner in which the social environment *influences* social activities to the extreme position that *all* activities are *determined* by that environment (which, itself, is usually categorised according to some broadly Marxist schema). Thus we find that that extremely useful coinage 'gender', originally used to refer to those distinctions between the sexes which *are* socially constructed, is now widely abused as a replacement for the word 'sex', thus effectively biasing discussion by assuming that *all* differences are socially constructed, and none dependent on biology. (In everyday speech, it is true, 'gender' has tended to become a synonym for the biological fact as well as the social construct since 'sex' in common usage has more and more come to have the, potentially embarrassing, connotation of 'the sex act'). That there are, as among individual human beings, great variations in sexual proclivities, and, among societies, great variations in sexual *customs* is not in dispute. But when the fundamental circumstances of human procreation, the fundamental biological differences between the overwhelming majority of males and females in any given society, and the fundamental nature of human sex drives are glibly swallowed up in the particularities of different sexual customs, theory really does part company from reality. A leading practitioner, Jeffrey Weeks notes that 'some cultures have made little distinction between heterosexual and homosexual forms' and that 'some cultures have seen no connection between sexual intercourse and conception'.[7] Quite so: but it is rather important to human affairs *everywhere* that there *is* a distinction, and there *is* a connection.

After Marxism, the most pervasive source of theory has been structuralism. Michael Lane has provided a useful summary of the distinctive characteristics of structuralism.[8] In the first place it is 'a method whose scope includes all human social phenomena'. This is made possible 'by the belief that all manifestations of social activity, whether it be the clothes that are worn, the books that are written or the systems of kinship and marriage that are practised in any society, constitute languages, in a formal sense.' Thus, and this, obviously, is absolutely central to the whole nature of structuralism 'their regularities may be reduced to the same set of abstract rules that define and govern what we normally think of as language . . .' But the most distinctive feature of structuralist method is 'the emphasis it gives to wholes, to totalities.' Structuralism seeks its structures 'not on the surface, at the level of the observed, but below or behind empirical reality'; the relationships it seeks to identify 'can be reduced to one of binary opposition'. This binary, oppositional, approach, of course, can (this is my own comment, not that of Lane) be very readily assimilated to Marxism with its notion of the dialectic and class conflict, while the aspiration after totalities also fits well with the ambitions of Marxism. The central emphasis on language takes one well away from traditional Marxism but the notion of regularities and abstract rules is certainly one to appeal to those who have a hankering after the 'respectability' that is one of the motivations, I have suggested, behind Marxist analysis. Most important of all is the structuralist search for truths lying below the surface, for Marxism has always claimed to penetrate behind the mask of bourgeois ideology. Now it happens that many of the leading structuralists (both in linguistics and in anthropology) had in any case a broadly Marxist outlook, believing in class conflict, believing that contemporary society is ruled by the bourgeoisie, and believing in the concept of ideology. Structuralism and Marxism very readily merged. It was both modish and sounded scientific, to talk of the centrality of language and of communication. As already noted, Marxism was having increasing difficulty with the refusal of history as it actually happened to conform to the Marxist plan. Thus, in place of crude materialistic conflict, there was substituted the notion of competing languages, competing discourses. This is not for a moment to say that there is not a great deal of truth in the conception that there are special discourses of authority, of the educated élite, etc. However, one school of interdisciplinary cultural studies would wish to reduce everything to the study of competing discourses. Much genuinely illuminating work has been produced. But the very severe limitations of the approach become clear if one reflects again on Marc Ferro's *The Use and Abuse of History*, and the very significant discoveries which historians have been making over the years. If historians actually did adopt the view that primary sources are not as I have defined them, but merely belong to different competing discourses, then they would very quickly stop making the kind of genuine discoveries which lie at the heart of the true achievement of history.

This section began with some reflections on why some historians are attracted to all-embracing theoretical approaches. At least such historians can claim to be defending their subject against the criticisms of scientists, philosophers, and others who wish to deny respectability to mainstream historical writing because of its lack of any coherent theoretical basis. Without any doubt, much very important work has been accomplished by historians working within the conceptual framework outlined above, and it can be argued that the enunciation of a clear theoretical position makes research more systematic and gives clarity to conclusions. The point of this section has not been so much to criticise these approaches (though it is impossible for me to conceal that I *am* critical of them) but to indicate that the foundations of these approaches, in the end a few Marxist assumptions, are not as secure as the great scientific fanfare would have one believe. Almost all historians, as I have already remarked, have been influenced by some aspect of Marxist thought. But the fact remains that a majority of working historians are neither Marxist, nor adhere to any other over-arching theory. This is not because they are overly individualistic, or intellectually sub-normal, but simply that given the problems with which historians are faced, and the sorts of answers they can get from their evidence, there simply is no grand theory which is intellectually fully persuasive. There are theories, but no theory. There are generalisations and conceptual frameworks. The notions, derived from Marxism, of establishing the conditions of cultural production and cultural consumption (discussed in Chapter 7) have been found by many historians to be very fruitful. Notions of social control (explaining, in the hands of conservative sociologists and historians, how stability and harmony is maintained in society, and, in the hands of left-wing historians and sociologists how dissident tendencies are repressed) are very useful, provided relationships are explored not simply asserted. The theoreticians may not always illuminate, but they usually stimulate. The deadly hand is that of those who maintain that history is simply the stories that individual historians, in their ineffable wisdom, tell.[9] History is a systematic subject which calls for a fully conscious and fully articulated statement of assumptions and methods, which employs generalisations, concepts, and theories (plural), which as and when necessary can be tested by empirical methods, and a subject which has complex, definable, but always expanding ranges of sources and means of exploiting them. But it is pointless to claim for history a theoretical basis which is neither appropriate to it nor produces results for it. If the handful of fundamental contentions of Marxism could be demonstrated as valid on the basis of existing evidence, and were open to the possibility of disproof on the discovery of further evidence, then they would indeed be analogous to the 'laws' of the natural sciences: but they cannot, and they are not. The point seems to have been fully taken by the editors of *Past and Present* (founded in Oxford in 1952 with a heavily Marxist editorial board) when during the seventies they abandoned the subtitle, 'a journal of scientific history'.

2. History and Science

Perhaps the previous section was too authoritarian, perhaps, it went a little beyond the experience of the general reader or the beginning student. Let the reader then pause for a moment here to reflect upon what he or she knows of the world of the natural scientist. Let us see if we can compile a list, on the basis of commonsense and ordinary observation, of obvious, if sometimes simple, differences between the history of the historians and the science of the scientists; it would be rather agreeable if we could also list anything that we feel the two have in common. If you feel the need to flex your fingers, you might care to jot down such a list now, before reading my own list which follows immediately. I have come up with nine points of difference, and one large point (perhaps two points linked together) of commonality.

1. There is a fundamental difference in the subject of study: the natural sciences are concerned with the phenomena of the physical universe, while history is concerned with human beings and human societies in the past. There is a difference in the

phenomena studied, and these phenomena are very different in character.

2. Historians do not conduct controlled experiments of the sort typically conducted in a science laboratory.

3. Historical study (though some, obviously, would disagree with this) is not governed by general laws and is not concerned with developing or refining such laws.

4. While scientific laws offer a power of prediction, history (though it should equip us to cope more intelligently with the world in which we live) does not have that power.

5. Science is 'useful' (it enables people to make television sets, or nuclear bombs); history has no such direct material pay-off.

6. Similarly it is fairly clear when scientists have got things right, or got them wrong (the television sets explode; the nuclear bombs don't); with historians there isn't quite the same sure way of telling whether or not they have got things right.

7. While the relationships and interactions studied by scientists are almost always best expressed mathematically, this is not generally so of those studied by historians.

8. History, the 'product' of 'interpretation' by historians, comes in the form of an extended piece of prose (article or book) in which the various discoveries and interconnections have to be woven together with some pretence (however modest) to literary form and elegance. Major scientific discoveries are often best reported in very terse articles, sometimes in a page or two of mathematical equations.

9. While scientists can report in a neutral way on the results of their experiments, historians, being concerned with human affairs in the past, are unable to avoid value judgements: describing certain events as 'a massacre' for instance, or analysing the motives of a particular politician.

10. Now, as to discerning the common ground: both historians and scientists are concerned with discovery, with bringing into being new knowledge about the world (in the widest sense) in which we live, with solving problems, using systematic methods (this is the second part of the point), involving rigorous checks and the presentation of evidence as well as conclusions.

In discussing these simple points one might well argue that the first one is the critical one, and that all other differences spring from the fundamentally different nature of the phenomena studied by the historian and the scientist respectively. Some of the other points deserve further development. Point 2 is self-evident, and I have already dealt with the question of general laws. As historians are concerned with the past, one should perhaps not expect them to indulge in prediction, though E. H. Carr did give an example of the kind of prediction historians might indulge in:

> People do not expect the historian to predict that revolution will break out in Ruritania next month. The kind of conclusion which they will seek to draw, partly from specific knowledge of Ruritanian affairs and partly from a study of history, is that conditions in Ruritania are such that a revolution is likely to occur in the near future if somebody touches it off, or unless somebody on the government side does something to stop it; and this conclusion might be accompanied by estimates, based partly on the analogy of other revolutions, of the attitude which different sectors of the population may be expected to adopt. The prediction, if such it can be called, can be realised only through the occurrence of unique events, which cannot themselves be predicted; but this does not mean that inferences drawn from history about the future are worthless, or that they do not possess a conditional validity which serves both as a guide to action and a key to our understanding of how things happen.[10]

Certainly, one would expect historians, and those with a historical training, to react perceptively to current crises. But this is really to move away from the kind of 'prediction' continuously practised by the professional historian in the normal line of business, a type of 'prediction' which in a small way is analogous to the prediction of the physical scientist. This comes about when a historian, using the evidence painfully accumulated, together with the feel for the way things happen in certain circumstances developed over the years, makes an inference about something for which he or she does not in fact have full and sufficient evidence. This historian is 'predicting' what will be seen to have happened if and when the full evidence is forthcoming. This in the end is certainly not the *same* as the scientist's prediction (indeed the special word *retrodiction*[11] has been coined for it): again we come up against difference at least of degree.

Naturally, given my contention about the social necessity for history, I do not agree that, compared with science, the subject is not useful, though of course there is force in the argument that scientific investigations can lead to the production of material goods, while the study of history never does. The production of such goods will actually be in the hands of applied scientists and technologists, most scientists not being concerned with immediate utilitarian results; however the point does stand. One might, though, make a parallel between the applied scientist and what one might call the 'applied historian', making use of historical knowledge as, say, a journalist or broadcaster.

The argument about scientists being found out, while historians are not, was put most forcefully to me some years ago by my Open University colleague, John Sparkes, Professor of Electronics and Dean of the Faculty of Technology. The difference between his subject and mine, he said, was that if he and his colleagues get it wrong it shows: rockets remain earth-bound, bridges collapse into the surf. Historians, by contrast, he reckoned, can get away with anything: who can tell whether their theories, their accounts of the past, are right or wrong? Again leaving aside the comment that such arguments in any case would be more relevant to applied scientists and technologists than to scientists in general, I would still express disagreement. In my view the test to be applied to a piece of historical writing is exactly the test to be applied to a scientific model or technological innovation: does it work? 'Working' in this connection means carrying conviction, corresponding with the evidence adduced, fitting in with what we know of the topic and period. These points will be developed more fully in Chapters 5 and 6. With regard to the role of mathematics in scientific explanation, one might counter with the argument that historical studies are becoming increasingly quantitative, and that in some areas resort is made to mathematical equations. But this would be to use rather minor, and often exceptional (though in both cases very important) examples in face of a broadly valid case: the overwhelming bulk of historical explanation depends upon citation of sources and structure of argument. For myself, I would go so far as to argue that it is the very fact that relationships, interactions, structures, in history are not mathematical (or certainly have not so far been shown to be so) which makes it impossible to apply general laws and overarching theory. The other, lesser, implication is the difference in form of discourse noted in point 8.

For historians there is no complete escape from involvement in moral and value judgements. These should be pronounced sparingly, and should be presented against clearly established criteria. The neat statement of David Knowles, 'The historian is not a judge, still less a hanging judge',[12] is acceptable and salutory; but when Michael Oakeshott joined with other misguided souls in demanding from the historian complete moral neutrality, he met his come-uppance from Alfred Cobban:

> It is admittedly difficult, says Professor Oakeshott, to avoid 'the description of conduct in, generally speaking, moral terms'. This I take to mean that, for example, we cannot help describing the September massacres as massacres. The important thing is to avoid any suggestion that massacres are a bad thing, because this would be a moral judgement and therefore non-historical.[13]

The historian cannot help but make moral judgements, if only by implication or by virtue of his selection of the facts: these judgements are of a type not encountered in the natural sciences.

The ultimate commonality of purpose between historians and scientists, that is to say the disinterested and systematic pursuit of knowledge in the belief that the more we know the greater our control over our environment, physical and social, actually emerges most distinctly if one does not set up a smokescreen of false similarities. As already noted the word 'scientific' has traditionally been used in different ways: today, however, it most usually means 'pertaining to the natural sciences'. History does not use general laws and theory in the way these sciences do, but, as I hope this book will demonstrate, it is a systematic discipline, employing methods and standards which, I believe, should command the respect of the most rigorous scientist. I would be content to leave it there; however, the reader should perhaps have some alternative formulations. First the American diplomatic historian Bernadotte Schmitt:

> Evidently much depends on what you mean by science. A recent English writer has remarked that science does not cease to be science because it sometimes fails to formulate its laws or adhere to the gift of prophecy. Thus meteorology cannot be denied the quality of a science because the laws according to which sunshine and storm succeed one another are as yet undiscovered . . . Science, in the mind of this writer, can be defined as 'systematised, organised, formulated knowledge', and history, the original meaning of which is investigation, is therefore a science if it is pursued with the sole purpose of ascertaining the truth, if all relevant facts are diligently searched for, if presuppositions and prejudices are eliminated, if the constants and the

variables are noted and plotted with the same care that is the rule in
the natural sciences. But do we really care whether the chemists and
the mathematicians accord our study the title and dignity of a science?
We believe that the critical methods which we use in the acquisition
of historical information are every whit as scientific as those of the
laboratory or the field expedition. For my part, I am willing to let the
matter rest there.[14]

E. H. Carr has been rather more definite:

> The word science already covers so many different branches of knowl-
> edge, employing so many different methods and techniques, that the
> onus seems to rest on those who seek to exclude history rather than
> on those who seek to include it . . . I am myself not convinced that
> the chasm which separates the historian from the geologist is any
> deeper or more unbridgeable than the chasm which separates the
> geologist from the physicist.[15]

The most challenging words were those of E. E. Evans-Pritchard,
the anthropologist: 'When will people get it into their heads that
the conscientious historian . . . is no less systematic, exacting and
critical in his research than a chemist or biologist, that it is not in
method that social science differs from physical science but in the
nature of the phenomena they study.'[16] We have come back to
the first and critical point, but we have also introduced the notion
of history as a social science.

3. History and Social Science

The one principle which united *Annales* historians of all generations was that historians should use to the full the discoveries
and methods of the social sciences (and, indeed, as relevant, the
sciences). François Furet, Braudel's successor as Director of the
École des Hautes Études, has spoken of his kind of history as a
'history reshaped on the pattern of the social sciences'.[17] Both
social scientists such as Evans-Pritchard and historians such as
E. H. Carr have been clear that history either was, or certainly
ought to be, a social science. In a most important book, in which
he lambasted the 'impressive ability' of sociologists 'to ignore the
fact that history happens in time', and denounced historians for
eschewing serious analysis for the mere magic of rhetoric, Philip
Abrams (till his tragically early death Professor of Sociology at

Durham University) urged that history and sociology should be merged into one discipline 'historical scoiology'.[18] John Tosh in his excellent *The Pursuit of History* declared 'the business of historians' to be 'to apply theory, to refine it, and to develop new theory, always in the light of the evidence most broadly conceived.'[19] However, what Abrams in fact wanted was a merging of *Marxist* history with *Marxist* sociology, while Tosh too is very much of the same persuasion. Abrams was very conscious of the two-way flow between the historical and the sociological approaches. Some earlier writers had argued that history is *the* central social science, off which all the others must feed; it is, H. C. Darby suggested, basic to social science rather in the way that mathematics is basic to natural science.[20] In fact it is a rather moot point whether the history of historians really is basic in quite this way. The real point is that everything has a past and a time dimension, so that history is basic to literature, philosophy and the arts as well as to social science.

Indeed as the discipline of history evolved historically its natural place seemed to be with the 'arts' or 'humanities', since it had very direct associations with literature and languages, and also with philosophy, art history and musicology. Have changes in historical methodology and approaches been so great in recent decades that history is now more accurately numbered among the social sciences than among the arts? The answers given are partly a matter of history, partly a matter of administrative convenience within universities, partly a matter of deeply held belief about the nature of historical study. Richard Hofstadter (one of the American postwar 'consensus' historians) saw the 'historian as having contacts with the social sciences rather than as being a social scientist'.[21] Others have reverted to the notion put forward from time to time by distinguished historians in the past, that history is 'both art and science'. Others again have resolved the issue – to their own satisfaction at least – with the reflection that history, being neither truly art nor science, is *sui generis*, so that if it can't be in a Faculty or School of its own, it might as well remain with the arts. Fritz Stern (whose collection of readings I refer to throughout this book) described the 'Solomon's judgement' which took place when the University of Chicago set up separate divisions of the Social Sciences and the Humanities, some historians opting to go to one division, some to the other.[22] In

British universities there not infrequently exists a split between economic history and, sometimes, social history, which are grouped with the social sciences, and general history, which remains with the arts. In theory a deplorable division in that it suggests a perpetuation of the sub-world of the sub-histories, this often works well in that almost inevitably there is a co-operation between different historians which transcends faculty barriers.

It would be tedious to rehearse the traditional arguments, which are largely those discussed in the section on history and natural science. It can reasonably be stated that history and sociology or economics stand closer to each other, being concerned with human beings and their activities in society, than sociology or economics stand to those sciences which are concerned with natural phenomena. The basic difference we postulated between history and natural science (that of the *phenomena* studied) can therefore be eliminated. But since the social sciences model themselves on the natural sciences in a way in which history so far, wittingly, has not done, four secondary distinctions are worth further examination. These concern (1) *experimental data*, (2) *theory, theoretical constraints* and *use of hypotheses*, (3) *value judgements* and *subjectivity* and (4) *communication*.

Social scientists do, in greater or lesser degree, conduct 'experiments', in the form, principally, of opinion samples, or studies of behaviour patterns and responses to controlled stimuli of small groups. Historians, of course, make extensive use of social surveys, census returns and so on conducted in the past by 'pure' or 'applied' social scientists; and they may, as we shall see, derive a great deal of benefit from participating in controlled surveys conducted in their own time. Nonetheless it remains true that the historian, as historian, does not conduct controlled experiments; his or her evidence is always that little bit more impressionistic than is that of the man or woman working on the frontiers of the social sciences.

Some of the misconceptions surrounding the use and non-use of generalisation we have already discussed. Yet when all qualifications have been made, it remains true that the social scientist far more regularly uses models and theoretical constructs than do historians, and that these constructs are nearly always of a more abstract character than historians would be happy with. The familiar platitude probably overstates the case but it nonetheless contains a vital kernel of truth: historians must always accommodate the unique and the contingent, social scientists are essentially orientated towards the universal, towards the recurrent pattern. Social scientists, too, tend to give certain abstractions an absolute value. Thus 'class' may be used with the explanatory value given to it by Marx; or it may, as decreed by Weber, be treated as connoting only the economic dimension of inequality, to be distinguished from position in the status and political hierarchies. Social scientists may make a distinction between class with its explanatory qualities, and what, in an ugly metaphor, they call 'social stratification'. Historians, on the other hand, may be interested in class in the distinctive forms it takes in different societies (how it actually affects life chances, and how it is actually perceived, in these societies). Historians may have difficulties with such pronouncements as this from a leading contemporary theorist:

> An initial distinction can be drawn between 'class awareness' and 'class consciousness'. We may say that, in so far as class is a structurated phenomenon, there will tend to exist a common awareness and acceptance of similar attitudes and beliefs, linked to a common style of life, among the members of the class. 'Class awareness', as I use the term here, does *not* involve a recognition that these attitudes and beliefs signify a particular class affiliation, or the recognition that there exist other classes, characterised by different attitudes, beliefs, and styles of life: 'class consciousness', by contrast, as I shall use the notion, does imply both of these. The difference between class awareness and class consciousness is a fundamental one, because class awareness may take the form of *a denial of the existence or reality of classes*.[23]

The use of 'class awareness' seems curiously rarefied. Historians, I think, would tend to use the phrase in the simple sense of 'being aware of belonging to a class' (as distinct from being 'class conscious' in the Marxist sense of taking up a position of conflict with a rival class). Those who wish history to assimilate itself to the social sciences enjoin, furthermore, that in presenting their interpretations historians should follow the method of first clearly stating their hypothesis. The fact is that most historians don't do this, and for the very good reason that the kinds of complex reconstructions of past happenings and all their subtle interconnections between individual, social, and environmental influences, and between short-term and long-term forces, in which historians specialise are simply not amenable to summary in the form of a hypothesis. Which is not to say that historians should not make very clear to readers what the aims and the conclusions of any piece of work are (historians who produce coruscating, but impenetrable layers of rhetoric are bad historians); simply that the formula of a hypothesis does not suit the structure of historical discourse.

Value judgements, inevitably, will intrude further into the work of social scientists than into that of natural scientists; but through their use of direct experimental data and abstract models social scientists will tend to avoid the frequent entanglement with them which besets historians. Much depends, however, on whether the social scientist is concerned with a carefully controlled, and limited, experimental study, or with large-scale generalisation as in, say, political sociology. In the latter it is hard to believe sometimes that value judgements do not intrude at least as much as they do with any historian. It's a question of evidence and scale. A very limited study can be highly objective. But interpretations of the type historians are usually involved in always, because of the imperfect and intractable nature of historical sources, leave scope for subjectivity. The matter of communication is not a clear-cut one. My bottom-line contention remains that it is more important that historians get things right than that they rely on literary finesse to carry them through. But it does sometimes seem to be in the nature of social science to produce cumbersome sentences and ugly jargon. On the whole, historical writing is still characterised by a belief in the need for clarity, simplicity, as well as elegance, of expression. And, as noted, historical study does not readily lend itself to the 'scientific' mode of statement of hypothesis followed by 'empirical' demonstration of it.

Historians, in my view, should not overly concern themselves with the precise technicalities of their relationships with the social sciences; better to keep in mind their relationship with *all* academic and creative pursuits, and consider all scholarly and creative activities as combining in the attack upon that which is not yet known, in the solving of problems, in the production of usable representations and interpretations. The forces are spread widely across the extensive plain of present knowledge. On one wing are the mathematicians, the mathematical physicists, then the physicists, the chemists and the biologists; somewhere towards the middle come the geologists. On the other wing are the painters, the musicians, the poets, concerned also (whether avowedly or not) with broadening humanity's perception of itself and of its environment. But the plain is really a continuum for it may well be, as is suggested by those who talk of 'the beauty' of mathematics, that the one wing touches closely upon the other. But let us proceed onwards from the geologists; soon we come to the social scientists, then to history, then to languages, literature and philosophy. Any model of this sort must seem contrived and arbitrary; where for instance do we put psychology? – long regarded as a social science, but now becoming more and more biological in content. And then we have such subjects as social biology, and social medicine. Beyond that, in literature, art history and musicology as currently studied, great emphasis is placed on the social context, on the conditions of cultural production and consumption; aesthetic considerations, it could be said, are giving way to historical and sociological ones. A whole new area of cultural studies has been opening up which brings sociology and *all* of the arts into an integrative relationship. So indeed there is a continuum. But the present divisions, provided they are taken as divisions within a deeper unity, serve a useful purpose, and have a certain commonsense validity. It follows, however, that each discipline, as traditionally conceived, must at all times be ready to make useful borrowings from other disciplines. Of no subject is this more true than history: it is to the detailed relationships between history and the individual social sciences that we now turn.

4. History and Geography

Between history and geography there are venerable ties. Diplomatic history and military history of the standard type obviously require some rudimentary geographical knowledge. National history, too, clearly requires to be set within the appropriate geographical context. In the preface to his *Histoire de France* (1833) Michelet stated that history in essence was founded upon geography; he himself spent a great deal of time wandering through France collecting first-hand impressions of the changing countryside. The preface to the 1869 edition contained the more positive assertion that:

Without a geographical basis, the people, the makers of history, seem to be walking on air, as in those Chinese pictures where the ground is wanting. The soil, too, must not be looked upon only as the scene of action. Its influence appears in a hundred ways, such as food, climate, etc.

This concern with the geographical context of history was later very noticeable in the work of Lucien Febvre and Marc Bloch, of that of Braudel, and indeed was something of a characteristic of French historical study in general. Bloch, who himself observed the precepts of Michelet, noted that:

> In certain of its fundamental features, our rural landscape, as has been previously mentioned, dates from a very remote epoch. However, in order to interpret the rare documents which permit us to fathom its misty beginnings, in order to ask the right questions, even in order to know what we were talking about, it was necessary to fulfil a primary condition: that of observing and analysing our present landscape. For it alone furnished those comprehensive vistas without which it was impossible to begin.[24]

In his study of *Tudor Cornwall* (1941) A. L. Rowse has remarked upon the fascination of attempting 'to decipher an earlier, vanished age beneath the forms of the present and successive layers that time has imposed':

> So it is that beneath the towns and villages, their roads and fields of today, we may construct under our eyes out of the evidences that remain, a picture of a former age.

The geographical context in fact is something of a commonsense matter, well in keeping with the old amateur tradition in history, requiring no professional expertise to unveil its significance: indeed professional expertise in the twentieth century often tended to obscure what had formerly been obvious: the dependence of history upon geography. The commonsense, amateur apprehension of this can best be seen in the famous third chapter of Macaulay's *History of England*, giving the cultural and geographical setting. J. R. Green, in his *The Making of England*, called landscape 'the fullest and most certain of all documents'. Maitland, the great professional, had a vivid understanding of the importance of geography to historical investigation. Many general histories since then have continued this tradition.

This use of geography has often been impressionistic and uninformed. Though history's close relationship with geography has been recognised more universally and over a far longer period than any other possible relationship between history and a social science, it is only recently that historians have turned to the geography of the geographers in place of their own undisciplined observation. One of the many strengths of Febvre and Bloch and the *Annales* school was that they did not just invent their geography but sought the co-operation of professional geographers. In his *A Geographical Introduction to History* (1925) Febvre declared that the study of the relationship of past societies to environment must rest upon 'a sound study of physical geography'. It is scarcely to be expected that historians, unless preoccupied with a specific environmental problem, will find the time to master the scientific (in the sense of natural science) intricacies of physical geography, but there can be no doubt as to the value for any historian of a knowledge of the classificatory categories employed by the geographer.

The climate of the British Isles is notorious: at times, as with the heat-waves of 1911 (associated with strikes and violence) and in 1959 (associated with Conservative electoral victory) or with the hard winter of 1946–7, or the east coast floods of 1953, it may have impinged directly upon political and social history. It is possible for the historian concerned with such matters simply to throw in a few references to variable climate and the influence of the sea. But how much clearer and simpler to borrow the geographer's classification of the four types of air-masses likely to invade the British Isles: the warm damp tropical maritime from the Atlantic, which often brings fog or heavy rain; the polar maritime, which usually brings periods of rain showers and sunny intervals; the polar continental which brings a cold, dry, biting wind, often provoking a 'temperature inversion' and fog; and the tropical continental, which brings dry, stable weather and occasional heat-waves.[25]

To describe the general physical geography of the British Isles, absolutely basic to an understanding of the processes of urbanisation and the processes of urban deterioration which are so critical in the last two hundred years of British history, what more economical method than to adhere to the geographer's classification of the country into three components: lowland, upland and highland?[26] In the lowland regions of the south lay the original agricultural wealth of England, while it was amid the mineral wealth of the upland areas of South Wales, the Pennines and central Scotland that the Industrial Revolution took place; the highland regions of central Wales and northern Scotland were steadily drained of their native rural populations and left to decay while the rest of the land was prospering; in the early, and mid-twentieth century, with the advent of new light industries, the movement of population was back to the lowland areas: in the period of post-industrialisation the economic and political geography of Britain had taken yet another twist. In the sub-discipline of urban history the spatial concepts, and the notion of networks developed by modern geographers, have proved of great value. Asa Briggs has stressed the impact on his own understanding of urban history of recent American work in urban sociology and urban geography.[27]

The sort of fascinating collaboration between historians and geographers which now takes place assisted by the most up-to-date computer technology is exemplified by the Analysis of Regional Settlement Structures in Ancient Greece carried through by the School of History and the School of Geography at Leeds University. Here is a brief statement of the initial basis of the project (footnotes omitted):

> The emergence of the *polis* symbolises the transformation from European prehistory to 'the Western Tradition'. The dividing line, for analytical purposes, is conventionally drawn at 700 B.C., the start of the Archaic period of Ancient Greece. Such a radical transformation, needless to say, involved social change at the level of structural principles – society was more or less completely reorganised along new lines.
>
> Cities are at the core of 'civilisation'; citizen, civic, civil and civilised are all historically and etymologically intertwined with the phenomenon of the city, and nowhere more so than in the city-states. Attempts to define 'the city' in terms of urban structure have now been abandoned by geographers and sociologists as futile and misdirected, and the city is instead conceptualised in terms of a storage container and crucible for the generation of power. Cities are, above all, loci of social interaction, places where social action is concentrated and focussed. To analyse why some settlements became cities whereas other did not, and why some cities became greater than others, we can enlarge the historical armoury with tailor-made spatial interaction and location models based on recent developments in geography.[28]

5. History and Psychology

Consciously or unconsciously historians have always dabbled, amateurishly and haphazardly for the most part, in geography. Similarly in their discussions and analyses of the motives and actions of men and societies they have had to venture into the realm of psychology. Trevelyan, we have seen, believed that history remained literature rather than science by virtue of its need for deep insights into the minds of men. Later commentators have rightly remarked that so long as the historian continued to back his own psychological insights without reference to the discoveries of modern psychology he was producing, if not literature, certainly fiction. Because of their preoccupation with the biographical approach to history and the doings of great men, historians of Trevelyan's generation had to make frequent recourse to their own amateurish 'psychological' insights. Today no historian could write a biographical study without betraying something of the influence of Freudian and post-Freudian psychology.[29]

Just how far the historical biographer should penetrate into the depth psychology of his subject is by no means a settled matter, even among those historians who are most receptive to the influences of the social sciences. For one thing the individual biography *in this sense* would not now normally be regarded as one of the most important forms for historical writing to take. Many of the greatest historical works of today have indeed been biographical in form; but in content they are almost always of the 'life and times' type; that is to say they use the biographical device to illuminate a far wider sector of human experience. If the main focus of attention in the biography is on the political and social achievements of the subject, on his relationships with various social groups, and with their reactions to him, there may be less need for detailed study of his own individual psychology than a purist might think. Further, many of the great contemporary biographies – Alan Bullock's *Hitler: A Study in Tyranny* (1952, 1962) is an obvious example – are concerned with men of quite extraordinary individual characteristics. Theories of psychopathology are almost all derived from the study of 'failures'; Hitler was no failure (or at least not till he had destroyed half a continent). The historian is concerned less with Hitler's private

fantasies than with his huge destructive achievements. Even with
more 'normal' figures, much of the detail which might be yielded
through use (retrospectively, of course, and therefore imperfectly)
of some of the techniques of psycho-analysis may well prove more
appropriate to the higher gossip than to an understanding of the
major problems which exercise, or should exercise, the mind of
the historian. Many of the nastier big men in history – the Nazis
are a good example – are widely believed to have been defective
in their sexual equipment. The same point is sometimes even
made about more conventional political leaders. The difficulties
in finding hard evidence (as distinct from inspired conjecture) are,
for the historian, immense; and even if he does find the evidence,
how much further does this take him?

These are merely qualifications, not in any way rebuttals of the
highly stimulating attempts which have been made to bring the
resources of psychology to the aid of historical biography (some
of which we shall examine in a moment). They are preliminaries
to the statement of one simple point about the uses of psychology
which is too often ignored. Although there is in practice no rigid
line between the *individual* psychology which we have been
discussing up till now, and the *group* and *social* psychology which
must be of the utmost value to the historian, the distinction is one
which should always be borne in mind. In brief, my argument will
be that just as the individual biography is a less significant area
of study for the historian than a society, or a substantial segment
of a society studied in totality, so individual psychology is less
directly relevant to the needs of the historian than is group
psychology. Individual psychology will provide illuminating
details; social psychology may in some cases be a *sine qua non*
of the intelligent analysis of certain historical problems. Where
individual psychology can probably be of most significant utility
is in helping to establish types of individual political leadership,
of 'great man' activity, and in explaining aberrations in political
behaviour.

Martin Luther was clearly a 'great man', in the sense of being
a man whose actions did demonstrably affect the course of history.
His stormy career has attracted legions of biographers, historical
and fictional. Before the First World War one of the most
distinguished of twentieth-century American historians, Preserved
Smith, published both a biography and a collection of Luther's

letters. He followed these up with an interesting paper, published in 1915, on 'Luther's Early Development in the Light of Psychoanalysis'. Forty years later the subject was treated with greater sophistication by a practising psychiatrist, Erik Erikson, in his much-acclaimed book, *The Young Man Luther: A Study in Psycho-analysis and History* (1959) (on which John Osborne subsequently based his successful play). The book makes fascinating reading and in its discussion of such matters as Luther's childhood conflicts with his father, his 'anality', his 'lifelong burden of excessive guilt', undoubtedly makes a major contribution to our understanding of Luther. I have suggested above that there are vast tracts of history, even biographical history, where individual psychology is not a specially useful tool (though clearly some knowledge of psychology must replace Trevelyan's literary intuition): Erikson's study is a triumphant signal indicating the area of applicability of psycho-analysis to history. But it is a book by a psychiatrist bringing his expertise to bear on materials collected and collated by generations of historians. More interesting in many ways is Sir Lewis Namier's study of *Charles Townshend* (1964), the brilliant English politician whose erratic political behaviour has sometimes been regarded as a contributory cause of the American Revolution: a study drawn from a mass of unsorted manuscript material, but openly employing the categories of Freudian psychology, and showing how conflicts between Townshend and his father 'produced a mental attitude towards authority which he carried over into the field of politics'. Another analogous relationship was persuasively explored by Bruce Mazlish, an American scholar who has been in the vanguard in urging historians to master the skills of psychology, *James and John Stuart Mill: Father and Son in the Nineteenth Century* (New York, 1975).

The most sustained, and scintillating, demonstration of the importance to history of psychology is Peter Gay's *The Bourgeois Experience: Victoria to Freud* (2 vols. New York, 1984, 1986), described by Gay, in his useful primer *Freud for Historians* (New York, 1985, pp. xi–xii) as 'a study of nineteenth-century bourgeois culture from a psychoanalytic perspective'. Certainly the book is a treasure-house, firmly grounded in an amazing range of family papers. Gay has more recently completed a highly praised biography of Freud.

Nonetheless it is social psychology, out of all the social sciences, upon which the historian today is most likely to call. That this science may be regarded as a branch of sociology rather than as a branch of psychology only shows that history is not alone in having its demarcation difficulties. Here I shall deal only with the more manifestly psychological elements, returning again to some other major contributions furnished by social psychology when I look at the crucial problem of the relations between history and sociology

When we look back over the human past, one obvious feature stands out: the amount of time, energy and human life which has been expended in that most destructive of all man's activities – war. Given their concern with the specific and the unique, historians will no doubt continue to place great emphasis on diplomatic exchanges, political and strategic calculations and immediate social and economic circumstances. Yet some of the broader generalisations made by some historians – about, for example, the 'will to war' to be detected in European societies on the eve of the First World War – cry out for analysis in the light of the important studies of human aggression produced by social psychologists. In general the works of Konrad Lorenz and his disciples[30] demonstrate how nasty a creature the human animal is, and describe the conditions in which the nastiness is liable to break out in the form of large-scale violence or war; one such condition is overcrowding. Historians can demonstrate the rapidity with which urbanisation was taking place in hitherto relatively pastoral European countries in the years before the First World War; they can also show impressionistically, through a study of popular reading-matter, music-hall songs, modes and language of public protests and demonstrations, as well as such high-culture phenomena as Futurist painting, that there was something that can fairly be termed a 'will to war'. With the assistance of the theorists of human aggression they may then perceive a correlation between the two, and, more tenuously, a possible explanation of the war as an objective fact, or at least of why the war *appeared* to be welcome when it came. This is another complex area. In fact individual psychology has been useful in driving home that human beings can simultaneously experience conflicting emotions: thus the men who went to war in 1914 were both joyful and terrified, full of patriotic sentiment, and worried about their families.[31] In the past historians have been fascinated by the origins of wars; more recently they have begun to pay due regard to the question of the consequences of wars. In this realm, too, there is much to be learned from the studies of the social psychologists. The phenomenon of mass hysteria in the form of jingoistic patriotism has often been noted; with the assistance of social psychology it can be discussed in a more rigorous and less impressionistic way. The effects of bombing upon civilian morale are a matter of interest to both psychologists and historians. Much of value can be found in the 'disaster studies' undertaken by social psychologists.[32]

An understanding of the significance of group psychology for the historian, we have seen, underlies much of the work of Bloch and Febvre. Indeed one of the most characteristic achievements of the French school was the emphasis it gave to the study of *mentalités* – the world view, the perceptions, the attitudes of mind of past peoples. Involvement in the problems of crowd psychology led George Rudé and others into some fascinating work on the role of the crowd in various revolutionary upheavals, and in other disturbances. Psychological insights into the effects of factory discipline, into the human consequences of creating a new emphasis on clocks and timekeeping, have brought a new qualitative element into assessments of the social consequences of the industrial revolution. The concepts of 'reference groups', by which people censor their activities or assess their standards of living, and 'relative deprivation' have helped to take some of the imprecision out of the traditional study of social conditions.[33]

As might again be expected, some of the most imaginative historical work bringing in social psychology has been carried out by French historians. The work of Leroy Ladurie in endeavouring to penetrate the 'mental outlook' of small communities in France in the early fourteenth century and in the seventeenth century has already been mentioned. Marc Ferro and Pierre Sorlin have brought psychological perceptions to bear not only in conventional historical writing, but also in their pioneering analyses of film.[34] After admitting to the unfashionable nature of biography, Sorlin said of his *Waldeck-Rousseau* (1966) that it might well be called an essay in psychological portraiture, save that such a title seemed a bit ambitious. His *'La Croix' et les Juifs (1880–1899): Contribution à l'histoire de l'anti-Sémitisme Contemporaine* (1967) was very much a work in the study of a collective psychological phenomenon, 'the passionate hostility of a community against a minority judged inadmissible'.

In my opinion, by way of a conclusion to this section, the books which have set out deliberately to provide exercises in the use of psychology, particularly psycho-analysis, are less rewarding than the wider studies, of the crowd, of the bourgeoisie, of war, which have put psychology to work as a tool in a greater enterprise. But then that is in keeping with my overall view of the relationships of individual social sciences to history – a view which would be hotly contested by many social scientists, and all assimilationists.

6. History and Economics

The relationship of economics to history is rather different from that of the other social sciences; curious as it may sound, this relationship in many respects comes close to that between history and literature. Economics, after all, is the science (in the broad meaning of the term) of something which people actually do; even if the science did not exist, people would still make economic decisions, economic predictions and participate in the various forms of economic organisation which, in part, it is the economist's function to describe. Similarly the disciplined study of literature is concerned with something which individuals would also do anyway even if the disciplined study did not exist: compose poems, act out drama, write novels and read them. Political science, or the discipline of politics, has, it is true, many similarities to economics, particularly where it is concerned with generalisation about political structures. But political science covers a great range of other topics as well: it does not stand in a simple relation to political history as economics does to economic history. Sociology clearly is an 'invented' subject in the sense that in everyday life people do not make 'sociological' decisions or join 'sociological' organisations (the sociologist, of course, may study the stock exchange, or trade unions, particularly with reference to traditional and psychological influences upon their structure; but at the base these organisations were founded for economic purposes).

The historian then is forced, whatever his period of study, to have some rudimentary knowledge of economics since so much of man's activity in societies is concerned with economic matters. In the same way a historian who seeks a thorough knowledge of any particular period must acquire a true familiarity with the literature of that period. In the earlier part of this century, a century much preoccupied with the economic problems of whole nations and with the economic needs of individual men, it is probably true that most historians did possess some basic knowledge of economics as the subject was then understood: in the amateurish atmosphere of the British and American univerisites the subjects were in fact held to lie pretty close together, as we saw from the early career of J. H. Clapham.

However, economics in the last generation has become a much more complex and difficult subject, with economic theory heavily dependent on mathematics taking over from the old commonsense approach. On the basis of the arguments at the beginning of this chapter it should still be true that the historian today ought to acquire a basic working knowledge of modern economic theory. However, such counsels of perfection must always be tested against practical utility: if in fact historians did try to acquire all the skills which they 'ought', they would have precious little time left for the writing and study of history. So again we come upon a necessary academic division of labour. We have already noted the evolution of the various sub-histories, of which economic history was one of the most important. Originally economic history was distinguished from other histories more by content than methodology; now, as Professor W. H. B. Court has put it, economic history is 'that part of history which requires a knowledge of economics for its full understanding'.[35] The question more and more economic historians are having to ask themselves is whether their primary loyalty lies to history or to economics: as a matter of academic convenience many university economic history departments now derive their main function from being a service department for economics. But whatever the immediate function, economic history remains a part of history, part of the attempt to increase that understanding of the past which is necessary to human society. In so far as the line between the economic and the general historian is not simply an educational and administrative device, economic historians are historians who have deliberately decided to study one part of history in great depth, that depth to be obtained primarily by use of economic tools. Their conclusions must be served up in clear and intelligible form, for they may then be used by the general historian interested in the totality of human experience in any given period. More usually general historians will themselves be carried by the questions which they wish to answer into territory where possession of certain economic tools will be necessary: they will then for specific, *ad hoc* purposes, need to acquire them.

Relationships between history and economics, therefore, take two rather different forms. First of all we have the question of the borrowings which the general historian from time to time and the economic historian (of the traditional type) all of the time will have to make from economic science. Right away we come upon the question of the historian's use of statistics ('Il faut compter', as Lefebvre said), which often is a matter of more or less sporadic borrowing. I can myself recall that while, as a young lecturer at Edinburgh University, wrestling with some conclusions which I wished to draw with regard to the quantitative consequences of the First World War for Great Britain, I literally shouted across the mews to a colleague in the department of economics, who also happened to be a neighbour, so that he could quickly check my extremely simple mathematical premises. However, the question of the use of mathematics and statistics, though fundamental to modern economics, really does take us beyond economics and will be considered separately in the next section. Another obvious and absolutely inevitable borrowing is that practised continuously by any historian concerned with twentieth-century history: impossible to deal with such crucial circumstances as, say, the Wall Street Crash of 1929, the policies of the New Deal, or the world trading structure established after 1945 without a knowledge of the relevant economic theory. Today it is important to know what it was J. M. Keynes said, and it is important to know why it is thought that some of the things he said were wrong.

A much more interesting style of 'borrowing', however, is that adopted by Professor Thomas C. Cochran and his associates when they embarked upon a history of the Pabst Brewing Company. First they asked Professor Arthur H. Cole, the Harvard economist, to draw up a list of questions which the economist would ask of business records. According to Professor Cochran this list immediately suggested a number of problems not generally dealt with by historians, and produced some of the most interesting aspects of the history. Cochran has cited the specific example of the use made of the economist's concept of 'location theory', as shown in this passage from the history as finally written:

> The most compelling locational advantage of Milwaukee over Chicago, Cincinnati, and St Louis was . . . the smallness of the population which restricted the company's home market. With all other factors favourable to large production and the growth of a shipping business, the Milwaukee brewers were forced into a contest for the national market in order to sell their surplus product at a time when their future rivals in the larger western cities were still content to sell at home.

Cochran himself deals with the objection that many traditional historians would make, that far from employing economic theory all he has done here is to use the historian's age-old standby 'informed common sense':

> The difference between the application of a well-structured group of related concepts, and the intuitive use of common sense is often subtle. The gain resulting from the more systematic procedures may appear mainly in the orderly presentation of the evidence and the explicitness of the conclusions. But granting the staggering problems of the historian, even this gain would seem sufficient to justify the method. Researchers unequipped with the concepts of location theory might have seen clearly the paradox of the Pabst brewery location, but then again they might not.[36]

The other form of involvement is that relating to 'quantitative history' (national aggregates) and econometric history. Some of the most interesting developments here, including the work of Simon Kuznets, Jean Marczewski, and the employment of the counter-factual conditional concept by R. W. Fogel and others, have already been summarised in Chapter 3: the reader with a specialist interest in economic history should refer back to this passage. In certain types of historical debate the mathematical formulations of the pure economist are indispensable. One such debate is that over whether late Victorian Britain was already betraying the signs of economic decline which have been so apparent to everyone in recent years. Here is a passage from a 1970 article 'Did Victorian Britain Fail?' by the Chicago economic historian D. N. McCloskey which presents an appearance familiar in the journals devoted to economic history (I have omitted the footnotes). McCloskey argued that a growth rate of 3.71 per cent per year, which critics of Victorian entrepreneurs said the economy ought to have achieved, was impossible:

> The supply of labour was in all likelihood insufficiently responsive to the pressures of export demand in the late nineteenth century to permit so high a growth-rate. Unemployment was low and the rural pool of underemployed labour was by this time small. Had all emigration from the United Kingdom ceased and had all these emigrants been of working age, the labour force might have grown at 1.6 per cent per year rather than at 1 per cent as it did from 1871 to 1911, but this is still low relative to the hypothetical growth of gross output. If capital and labour were not substitutable, then, the slow growth of the labour force in the United Kingdom would have limited output growth. To put it the other way, had output grown at 3.71 per cent per year from 1872 to 1907 instead of 1.69 per cent the labour force at the end of the period would have had to have been twice as large as the actual labour force and two-fifths larger than the entire population aged 15 and over.

> If capital and labour *were* substitutable, an increase in capital per man could substitute in some degree for these improbable increases in the labour force. The magnitude of the necessary capital accumulation, assuming that the elasticity of substitution between capital and labour was unity, can be estimated from an equation of the sources of growth:

$$\overline{Q}go = S_k \, \overline{K} + S_l \overline{L} + \overline{T}^l$$

> in which $\overline{Q}go$ is the proportional growth-rate of gross output in the economy, $\overline{K}$ and $\overline{L}$ the growth-rates of capital and labour, S_k and S_l their shares in national income, and $\overline{T}^l$ the rate of productivity change defined to correspond with gross output. The growth equation can be solved for the rate of growth of capital.

$$\overline{K} = \mathit{1/S_k} \, [\overline{Q}go - S_l \, \overline{L} - \overline{T}^l]$$

> and placing the appropriate values in the right-hand side of the new equation yields the necessary rate:

$$\overline{K} = \mathit{1/0.442} \, [0.0371 - 0.52 \, (0.0102) - 0.0050] = 0.0609$$

This 6.09 per cent per year rate of capital growth (needed to produce a growth rate of 3.71 per cent per year), McCloskey pointed out, was around four times the actual rate in the late nineteenth century, and would have needed incredibly high savings of 42 per cent of income. McCloskey's final conclusion was that the British economy was growing as fast as circumstances permitted and that therefore British businessmen of the time should not be condemned for lack of vigour. There are other arguments, of course, which historians on the other side of the debate have continued to make: failure to invest in technical education, for instance; or the absence of a satisfactory relationship between the banks (as sources of investment) and British industry.

How far should historians employ economic models?

> An economic model is not a precise description of reality, but rather an abstract characterisation of the way in which an economic system works: a characterisation that, it is hoped, captures the essence of the economic system.[37]

Useful – but to be treated cautiously! The direct application of the techniques of economic science to historical problems can yield rich harvests. General historians necessarily are familiarising themselves with the arguments and conclusions of the econometric historians; but that does not mean that they must all become econometricians forthwith. The manner in which today's historian seeks to integrate fundamental economic analysis with a subtle appreciation of social and cultural trends is well exemplified in Alan Milward's *Reconstruction of Europe* (1984).

This section has been concerned with economic history: that is, however valid the various approaches discussed here, they are irrelevant to vast tracts of the historian's territory. Statistics, certainly, can be applied to other sectors of human experience than the economic; to statistics we must now turn.

7. History, Quantities and Computers

In the first two editions of this book, this section was entitled 'History and Statistics'. The original section covered a bare two pages, the revised version ran to three. This new section contains a few more pages, and its title introduces the word 'Computer'. Of course, the need for quantification had been recognised, and acted upon, long before the development of modern computers. In fact, the threatening age of the computer has been threatened for a long time, though it really only arrived in the 1980s (the better formulation would be 'age of information technology'). As far as historical studies are concerned, one can distinguish three phases. From the time of the first *Annales* group, and of Lefebvre and Labrousse, and of Clapham, some leading historians were insisting that 'one must count', even if they went no further into mathematical manipulation than long division or perhaps the use of logarithmic tables One of the most interesting comparative statistics thrown up by R. R. Palmer in his 1950s study of the 'Atlantic Revolution' was that in relative percentages there were more émigrés from the American Revolution than from the French: this was easily computed with pencil and paper by simple long division.[38] It was in the 1960s that the first great passionate involvement with the computer became evident, with the work of Fogel, the demographers, and the other studies already noted. Some historiographers were commenting in the seventies that the romance was over, and were detecting a revival of qualitative history. This silly, and inadequately based prediction (it was not in fact the case that in the 1960s a majority of historians had rushed into the arms of computation) was swamped in the widespread application from the early eighties of the possibilities released by the development and use of the microchip. The use of computers continued to require effort in the learning of new skills and much laborious work in the compiling of initial databases, but undoubtedly the new generations of computers and the new software programmes made the employment of computers more accessible and less grinding than it had been for pioneers in the 1960s.

In the earlier phases quantitative history had produced a number of important triumphs, though also much routine stuff, and also some hot contention. In the wide historical perspective the final destruction of old myths about population increase in the eighteenth century being basically due to people living longer was of great importance, as also was the establishment of precise (and smaller) figures about the numbers involved in the African slave trade.[39] Informed discussion of population movement, births and deaths, fertility rates and immigration would not have been possible without the means to process and correlate the complicated data which have been thrown up by detailed research among the relevant records. A useful summary of the state of the art at the end of the 1960s was provided by Marshall Smelser and William I. Davisson. Smelser and Davisson summarised the virtues of the computer under two heads: first the simple point that a computer could handle enormous quantities of fact at several million separate operations per second; second, the indirect point that in preparing their material for the computer students are forced to ask precise questions.[40] This latter point is often made and repeated, though, personally, I am not sure that it really deserves the force it has been given. Historians are actually capable of formulating precise questions (though admittedly not all of them have always done so) entirely without having to meet the demands of the computer, sometimes the 'precise questions' are not necessarily the questions that ought to be asked, were it not for the constraints of whatever programmes exist, or can be created. Smelser and Davisson gave the example of the inventories of estate in the records of Essex County, Massachusetts, for the years 1640–82, which can be reduced to 26,000 data cards which together contain all that can now be known of the wealth of the county in those forty-two years. Whereas the computer could print seven one-page tables and eighteen explanatory graphs, presenting this information in systematic form, in about ten minutes, a manual worker would have to spend at least 500 hours organising the material and making about 125,000 calculations.

Two basic questions were asked of the material: first, did the number of draught animals (horses and oxen) increase between 1640 and 1682? and second, did the number of ships increase over the same period? Then these sets of answers were integrated in one graph showing the increase or decrease of draught animals and ships on the same scale at five-year intervals. The number of draught animals was in fact shown to be decreasing, while the number of ships was increasing, demonstrating that the main population centre, Salem, was changing from a farm village to a commercial centre. This not very surprising conclusion no doubt was, on the basis of impressionistic evidence, known to historians anyway: such is often the way with elaborate statistical demonstrations; nonetheless it is still valuable to have concrete supporting evidence for a previously held thesis. Smelser and Davisson did given one example of how their statistical methods undermined another long-held thesis, that of the triangular pattern of trade out of the northeastern colonial ports, a thesis based on various fragmentary pieces of evidence such as the odd surviving ship's log book. By processing the data for every ship (instead of the distinctly non-random sample on which historians had previously depended) for two three-year periods, 1733–5 and 1749–51, the authors were able to suggest that an 'H-shaped' trade pattern was more in accordance with the facts than a triangular one.

In the sixties, if not earlier, historians became aware of the danger of a promiscuous citation of 'averages' and indeed of the difference between an 'average' and a 'median' figure (extremes at either end may grossly distort a mathematical average; the median is a more genuine representation of what was 'normal' or 'representative'). They now had some idea of the type and magnitude of error which can be involved in the old impressionistic sample methods, and they became aware of which fluctuations are statistically significant and which are likely to be due to random error. The broad impact can be seen by comparing the general histories as they still were in the early sixties, and as they became from the seventies onwards: almost all authors treating of social, as well as economic matters, and not a few dealing with politics, felt bound to include statistical tables in their texts. No longer was it good enough to interweave the odd figure into the general argument; tables had to be set out so that readers themselves could observe the broad trends. It does, however, have to be said that sometimes the relationship between tables and written text was not always made very clear. Nonetheless the movement towards an increased awareness of the significance of statistical evidence and towards precision in the handling of quantities was very evident, even among the great majority who were not making use of computers. In introducing his *The Crisis of the Aristocracy* (1965) Lawrence Stone explained:

> Statistical measurement is the only means of extracting a coherent pattern from the chaos of personal behaviour and of discovering what is a typical specimen and what a sport. Failure to apply such controls has led to much wild and implausible generalisation about social phenomena, based upon a handful of striking and well-documented examples.[41]

However, in the major issues with which historians concern themselves there are no ultimate courts of appeal: the computer – or at least the historian's use of it – is no more infallible than any of the other methodologies or types of source material used by historians. The point was brought out with pyrotechnic effect in one of the most colourful historical controversies of the 1970s, that over *Time on the Cross: The Economics of American Negro Slavery* (1974) by R. W. Fogel and Stanley L. Engerman. Fogel and Engerman claimed that over the previous fifteen years or so 'the cliometricians' had been able to amass, and make use of, a more complete body of information on the operation of the slave system than had ever been available previously; 'this enormous body of evidence' was the source of many new discoveries – basically, taking further the work of Meyer and Conrad (see Chapter 3), that slavery was a rational and economically viable institution and, more controversially, that conditions among slaves were no worse than those of poor white workers with family life among slaves being stable and healthy. Paul A. David, Herbert G. Gutmann, Richard Sutch, Peter Temin and Gavin Wright devoted a whole volume *Reckoning with Slavery: A Critical Study in the Quantitative History of American Negro Slavery* (1976) to a blow-by-blow refutation of *Time on the Cross*:

> The authors of this volume have sought to judge *Time on the Cross* on its own merits, according to the standards of the discipline from which it claims to derive. Toward this end we have attempted, collaboratively, to reproduce every important statistical manipulation, check every significant citation, re-examine every striking quotation, re-think every critical chain of inference, and question every major conclusion in Fogel and Engerman's book. To our surprise and dismay, we have found that *Time on the Cross* is full of errors. The book embraces errors of mathematics, disregards standard principles of statistical inference, mis-cites sources, takes quotations out of context, distorts the views and findings of other historians and economists, and relies upon dubious and largely unexplicated models of market behaviour, economic dynamics, socialization, sexual behaviour, fertility determination, and genetics (to name some).
>   . . . When the faults are corrected and the evidence is re-examined, every striking assertion made in *Time on the Cross* is cast into doubt. The effect in many instances is to restore and reinforce more orthodox conclusions hitherto shared by conventional and quantitatively orientated students of the peculiar institution [i.e. slavery] (pp. 339–40)

Those who live by the computer, one might well believe, shall perish by the computer!

However, it would be absurd to deny that the computer, with its extensive new facilities, and in its many convenient forms, has captured the imagination of the generation of the 1980s. Historians who work with computers have a feeling of being in the swim, of joining in a basic activity common to scientists, business executives, social administrators and social planners. Much important research which historians undertake, and which they will continue to undertake, is not, in its more significant aspects at any rate, amenable to the exploitation of the resources of the computer. Where many kinds of often fragmentary information are accumulated from a vast range of different kinds of archives there will be little possibility of the rational compilation of a database. Where issues of perception, mental attitudes, quality of life, rather than quantities, are being investigated, then the computer will remain on the sidelines. But certainly whole new areas, which ten or fifteen years before could only be broached in a most painstaking, and sometimes imperfect, way, are now opening up. The feeding into electronic data banks of whole texts, or classes of texts, is having implications similar in kind to the great ventures in the publication of national texts of the nineteenth century. There are a number of guides to the sort of work which is being done, one of the most useful being the compilation *History and Computing* edited by Peter Denley and Deian Hopkin. Anne Gilmour Bryson in her essay on 'Computers and Medieval Historical Texts: an overview' indicates the kind of analysis, and their uses, which different kinds of programmes can provide once the texts themselves are on computer. Much glamour, and indeed even news value, has attached to the computerising of the most famous of all of medieval documents, *Domesday Book*. In the Hull University Domesday Project, as described by Andrew Ayton and Virginia Davis, the user may 'search for words or phrases in specified contexts' and 'display on the screen the pieces of text in which they appear sorted according to pre-defined criteria (for example, in village order within the administrative unit rather than in the tenurial order of the Domesday text).' Selected texts may then be amended and supplemented or statistical values may be abstracted 'for analysis, displaying the results in tables, graphs or maps as required' (pp. 21–2).

One of the most impressive, substantial and sustained pieces of work bringing statistical techniques to bear on vast amounts of data, by employing a computer, also relates to that prime medieval databank *Domesday Book*. Important work as *Domesday Economy: a new approach to Anglo-Norman History* (Oxford, 1986) by John McDonald and G. D. Snooks undoubtedly is, it is, it should be stressed, purely and simply economic history and the methods used are entirely those appropriate to economic history rather than to the kind of textual analysis already mentioned. It also has to be stressed that the study is confined to two counties, Essex and Wiltshire: computers, it is too often forgotten, create masses of work before eventually yielding an enormous saving in work. McDonald and Snooks set out to test the traditional view, originating with the Victorian scholar, J. H. Round, that the Anglo-Norman tax, the geld, was imposed in arbitrary fashion, in accordance with administrative convenience rather than capacity to pay. As they comment:

> the great volume of information in Domesday Book poses substantial problems in terms of transferring the data to the computer and in writing programs that can subject it to analysis. The cost involved in overcoming these problems had to be balanced against the possibility that, if the traditional interpretation were correct, then the data in Domesday Book would be meaningless (p. 4).

McDonald and Snooks were able to make calculations as to manorial income and capacity to pay, and then show a direct correlation between this and the tax levied; applying basic economic theory, economic production functions – i.e. the technical relationships between the quantities of various resources (or inputs) and the quantity (or value) of output produced – to analyse the system of manorial production. The direct conclusion was that contrary to the views of Round and his followers, the geld was based on the capacity of the manor to pay, which, in turn, implies a challenge to the view of the more recent medievalist H. R. Loyn that the village, rather than the manor, was the more important administrative unit. Overall, the findings suggested that the Anglo-Norman bureaucracies were rather more sophisticated than had hitherto been thought in their ability to calculate manorial income accurately.[42]

So many, now, are the works based on the complex, computer-assisted analysis of texts, on the processing of vast quantities of data and the establishment of complex correlations, that there is no possibility here of summarising, let alone cataloguing, the work that is being done. In no way is it confined to economic history. The social origins of particular professional groups (servants in medieval France, for example) or the recruitment of élites are two areas in which social history is being assisted by computer-based research.

More generally it can be said that as new research projects, particularly group projects, are set up, the great likelihood is that they will involve the compilation on computer of a database (still rather a laborious human process – historians on the whole still have to seek out their sources – though the latest laser technology does offer the possibility of the machines themselves actually inputting the texts, whatever form they are in), and the use of computer programmes to analyse them. On the whole, very high prestige attaches to such projects. Training in computer techniques will almost certainly become an inevitable part of post-graduate courses in historical research methods, and is also likely to assume a place in undergraduate courses (though almost certainly as an option). Yet, as I have already said, numerous aspects of the attempt to understand the human past will continue to be conducted along lines which do not need, and would not be helped by, the assistance of computers. In the 1960s enthusiasts, and more usually those who really did not know what they were talking about, made exaggerated claims for the way in which quantitative methods would soon take over all historical study. There was then something of a reaction. Computers are now established much more firmly than perhaps was ever really envisaged in the 1960s. But no one would now claim that computers offer solutions to all the problems with which historians wrestle, or even that they will exercise a dominant influence over historical studies.

8. Sociology, Anthropology and Politics

After taking so long to work back round to sociology, it may seem cavalier to lump into this section anthropology and politics as well. But, speaking of course from the outside as a historian, it does seem that although the balance of material studied differs in these three disciplines, the methods employed are essentially similar.[43] Here I shall most often speak of sociology, though some of the techniques discussed may more properly belong to the other disciplines, or to social psychology. Sociology embraces much of what, separately, is taught in social anthropology and politics: it does not seem desperately important whether psephology be strictly allocated to politics or be allowed to align with sociology. This interaction has been specially strong in France, where Emile Durkheim exerted a strong influence over generations of historians. The career of Durkheim (1858–1917) illustrates the way in which sociology only slowly established itself as an autonomous discipline. In 1887 a special course in social science was created for Durkheim to teach at the University of Bordeaux; and in 1896 he was elevated to the first Chair of Social Science in France. In 1898 he founded the periodical *L'Année Sociologique*, which was to have a tremendous influence on the later development of historical studies in France: among its most important contributors from the historical side later on was Lucien Febvre. When Durkheim achieved the eminence of a chair at the Sorbonne, so great still were the resistances to new-fangled subjects that it was a Chair of Education. Not till 1911 was the title changed to Education *and* Sociology, the first time the tag sociology had been attached to any chair in France, although there were already such chairs in Germany and the United States.

Durkheim was preoccupied with the problem of the irrationality of human actions and with the question of collective consciousness, or group psychology. These concepts, we have seen, greatly influenced Lefebvre, Febvre and Bloch, while there was a direct train of influence between Durkheim and his younger contemporary (who outlived him by thirty-seven years) Henri Berr. Berr saw sociology as 'primarily a study of what is social in history'; its point of departure, he thought, 'must be the concrete data of history'. Durkheim he particularly admired for applying 'a precise, experimental, comparative method to historical facts'.

The most influential of all twentieth-century sociologists was Max Weber (1864–1920). Weber, who was appointed Professor of Economics at Freiburg University at the age of thirty was a man of astonishing erudition who could read eight languages. His 'interests and skills' included law and economics, Biblical studies and the interpretation of religious doctrines, the land-surveying techniques of ancient Rome, medieval trading companies, the modern stock exchange, the comparative history of urban institutions, east German agriculture, the medieval origins of Western music, and conditions in the West German textile industry.[14] Flitting from topic to topic, constantly throwing up illuminating ideas, Weber coined concepts and produced basic studies of certain institutions which have dominated sociology and history ever since. From Weber originate the concept of the 'ideal type', of 'bureaucracy' and of the 'status group' as being as important a category as 'class'. He was the first to suggest the correlation between the Protestant ethic and the spirit of capitalism, the suggestion which so influenced Tawney; he was a pioneer in studying the importance of bureaucracy in the growth of the modern state; he virtually created urban sociology and the sociology of law. Like Durkheim he was specially interested in the non-rational foundations of human action: he invented the *charisma*, the 'magical', irrational quality which gives certain men the power to attract the loyalty and devotion of their followers. Most of this was served up in scattered articles, all of them appallingly written and, at times, extremely difficult to follow. As Weber's wife explained:

> He was entirely unconcerned with the form in which he presented his wealth of ideas. So many things came to him out of that treasurehouse of his mind, once the mass was in flow, that many times they could not be readily forced into a lucid sentence structure. And he wants to be done with it quickly and be brief about it on top of that, because ever new problems of reality crowd in on him . . . Therefore, much must be pressed hurriedly into long involved periods and what cannot be accommodated there has to be put into the footnotes. After all, let the reader take as much trouble with these matters as he had done himself.[45]

This is fine for a sociologist of genius (though it explains why Weber is more quoted than read): historians might be tempted to argue that only when their ideas make sense to their readers can they be sure that their ideas make sense at all.

Already during the period of Weber's greatest influence the lines between history and sociology were hardening. It became clear that sociologists were themselves engaged in two rather separate types of activity of which the second, and increasingly more usual, seemed a far cry from history. The first activity continued the traditions of Durkheim and Weber, the production of broad general formulations covering significant areas of human action and drawing upon historical material. This traditional aspect of sociology, it could be said, acknowledged an initial dependence upon history, though history in turn could, and frequently did, benefit from the syntheses produced by the sociologists. The second aspect of sociological study, which developed in the years after the First World War, was the detailed study of some very narrow area of human activity. In such studies the 'scientific' element could be much more pronounced, particularly as sampling techniques and questionnaires were developed in a manner which minimised subjective influences. Early examples of this style of sociological inquiry were the famous *Middletown* studies of the Lynds.[46] Since then smaller and smaller areas of study have been delimited: single educational institutions, even small controlled groups of human beings. Traditional sociology yielded much theory on the nature of social class, which historians might or might not find helpful. But there can be no doubt whatsoever that historians studying class or social attitudes, in the twentieth century owe an incalculable debt to the surveys sponsored by the second type of sociology. Such studies as W. Lloyd Warner and Paul S. Lunt, *The Status System of a Modern Community* (1942), Charles Bettelheim and Suzanne Frère, *Une ville française moyenne: Auxerre en 1950* (1950), and Gordon Marshall, Howard Newby, David Rose and Carolyn Vogler, *Social Class in Modern Britain* (1988) are invaluable treasure-houses of source material. Historians of earlier societies look instead to the empirical studies of the anthropologists, trying to find work relating to societies, or institutions, or kinship patterns, say which are at analogous levels of development to the society, institutions, or practices they are studying.

In one fashion or another historians have had to cope with such fundamental data as shifts in population. Demography is now a highly developed social science in its own right, and also, in its historical aspect, a sub-branch of historical study. Historians are accustomed enough to using phrases like 'birth rate' and 'marriage rate' and for many of their purposes these rather blunt concepts are perfectly satisfactory. But should it be necessary to establish a real level of fertility then such concepts as *age-specific fertility* become necessary. This forbidding term means 'the number of children born in relation to a woman's age, and this varies, being higher in the mid-twenties than in the mid-thirties, or indeed in the late teens, and very much higher than in the mid-forties'. And that, Peter Laslett has told us, 'is only one amongst a whole series of new terms which we hope will come to have a place in the universe of historical discourse':[47]

And for each term there is a corresponding statistic. Infant mortality, that favourite measuring-rod of welfare, should soon become a commonplace of accurate estimation rather than a matter of fragmentary and somewhat wistful guesswork. Expectation of life at birth; the chances of a woman being pregnant at the time of her marriage; the rate of illegitimacy; the size of families; the lesser (or greater) liability of gentlemen to die than craftsmen and peasants; movement of individuals from place to place about the country; perhaps, ultimately, their movement from position to position on the scale of social differences in England, the best graduated of all societies: all these and more are on the way to demonstration.

In analysing social groups great assistance is to be had from what in sociology is termed *rôle theory* (involving Weber's 'ideal types' mentioned above), the idea, in the words of Walter P. Metzger, that

> Every society, in order to achieve its goal, requires its members to play standardised roles, these being assigned in the main on the basis of age, sex, class and occupation.[48]

Thomas C. Cochran, whose application to historical study of other social science tools we have already noted, has made most effective use of the role theory in such important pioneering works as *Railroad Leaders, 1845–1890: the Business Mind in Action* (1953). He has summed up in the following illuminating fashion:

> Role analysis applies to a central problem of the historian: What makes for permanence and for change? Sharply defined roles with strong defining groups make innovation more difficult, while loosely defined roles invite variations in behaviour. The difference in roles gives meaning to such clichés as 'a young country' and 'an old country'. In new situations roles are still fluid; in old traditional situations they tend to be well defined. The American promoter on the unsettled frontier governed his conduct largely by expediency, while the Congregational minister in New England knew rather precisely what was expected of him.[49]

Sociology made its declaration of independence late in the nineteenth century, and by the mid-twentieth century felt itself in a position to look with some scorn upon the pretensions of history. Political science (or 'politics'), generally, was slower to make good its claims to autonomy. Up until the most recent past it was usual in both British and American universities for political science teaching to be included within the history departments. Quite late in the day politics has developed somewhat in the same direction as sociology. Again there are useful borrowings for the historian to make. Much attention in the 'Is history a social science' debate has been focussed on the question of public opinion polls. Undoubtedly opinion polls taken today will form valuable source material for historians in the future, but of course for the vast sectors of the past with which the historian is concerned there can be no question of quizzing the opinions of the dead. Where history has been beneficially influenced is through the insight recent polls give into electoral behaviour in general: it is a little less easy now for historians to deliver those fatuous judgements about 'the people thought this' or 'the electorate wanted that', which were pure guesses and pretty shoddy ones at that. Other techniques developed by the political scientists deserve attention. Samuel H. Beer, for example, has developed some interesting techniques for measuring such difficult quantities as party cohesion.[50]

In the seventies the American Social Science Research Council sponsored interesting work on the concepts of 'modernisation' and on 'crises in political development'. Much of the work on modernisation was criticised as presenting rather naïve praise of Western-style capitalist development, but the concept has been taken over and used successfully by social historians who emphasise the social and cultural implications as much as the economic ones. In 1978 a collaborative venture written by historians, *Crises of Political Development in Europe and the United States* (edited by Raymond Grew) was published. Based on the hypothesis that in the evolution of the modern state each polity will encounter five 'crises' – of identity, legitimacy, participation, penetration and distribution – the book turned up some illuminating comparisons and contrasts; the question of 'legitimacy' had become a central one in much recent historical discourse. Writing on the United States, J. Rogers Hollingsworth pointed out that the high level of participation before the onset of industrialisation helps to explain the low level of class consciousness among American workers, and also the emotional chaos of much American political campaigning. David D. Bien and Raymond Grew noted the significance of the separation of the notions of identity and legitimacy in post-revolutionary France: regimes crumble, the state marches on. No doubt these perceptions were far from new; but the point was that through being set in a defined analytical framework they stood out very clearly. While Grew and Bien noted that an emphasis on politics and the state implied a justified return to the preoccupations of earlier generations of historians, most of the authors were forced to comment on the impossibility of treating political processes as if autonomous, agreeing with Keith Thomas (whose essay on the United Kingdom was the most successful in the book) that 'we have to leave politics altogether and look at society, or rather look at politics as a part of society.' So, in the end, this interesting collaborative venture was a fine affirmation of the importance of history as against political science; but it was also a keen demonstration of the value of comparative study employing concepts originally developed by political scientists. If the social scientists make the kites, then, one might say, let the historians fly them.

9. Last Words

With great wit the American historian C. Vann Woodward some years ago pointed out the frequency with which historians have met in solemn resolve to pay closer attention in future to the discoveries of the social scientists, and have then carried on exactly as before.[51] Another American, Bruce Mazlish, argued that all historians should undergo a training in psychology before embarking on their researches;[52] the British writer, S. F. Holloway, agreed with Philip Abrams that history and sociology should merge, that is that historians should become sociologists, not mere borrowers;[53] many others have suggested even more arduous courses of apprenticeship. In fact, historians continue to borrow, while social scientists look on coldly. 'Either social history,' warns American anthropologist John W. Adams, 'is anthropology or it is nothing. Dabbling with it,' he continues grimly, 'will do no good.'[54] Now perhaps is the time to make the point that if history has imperfections, so indeed have most of the social sciences. Historians in earnest and laborious pursuit of the insignificant are rightly mocked; but some of their puny labours are made to seem positively significant compared with certain social science projects where vast statistical resources are brought into play in the interest of restating the obvious in the most obscure fashion possible. Among those sociologists who go in for model-building on the wider scale it is often to be noted that their handling of historical material is cavalier in the extreme; and one frequently finds a curiously naïve reliance on the sort of narrative source material which historians for fifty years have been viewing with grave scepticism. Occasionally we find among those who depend heavily on theory, whether they call themselves historians or social scientists, a dismaying reliance on what is in effect purely anecdotal material: because the material can be made to fit some a priori theory, such as that, say, of social control, the highly impressionistic evidence is taken to have acquired respectability, without any assessment as to how truly representative it really is.

In support of his plea for a merging of history and sociology Dr Holloway approvingly quotes the advice of the distinguished social scientist Robert K. Merton:

> The report of data would be in terms of their immediate pertinence for the hypothesis and, derivatively, the underlying theory. Attention should be called specifically to the introduction of interpretative variables other than those entailed in the original formulations of hypotheses and the bearing of these upon the theory should be indicated . . . The conclusions of the research might well include not only a statement of the findings with respect to the initial hypotheses but, when this is in point, an indication of the order of observations needed to test anew the further implications of the investigation . . . One consequence of such formalisation is that it serves as a control over the introduction of unrelated, undisciplined and diffuse interpretation. It does not impose upon the reader the task of ferreting out the relations between the interpretations embodied in the text. Above all, it prepares the way for consecutive and cumulative research rather than a buck-shot array of dispersed investigations.[55]

There is, of course, a valid case being made out here, but in so far as the reader is left to 'ferret out' what the hell Merton is trying to say, this passage is a fine example of that to which history never has aspired, and never will aspire.

Notes

1. *Times Literary Supplement*, 7 November 1975.
2. For 'social control' see: Jack P. Gibbs (ed.), *Social Control: views from the social sciences* (1982); Stanley Cohen and Andrew Scull (eds.), *Social Control and the State* (Oxford, 1983).
3. Good introductory works are Mark Poster, *Foucault, Marxism and History* (1984), and John B. Thompson, *The Theory of Ideology* (1986).
4. Among the best-known works by Michel Foucault available in English are: *The Archaeology of Knowledge and the Discourse on*

Language (1972); *Discipline and Punish: The Birth of the Prison* (1977); and *The History of Sexuality* (3 vols. 1978–87).

5. E. P. Thompson, 'The Poverty of Theory' in *The Poverty of Theory and Other Essays* (1978), pp. 1–205.

6. The classic statement is Peter L. Berger and Thomas Luckman, *The Social Construction of Reality* (New York, 1966). Sexuality is discussed on p. 202; the direct quotation is from p. 67.

7. Jeffrey Weeks, *Sex, politics and Society: the regulation of sexuality since 1800* (1981), p. 11.

8. Introduction to Michael Lane (ed.), *Structuralism: A Reader* (1970) pp. 13–14.

9. This view has been restated, at length, in Paul Veyne, *Writing History: Essay on Epistemology* (Paris, 1971, English edition, Manchester, 1984); see also Lawrence Stone, 'The Revival of Narrative; Reflections on a new old history'; *Past and Present* (1979).

10. Carr, p. 69.

11. See W. H. Walsh, *An Introduction to the Philosophy of History* (1967 edn), p. 41.

12. M. D. Knowles, *The Historian and Character* (Cambridge, 1963), p. 6.

13. Irish Committee of Historical Sciences, *Historical Studies*, III (1961), p. 1.

14. Schmitt, *Fashion and Future of History*, p. 23.

15. *What is History?*, p. 84.

16. E. E. Evans-Pritchard, *Anthropology and History* (1961), p. 18.

17. Furet, p. 10.

18. Philip Abrams, *Historical Sociology* (Shepton Mallet, 1982), chaps. 1, 7 and pp. 306–9.

19. Tosh, p. 149.

20. In H. P. R. Finberg (ed.), *Approaches to History* (1966), p. 144.

21. Quoted in Stern, p. 360.

22. Stern, p. 347.

23. R. S. Neale, *Class in English History 1680–1850* (1981), pp. 155–92; Anthony Giddens, *Class Structure*, p. 111.

24. Bloch, p. 46.

25. See, for example, J. B. Mitchell (ed.), *Great Britain: Geographical Essays* (1962) pp. 17–31.

26. Ibid., pp. 3–16.

27. Asa Briggs in an Open University radio talk, A102 Radio 1.

28. T. E. Rihll and A. G. Wilson, 'Model Based Approaches to the Analysis of Regional Settlement Structures: the Case of Ancient Greece' in *History and Computing*, edited by Peter Denley and Deian Hopkin (1987).

29. A good starting-point is Miles F. Shore, 'Biography in the 1980s: A Psychoanalytic Perspective', in Rabb and Rotberg, pp. 89–113.

30. Konrad Lorenz, *On Aggression* (1966); in general see, Leon Bramson and George W. Goethals (eds.), *War: Studies from Psychology,*

Sociology, Anthropology (New York, 1968); see also Marc Ferro, *The Great War*, Chapter I.

31. Among historical studies see Ferro, loc. cit., and Jean-Jacques Becker, *1914: Comment les Français sont entrés dans la guerre* (Paris, 1977).

32. See, e.g., G. W. Baker and D. D. Chapman (eds), *Man and Society in Disaster* (1962); A. H. Barton, *Social Organization under Stress* (1963); F. C. Iklé. *The Social Impact of Bomb Destruction* (1958).

33. Examples are George Rudé, *The Crowd in History* (1964); E. P. Thompson, 'Time and Work-Discipline' in *Past and Present* (Dec. 1967); W. C. Runciman, *Relative Deprivation and Social Justice* (1966).

34. See, for example, M. Ferro, 'Le film, une contre-analyse de la société?', *Annales*, 28 (1973); P. Sorlin, 'Clio a l'écran, ou l'historien dans le noir', *Revue d'histoire moderne et contemporaine*, 21 (1974).

35. In Finberg, *Approaches to History*, p. 17.

36. Thomas C. Cochran, *The Inner Revolution* (1964), pp. 20–3.

37. McDonald & Snooks, *Domesday Economy: a new approach to Anglo-Norman History* (Oxford, 1986), p. 98.

38. R. R. Palmer, *The Age of the Democratic Revolution* (1959), p. 30.

39. Philip Curtin, *The Atlantic Slave Trade: A Census* (1969). See Tosh, p. 153.

40. Marshall Smelser and William I. Davisson, 'The Historian and the Computer: A Simple Introduction to Complex Computation' in *Essex Institute Historical Studies*, CIV 2 (1968), 111 ff.

41. Lawrence Stone, *The Crisis of the Aristocracy 1558–1641* (1965) pp. 3–4.

42. McDonald and Snooks, esp. Chaps III and VI.

43. For a closer look at anthropology, see Evans-Pritchard, *Anthropology and History*, and Keith Thomas, 'History and Anthropology' in *Past and Present*, XXIV (April 1963), and contributions on 'Anthropology in the 1980s' by Bernard S. Cohn, John W. Adams, Natalie Z. Davis and Carlo Ginzburg in Rabb and Rotberg, pp. 227–78. Professor Evans-Pritchard seems to make little distinction between social anthropology and sociology.

44. Reinhard Bendix, *Max Weber: An Intellectual Portrait* (1960). See also the introduction to H. H. Gerth and C. Wright Mills (eds), *From Max Weber* (1948).

45. Quoted by Bendix, p. 18.

46. R. S. and H. M. Lynd, *Middletown: A Study in Contemporary American Culture* (1929) and *Middletown in Transition: A Study in Cultural Conflicts* (1937).

47. In E. A. Wrigley, D. C. Eversley and Peter Laslett, *An Introduction to English Historical Demography* (1966).

48. Walter P. Metzger, 'Generalizations about National Character' in Gottschalk (ed.), *Generalization in the Writing of History*, p. 90.

49. Thomas C. Cochran, 'The Historian's Use of Social Role' in Gottschalk, pp. 109–10.

50. S. H. Beer, *Modern British Politics* (1965) pp. 257 ff.

51. 'History and the Third Culture' in *Journal of Contemporary History*, III 2 (1968) 23–5.

52. '*Group Psychology and Problems of Contemporary History*' ibid., p. 177.

53. Burston and Thompson, p. 18.

54. In Rabb and Rotberg, p. 265.

55. Merton, *Social Theory and Social Structure*, p. 100; Holloway, in Burston and Thompson, pp. 17–18.

Chapter 5 The Historian at Work: Historical Facts and Historical Sources

1. Facts

Some very curious remarks have been made, and, apparently, believed, about historical facts. Even today some writers (e.g. educationist P. J. Rogers in the excellent *Learning History*, and John Tosh in the textbook I have cited several times) take it for granted that E. H. Carr in his *What is History?* had the last word on the subject.[1] In delivering the G. M. Trevelyan lectures at Cambridge in the spring of 1961, Carr was concerned to clear up some misapprehensions he felt to be then current, and to put over the case for the kind of history in which he believed. In order to move on beyond Carr's discussion of historical facts, we shall have to spend a moment or two on *What is History?* As was to be expected in a course of lectures delivered to a Cambridge audience it is urbane, witty, full of anecdote, metaphor, elegant phrases and occasional cracks at the expense of Oxford philosophers and historians. Carr wanted to bring out that different historians present different interpretations, that 'the facts do not speak for themselves', that in everything they do historians are affected by their own subjective views. Like so many others who denounce the subjectivity of the history with which they do not agree, Carr believed that he personally had the secret of objective history. No one could disagree with the first characteristic of the objective historian identified by Carr: 'he has a capacity to rise above the limited vision of his own situation in society and in history – a capacity which . . . is partly dependent on his capacity to recognise the extent of his involvement in that situation, to recognise, that is to say, the impossibility of total objectivity.'[2] Much more dubious is the second characteristic, cited in support of the general principle that the point about an objective historian is not 'simply that he gets his facts right, but rather that he chooses the right facts, or, in other words, that he applies the right standard of significance':

> he has the capacity to project his vision into the future in such a way as to give him a more profound and more lasting insight into the past than can be attained by those historians whose outlook is entirely bounded by their own immediate action . . . Some historians write history which is more durable, and has more of this ultimate and objective character, than others; and these are the historians who have what I may call a long-term vision over the past and over the future.[3]

That 'long-term vision over the past and over the future', as might be guessed, was in fact a kind of woolly upper-class Marxism blended with an absurd respect for 'great men' in history. Carr speaks of 'basic facts', such as the fact that the Battle of Hastings was fought in 1066 not in 1065, and at Hastings not at Eastbourne or Brighton, or the fact of the exact origin and period of a fragment of pottery or marble. These so-called 'basic facts, which are the same for all historians,' he continues, 'commonly belong to the category of the raw materials of the historian rather than of history itself.' He then observes 'that the necessity to establish these basic facts rests not on any quality in the facts themselves, but on an a priori decision of the historian.' At rather great length Carr makes the point that certain 'facts' in the past are held by historians to be very important, while other ones, such as that millions of other people apart from Caesar crossed the Rubicon, are of no interest. One might perhaps comment that the ability to separate out the significant from the trivial is not necessarily a sign of a priori subjectivity and that really Carr brings a sledge hammer to bear in cracking a nut: 'The belief in a hard core of historical facts existing objectively and independently of the interpretation of the historian is a preposterous fallacy, but one which it is very hard to eradicate.'[4] Carr then moves from the notion of 'basic facts' to a distinction between 'a mere fact about the past' and 'a fact of history', and produces the famous anecdote and metaphor which purports to show how the former is transformed into the latter:

> At Stalybridge Wakes in 1850, a vendor of gingerbread, as the result of some petty dispute, was deliberately kicked to death by an angry mob. Is this a fact of history? A year ago I should have unhesitatingly have said 'no'. It was recorded by an eye-witness in some little-known

memoirs; but I had never seen it judged worthy of mention by any historian. A year ago Dr Kitson Clark cited it in his Ford lectures in Oxford. Does this make it into a historical fact? Not, I think, yet. Its present status, I suggest, is that it has been proposed for membership of the select club of historical facts. It now awaits a seconder and sponsors. It may be that in the course of the next few years we shall see this fact appearing first in footnotes, then in the text, of articles and books about nineteenth-century England, and that in twenty or thirty years' time it may be a well-established historical fact. Alternatively, nobody may take it up, in which case it will relapse into the limbo of unhistorical facts about the past from which Dr Kitson Clark has gallantly attempted to rescue it. What will decide which of these two things will happen? It will depend, I think, on whether the thesis or interpretation in support of which Dr Kitson Clark cited this incident is accepted by other historians as valid and significant. Its status as a historical fact will turn on a question of interpretation. This element of interpretation enters into every fact of history.[5]

This is amusing, rhetorically satisfying, but complete rubbish. Carr believed that the positivistic historians of the nineteenth century were unduly obsessed with facts. Actually, in his obsessive discussion of what he takes to be facts, Carr reveals himself also a prisoner of the nineteenth century. The greatest weakness of his *What is History?* is that nowhere does he analyse the processes that historians actually go through in writing a book, or an article, or even a lecture. Carr often writes in the manner of those philosophers of history who generalise from second rate secondary authorities without ever considering what it is historians actually do. Let us look at the story of the vendor of gingerbread. 'Is this a fact of history?' asks Carr. The answer Carr gives is highly eccentric. The proper answer of a trained historian would be that this depends upon a critical analysis of the evidence. How reliable is this eye-witness?; is there corroborating testimony?; perhaps in fact the poor chap wasn't kicked to death at all; perhaps the alleged eye-witness account was an inflated piece of hearsay. That a cautious professional historian such as Dr Kitson Clark vouches for the reliability of the evidence is impressive, but it is reliability which is, or should be, the issue, not a lot of junk about being proposed and seconded for a club. Whether the event is a historical fact or not depends entirely on whether it is supported by the evidence, not on whether it is used by Dr Kitson Clark or any other historians. Its status as a fact is not dependent on whether other historians support Kitson Clark's thesis (about violence in mid-Victorian England). They might well accept the accuracy of the fact, yet use it in producing entirely different interpretations: that, for instance, this was a purely isolated incident in a generally tranquil society, or (I speculate wildly here) that gingerbread was a notoriously adulterated commodity, and that therefore vendors were particularly unpopular. Facts themselves are established by basic principles of source criticism. The *use* that is made of them may then be determined by the particular interpretation the historian is developing. This, also, may determine which facts are considered to be important and which unimportant. But the facts remain facts, or not facts, irrespective of the interpretation. Every historian knows that in writing a book or article he or she accumulates vast amounts of information which in the end will be discarded in producing the final interpretation; but quite often a particular fact, not at first thought to be of great importance, will be brought in as a necessary link in a chain of argument. Facts may be used, or not used, may be used by some historians, ignored by others. But they are, for what they are worth, all facts. Carr's statement that an 'element of interpretation enters into every fact of history,'[6] simply isn't true; what is true is that it takes the labour of historians to establish such facts (and, sometimes disestablish them).

The alleged distinctions between 'basic facts', 'facts about the past', and 'facts of history' are not helpful ones. Establishing 'basic facts' can be a difficult and highly technical task. That historians today can take certain facts for granted is a tribute to the labours of their predecessors (all working without the aid of the wit and wisdom of E. H. Carr, or, for that matter, of François Furet). The establishment of such facts in less explored areas (African history, family life in the Middle Ages, British Intelligence in the last five years) is still complex and taxing work. To go further I must again (sorry!) refer to how the phrase 'the past' is used and to the five (or six) interrelating meanings of the word 'history'. Self-evidently the past contains almost an infinity of facts. No one can possibly know all of them – though we can quite readily perceive what some of the most trivial of them might be: individuals getting up, having breakfast, etc., etc. For the historian of family life, or of diet, some of these presumed facts may come to acquire historical significance. But it will not be enough for that historian to assume these facts: evidence, and persuasive exposition of how inferences have been drawn from that evidence, will have to be presented. It is the validation which makes the fact 'historical': whether it is shown to be significant or not depends upon the use made of it. There will always be facts, not yet known, which may well be discovered and validated in the future ('waiting to be discovered' misrepresents the process). There will be (the popular parlance is entirely apposite) 'neglected facts', 'little-known facts', perhaps 'half-explored facts'. Historians often throw up facts (and substantiate them) without knowing quite what to do with them. Carr, with his passion for social engineering, forgot that the passion simply to find out is a strong, and not reprehensible one. Sometimes previously accepted facts will, through the processes of source criticism, be disproved: they then cease to be historical facts, indeed they cease to be facts *tout court* – Carr's distinctions, as I say, are not helpful.

So far so obvious. But what exactly are these facts? Can they be reduced to some basic unit, analogous say to a chemical element, or to an atom, or to a molecule? They can't – which is the final and clinching reason for writing off (my main purpose in this section) the arguments of Carr and his like as scholastic foolery irrelevant to an analysis of what history is; Rogers seems to sense this, for with rare discretion, he merely blesses Carr ('Essentially, . . . Carr's point seems to hold') then rushes on ('It is not possible to go into the matter in detail here'[7]). When Peter Gay, articulating the voice of sober mainstream history (yet what fun there is in his volumes on bourgeois sex) criticises Foucault for paying scant regard to facts,[8] he means that Foucault avoids detailed discussion of what actually happened (as distinct from imaginative speculation), does not cite precise examples, and gives little sense of the evidence on which his conclusions are based. The 'facts', as everywhere in history, are of a considerable variety in nature, and in complexity. There are the 'simple' 'public' facts (date and place of Battle of Hastings), the complex 'private' facts (the psychological state of a particular individual at a particular point in time). Are 'The Renaissance', 'The Reformation', 'The Counter-Reformation' facts? If they are clusters of facts, what are the basic individual facts (the 'atoms' or 'molecules') which make them up? The French Revolution, presumably, is a fact – yet what a complex one! There are facts within facts: Was it really *gingerbread*, the poor fellow was selling? I have (by implication here, specifically elsewhere) described Carr as an 'upper-class socialist'.[9] Presumably the socialist bit is fact (though, 'socialist in what sense?' would be an obvious secondary question requiring the seeking out of 'smaller' facts). The 'upper-class', however, is interpretation, dependent upon: (a) how I interpret *the facts* about Carr (family background, education, etc., etc. – as 'facts' by no means simple); and (b) how I interpret *the facts* about the British class structure of his day (as 'facts', even more complex). I hope I have demonstrated the futility of any abstract (let alone metaphorical) discussion of historical facts. What we need to do is look at what historians actually do.

Historians, as we know, produce reconstructions or interpretations of the past: in doing this, their essential 'raw material' (the phrase which Carr mistakenly applies to 'basic facts') is the accounts, relics, traces, sources left by the past itself. The central activity is not that of manipulating 'facts', but of teasing out information from often highly intractable sources, discovering new sources, and developing new techniques for analysing them, thus establishing new 'facts', and dethroning old ones; in many of the most crucial areas uncertainty and disagreement will remain, these not necessarily being matters of interpretation, but may well relate to the difficulties inherent in the source material. The critical relationship which has to be studied, then, is not that between facts and interpretations but that between interpretation and *sources*.

2. Primary and Secondary Sources

Frequently at the end of a television programme, broadcast on any of the major channels, there will, in addition to credits for script-writer, cameraman, director, producer, be a credit for 'research by . . .' The 'researcher' here will have helped to provide the material on which the programme was based, by looking up various books, consulting various experts, making contacts with archives or museums or business organisations, setting up personal interviews, and so on. Sometimes students talk about their 'research' as, in preparing an undergraduate essay, they set to work in their college library. Common to 'research' in its various uses is the activity of 'finding out' or 'digging out' information.

Research in academic study has a rather deeper and more rigorous meaning. In many science subjects, obviously, research involves the setting up and operating of laboratory experiments. In history, research involves:

> diligent and systematic investigation in all potentially relevant primary and secondary sources, including research for hitherto unknown primary sources, conducted with the aim not merely of 'making a book' but in order to address precise problems and extend human knowledge in a particular area.

Before getting to the heart of this, let me clear up the point about 'making a book'. People write books for several reasons, not least of these being the desire to see themselves in print, or the hope of making a little money. There are, as we shall see in the next chapter, various types of perfectly respectable historical work. But the true work of research, whether dissertation, article, or book, will set out to extend knowledge, not simply remain within the comfortable territory of a topic which has already been fully explored by other historians.

Let us just remind ourselves that primary sources are sources which came into existence during the actual period of the past which the historian is studying, they are those relics and traces left by the past, while secondary sources are those accounts written later by historians looking back upon a period in the past. Students, and lay readers, who have neither the time nor the specialist skills to deal with primary sources, will perfectly naturally and properly derive most of their knowledge from secondary sources. As the definition makes clear, serious researchers will need to master all the relevant secondary material before proceeding to study, and in some cases discover new, primary sources. But a historical work is generally esteemed serious and scholarly to the extent that it is properly based on the primary sources. It may happen that when a historian is concerned to increase knowledge on some large and general topic (such as, say, 'The Nature of Revolutions' or 'The Causes of Industrial Progress'), perhaps by illuminating new themes, or indicating new contrasts and comparisons, he or she will depend mainly on the secondary works of other authors. But in the main the notion of historical research implies research in primary source material. Study of primary sources alone does not make history; but without the study of primary sources there is no history.

Certain materials do not fit neatly into the categorisation as primary or secondary sources; some are primary sources from one point of view, secondary from another; as so often in all aspects of historical study, much depends upon the precise questions which are being asked. The outstanding instance is the autobiography. Frequently listed in bibliographies as a primary source, an autobiography often assumes the proportions of a secondary history of the times through which the writer has lived as well as a primary account of his or her own experiences and thoughts. Usually composed long after the events described, an autobiography will usually have to be treated with even greater circumspection than the more straightforward primary document. In somewhat similar case is the contemporary history, that is to say a history actually written during the period which is being studied, a history which may have some of the eye-witness quality of a primary record. Actually contemporary histories fall into two types: those written in the normal, detached (as far as this is ever possible) fashion of any reputable historian writing about any period, and those written by actual participants in the events narrated. A. J. P. Taylor's *English History 1914–1945* (1965) is an instance of the former; Clarendon's *History of the Great Rebellion* and Winston Churchill's volumes on the two World Wars are classic instances of the latter. *English History 1914–1945* is uniformly valuable as an authoritative secondary work by a distinguished professional historian: Churchill and Clarendon, when they deal with the wider sweep of events, are much less authoritative. They are of most value when dealing autobiographically with events with which they themselves are intimately associated; and where, demonstrably unreliable on detail, they nonetheless convey something of the atmosphere of the time in which they lived, something of the excitement of direct involvement, something of that quality of seeing events as they seemed to contemporaries which historians must labour for years to attain. The comment of the Tory elder statesman A. J. Balfour on Churchill's account of the First World War was apposite: 'Winston has written an enormous book about himself and called it *The World Crisis*.'

A further example of this kind of hybrid source is a work of contemporary politics such as Engels's *Condition of the Working Class in England* (1845). Engels was concerned to paint as black a picture as possible of working-class conditions and of the wicked-ness of their capitalistic exploiters. We cannot take his descriptive matter entirely at face value, though his eye-witness accounts, however critically they must be assessed (and all primary sources must be assessed in this way), stand as primary sources. Much of the book, however, is taken from newspaper accounts and from government papers, and in that sense is secondary: historians must themselves go directly to the sources from which Engels quotes and, in some cases, misquotes. But from the point of view of a rather different topic, *The Condition of the Working Class in England* is a most important primary source – that is from the point of view of the study of the development of socialist thought.

The example is instructive. Engels essentially wrote his book with a specific, definite purpose – the exposure of the evils of capitalism. He was not consciously writing a source book for the study of the history of socialism. Historians, however, do not take from the book what Engels wanted readers to take, they do not regard it as a completely authoritative source for what it consciously purports to be about. But historians do value the book in a manner that was not in Engels's mind at all. This gives us a further clue to the nature of primary sources. They are contem-porary, of course; they belong to the period which the historian is studying. But just as important, they are not deliberately designed for the benefit of the historian. Every primary source served a real purpose for those who created it: their purpose is a quite different one from that of the historian coming along later. The Declaration of Independence was a masterly piece of political propaganda serving a tremendously important immediate political purpose: no doubt vague thoughts of posterity were in the minds of its framers, but it was certainly not written for the benefit of future students of the American Revolution. Magna Carta was designed to meet a particular political crisis in early thirteenth-century England: it was not drawn up so that future historians could learn about the assumptions of society at that time, though in fact historians do learn much along these lines from it. Domesday Book was compiled for very mercenary reasons by William the Conqueror, desirous of knowing the potential wealth of his domain: but it has proved a godsend to historians seeking all kinds of information about the structure of eleventh-century society. On the whole it can be said that a primary source is most valuable when the purpose for which it was compiled is at the furthest remove from the purpose of the historian. (This is not absolutely true: census-takers may most usefully be asking the same kind of questions as the historian wishes to, though in a most tantalising way they often do not.)

At a commonsense level the distinction between a primary and a secondary source is obvious enough: the primary source is the raw material, more meaningful to the expert historian than to the ordinary reader; the secondary source is the coherent work of history, article, dissertation or book, in which both the intelligent general reader and the historian who is venturing upon a new research topic, or keeping in touch with new discoveries in his chosen field, or seeking to widen his general historical knowledge, will look for what they want. Of course ordinary readers interested in history may find the scholarly secondary work too forbidding and turn to textbooks or popularisations. There is in fact a kind of hierarchy of scholarly acceptability among secondary sources, running from the academic monograph at the top to the sensationalised popular work at the bottom, which, indeed, will scarcely be allowed the title of 'secondary source'. The line between what passes muster as a secondary source (or secondary 'authority') and what has no authority can be seen from the bibliography of any important historical work; the books included are secondary sources; books omitted, though the author may in fact have read them, are *de facto* not acceptable as sources or authorities. The highly esteemed secondary source is itself dependent on primary sources: textbooks and popularisations tend to be dependent on secondary sources, or indeed upon other textbooks and popularisations. We shall return to this hierarchy in the next chapter; meantime we must look in more detail at some of the more important types of primary sources. They too are often organised in some kind of hierarchy.

The informing principle behind this hierarchy is the idea that something which is handwritten, and of which there may be only one copy, is somehow more *primary* than something which is printed, and of which there may well be many copies. Behind this idea there lies the more fundamental and perfectly reasonable one that the historian who has searched around, travelled far, written the necessary ingratiating letters to secure access to a rare document, has put in more sheer leg work than the historian who has relied on printed documents obtainable in all the major libraries (I am not here referring to a printed edition of the rare document, but to, for example, a government paper which began life in print and in many copies). Possibly there is an element of the feeling that it is in the study of rare documents that historians assert their professional autonomy: printed papers are more readily open to inspection and use by scholars in other disciplines – economists, lawyers, sociologists – and indeed to the vulgar mob. At one stage in the development of historical studies it was held – and this is how the hierarchy arose in the first place – that a document written in a man's hand was more immediate to historical reality, closer to how it really was, than a document that had suffered the less direct method of production on a printing-press. This distinction is scarcely a valid one: a document written in one man's handwriting may be a genuine record of a transaction which actually took place, or a record in good faith of something the writer has seen with his own eyes, or it may be the record of a statement dictated by one man to another, or the record of a collective decision, or it may be a complete invention on the part of the writer. It will in any case yield answers only to certain questions; if what one requires is the final statement of government policy on a particular issue, the printed document may well prove a much more valuable primary source *for that particular topic*. Primary sources do not have an autonomous value entirely apart from the questions which the historian wishes to ask and the context in which he or she wishes to set them.

The accepted hierarchy of primary sources, nonetheless, can be seen in the bibliography of any substantial piece of historical scholarship. First the manuscript materials: thus, E. P. Thompson in the bibliography of his *The Making of the English Working Class* (1965) first lists various papers found in the Public Record Office in London: the relatively well-sorted Home Office papers, of which he made special use of those catalogued as series 40 and 42; miscellaneous bundles of papers relating to the London Corresponding Society, food riots and other working-class topics found among the less well-sorted Privy Council Papers; and the Treasury Solicitor's Papers which (among a mass of material of no direct use to Thompson) contain some of the evidence, such as informers' reports, depositions, intercepted letters, from which the Crown briefs against State prisoners were prepared. In the

Manuscripts Room of the British Museum Thompson consulted the much-worked-over Place Collection, which includes Minute Books and Letter Books of the London Corresponding Society. In the Sheffield Reference Library Thompson used the Fitzwilliam Papers, where the relevant material for his study included part of the correspondence on public affairs of Earl Fitzwilliam, and reports from Yorkshire Justices of the Peace and other informants during the time when Fitzwilliam was Lord Lieutenant of the West Riding of Yorkshire. At a private country mansion, Rudding Park, Harrogate, Thompson consulted the Radcliffe Papers and made use of the correspondence of Sir Joseph Radcliffe, a Huddersfield magistrate responsible for bringing Luddite agitators to trial. In the Nottingham City Archives Thompson consulted the Papers of the Framework-Knitter Committee.

Having listed and discussed his manuscript materials. Thompson then proceeds to the next level of the primary hierarchy: contemporary pamphlets and periodicals, discovered mainly, the author tells us, in the British Museum Reading Room and the John Rylands Library, Manchester. A historian concerned with similar problems in a slightly later period (Thompson is concerned with the late eighteenth century and early nineteenth century, when the governmental system was pretty rudimentary) would also include on this level (published) government reports and reports of parliamentary debates. The bound volumes of Acts of Parliament could also be included here. A diplomatic historian, having put private manuscript collections and archival material from the various embassies, state departments and foreign offices first, would, on the second tier, list published collections of foreign correspondence. Finally, the historian mentions the secondary authorities; in Thompson's case, such books as J. L. and B. Hammond, *The Skilled Labourer*, J. H. Clapham, *The Economic History of Modern Britain*, and I. Pinchbeck, *Women Workers and the Industrial Revolution* (and, of course, masses more).

The bibliography of a scholarly work will give a broad impression of the relationship between primary and secondary sources. A more detailed impression can be derived from noting the way in which quotations from and references to primary materials are woven into a secondary account, it being the function of footnotes to reveal the precise nature of the particular primary sources involved. Here are a couple of extracts from another important secondary work, this time on, not the nineteenth century English working class, but the nineteenth century English landed aristocracy. The first is from the main text, and includes the footnote reference; the second is the footnote reference itself (the author, F. M. L. Thompson, is no relation of E. P. Thompson).

> Behind all these changes in the balance of forces within the community lay the fact that in the 1880s the landed interest still possessed an influence altogether out of proportion to their numbers. This they owed to the great social consequence which continued to attach to the owners of landed estates, a feeling· of respect which had not been greatly affected by half a century's experience of adjustments to the new forces and new necessities thrown up by the industrial revolution. Several landowners had appreciated, by the middle of the century, that land was a luxury which gave very poor financial returns to its owners, and had wondered whether the time had not arrived to put their wealth to more remunerative uses. Sir James Graham in 1845 contemplated retreat from the position of a great landowner. Evelyn Denison expatiated to Lord Fitzwilliam in 1847 'about that "expensive luxury" Land. It is about to become infinitely more expensive than ever', he wrote, 'so great a luxury that many now in possession of it will be obliged to resign it'. This was because, he felt, interest rates on mortgages were about to be pushed to unprecedentedly high levels by the competition of railway debentures, 'which will put a pressure on encumbered estates (that is, speaking generally, on half or two thirds of the land of England) to which they have never before been subjected'. He himself, however, was going to sell land 'not because I am of the class of encumbered landlords, for I have luckily extricated myself from that, but because I do not think it worthwhile to keep a security paying 2 percent, when I can get an equally good one paying 5.' Lord Monson put the matter more succinctly when he burst out in 1851: 'What an infernal bore is landed property. No certain income can be reckoned upon. I hope your future wife will have Consols or some such ballast, I think it is worth half as much again as what land is reckoned at'.[1]

[1] D. Spring, 'A Great Agricultural Estate', p. 81. Wentworth Woodhouse MSS, G. 20, J. E. Denison to Lord Fitzwilliam, 18 Aug. 1847. Monson MSS, 25/10/3/1, no. 19, 22 Nov. 1851.

Thompson is making a statement about the continuing importance of the landed aristocracy, supporting it with two references to manuscript letters, one in the archives of the City Library, Sheffield, the other in the County Record Office in Lincoln, and to another secondary source, an article by another historian, David

Spring, which contains yet more evidence, based on *his* primary researches. I'll explore these questions of relationships between research and secondary sources, and between sources, footnotes, and the writing of a secondary book in the next chapter.

Some will say that I make too much of the importance of primary sources, that I am an old-fashioned victim of what critics like to define as out-dated nineteenth-century positivism. I will simply repeat that the great successes achieved by historical study have been based on the systematic study of sources, and add that those who declaim loudest on the superiority of theory have usually contributed least to the sum-total of historical knowledge. François Furet has expressed impatience with the traditional emphasis on archives and their contents.[10] Vital sources, certainly, are to be found elsewhere than in the archives of those who rule, but where on earth does Furet think his much vaunted statistics come from, but from documents in the archives? They certainly cannot be conjured out of theory, or should not be. 'What, when we get down to it,' E. H. Carr asks in another famous rhetorical passage, 'do these documents – the decrees, the treaties, the rent-rolls, the Blue Books, the official correspondence, the private letters and diaries – tell us?' He continues:

> No document can tell us more than what the author of the document thought – what he thought had happened, what he thought ought to happen or would happen, or perhaps only what he wanted others to think he thought, or even only what he himself thought he thought.[11]

This sounds clever, and no doubt brought many guffaws from Carr's Cambridge audience, but once again it is nonsense. Let's take these documents itemised by Carr. Decrees record a definite decision by a ruler or government: whether the decrees are carried out will be a matter for further investigation, but a decree was certainly more than just one person's thought: for instance, medieval Jews would know when yet another decree was passed expelling them or confiscating their goods. Treaties record what has been agreed between two powers; again the provisions of the treaty may well not be carried out, but the significance to the historian of, say, the terms of the Treaty of Versailles at the end of the First World War goes far beyond Carr's silly trivialisation (think about the re-shaping of Europe, the notions of national self-determination, and their negation, the rights of labour, the ideal of a League of Nations, then read Carr's sentence again: is it any wonder I am so sceptical about the reputation attained by *What is History?*). Rent rolls are likely to be a most important source for statistical information, and will offer clear evidence for social and economic relationships into which the element of thought stressed by Carr scarcely enters. 'Blue Books' are the reports of the commissions and committees of investigation which figured prominently in nineteenth century British politics: a report on the conditions of women and children in the mining industry quite patently has a significance for historians far beyond what Carr allows. Official correspondence, private letters and diaries may come rather nearer to matching the specification Carr gives, yet even here official correspondence usually amounts to rather more than the personal thoughts of one person, while private letters and diaries often reveal information historians could not find elsewhere. With all of these kinds of document, historians find much of value in the assumptions which lie behind what is written as well as in the overt thoughts being expressed. Carr said nothing about archaeology, place names, the landscape, physical artefacts, visual sources, film, and all the other non-traditional sources which historians use: but then it's rather difficult to indulge in the joke that the field plan of a medieval village shows only what someone 'thought he thought'. The overwhelming majority of working historians, I believe, would not agree with Carr, or even with Furet. The appeal to the actual practices of the profession is much clearer in the elemental hunting call sounded by the two medievalists H. G. Richardson and G. O. Sayles when they unleashed their vigorous attack on what they believed to be the myth surrounding the early English parliaments which they claimed had held the field since the time of Stubbs:

> It is to the sources, to a representative assembly of texts at the very least – not, we may emphasise, a selection carefully chosen to bolster up some foregone conclusion – that we would direct the reader who would know the truth. And we shall have failed in our aim if we do not persuade some of our readers to look, or look again, at the sources. If with the aid of texts unknown to us or perchance misunderstood by us, they are able to confute us, none could more willingly submit to correction. We would, however, be spared the censure of those who may be moved to contradict without examining the texts we have cited in our notes.[12]

Let it be absolutely clear, however, that what I speak of here is the *critical* study of primary sources, the analysis of one source, or set of sources, in the perspective of what is contained in all the other relevant sources. It is possible to make an enormous display of source material, sometimes material that no other historian has consulted, and write history which is naïve, incoherent to the point of gibberish, or bigoted beyond belief. David Irving, amateur historian (in the sense that he does not occupy a professional academic post) of Nazi Germany and, more recently hostile biographer of Churchill, does immense work in German archives, and sometimes turns up collections unknown to other historians. His tone is often reminiscent of Richardson and Sayles: his interpretations fail to persuade.[13]

3. The Variety of Primary Sources

Helped perhaps by various hints and references made in the previous section, you, my reader, may now care to try your hand at noting down on a piece of paper as many kinds of primary source as you can think of. A rather more difficult task would be to try to group the different sources that actually exist into 'families' or groups of similar sources. Although in any one research project the sources will probably be organised in the sort of hierarchy already discussed in connection with E. P. Thompson's bibliography for *The Making of the English Working Class*, such a hierarchy is not very adequate for organising and categorising *all* the sources which there are dating from *all* periods of history, and *relevant to all* types of historical problem. I invite readers to do their best at this stage, and then will provide my list, grouped under the headings which I believe to be most useful in such a wide ranging exercise as this.

Here is my list:

1 *Documents of record*

Central government sources: government edicts, laws, charters, records of exchequer, chancery and other government departments. Records of parliaments, estates or other representative institutions. Council and cabinet records. Records of central law courts, central police records.

Local records: manorial records, local legal cases and reports, parish registers, local police reports, parish poor relief records, local government records, local electoral records (e.g. poll books).
International records: treaties, protocols, charters (e.g. of the United Nations, etc.); ambassadors' reports, diplomatic dispatches.
Other formal records: records of the Papacy, of other religious bodies, reports of the Inquisition; university records, records of societies, records of political parties, trade union minutes and reports.
Private business records: estate records, rent-rolls, wage returns, contracts, prospectuses, minutes of board meetings and so on.

2 *Surveys and reports*

Centrally organised: Reports of royal commissions and parliamentary committees of inquiry; reports from localities commissioned centrally; tax inspections, Domesday Book, etc.
Private and individual surveys: studies of folklore and customs; investigations by writers and social critics; reports by private bodies, directories and handbooks; (for the very modern period) opinion surveys and polls.

3 *Chronicles and histories*

Monastic chronicles, 'chivalric' chronicles, town chronicles, civic histories and other contemporary histories, memoirs and autobiographies.

4 *Family and personal sources*

Letters, diaries (memoirs and autobiographies might equally well be included here).

5 *Polemical documents*

Pamphlets, treatises and polemical writings, sermons.

6 *Media of communication and artefacts of popular culture*

Newspapers, cartoons, etchings and other illustrative material, posters and advertisements, films, radio tapes, television tapes.

7 *Guides and works of reference*

Codifications of the law, guides on parliamentary procedure, social customs and etiquette, fashion, etc. Educational manuals, guides to the contemporary social scene, etc.

8 *Archaeology, industrial archaeology, history-on-the-ground, and physical artefacts*

Inscriptions (where the inscription is an edict of government – e.g. the Roman government – it is in fact a document of record), entire or part remains (buildings, walls, and so on), pots and other artefacts, coins, paper money, entire or part remains of factories, old machinery, work-people's houses, remains of transportation systems, complete towns or sections of towns, furniture, old costumes, and so on.

9 *Literary and artistic sources*

Novels, romances, operas, plays, poems, philosophical writings, painting, sculpture, architecture (films might perhaps be included here, though the medium itself has special characteristics of its own; by a different categorisation one might perhaps distinguish between documentary and newsreel films on one side, and feature films on the other).

10 *Sources that are techniques as much as sources*

Place names, maps, aerial photography, statistics, serology, palaeobotany, processes and techniques (for example, surviving industrial processes and craftsmen at work).

11 *'Oral history' and oral traditions*

Written or taped records of interviews or personal reminiscences, folk sayings, folk songs, jokes, traditions.

12 *Observed behaviour*

The way things (e.g. courtship and marriages, ploughing the fields) are still done in present-day communities; children's games, etc.

If you did try your hand at my little exercise, I don't suppose you thought of as many types of primary source as that, and I certainly don't suppose you organised your list under the headings I have used (I'll explain them in a moment). Even so, this cannot claim to be an exhaustive list (perhaps you have thought of items which I have omitted): to put the matter at its simplest, *anything* which came into existence during the particular period the historian is studying is a primary source for that period (with the addition of the last three types whose real existence may actually be confined to today, but which represent genuine survivals from the past). Obviously, sheer practicality and utility demand that a line be drawn somewhere. Thus the wrapping paper of a bar of chocolate will be in the strictest sense a primary source for the future historian studying the age in which we now live; on the other hand since there will be such a wealth of other primary sources we could easily forgive the future historian for ignoring the chocolate wrapper on the grounds that it is completely insignificant compared to these other sources. On the other hand, a historian of the chocolate industry, or of diet, or of design might very well be interested in the chocolate wrapper. As I have already suggested the value of a particular source depends upon what particular topic is being investigated.

Now let me explain and justify my headings. By *Documents of record* I mean sources that formally record decisions whether taken by a single ruler, such as a king or emperor, or by a committee or council or parliament; in the latter case, the document may also give a formal account of the discussions and proceedings. I have made rough, and fairly obvious distinctions between records of central government, local government, and records of other institutions. These include Carr's edicts and treaties, and record, not simply thoughts, but decisions and agreements, events which actually took place. In more recent times they will be on paper, and in most recent ones they will be printed; but they can as well be inscribed in stone or written on parchment. I have included documents relating to private business transactions since these all are, or purport to be, records of something that definitely happened. Perhaps this sort of source sounds rather dreary. Far from it: court records can be a colourful source for ordinary social life; one of the most fascinating sets of sources for French life in the *ancien régime* are the *déclarations de grossesse*, statements required by law from unwed mothers.

Then I moved on to *Surveys and reports*. Such documents come into existence when a government or some other institution (e.g. in Britain, the Royal Statistical Society) or individual (e.g. the journalist Henry Mayhew in Victorian London) sets out to collect information, on financial assets, social conditions, etc. These *record* information, and probably a fair dose of opinion as well (which was perhaps what Carr was trying to get at in his reference to 'Blue Books'), but they are not records *of* actual decisions, transactions, agreements, or testimony. A standard source for the study of the French Revolution is the *cahiers de doléances*, the petitions of grievance which the first constituent assembly invited to be sent in to the centre from the provinces through the elected members of the assembly. Folklorists, particularly for the early modern, and early industrial periods, can be a very fruitful source of popular behaviour, belief, and custom. Later I cite works by Ruth Richardson and Eugene Weber which have made profitable use of them.

Next came *Chronicles and histories*. Of course, to qualify as primary sources these must have been produced within the period being studied. Such sources are not much used in modern history, but they are valuable for the medieval period. However, memoirs and autobiographies are very much a feature of the modern world. Autobiographies may be of leading political figures, or of course they may be entirely confined to family and personal matters. But I prefer to include them under this heading because autobiographies, usually written up long after the events they describe, do not have the immediacy of letters and diaries actually written at the time.

Family and personal sources could of course include the sort of business transaction I have listed separately, as well as autobiographies and memoirs. But as the detailed list shows, I'm thinking here of items like personal letters, private diaries and so on, which, obviously, are less a direct record of transactions or listing of information. Again such sources don't just reveal what an individual thought, or thought he or she thought: they tell us about family structures, attitudes to children, the role of women.

Next come two headings, *Polemical documents* and *Media of communication and artefacts of popular culture* which in the previous edition of this book I combined into one. The distinction I have now made is partly (but not exclusively) between materials which are written, and materials which are in some other format, and partly (but not exclusively) between materials which are intended for relatively limited audiences, and materials which are intended for mass audiences. Cartoons, to pick one example, may be designed to make polemical points, or may be designed purely to entertain. The value of both sets of sources (ignored by Carr) lies in what the historian can deduce from them about attitudes, assumptions, mentalities, values. Newspapers are richer and more complex sources than is often thought. Large parts of them may well only be expressions of the opinions or thoughts of one powerful individual. But newspapers also contain accounts and discussions of events and happenings which can be very useful indeed. Advertisements may tell us about the commercial ethics of the period, and about taste and values.

Many of the same points could be made about my next heading, *Guides and works of reference.* What one person thought about the nature of the law, or the class structure, or fashion, might not seem of much importance, but then a book which was merely personal and eccentric would be unlikely to sell in the contemporary market. If a range of such sources is available, it is often not too difficult to separate the widely applicable and representative, from the idiosyncractic. Often the most grindingly utilitarian of reference works are the most useful to historians, lists by rank, say, of military officers, or of apothecaries in seventeenth century Bologna.

Archaeology, industrial archaeology, history-on-the-ground, and physical artefacts: the uses of such sources for very early periods are well known. We can learn a lot about more modern periods too, particularly about life-styles and living conditions, from, for example, household utensils, furniture and surviving buildings. Large and elaborate inn signs dating from the early seventeenth century indicate that in that period literacy was still not widespread: an ideographic (or visual) and easily recognised sign was of more use to the majority than a written one. Such sources may often be of use for rather specialised history, such as, for instance, the history of costume and fashion. But they can play their part too in the study of the wider questions of attitudes and mentalities. Coins have all sorts of subtle uses. Sometimes the actual illustrations and inscriptions on them tell us something about what matters seemed significant to the particular society which used the coins. The Roman Emperors used coins for disseminating propaganda. More often coins serve as a basic source of precise information which can help to illuminate the significance of a whole host of other archaeological finds by, for example, giving an exact dating.

With regard to *Literary and artistic sources*, two key points may be made. Again we are in the realm of attitudes, sensibilities, values (though, of course, the historian will want to consider very carefully whether the poet or painter is simply rendering a highly personal vision); but there is also the point that architecture, novels, poems, paintings, sculpture are distinctive products of the society which is being studied, so that the historian who fails to pay attention to them will fail to understand that society in its totality.

The next heading, *Sources that are techniques as much as sources*, must sound particularly puzzling. Old maps do, of course, have an actual existence, and perhaps should have been referred to as a kind of visual guide or work of reference. But often a specially created, and more reliable, map will be of more use to the historian, while at the same time surviving older maps may best be used as a basis for other techniques, such as the analysis of place names. Place names and, say, aerial photography do not have an actual independent physical existence dating back to an earlier age, though they are both used as sources for medieval history. The taking of an aerial photograph is a *technique* for making clear the contours of a medieval village, say, or of prehistoric field plans which are not apparent to someone standing on the ground. To be absolutely accurate one should probably say that the actual contours of the landscape, invisible as they may be, form the true primary source, while the taking of the aerial photograph is merely a modern *technique* for making use of this particular source. The true primary sources for the analysis of place names are old maps, together, however, with charters and oral traditions which provide our knowledge of the names. Good examples are surviving place names with such distinctively Scandinavian endings as -*by*, as in Whitby, and -*thorpe*, as in Scunthorpe, which give the historian a very good idea of the extent of Viking settlement in England. Chiswell Street, where the Whitbread Brewery founded in the eighteenth century still stood in Victorian London, *may* imply that there was once a 'choice well' there. As with any other source, place names are not infallible in giving the date and sequence of settlement by a particular national group: the date we first hear of the place name may not be the same as the date at which it first came into existence. P. H. Sawyer has made considerable use of this discrepancy in arguing that the pattern of English settlement had established itself by the seventh century, and not, as usually thought, only in the eleventh century.[14] Statistics are the most significant example of the type of source which is as much method as source. Certain statistics in the form of, say, pages of royal revenues, or estate accounts, or details of a country's balance of payments over several years, do have a concrete physical existence. But quite often historians extract their statistics from a wide range of different sources. What makes them *usable* is the application of statistical techniques and, usually, the employment of a computer. Serology uses the distribution of different blood groups in societies of today, to indicate settlement patterns of say (in Africa) different tribal groups or (in early England) of different nationalities (Angles, Saxons, Norsemen, etc.). The method, however, depends upon the stability of blood group frequencies through time, which can be quite a large assumption.[15] Palaeobotany is the study of pollen cores from peat bog and lake sediments, giving knowledge of vegetational (and therefore cultivational) change.

My final entry may have seemed particularly obscure. But if we want to learn something, say, of village life in earlier times we would find it very useful indeed if we could find a village blacksmith today still practising the craft of his ancestors. The *medium* of video recording is particularly useful for capturing such processes.

In my second last heading I deliberately put 'oral history' in quotation marks because this phrase, though now absorbed into everyday speech, can be misleading. What is usually meant is 'oral testimony' or 'oral sources', the recording, whether on tape, by shorthand, or by any other means, of personal recollections (though sometimes what is meant is a fully written-up history based almost exclusively on such sources). For some areas of historical study, relating to the poor and the underprivileged, this kind of source may be the main one available; the evidence it offers should, as far as is possible, always be checked against other kinds of source; it is, naturally, available only for the study of periods within living memory. For Black Americans in the Deep South, working-class wives in Edwardian Britain, Italian peasants in the First World War, and for much recent Third World history, oral testimony really is invaluable, since there is so little other source material to go on. The topic may be explored further in the new edition of the standard work by one of the pioneers of oral history, Paul Thompson's *The Voice of the Past: Oral History* (1988). Oral traditions (which take us back beyond living memory) are specially valuable for societies where the written word is little used. Folk songs and folk sayings, carefully analysed, can give insights into the attitudes and mentalities of ordinary people in the past.

Finally, we have what might well be described as an 'anthropological' source. Bloch believed that in studying the French peasants of his day, he would learn about their past. A twist to this, is the study of behaviour patterns in the less developed societies of today in the Third World in the hope that this will throw light on behaviour in the Europe of earlier times. Change in the West has been so rapid since the 1960s that there may now be little scope for Bloch's approach. How far children's games are unchanging merits study in its own right.

4. Witting and Unwitting Testimony

This simple phrase, I believe, offers a very sharp illumination of the activities historians are engaged in when they grapple with their primary sources, though, of course, it does not in any way make these activities more simple. The phrase is one which I, twenty years ago, borrowed from the distinguished American historian of science, Henry Guerlac, polished up, and codified: Guerlac had originally spoken of a distinction between the 'intentional record' and the 'unwitting testimony' of official records and private correspondence.[16] 'Witting' means 'deliberate' or 'intentional'; 'unwitting' means 'unaware' or 'unintentional'. 'Testimony' means 'evidence'. Thus 'witting testimony' is the deliberate or intentional message (more, often, than merely 'intentional record') of a document or other source; the 'unwitting testimony' is the unintentional evidence that it also contains. Actually, it is the writer, creator, or creators of the document or source who is, or are, intentional or unintentional, not the testimony itself, so these phrases are examples of a figure of speech, the transferred epithet, where the adjective, which strictly speaking should apply to a person, is transferred to what the person produced – the phrase is all the more effective for that. Witting testimony, then, is the information or impression that the person or persons who originally compiled or created the document or source intended to convey, or in some cases, to record. Domesday Book came into existence because William the Conqueror wanted to know exactly how much the land he had conquered was worth: thus he sent his investigators to every part of England to collect details of every village from the sworn testimony (a good example of the normal usage of this word!) of local men, details about who held what land and about the value of each holding and its stock. The witting testimony of Domesday Book, then, consists of these factual details of who owned what, how much cattle, how many sheep, what fields, and so on. But, though this was no part of William the Conqueror's intention, Domesday Book also gives historians fascinating insight into the structure, attitudes and life of the various communities of eleventh-century England. This is its unwitting testimony, which may well be more important to historians than the witting testimony. Magna Carta, in intention, was a record of the bargain imposed by the Barons on King John in 1315. The nature of that bargain, the witting testimony, is of great interest to historians. But Magna Carta also, unwittingly, reveals much about social relationships and social assumptions in early thirteenth-century England. Neither Magna Carta nor Domesday Book were drawn up in order to enlighten historians about conditions in medieval English society.

Hansard's published volumes of Victorian parliamentary debates were intended to inform all interested of exactly what different ministers, and ordinary MPs, had said in the House of Commons: that is their witting testimony and it is of profound interest to political historians. But this publication also tells us something about the way in which parliamentary debates were conducted, about the procedures and conventions of the Victorian parliament. This is unwitting testimony, interesting, though perhaps in this case not as important as the witting testimony. However, where the basic assumptions of Members of Parliament are also revealed – for example, their almost automatic acceptance of the forms and beliefs of revealed religion, taken for granted by them, but very striking to *us* – then such unwitting testimony can be of great importance. Most Victorian documents do not say much about women, the clear understanding being, and this is supported wherever there are casual references to women, that women occupied an inferior place in society and were excluded from public life. The Victorians did not usually feel the need to express this openly (though sometimes they did); they took it for granted. But we, 'reading between the lines' as it were, that is to say reading the unwitting testimony, the unspoken assumptions, can derive a very clear impression of the role and status of women in Victorian society. Witting testimony, then, is the message a document deliberately sets out to convey to contemporaries; the unwitting testimony is evidence which historians find very useful, but which the originator of the document is not conscious might be conveyed to later historians, for it would be known anyway, or taken for granted, by contemporaries.

The notion of 'unwitting testimony' has, to give one example, been taken up usefully by Danish film historian Karsten Fledelius:

> Often the most interesting evidence is the 'unwitting testimony' of the cinematographic recordings, all those incidental aspects of reality which have just 'slipped' into the camera without being consciously recorded by the cameraman. The 'evidence by accident' may be extremely valuable to the historian.[17]

Evidence also 'slips' into written documents 'by accident' – that is to say without the writer of the document being aware that matters he unconsciously includes will be of great value to historians.

Once again the best procedure might be for the reader to pause and attempt to make this distinction for himself or herself. I am now going to print a brief extract from a commentary a leading figure in the Church of England, Horace Mann, wrote on the results of a Religious Census conducted by the Church of England in 1851. I would like readers to consider this extract with great attention, and see if they can distinguish between its main witting testimony and its most important unwitting testimony.

> The most important fact which this investigation as to attendance brings before us is, unquestionably, the alarming number of the non-attendants. Even in the least unfavourable aspect of the figures just presented, and assuming (as no doubt is right) that the 5,288,294 absent every Sunday are not always the same individuals, it must be apparent that a sadly formidable portion of the English people are habitual neglecters of the public ordinances of religion. Nor is it difficult to indicate to what particular class of the community this portion in the main belongs. The middle classes have augmented rather than diminished that devotional sentiment and strictness of attention to religious services by which, for several centuries, they have so eminently been distinguished. With the upper classes, too, the subject of religion has obtained of late a marked degree of notice, and a regular church-attendance is now

ranked among the recognised proprieties of life. It is to satisfy the
wants of these two classes that the number of religious structures has
of late years so increased. But while the *labouring* myriads of our
country have been multiplying with our multiplied material prosperity,
it cannot, it is feared, be stated that a corresponding increase has
occurred in the attendance of this class in our religious edifices. More
especially in cities and large towns it is observable how absolutely
insignificant a portion of the congregations is composed of artizans . . .
the masses of our working population . . . are never or but seldom
seen in our religious congregations; and the melancholy fact is thus
impressed upon our notice that the classes which are most in need of
the restraints and consolations of religion are the classes which are
most without them . . .

The witting testimony, the message which comes through loud
and clear, the one which Mann is obviously striving to put over,
is that the alarming problem of non-attendance is concentrated in
the working masses: they, he passionately feels, need religion
most, yet heed it least. That is the problem *he* wants *his* readers to
give their attention to. One obvious piece of unwitting testimony is
the profound belief in the importance of religion held by Mann
and those to whom he is addressing this commentary. He clearly
takes this for granted (he does wittingly tell us that religious
observance is not a problem with the middle class, and, if it once
was one, has now ceased to be one with the upper classes – but
the evident belief in the significance of religion goes beyond this
factual, witting, information). But the more important piece of
unwitting testimony has got nothing to do with the ostensible
subject of religion: Mann takes it for granted that society at the
time is divided into the upper classes, the middle classes, and
the labouring masses. He is not intending to tell his Victorian
contemporaries, still less future historians, anything about the
class structure, but, unwittingly, his picture of it emerges. Now
this is only one man's picture, though if it was wildly wrong, or
eccentric, he could hardly expect his deeply felt appeal to be
heeded by his readers – so one would have strong grounds for
presuming that his picture was shared by his readers. It would
have to be put with other perceptions of class structure at the
time and, more important, would have, if the historian is to get
beyond mere perceptions to the actual nature of the mid-Victorian
class structure, to be integrated with more solid statistical

evidence. Still, we have here an important example of unwitting testimony.

If the point is still not clear, here is a simple little invented example which ought to drive it home. Imagine that a king in some medieval society wishes to get rid of a courtier who has displeased him. He sends the courtier to a neighbouring kingdom with a sealed message which asks its king to put the bearer of the message to death (a plot device which, it may be remembered, is used in Shakespeare's *Hamlet*). If by any chance that message fell into the hands of a present-day historian, its witting testimony would be that, for whatever reason, the courtier had so displeased his king that the king wished him put to death. Unless the courtier was someone of importance, that piece of witting information might not be of great significance. But the historian might wish to go beyond this and say that this piece of evidence revealed something of the callous morality, the autocratic attitudes, and the absence of due legal processes in these medieval societies. Now that would be unwitting testimony, going beyond what was actually written in the message itself, since the king did not actually write: 'I being, as is the custom in our societies, a callous and autocratic king, with no respect for due legal processes, hereby ask you . . .'.

5. The Criticism and Evaluation of Primary Sources

In defining 'research' I stressed that as well as the all-important work in primary sources, it also involved the reading of all relevant secondary sources. The fact is that when historians come to the evaluation and interpretation of particular primary sources they usually already have a deep knowledge of their chosen period of study, based on other primary sources as well as on the secondary sources, and this is knowledge which they bring to bear in interpreting these sources. Still, younger historians have to begin somewhere, and older ones sometimes venture into completely new territory. What happens then is that sometimes the first primary documents analysed are not fully understood or exploited; as a historian gathers knowledge of his or her field he or she may well come back to re-scrutinise documents in the light of what has been learned from other sources. Here my aim is simply to state the basic elementary principles of the analysis and criticism of primary sources. To do this I am going to set out in schematic form each of the questions which have to be asked of any primary source, though in practice professional historians will deal with many of these questions instinctively without having to work through them systematically, and in many cases will already know the answers to some of the questions. And professional historians will always have a particular topic, or particular questions in mind, when analysing primary sources. The answers depend not just on the techniques employed, but also on the broader historical questions asked. Here I am going to set out a numbered list of the points which have to be established, or questions answered, before a historian can use, interpret, derive, information or meanings from, a particular primary source.

1. Is the source authentic, is it what it purports to be? Take for example a medieval charter apparently dated early in the eleventh century and purporting to make a grant of land from the king to a monastery. It is always possible that the charter was actually forged by the monks late in the twelfth century (say) in order to establish a right to the land. The document will still be of value to the historian as a genuine twelfth-century forgery which will tell him a good deal about that century, but he will have to be very circumspect in his use of it if his subject of study lies in the early eleventh century. To establish authenticity the historian will have to deploy his or her technical knowledge: he or she will be familiar with the characteristic forms of an early-eleventh-century charter, the script used, the style of language, and the legal forms; if the charter being studied departs from these the historian will on *internal* evidence suspect its authenticity. There will also be certain *external* evidence which can be applied: was the king actually in the part of the country where the charter was supposedly issued at the date when it was apparently issued; was he in the habit of making grants of this type; does this purported fact, in short, accord with other known facts? If it does not, the historian may well be on the track of a revision of hitherto accepted versions of events, in which case there is a great deal more work to be done; for the historian may decide, especially if the internal evidence suggests this as well, that the document is not authentic.

An interesting case in point is provided by the biography of the

Victorian novelist Thomas Hardy, *The Life of Thomas Hardy*,
by his second wife. Scholars subsequently established that the
biography had in fact been written by Hardy himself, which, of
course, changes its whole nature as evidence. As a relatively
objective, factual account by a woman who knew him only in later
life it is not *authentic*; in fact it contains the modified version of
events which Hardy wished to convey to posterity. On the other
hand, as an autobiography by Hardy himself it is authentic, and
where compared with the real facts as we know them, gives interesting insights in Hardy's thought processes.

The question of authenticity is not one that can ever be totally
ignored, though actually the vast majority of the sources used by
working historians do not raise this problem. Often it is known
that a particular document has been safely housed in a particular
collection from the very moment it was created, and sometimes
that there were actually witnesses to its creation; there are many
obvious checks on the authenticity of published documents. Still
the issue can crop up, as it did rather spectacularly in 1985 when a
British Sunday newspaper published as authentic the quite cleverly
faked 'Hitler Diaries'.

2. Connected to authenticity is the question of provenance.
Where did the source come from, where was it originally found?
This is particularly important in regard to physical artefacts or
archaeological sources. If a Mediterranean pot is found in Roman
excavations in London, it is this location that gives the pot its
special signifidance (suggesting, for instance, something about
trade routes and commerce between the Mediterranean and
London). Much of E. P. Thompson's material on early working-
class figures, we noted, was found by him in police files: that in
itself is very significant in showing the suspiciousness, and even
fear, with which the authorities looked upon working-class
activism. Sometimes, therefore, provenance can throw extra light
on the significance of a written document. We can be more sure
about the authenticity of any type of source the more we know
about its provenance.

3. When exactly was the source produced? What is its date?
How close is its date to the date of the events to which it relates,
or to dates relevant to the topic being investigated? How does this
particular source relate chronologically to other relevant sources?
How does it relate to other significant dates? – for example, there

is a famous charter (in the Guildhall Museum, London) from King John to the citizens of London whose date, May 1215, is shortly before that of Magna Carta itself, so that the grant of this charter can be related to King John's need to find supporters in the City of London against the barons; the date of the Horace Mann commentary already studied might be related to those of other significant events and developments, for instance while its tone is extremely pessimistic, 1851 is often seen as a time of gathering optimism among the middle and upper classes, represented by the Great Exhibition of that year. What, in short, is the significance of the date of the particular source being studied? In some cases precisely dating a document or, more particularly a building or physical artefact, is an extremely difficult task in itself. But if the historian cannot date his source it is very difficult indeed for him to make much use of it. The more he knows about its date, and other related dates, the more use he will be able to make of it.

4. What type of source is it? A private letter? Or an official report, a public document of record, or what? Usually the answers will be obvious, but it is important to be clear about the type. An official letter sent by a foreign secretary will contain different kinds of information, and will need different types of analysis, from a private letter sent by the same foreign secretary to his wife, which may, in some circumstances, actually contain more frank, and more usable information. Historians come to recognise the conventions, the codes, if you like, of particular types of sources, and these will have to be taken into account.

5. What person, or group of persons, created the source? What basic attitudes, prejudices, vested interests would he, she or they be likely to have? How and for what purposes did the source come into existence? Who was it written for or addressed to? An ambassador's report on conditions in the country in which he is stationed may be biased in various directions: if he is a Catholic in a Protestant country he may tend to exaggerate the evidence of a Catholic upsurge; he may send home the kind of information he knows the home government wants to hear; he may, as for instance Nevile Henderson, British Ambassador to Hitler's Germany was, be over-anxious to maintain peaceful relations between the two countries; on reporting on a potential enemy he may give a hopelessly optimistic account, say, of the likelihood of unrest among the general populace. If we are dealing with a

private letter, was it written with the genuine intention of conveying reliable information, or, maybe, to curry favour with the recipient? Here knowledge of the respective social positions of writer and recipient will be useful. If we are dealing with some kind of report or investigation, what were the sympathies of the writers of the report? And so on.

6. How far is the author of the source really in a good position to provide first-hand information on the particular topic the historian is interested in? Is the writer dependent, perhaps, on hearsay? How far is Horace Walpole, a Whig aristocrat, reliable in describing the mainsprings of the 'Wilkes and Liberty' movement? Can middle-class writers really understand the feeling of the poor? John Reed's *Ten Days That Shook the World* (1919) is an exciting on-the-spot account of the Bolshevik Revolution: but, in using it as a primary source, can we be absolutely certain that in fact he ever left his hotel bedroom?

7. How exactly was the document understood by contemporaries? What, precisely, does it say? Certain branches of historical investigation require the skills of palaeography, diplomatics and philology. There may be problems of deciphering inscriptions, hieroglyphics and certain types of handwriting. There can be problems arising from archaic or obscure languages. Some of the controversies in medieval history centre on the shade of meaning to be allotted to a specific passage in dog-Latin or medieval French: I have already quoted in Chapter 2 from the Anglo-Saxon chronicle (written, of course, in Anglo-Saxon) the phrase about the state of religion in William the Conqueror's time being such 'that every man who wished to, whatever considerations there might be with regard to his rank, could follow the profession of a monk'. An alternative translation, which gives a much narrower meaning, reads 'Christendom was such in his day that every man who so desired followed what pertained to his order.'[17] Any technical phrases, esoteric allusions, or references to individuals or institutions will have to be fully elucidated in order that the full meaning of the document can come through. Thus when an Elizabethan document refers to the Star Chamber, whoever is interpreting the document has to know exactly what the Star Chamber was. A Renaissance letter will usually be loaded with references to classical mythology: the historian has to be completely clear about their meaning and significance for contemporaries.

In analysing primary sources historians must be critical, but they must have understanding. Before seeing how all of this might work out in practice, let me share the general message I always give my students when we work together on primary sources: always be sceptical, never cynical. Now imagine that, as a rather raw and inexperienced researcher, you have taken it upon yourself to investigate the topic 'Was There Really a Renaissance?'. You are studying the letter which follows, written in 1492 by Marsilio Ficino to Paul of Middleburg. The letter was actually written in Latin, which of course relates to point 8, and which you would have to be able to understand if you were to undertake research in this sphere. For the purposes of this exposition, I give the letter in a well-known English translation:

What the poets once sang of the four ages, lead, iron, silver, and gold, our Plato in the *Republic* transferred to the four talents of men, assigning to some talents a certain leaden quality implanted in them by nature, to others iron, to others silver, and to still others gold. If then we are to call any age golden, it is beyond doubt that age which brings forth golden talents in different places. That such is true of this our age he who wishes to consider the illustrious discoveries of this century will hardly doubt. For this century, like a golden age, has restored to light the liberal arts, which were almost extinct: grammar, poetry, rhetoric, painting, sculpture, architecture, music, the ancient singing of songs to the Orphic lyre, and all this in Florence. Achieving what had been honoured among the ancients, but almost forgotten since, the age has joined wisdom with eloquence, and prudence with the military art, and this most strikingly in Federigo, Duke of Urbino, as if proclaimed in the presence of Pallas herself, and it has made his son and his brother the heirs of his virtue. In you also, my dear Paul, this century appears to have perfected astronomy, and in Florence it has recalled the Platonic teaching from darkness into light. In Germany in our times have been invented the instruments for printing books, and those tables in which in a single hour (if I may speak thus) the whole face of the heavens for an entire century is revealed, and one may mention also the Florentine machine which shows the daily motions of the heavens.[18]

Now, once more, readers might care to have a stab at raising (and where possible, answering) the questions which would have to be asked in interpreting this letter. I will myself again set out the points schematically:

(1) *Authenticity?* This actually is a well-known letter which has been much used by historians, so its authenticity can be taken as

assured. (2) *Provenance?* Given that authenticity is established, this is not of pressing concern. (3) *Dating?* Well we have the date. The significance would relate to an essential ancillary to the main question – if there was a Renaissance, when was it? This letter dated 1492, would have to be related to the dating of other letters, poems, paintings, etc., suggesting, or not suggesting, the existence of a Renaissance, leading to an argument along one of the following lines: the Renaissance had already begun well before 1492, had reached its peak in 1492, was not really apparent yet in 1492, etc., etc. (4) *What type of source?* It's a private letter, though written in the rather elaborate formal style of the time. (5) *(a) Who created it?* Marsilio Ficino, a serious, even if raw, scholar in this field would know, was a protégé of Cosimo de' Medici, the virtual ruler of Florence, and the son of his physician. Ficino's house became the centre of an enthusiastic group of Platonist scholars and Ficino himself translated all Plato's *Dialogues*, wrote a commentary on Plato's *Symposium* and an original work *The Platonic Theology*. (b) *What prejudices etc?* We might expect Ficino, as a Florentine, to be biased in favour of Florence. Obviously, also, he was a committed Platonist. Possibly (I can only say *possibly*, because we'd need much more evidence on this slightly speculative point) as the son of a physician he might be unduly respectful towards such princely figures as Cosimo de' Medici, to whom, anyway, he was deeply indebted. (c) *Why was it written, and to whom?* It seems reasonable to assume that this letter was written with the genuine intention of conveying what Ficino believes to be true (not *necessarily* exactly the same as reliable information of course). Furthermore, there seems to be a genuine note of affection as between Ficino and Paul, also suggesting that he would write genuinely. (6) *How far does it provide good first-hand information?* We know that Ficino was right at the centre of intellectual developments in Florence, so he is a very good source for these. Possibly his knowledge of German developments was less good. (7) *Technical points, contemporary allusions, etc.?* There are a lot of these which, to get the full contemporary meaning and flavour of the document, would need to be understood, as presumably you would if you were genuinely a student of the Renaissance period. The points that need clarifying are:

(a) Who are the poets in the first line?

(b) What is the exact reference in Plato's *Republic*? What is its significance?

(c) What is the full implication of the phrase 'liberal arts'?

(d) What is the force of 'has restored' . . . 'almost extinct.'? This, actually is central. What Ficino is speaking of is (as he sees it) a restoration of the achievements of Ancient Greece after their near extinction in the Middle Ages. This notion is central to the concept of a Renaissance (or Rebirth). It's a simple point, but the student who didn't understand would miss much of the historical significance of the letter.

(e) What is the force of the (classical) allusion to Pallas?

(f) What exactly is Platonic teaching?

(g) If 'instruments for printing books' are obvious, what are the tables' and the 'Florentine machine' also referred to? (Though he puts all three in the same breath, we today would see printing as far more important than the various astronomical devices upon which Renaissance scholars set such store.)

(h) Who are Federigo, Duke of Urbino, and his son and brother? As a scholar of the period, you would know that Urbino was one of the smallest Italian city states, but often considered the quintessence of the Renaissance city, that Federigo and his son were great scholars, and that Federigo provided the model for Castiglione's famous *Book of the Courtier*, a work which, among other things, greatly influenced Elizabethan ideas about the Renaissance gentleman.

What then does the document contribute to answering the major question being addressed? The message that comes through loud and clear is that a leading and representative Florentine scholar of the late fifteenth century is sure that a Renaissance ('a golden age' which has 'restored to light' Classical achievements) has taken place in his century. This is a first-class piece of evidence demonstrating that men of the time were aware of a Renaissance, and that they looked back to the wisdom of 'the ancients' while believing the period in between had been something of a dark age with the liberal arts 'almost forgotten'. More than this, Ficino gives pride of place in this development to Florence (though here he may be biased, as we have noted); yet he sees Federigo (not a Florentine) as the acme of Renaissance man in all his aspects: the stress on the individual is significant since this is often seen as a major new characteristic of Renaissance thought. (Ficino was at the centre of Florentine intellectual developments, so that it is highly unlikely that he would be expressing an eccentric individual opinion of his own.) It would then be necessary to find out whether there were a large number of other statements making a similar point. As in fact there are, it would then become possible to say that intellectual figures of the time certainly *believed* that a Renaissance was taking place. However that is only a step, and not necessarily a secure one, towards establishing that a Renaissance did take place. The use of the word Renaissance implies some kind of striking change, so that all sorts of sources, including quantitative ones, would have to be referred to with a view to establishing whether or not, around this time, significant changes in important aspects of life and culture were taking place.

Before leaving sources in general, I must repeat again that the sources historians use are often imperfect, fragmentary, and intractable. They were, as we have seen, created for purposes utterly different from those of the historian. Often sources have been destroyed in the course of time. So apart from the complex range of questions which have to be posed, there is the problem of the unavailability, or unsatisfactory nature, of sources for the questions historians wish to address.

6. Literature and Art as Primary Sources

The use of literature and art as historical sources raises problems which are not always fully recognised. Right off we can make one obvious point: a novel or poem or painting, if it is a source at all, is a source for the period in which it was written or painted, not for the period about which it is written or what it is purporting to represent. A Renaissance painting of the Crucifixion may be a marvellous primary source for the Renaissance, but it will in no sense be a primary source for the first century A.D. Shakespeare's history plays are good sources for contemporary attitudes towards politics and society and, in particular, for Tudor attitudes to English history: they are not, obviously, primary sources for the historical Macbeth, Hamlet or Richard II. The same point, obviously, applies to feature films: the *Battleship Potemkin* tells much about Soviet Russia, but not a lot about the revolution of 1906. The novels of Sir Walter Scott may tell us a great deal about the early nineteenth century; but though Scott was undoubtedly historically minded, a novel such as *Ivanhoe* will not tell us much about the twelfth century that we could not better and more reliably find elsewhere, though it might (and this is true of all great novels), through the author's creative insight, suggest lines of inquiry which should be checked against the other sources. Among novels set in past time we would (as historians) tend to pay most direct attention to novels drawing directly upon childhood experiences and, perhaps upon the memories of still earlier times passed on then by parents and grandparents.

Nonetheless, the use of imaginative literature did fall rather seriously into disrepute in the wake of a spate of popular, chatty 'social histories' drawing their evidence, say, for social conditions in early nineteenth-century England almost exclusively from the pages of Dickens. Which takes us to one basic rule in the handling of imaginative literature: for the concrete facts of everyday existence, wage rates, living standards, environmental conditions, spurn the novelist, and turn instead to government papers, statistical series, company records, trade union archives, private correspondence, houses still in existence from the era being studied, or their remains (industrial archaeology). Once the record has been established from such sources, the historian may well use a vivid example culled from a novel or poem to *illustrate* (not *prove*) that record. Thus it is fairly easy to establish from bills of mortality, private diaries, and the like, the truly noisome conditions of eighteenth-century England: but *communication* with the reader may well be intensified by a judicious quotation from Fielding's *Tom Jones*. One of the most famous examples of a false trail established by a great creative writer lies at the door of Shakespeare himself: Juliet was married to Romeo at the age of fourteen; her mother, as apparently the other ladies of Verona, had been married even earlier; Miranda in *The Tempest* was married at fifteen. Arguing from these and other plays, historians at one time deduced that the marriage age in Elizabethan and Jacobean England must have fallen consistently in this age range. In fact demographic research in the fifties and sixties showed that in that era the marriage age was higher, not lower, than at present: the commonest age of first marriage for women being at least twenty-two.[19]

A painting (or etching, or other form of visual art involving elements of landscape or townscape) *may* provide reliable information on what a particular environment looked like at the time it was painted – for instance, much of our knowledge of the appearance of seventeenth-century London is derived in this way; a genre painting *may* contain information on the food eaten by particular social groups. But it must always be borne in mind that the painter will quite certainly have been affected by prevailing stylistic conventions, and will have non-informational artistic purposes of his own, so that the painting is most unlikely to be an exact factual record. While concrete facts of everyday existence should be sought elsewhere, a novel, provided it is set in the novelist's own age, may well provide insight into the attitudes, morals, assumptions and even customs of that age. Certainly, if historians are to understand a past society from, as it were, the inside, the essence of true historical thinking, they must saturate themselves in the art and literature of that society. But they should be sparing in drawing direct references from these always highly problematic sources. Literature is never a good source for political developments, even if such a novel as Trollope's *The Prime Minister* gives clear suggestions of the changing attitudes at mid-century of aristocratic political figures towards the rights of electors, suggestions which, of course, have to be verified from more conventional sources. Literature has not been helpful on the nature of electoral politics earlier in the century. Once historians made much of the fact that the Eatanswill election (in *Pickwick Papers* by Dickens) was set in the pre-1832 era. Actually the Great Reform Act of 1832 had little effect on the conduct of elections, and, in any case, Dickens erred on the side of restraint. As Professor Gash has written: 'The electoral mob at the time of Victoria's accession to the throne was in many ways more akin to the London of Barnaby Rudge than the Eatanswill of Mr Pickwick.'[20]

The greatest danger in bringing art and literature into historical study is that of developing a circular argument about the relationship between the arts and society. A particular period in British history is defined as the 'Victorian Age', with certain characteristics drawn in part from Dickens, Trollope, the pre-Raphaelite painters, etc.; then the art and literature are studied more systematically, when, lo and behold, they are found to reveal striking examples of the characteristics already defined; but in fact these 'characteristics', in part at least, came from these same sources (see diagram).

Establishing meanings in art and literature requires the formal skills of art historian and literary scholar. That said, a piece of literature or art calls upon the historian to address the same list of basic questions as are raised by any type of source. When a novel is being studied, two questions are paramount:

1 When was it written, and how does that date relate to the period being written about?

2 Was the author in possession of first-hand experience or childhood memories, or family recollections of the events and circumstances being described or 'constructed'?

Here my concern has been purely with the technicalities of source criticism. There is much more to say about the connections between the arts and their social and historical contexts, a matter to be taken up in Chapter 7.

7. The Imperfect and Fragmentary Nature of Primary Sources

Geoffrey Barraclough once defined history as 'the attempt to recreate the significant features of the past on the basis of imperfect and fragmentary evidence'.[21] That historical sources are fragmentary and imperfect is something of a central theme of mine: I conclude this chapter by offering a few examples. It is very seldom indeed that an archaeological dig uncovers complete, undamaged relics of past ages. And even when the relics are in a perfect condition they are likely to provide only a few tiny clues to the total picture of what life was like and what events were taking place in that bygone age. Archeological sources are not the only ones to suffer from the depredations of time. Frequently charters and other written documents have survived in a form which renders them practically unreadable. Even where a document is complete, or relatively complete, there are often still, as we have already noted, problems of comprehending archaic languages or strange scripts and hieroglyphics. Sometimes there are occasions when historians can never be absolutely sure that the meaning that they have given to certain strange words is the one understood by people of the time. Many of the claims which Victorian historians made on behalf of Magna Carta as being

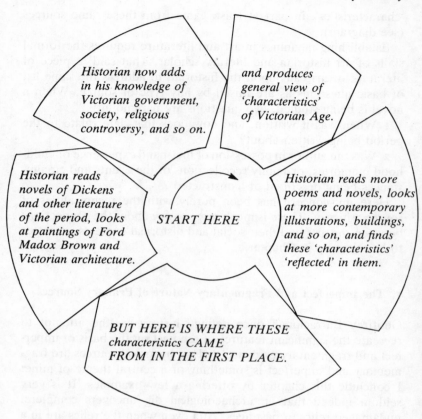

Historian now adds in his knowledge of Victorian government, society, religious controversy, and so on.

and produces general view of 'characteristics' of Victorian Age.

Historian reads novels of Dickens and other literature of the period, looks at paintings of Ford Madox Brown and Victorian architecture.

START HERE

Historian reads more poems and novels, looks at more contemporary illustrations, buildings, and so on, and finds these 'characteristics' 'reflected' in them.

BUT HERE IS WHERE THESE characteristics CAME FROM IN THE FIRST PLACE.

a basic charter of English liberties, establishing parliamentary government and trial by jury, were due to placing an unjustifiably modern interpretation on certain Latin phrases.

However much material historians have at their disposal they will never find everything necessary for answering the particular questions they wish to ask. It is in the nature of historical sources that the concerns of their originators differ greatly from those of the historians who study them. The problem is particularly acute when the attempt is made to describe the social structure of a past society, or to determine standards of living. Men in past ages did not have our interest in these problems, and therefore tended not to leave the kind of primary source material which would yield answers to them. Frequently this can mean that historians concerned with such problems have to deduce their interpretations in very indirect ways. For example, Eric Hobsbawm tried to make up for the lack of direct statistical evidence on the general standard of living in Britain in the early nineteenth century by seeking to derive this indirectly from the sales of meat at the Smithfield Meat Market in London. Because he could say with fair certainty that sales of meat were not increasing when population definitely was increasing, he argued that the standard of living for the majority could not have been rising, and probably was falling.[22] R. M. Hartwell, however, argued that the Smithfield figures are insufficient in themselves, that we need to know more about meat markets in other parts of the country, and that we must take into account imports from abroad and increased consumption of fish.[23] Hartwell came to opposite conclusions from Hobsbawm. How much simpler if early nineteenth-century governments had had our interest in compiling cost-of-living indices.

With regard to quantity and range of source materials, historians of the contemporary world have an opposite problem to those of the medieval and classical world. While medieval and classical historians usually suffer from extreme fragmentation in their evidence, frequently having to build up interpretations from only a handful of documents and a few pieces of non-traditional source material (archaeology, place names, aerial photographs), modern historians often have more material than they can cope with. Nonetheless there is the curious paradox that the increasing use of the telephone in the twentieth century has meant that for certain crucial decisions there is *no written (or any other) record at all*. Whatever different problems historians of different periods encounter, there always comes a point when a historian has to *squeeze the last drop* of information out of the evidence. This is a good image, and worth remembering.

Notes

1. P. J. Rogers in A. K. Dickinson, P. J. Leed and P. J. Rogers (eds.), *Learning History* (1984), pp. 22, 37 (n. 5); Tosh, p. 113. For a powerful and witty counterblast, see G. R. Elton, *The Practice of History* (1967), pp. 55–61.

2. Carr, p. 123.
3. Ibid.
4. pp. 10–11.
5. p. 12.
6. p. 13.
7. Rogers, p. 37.
8. Peter Gay, the *Education of the Senses*, p. 468.
9. *Times Higher Education Supplement*, 16 November 1984.
10. Furet, pp. 12–13.
11. Carr, p. 16.
12. H. G. Richardson and G. O. Sayles, *The Governance of Medieval England* (1958) p. vii.
13. For the elaborate presentation, and total misuse, of primary sources, readers are referred to David Irving, *Hitler's War* (1977), for example p. 331 where the paragraph beginning, characteristically, 'No documentary evidence exists . . .' continues with Irving's theme that Hitler had no responsibility for Nazi extermination policies towards the Jews.
14. P. H. Sawyer in P. H. Sawyer (ed.), *Medieval Settlement: Continuity and Change* (1976), p. 2.
15. W. T. W. Potts, 'History and Blood Groups in the British Isles', in Sawyer, pp. 236–53, and 'Comment' by E. Sutherland in ibid., pp. 254–61.
16. Henry Guerlac, 'Some Historical Assumptions of the History of Science' in A. C. Crombie (ed.), *Scientific Change* (1963), p. 799.
17. See Karsten Fledelius, 'Film and History – An Introduction to the Theme' in Comité International des Sciences Historiques, *XVIe Congrès International des Sciences Historiques: Rapports*, 1, p. 186.
18. Printed in James Bruce Ross and Mary Martin McLaughlin (eds.), *The Portable Renaissance Reader* (New York, 1968, Harmondsworth, 1978).
19. Peter Laslett, *The World we have lost*, pp. 81 ff. The ages suggested by the plays may, however, have been relevant to a small, wealthy minority.
20. Norman Gash, *Politics in the Age of Peel* (1953).
21. Geoffrey Barraclough, *History in a Changing World* (1955), p. 2.
22. E. J. Hobsbawm, 'The British Standard of Living – 1790–1850', *Economic History Review* (1957).
23. R. M. Hartwell, 'The Rising Standard of Living in England 1800–1850', ibid., (1961).

Chapter 6 The Historian at Work: The Writing of History

1. Basic Activities and Basic Concerns

Historical writing is concerned with human societies in the past. The 'societies' needs to be stressed since, although it is perfectly proper for historians to pay attention to the exploits of significant individuals, a history which concentrated solely on the activities of individuals would be a naïve and unsatisfactory history: human beings *do* live in societies, the social factors which operate both on individuals and on all communities are complex and require much patient examination. Many social science disciplines, of course, are concerned with human societies – sociology and social anthropology, for instance. What particularly characterises historical writing is a concern with change through time (purists may argue that this phrase is tautological: *all* change is 'through time', that is 'over a period of time': the historian's concern is with *extended* periods of time – not with seconds and minutes, but with years, not so much with days, but with centuries). Put very broadly, social scientists look for the common factors and the regular patterns, discernible in human activities in society; historians look at the way societies differ from each other at various points in time, at how, through time, societies change and develop, or change and decline. Thus historical writing must in some sense *tell a story*: it must contain narrative, a sense of movement through time. Of course, explanation and analysis are required as well. A mere list of dates or events is chronicle, not history: a writer of such a list is a chronicler or annalist, not a historian. That said, the establishment of when exactly events took place, and in what order, can be a challenging enough task in itself. Without analysis, history is incomplete; without chronology it does not exist. Historical writing, I have argued, is concerned with the particular and the unique, not with the establishment and refinement of theory: sometimes discerning alleged general patterns is actually simpler than teasing out how things actually were, or actually happened. Yet interrelationships and structures are important, so that a mere catalogue of particular and unique events is utterly unsatisfactory as history. The difficulties and dilemmas of him or her who would write history are, I hope, becoming clear.

The actual writing of history in fact is a challenging task. Schematically, one could perhaps say that historians have four tasks. They have to find their sources; to these sources they have to apply both their existing expertise in the society being studied and the techniques of source criticism; out of this they have to produce an interpretation; and finally they have to communicate this interpretation in the form of a piece of written history. Young researchers often approach this final task much too lightly. The need to observe the time dimension; the need to observe the uniqueness of events and circumstances yet offer persuasive explanations and interrelationships, the imperfect and fragmentary nature of evidence; and the need to bring the divergent elements together into a satisfactory structure: together these impose heavy burdens. Historians need to allow much time for reflection; once they have started writing, they will often find that only then do they really know what they are looking for, and that they will have to return to their researches; above all, they will need to be prepared for many revisions and many re-writes of their original draft. It is an enormous moment of relief when one has completed a substantial book, and for a time one is blinded by the knowledge of one's own excruciating endeavours, and by one's conviction that one really has something of significance to say. Then the gaps, the infelicities, the inconsistencies begin to become apparent. This happens with the most experienced of historical writers. All Ph.D. students need to be warned that three or four drafts may not be enough, and that one certainly will not be.

Before coming to some of the detailed problems of writing history, I want to look at how fragments of information derived from the sources become incorporated in a piece of historical writing. I am now going, in the hope again of involving readers actively, to list some invented (though not completely nonsensical) information on the somewhat shadowy Elizabethan figure Sir Christopher Bentlowe (actually completely fictitious). My invitation to readers is to try to compose an account of the life of this figure based on the 'information' which follows. Imagine that from your researches you have discovered:

1. A hitherto unknown play *The Virgin King* which you know was first performed in 1589. In certain aspects it seems almost to go beyond the contemporary Shakespeare in quality, and it has original characteristics which in conjunction with some external evidence confirm your view that it was written by Bentlowe.

2. Some poems of a highly erotic character which, though you cannot date them, you can firmly attribute to Bentlowe.

3. Certain household accounts showing that over a fifteen-year period Bentlowe consumed fifteen gallons of sack (sherry) a week.

4. Privy Council records of 1591 which show that Bentlowe, as a member of the Privy Council, had ambitious ideals for a new Poor Law.

5. A religious tract of 1592 attacking Bentlowe for licentiousness and ungodliness.

6. Memoirs of William Cecil, Lord Burghley, principal adviser of the Queen, referring to Sir Christopher Bentlowe, in 1588, as a very able member of the Privy Council and wise statesman.

7. Contemporary accounts of Bentlowe's death in a tavern brawl in 1595.

8. Persistent fragments of information 1588–95 showing Bentlowe's interest in the social problems of vagrancy and the deserving poor.

9. Parish records indicating Bentlowe's birth in 1555, as the son of a small tradesman.

10. By comparing the parts of the Poor Law of 1598 dealing with the deserving poor with Bentlowe's ideas, you can see very marked similarities.

Here now are three very different attempts which, as will be immediately apparent, are of very different levels of attainment.

A. Bentlowe wrote a play, *The Virgin King*, first performed in 1589, which is Shakespearean in quality. He also wrote poems (date uncertain) of an explicitly erotic character. His household accounts suggest that he was a heavy drinker. In 1591, as a Privy Counsellor, he had ambitious ideas for a new Poor Law. He was attacked as licentious and ungodly in 1593 though regarded very highly as a statesman five years earlier. He died in a tavern brawl in 1595. He seems to have been consistently interested in Poor

Law problems. He was born in 1555 in relatively humble circumstances, and must have risen in the world to receive his knighthood in or before 1588. He seems to have influenced the Poor Law of 1598.

B. Bentlowe was born in 1555, the son of a small tradesman. By 1588 he had achieved some reputation as a statesman, and a knighthood. He was also a poet and playwright and the following year his great play *The Virgin King* was produced. In 1591 he presented the Privy Council with ambitious ideas for Poor Law reform. He was attacked as 'licentious and ungodly' and he seems to have been both a drunkard and a rake. He continued his interest in the Poor Law. He was killed in a tavern brawl in 1595. The Poor Law of 1598 shows signs of his influence.

C. Born in 1555 in relatively humble circumstances, Christopher Bentlowe rose rapidly in the world becoming a Privy Counsellor and a knight by 1588, when he earned the praises of William Cecil. In 1591 he put forward ambitious ideas for a new Poor Law, a question which had preoccupied him, and continued to preoccupy him, for several years: some of these ideas seem to have influenced the Poor Law eventually enacted in 1598. Bentlowe was also a poet and playwright, and in 1589 his masterpiece *The Virgin King*, which in some respects rivals, or even outdistances, Shakespeare, was produced for the first time. Yet he died an obscure death in a tavern brawl in 1595. Some clues to his dramatic rise and fall may lie in his private life: he was attacked as licentious and ungodly and there is evidence that he was both a heavy drinker and a rake.

C is obviously the best of these three passages: it is clear, orderly, and it reads smoothly. B is not so good, though it is preferable to A which is very bad as a piece of communication. From a close look at C it will be noted that even in so short a piece of historical writing as this it is practically impossible (and probably not desirable) simply to recount information in a completely neutral way. The phrase 'some clues . . . may lie in his private life' is a cautious one, but it does show the introduction of an element of *interpretation*.

All writing, even of quite short pieces, presents problems. In their important work, *The Modern Researcher* Jacques Barzun and Henry F. Graff make some pertinent comments on the necessity for *form* and orderliness in writing:

Facts and ideas in disorder cannot be conveyed to another's mind without loss and are hardly likely to carry much meaning even for the possessor. This is because the mind is so constituted that it demands a minimum of regularity and symmetry, even in the arrangement of toilet articles on top of a bureau.

In written matter, Barzun and Graff continue, 'the most frequent and visible failure of *form* is that which comes from wrong emphasis':

> Organisation distributes emphasis in the right places. The mind cannot give equal attention to every part; it must be guided to those parts – of a sentence or a book – which it should attend to for a correct understanding.[1]

Such advice, perhaps, is more relevant to the undergraduate student than to the Ph.D. writer or professional historian. My Sir Christopher Bentlowe was an invention. Barzun and Graff quote a passage from a real book (*History of the Elizabethan Stage* by E. K. Chambers) in order to show what a piece of writing lacking in form reads like. Again you the reader might like to comment yourself on what is wrong with this passage and (if particularly enthusiastic and energetic) make an attempt at re-writing it in a more satisfactory way.

> The great spectacles of [Elizabeth's] reign were liturgies, undertaken by her gallants, or by the nobles whose country houses she visited in the course of her annual progresses. The most famous of all, the 'Princely Pleasure of Kenilworth' in 1575, was at the expense of Dudley, to whom the ancient royal castle had long been alienated. Gradually, no doubt, the financial stringency was relaxed. Camden notes a growing tendency to luxury about 1574; others trace the change to the coming of the Duke of Alençon in 1581. Elizabeth had found the way to evoke a national spirit, and at the same time to fill her coffers, by the encouragement of piratical enterprise, and the sumptuous entertainments prepared for the welcome of Monsieur were paid for out of the spoils brought back by Drake in the *Golden Hind*. The Alençon negotiations, whether seriously intended or not, represent Elizabeth's last dalliance with the idea of matrimony. They gave way to that historical part of unapproachable virginity, whereby an elderly Cynthia, without complete loss of dignity, was enabled to the end to maintain a sentimental claim upon the attentions, and the purses of her youthful servants. The strenuous years, which led up to the final triumph over the Armada in 1588, spared but little room for revels and for progresses. They left Elizabeth an old woman. But with the removal of the strain, the spirit of gaiety awoke.[2]

What is wrong with this passage is that it is totally disorganised. Facts and ideas tumble out in a very disorderly way. Thus although it obviously contains a good deal of valuable information, that information is almost impossible to grasp since the presentation is so bad. Clearly the author has done what writers of all levels of experience are sometimes tempted to do, that is to say simply serve up their notes as they stand, without any attempt to organise them in a manner which will communicate successfully with readers.

Here now is the passage re-written:

As rich men in classical Athens paid for the tragedies and comedies, so the great spectacles of Elizabeth's reign were paid for by her gallants, or by the nobles whose country houses she visited in the course of her annual progresses. The most famous spectacle of all, the 'Princely Pleasure of Kenilworth' in 1575, was provided by Dudley, who had long had possession of the ancient royal castle of Kenilworth. Although depending at first on the pockets of her nobles, Elizabeth gradually began to spend money more freely herself, especially as she found that the encouragement of piratical enterprise not only evoked a national spirit, but also filled her coffers. While Camden [a contemporary writer and historian] notes a growing tendency to luxury about 1574, others have traced it to the coming of the Duke of Alençon in 1581; certainly the sumptuous entertainments prepared for the welcome of Monsieur were paid for out of the spoils brought back by Drake in the *Golden Hind*. However the Alençon negotiations, whether seriously intended or not, represent Elizabeth's last dalliance with the idea of matrimony. Thereafter she assumed the part of unapproachable virginity which enabled her, as an elderly Cynthia, [This is a somewhat pedantic classical allusion, not altogether unexpected in someone who is writing about Renaissance theatre] to maintain a sentimental claim upon the attentions, and the purses, of her youthful servants, without complete loss of dignity. At the same time these later years, which led up to the final triumph over the Armada in 1588, were too strenuous to leave much room for revels and for progresses. Elizabeth was an old woman by the time they were over; yet now with the removal of the strain, the spirit of gaiety could break out in full flood.

Re-writing the passage is not nearly as easy as saying what is wrong with it. The secret (as with all writing) is breaking the material down into separate single ideas. Though one cannot be absolutely sure, through the obscure haze of the passage, just what exactly was in the author's mind, it seems to contain at least twelve separate ideas. In many cases Chambers has: (1) run separate ideas together in one phrase; (2) failed to distribute the correct emphasis between important ideas and less important ones; and (3) failed to establish a logical sequence between different ideas showing the manner in which they are related to each other. Apart from his failings in *form*, Chambers uses obscure words ('liturgies') and vague, elaborate phrases ('financial stringency') which serve to hide his meaning rather than clarify it.

In the revised passage the first sentence is allowed to stand, save for the obscure word 'liturgy'. Liturgy is a technical term from ancient Greece meaning 'a public service undertaken by private citizens at their own expense'. It referred, among other things, to financing the great tragedies and comedies. Chambers means (1) that the spectacles were paid for by private individuals (2) that the Elizabethan Age was comparable to the Great Age of Athens. The next sentence, apart from slight rephrasing of possible obscurities is allowed to stand. There is a main idea: (3) that the most famous spectacle was provided by Dudley at Kenilworth; and a minor one (4) (almost an aside in fact) that the former royal castle at Kenilworth had long been in the hands of Dudley. The next sentence has been drastically altered. In the original the idea about financial stringency being relaxed (5) seems to be incomplete and isolated. In the revised version it is related back to idea (1) and linked with idea (6) (which comes in rather later in the original) which explains how, through encouraging piracy, Elizabeth was herself able to afford more lavish spectacles. The next idea (7) concerns the two different views as to when the new tendency to lavish expenditure began: in the revised version the use of 'while' introduces the idea of two different views; in the original they are simply set down bluntly without any attempt to fit them in with the rest of the passage. In the revised version we then proceed, without starting a new sentence, to link the luxurious spectacle provided for Alençon with piracy (in this case Drake and the *Golden Hind*) already mentioned (this is 8)). In the original it comes in rather clumsily, the second reference to the Duke (Monsieur) being separated from the first by a rather different general idea (6) about piracy.

The sentence which follows is practically unchanged save for the addition of the very helpful 'however', which softens the transition from the previous idea, and brings out that having raised the question of luxury we are now turning back to something different, because (9) this is Elizabeth's 'last dalliance'. The idea (10) of Elizabeth's new part, 'unapproachable virginity' is slightly rephrased in order to keep the flow going. For we now move to the idea (also rephrased for the same reason) that we are back again to a period unfavourable to revels and progresses (11). The final idea (12), badly expressed in two separate disjointed sentences in the original, is that although Elizabeth herself is now an old woman, gaiety could again break out: we have already been talking of luxury (and by implication, gaiety) earlier in the reign so the phrase about how 'the spirit of gaiety awoke' (implying that it now appeared *for the first time*) is confusing; the point, apparently, is that it is bigger and better gaiety than before, gaiety 'in full flood'.

However, that is only the start; the writing of history presents certain important problems of its own, many of which are encountered at every level of historical writing. Because of the intense richness and complexity of historical experience, the problem of selection is a particularly acute one. Information provided for the sake of information is not really information at all: the writer must be aware of its significance and make that significance clear to the reader. The phrase 'it is important to note that . . .' is often a warning that the writer has a piece of information which he feels he'd better set down, but about the importance of which he is not really at all clear. As Kitson Clark has remarked: 'One of the earliest and most painful lessons which a young researcher must master is that much that he has discovered with difficulty, and with some exaltation, will prove in due course to be of no significance and of no imaginable interest, and in the end will have to be left out.'[3]

2. Narrative, Description, Analysis, Explanation, Rhetoric and Structure

Good historical writing should present a balance between narrative and analysis, between a chronological approach and an approach by topic, and, it should be added, a balance between both of these, and, as necessary, passages of pure *description* ('setting the scene', providing routine but essential information, conveying the texture of life in any particular age and environment). When S. R. Gardiner wrote his massive seventeenth-century *History*, he composed it year-by-year, completing his study of one year before he would even allow himself to turn to the documents he had amassed for the study of the succeeding year. Thucydides and the other ancients never departed from the strictly chronological approach. Diplomatic and political historians may sometimes find the purely chronological method the most satisfactory one. On the whole, however, it can be said that any historical writer, whether at the undergraduate or the highest professional level, who reduced his subject entirely to chronological narrative would incure the risk of being accused of intellectual naïvety – though it is too easily forgotten that the establishment of the sheer chronology of events can in itself be a difficult task. However, generally speaking, straight narrative is the easiest form of historical writing, though often a very inadequate one. Its fault, say Barzun and Graff is

> that it mixes events great and small without due subordination, and that it combines into a parody of life incidents that occur only once with permanent truths about habits and tastes, character and belief.[4]

On the other hand it *may* be possible (contrary to the views of Barzun and Graff) to produce an excellent historical study based entirely on analysis by topic: Namier did this in his studies of the structure of eighteenth-century politics (though, in terms of his original intentions, they *were* incomplete). Undoubtedly there is a danger in the purely analytical approach, for it may easily forfeit the important element of change through time. Furthermore an analytical study spread over too long a period may seriously distort the past as it actually happened if it treats on the same footing material culled throughout the period on topics which may have been undergoing significant change, as, for instance, might happen in a book covering the three hundred years from 1500 to 1800 which allocated one analytical chapter to each of 'the merchants', 'Puritan attitudes', 'the constitution', and 'the price of corn', and treated each one as if fixed in time. In general, therefore, the writer of history will usually strive for the combination of narrative and analysis which best conforms to the requirements of his subject and to the requirements of form.

One method, useful, if not always very elegant, is to alternate chunks of narrative with chunks of analysis: by and large this was

the pattern of the older volumes of the *Oxford History of England*.
Another effective technique involves breaking the entire chronological period of study into a number of sub-periods, chosen, not
arbitrarily, but on the basis of some logic of historical development
perceived by the historian in the course of his inquiry: then, within
each sub-period the material is analysed topic by topic, one topic
possibly being given primacy in one sub-period, while perhaps
a completely new topic is introduced in a different sub-period.
Christopher Hill's study of the seventeenth century, *The Century
of Revolution* (1961), is a good example of this method at its most
straightforward. The separate sub-periods taken are 1603–40,
1640–60, 1660–88 and 1688–1714: within each sub-period he
discusses in turn 'Economics', 'Politics and the Constitution' and
'Religious Ideas'. An effective compromise which keeps up the
narrative flow throughout the book is that adopted by Asa Briggs
in his study of Britain in the period 1780–1867, *The Age of
Improvement* (1958), where the material is grouped round a
succession of key concepts which form the chapter headings, with
a flexible range of sub-sections within chapters allowing for a
balance between narration and analysis. An early chapter, for
instance, is fixed on 'The Impact of [the French Revolutionary]
War'; there are two later ones which in fact cover the same
chronological period, the 1830s and 1840s, first from the aspect
of guided political change – 'Reform' – then from the aspect of
the nature of society at the time – 'Social Cleavage'. Denys Hay's
Europe in the Fourteenth and Fifteenth Centuries (1966) adopts a
tripartite design: the early chapters display and analyse the main
social groups; the long middle section carries the narrative forward
by outlining the main changes in political life; finally thematic
unity, which political narrative always threatens to tear apart, is
restored through a survey of the main unifying forces, religious,
cultural and commercial.

These, however, are examples of very high level textbooks
(incorporating much of the author's own research, certainly, but
covering periods of history which have already been thoroughly
charted). The problems of organisation and structure (always
serious) become particularly intense where the historian has been
involved in very detailed research in a new area of investigation.
The categories and headings, the balance between topics, analysis,
and the necessary sense of change through time, will only emerge

as the research progresses, and only then if the historian reflects long and hard upon the discoveries that have been made. I can still recall (quarter of a century later) how, having completed drafts of the first six of the eight projected chapters of my study of the effects of the First World War on British society (a relatively unexamined topic in the early 1960s) I came to a point of complete collapse in agony and despair because my attempt to distinguish both the main areas of society which were affected by the war, and to distinguish between the different chronological phases of the war (the first eight months or so; 1915/16; 1917/18; and then, of course, the aftermath) simply did not fit together coherently and persuasively (that is how it goes: one must at some stage settle on chapter headings; one must then get on and write the chapters, without at that stage being really sure that one chapter will logically lead on to the next). Then came the revelation: I needed to take much of the material out of Chapters 5 and 6, where increasingly it did not relate to any structure, reorganise it, and put it into a completely new Chapter 4 – so that eventually the book had nine chapters not eight. My next book of any significance, commenced a decade later, endeavoured to develop a non-Marxist approach to class which would pin down class as actually perceived *and* experienced by people in contemporary British, French and American society (since 1930 that is), and would establish the significance of class in, say, political behaviour, and as against such other sources of inequality as race and sex. Here the categories I used were only hammered into final shape after very many papers had been given, and attacked, at very many seminars. The first draft of the book, as I still recall with a shudder, was quite unspeakably awful. In the end the problems resolved themselves by forcing me to consider at every step what exactly I was trying to say and trying to say it clearly and straightforwardly (in place of the half-baked verbiage which concealed, or rather failed to conceal, uncompleted thought processes), making sure that every controversial utterance could be supported (or, alternatively, was simply dropped), and adding a good deal of additional linking material making the stages of my argument fully explicit. I know that colleagues who have written more important books go through the same agonies; I personalise because that is the simplest way for me to make points of universal validity.

A piece of historical writing which simply makes available new information is not to be scoffed at (given the intractability of historical sources new information is often won only through sweat and tears, if not actually blood), but in a substantial historical work one rightly looks for analysis and explanation. On the one hand we have the Furets and the Toshes, insisting that the hypothesis must be painstakingly spelled out, on the other the historian as artist, captivating the reader with the brilliance of his rhetoric, his mastery of metaphor and paradox. A plague on both their houses has been my motto, though a more rotten and debilitating one upon the latter. Historians will bring to their writings certain ideas about the way things were likely to happen (and unlikely to happen) in their chosen areas of study, and certain ideas about how to communicate these 'happenings' in a manner which both satisfies the demands of form and yet does not do intolerable violence to the complexities of the subject. The English historian and disciple of Namier, Richard Pares once defined history as 'a series of bright ideas'.[5] This could be a dangerous endorsement of the rhetorical approach to historical writing, but in fact there is all the difference in the world between vividly expressed insights based on thorough research and long reflection and those witty aphorisms and coruscating generalisations which are all effect and no substance. One of the results of the amateur tradition in British and American universities is that students are too often given high praise for wit and verbal felicity even when these gifts are unsupported by powers of serious historical analysis.

Practised historians learn to avoid the naïvety of monocausal explanation, of *post hoc, ergo propter hoc*, or of indiscriminately listing a haphazard series of 'causal factors'. One should treat with caution the kind of historical writing which argues that because somebody recommended a certain course of action centuries or decades before the course of action was actually taken, that person automatically becomes a 'cause' of the course of action: thus Wycliffe, without further thought, is a 'cause' of the English Reformation. Much bad so-called intellectual history is still written along the lines of 'so-and-so said it first, therefore he must be important', though the actual implementers of the Act, Revolution, or whatever it is that is being 'explained', may quite probably never even have heard of so-and-so. 'Ball-of-string' history of this sort is the easiest history to write. Lucien Febvre who spoke of the 'multiplicity of profound causes', defined the three variables in historical causation as contingency, necessity and idea. Richard Pares thought there must be at least four or five independent variables: climate, war, religion, technology and science, and the 'conditions of production'.[6] But it is questionable if we are here dealing with ultimate, autonomous variables, or indeed with variables of equivalent philosophical status. Rather than seeking ultimate variables, one is probably better off with certain simple analytical distinctions. There is the distinction between long-term trends, and immediate short-term causes. Long-term trends may be divided into the material, or structural (economic, industrial, and technological) and ideal or ideological. But these are not ultimate distinctions: technological innovations, and indeed important economic decisions, may result from new ideas developed in the minds of individuals or groups; ideas may be prompted by changing material circumstances. Short-term causes may take the form of political decisions (but these may be the results of longer-term ideological developments), or such particular occurrences as wars or revolutions (but these again will have longer-term causes).

The problems of how things happen are often crystallised into arguments over the significance of individual action, contingency, or accident. In a very profound sense, what happens is the consequence of the actions of individuals. But there is nearly always a multiplicity of individual actions which, interacting together, produce consequences which no single individual willed. It is very difficult to define what exactly is sheer contingency, even more difficult, what is sheer accident'. Where communities or states are ruled by absolute or powerful individuals, much significance will attach to the actions and decisions of such individuals. Where such an individual is drowned in an accident at sea, or succumbs to some disease, these can be termed accidents, and they may have quite important consequences. But many contingencies or accidents fit into longer-term trends. The assassination of the Archduke Franz Ferdinand was important as the occasion which brought to crisis point other forces making for a warlike situation in 1914. Insofar as the assassination was an action of Serbian nationalism against the Austro-Hungarian empire it was in that sense not a pure accident in the manner of someone being drowned at sea, or falling under a bus. A natural calamity, such as a flood or an earthquake, can reasonably be accounted an 'accident'. But when it comes to wars, revolutions, invasions, we have more complex circumstances which are themselves related to longer-term trends. It is, nevertheless, reasonable to make a distinction between longer-term trends operating without manifest violence or disruption, and the more violent and disruptive events which may produce separate consequences of their own. Much depends on the perspective. If one takes a short period of time, individual actions or particular events, may have quite profound effects within the lifetime of one or several generations. If one takes the perspective of centuries, then individuals, accidents, and events may not be so significant.

Such considerations will be involved in the written history which historians produce. Every now and then they will be distilled into such suggestions as that of Herbert Butterfield in his *Origins of Modern Science* that the development of modern science was inspired by the *idea* that natural phenomena were not unpredictable (though it is quite possible that this idea, part of what some historians might refer to as the 'Renaissance mentality', and what followers of Max Weber would call the process of *Entzauberung* ('demagification') was in turn inspired by material changes in conditions of production). As the reader will have come to expect, I offer no universal generalisations about structures of explanation. I do believe that systematic, informed investigation of past problems and past developments may, source material permitting, reveal coherent structures. I commend the discussion in Michael Stanford's *The Nature of Historical Knowledge*, based on a simple dictionary definition of structure as: 'The mutual relation of the constituent parts or elements of a whole as determining its peculiar nature or character.'[7] I will simply repeat that the structural relationships revealed will depend on the period, topic, society, or societies studied, and will not have universal validity.

More basic is the distinction between genuine explanation and psuedo-explanation by mere cataloguing of miscellaneous influences and consequences, or by metaphor. To say that relationships between men and women are always represented by a double helix, with women always coming out in the disadvantaged position,[8] may be a striking summary of what actually happens, but it is not in any sense an explanation. To say that a certain war acted as a *catalyst* for social reform, or *accelerated* improve-

ments in the conditions of the lower orders may be excellent
metaphorical descriptions (borrowed from the chemical and
physical sciences respectively) of what actually happened, but they
do not explain *why* they happened. Consider this passage from a
widely used textbook of twentieth-century American history:

> As for the war, it had raised the living standard of factory workers and
> built a powerful labor movement; it had created great shifts in popu-
> lation and accompanying tensions. It had given a temporary bonanza
> to the farmer, stepped up mechanization of agriculture, and brought
> the plow to tens of thousands of acres of semi-arid prairie grasslands.
> Much of this transformation had been painful, and led to further
> difficult adjustments in the twenties. War also had changed styles and
> fashions, and molded consumer demands into new channels. In little
> ways (such as in the introduction of wrist watches for men, shorter
> skirts for women, and cigarettes for both) and in major ways that
> involved basic shifts in the economy, it was changing the pattern of
> life for most Americans.[9]

This is a splendid summary of changes which took place over the
period of the First World War, but, of course, it does not in
any way explain why the war should have brought such changes:
although as narrative it penetrates below the mere surface flow
of events, it is nonetheless narrative, innocent of analytical or
explanatory power.

'Bright ideas' can sometimes be an effective means of historical
explanation, both of *why* something came about, and of *what*
something was. An example of the first is the notion developed
in A. V. Dicey's *Law and Opinion in England* (1902) of the *fait
accompli*, that is to say the notion that once something is done
by a government, however little advance support there may have
been for the action, it will generally gain the approval of the
populace at large as a *fait accompli*; opinion research conducted
more recently by political scientists has provided empirical validation for this 'bright idea'. Marc Bloch developed the fertile
notion that the traditionalism inherent in peasant societies was
basically due to the manner in which young children were mainly
in the company of their grandparents, since working conditions
kept their mothers and fathers out most of the day. An example
of the second sort of bright idea, explaining *what* something was,
is Maitland's brilliant elucidation of the meaning of *sake* in the
medieval phrase *sake and soke*: though the word has practically
gone out of existence, it still appears in what must be its medieval

sense, as Maitland pointed out, in the phrase 'for my sake'. Bright ideas in another form often spring from the historian's function as communicator, from his search for form at its most economical and elegant, and from his desire to arrest attention for a particularly important point. The test to be applied here is whether the bright idea is designed purely for literary effect, or whether it throws genuine light on a genuine problem. Sometimes the attempt at elegance, the effort to arrest attention, collapses into the same meaninglessness which tends to afflict the cautious historical writer who seeks never to give a precise evaluation of anything, never to give one thought preponderance over another, never indeed, to have any thoughts at all. A metaphor, intelligently and aptly used, can be a great aid to communication and understanding. But equally metaphors can be used to conceal meaning, or lack of it. Here is a quotation within a quotation where it is hard to say which is feebler, the absurd metaphor or the would-be balanced, though in fact meaningless, assessment of it (*what* exactly is 'exaggerated', and how much is a 'modicum'?)

'All the cards in the hand of her [France's] post-liberation destiny', says . . . (Mr R. Mathews in *The Death of the Fourth Republic*) 'had been dealt by April 1945; it only remained for time to play them.' Such a view, though exaggerated, does contain a modicum of truth.[10]

When the reader encounters a torrent of tortured metaphors he may well suspect that the historian himself no longer quite knows what he is talking about. The protracted metaphor is usually to be distrusted: the causes of a war may, if the writer has a liking for particularly hackneyed metaphors, be equated with a long fuse leading to a powder keg, or to runaway trains set on collision course, but it will be unwise to force every single circumstance or development to fit the metaphor. Regrettably, historical discourse, as the writer tires or coasts unthinkingly across seemingly familiar territory (I am being charitable), is readily invaded by the deadly virus of dead metaphor: spectrum of opinion, climate of ideas, tool of analysis, frontiers of knowledge, spectre of defeat, etc., etc. Worst of all, in my view, is the routine use of 'dramatic' which presumably ought to mean something like 'with the force and emotion of a drama': never a rise in prices, nor a fall in stocks, never a religious revival nor a political recovery, but each must be 'dramatic'.

My little homilies apply to historical writing at all levels: under-graduate essays, Ph.D. dissertations, the various products of the professional historians. But the really taxing problems, it seems to me, emerge in the larger scale research-based book. The characteristic product of the professional historian is the learned article. Historians also produce editions of texts, collections of documents, collections of essays. All call for many skills. But historical talent at its highest is deployed in the substantial work of original scholarship which, at its best, should be comprehensive and coherent, persuasively structured, and yet reflective of the contradictions and ambiguities within human behaviour. In the hope of conveying some sense of what I mean I am going to look in some detail at a highly professional work, by a hitherto unknown historian, which happened to be published as I was about to start the writing of this chapter.

Ruth Richardson's *Death, Dissection and the Destitute* (1988) sought to resolve a number of problems. Working on Mary Shelley's *Frankenstein* she had become interested in the eminently non-fictional Burke and Hare, infamous grave robbers and murderers. The standard medical histories told her that body snatching (to provide bodies for anatomical study) came suddenly to an end in 1832, which seemed surprising, particularly when no clear reasons were given. At the same time, at another, and perhaps deeper level of interest, Richardson was very aware of the deep fear which the poor had had all through the nineteenth century and well into the twentieth century, of dying in a poor house, and in the obsession to be found among all members of the working class with having a proper funeral. She became preoccupied with the status in popular culture of the newly dead corpse, and with popular attitudes towards it. Wider issues which seemed worth further exploration related to the development of medical science, and to the reordering of society in the early nineteenth century along utilitarian lines. She quickly became aware that the Anatomy Act of 1832, though touched on occasion-ally by other writers, had never been systematically studied.

The Anatomy Act was passed during the crisis over the 'Great Reform Bill' of 1832, and within the longer period of 'utilitarian reform' whose most famous (or notorious) achievement was the Poor Law Amendment Act of 1834. The Anatomy Act made it lawful for the corpses of those whose bodies were unclaimed at death, and particularly those who had been living 'at public expense' in hospitals (or, subsequently, in the new Poor Houses established by the 1834 Act) to be handed over for medical dissection. Already one or two advanced figures among the richer classes had, in the interests of medical science, bequeathed their bodies for this purpose; but among rich and poor alike there was a general horror of the whole idea. The Act made sure that the horror would fall exclusively on the poor. In the years before the Act, the legal supply of corpses for dissection had come from the hangman: for murderers dissection was an explicit part of the sentence, deliberately designed to terrorise the criminal. The new Anatomy Act, which was deliberately wrapped in ambiguity and deceit, the better to prevent the poor from claiming the corpses of their relatives or friends, became part of nineteenth century bureaucracy: its scarifying effects on the destitute endured well into the twentieth century.

At first sight, the structure of Dr Richardson's study (on which she spent ten years) seems very simple; but then the best structures, once the author has worked them out, usually do *appear* simple. The centrepiece of the book is the Act itself, but Richardson had both to explain how it came about, in relation (a) to medical history and (b) to the politics of the time, and to explain why, when it came, it had such enormous significance for the poor. She had also to analyse how, within the Victorian bureaucracy, the Act actually operated, and to work out the detail of its impact right into the twentieth century. Thus, the book is divided into three parts, the most important being the middle one entitled 'the Act'. The first part is entitled 'The Body', and in three separate chapters sets up three analytical, and to some extent chronological, themes. First, there is a study of 'the corpse and popular culture', which establishes a long historical perspective, and, making effective use, in particular, of the studies of contemporary folklorists, brings out the reverential treatment accorded to the corpse which was believed to have some kind of life still in it immediately after death. The second chapter moves into the realm of medical history, analysing how medical men had to combat popular sentiment in trying to achieve a sense of scientific detachment towards the corpse. The third chapter is entitled 'The Corpse as a Commodity' and traces the way in which, as the growth of medical schools raised the demand for corpses, the supply from hanged felons proved insufficient, and a trade in corpses, usually stolen from graves, grew up.

Part Two is a brilliant weaving together of topics and detailed chronology. In Chapter IV, 'The Sanctity of the Grave Asserted' the three themes of Part One are most effectively built upon to explain the immediate context, in the 1820s, for the arguments and discussions leading to the Act. Chapter V is as good an example of technical source criticism as could be found anywhere, concentrating in particular on the Proceedings and Report of the Parliamentary Select Committee appointed in the spring of 1828 to examine the problem, and on the ancillary documentation; a persuasive and lucid analysis justifies the chapter title, 'Foregone Conclusions'. There then follows a complete change of pace and content, perfectly integrated, however, into the overall analysis. It was soon after the Select Committee reported, that the Burke and Hare murders reached their climax, the full story becoming known in February 1829. Chapter VI 'Trading Assassins' is an exciting piece of narrative which at the same time relates the sordid events to the broader themes and to the political manoeuvres leading to the Anatomy Bill itself. Chapter VII discusses alternative means which might have been employed to secure the necessary anatomical specimens, while at the same time demonstrating the interaction between agitation over parliamentary reform and the shaping of the second Anatomy Bill (the first having been withdrawn): the Bill in its final form, Richardson explains, was a product of fear of, and contempt for, the poor. Chapter VIII follows through in detail to the actual enactment of the Act on 1st August 1832.

Part Three is a most impressive attempt, on the basis of particularly fragmentary and intractable evidence, to analyse the effects the Act had on the poor and, in particular, their fear of dying in the workhouse. Chapter IX brings out forcefully the supreme, and apparently deliberate, cruelties of the Act, both for friends and relatives not in a financial position to 'claim' the body as the law required, and for the dead persons themselves, who were well aware in advance of the fate that awaited their corpses. Chapter X 'The Bureaucrat's Bad Dream' details a story of 'opposition, riot, shortage, maldistribution, speculation, disinterment and noninterment of corpses, indecency, misconduct, collusion, corruption.' The final chapter, coming up to and after the advent of the Welfare State drives home the theme of dissection as punishment for 'the unpardonable offence' of destitution, and explains both the terror inspired by the Act and the fact that hitherto it has been almost completely ignored by historians: 'over the course of Victoria's reign, the fact that the misfortune of poverty could qualify a person for dismemberment after death became too intensely painful for contemplation; became taboo. The memory went underground of a fate literally unspeakable.'

Here there is only space for one further brief analysis of how a substantial monograph is organised or structured (though at the very end of the chapter I shall try to bring my entire analysis of the writing of history together by discussing James J. Sheehan's *German Liberalism in the Nineteenth Century* (1978)). Eugen Weber was stimulated to write his massive *Peasants into Frenchmen: The Modernisation of Rural France 1870–1914* (1976) by re-discovering literary and folklorist sources indicating that French peasants, even in the second half of the nineteenth century, belonged to distinctive local communities, rather than to one unified nation. Weber's book has a tripartite structure (three is *not* a magical number, the books by Hill, Briggs, and Sheehan, depending upon the demands of periodisation, have more sections). Part I 'The Way Things Were', uses material going back to the early nineteenth century, and overlapping into the 1890s: it discusses such topics as 'Languages', the 'Working of the Land', and 'The Family'. Part II identifies 'The Agencies of Change', including economic forces, in which Weber includes the building of roads, military service, and schooling (both of these are stressed by Weber as agencies fostering a sense of nationhood). Part III, 'Change and Assimilation' examines the effects of the agencies of change on the old society by looking at such topics as 'Feasts', 'Markets and Fairs', reading matter, etc.

I hope these examples make clear how the historian, from the knowledge derived from both primary and secondary sources, establishes categories and creates a structure which will link arguments together into a logical and persuasive whole, yet will not distort the subtleties and contradictions inherent in the subject matter. Of course as research proceeds and, perhaps even more important as the actual writing and revisions of the writing take place, the structure will almost certainly be modified. What I am at pains to stress is that the development of a structure to underpin a substantial piece of original historical scholarship is one of the most important and difficult tasks of the historian, and one by which, at the highest level, historians should be judged. There are many other ways of getting into print and simple textbooks, or collections of essays, all have their important uses: but as history, they are essentially in a lesser category than the substantial unified work of original scholarship.

3. Quotations and Scholarly Apparatus

Because of the relationship between 'history', 'the past', and 'sources' almost every piece of historical writing will contain direct quotations from source material. According to Barzun and Graff, in their advice to young researchers, quotations 'must as far as possible be merged into the text'.[11] Insofar as they are speaking of quotations from *secondary* works this is quite sound advice. There are few more tiresome, or less persuasive, confections than assemblages of direct quotations from other writers. With regard to primary sources it is broadly true, as Barzun and Graff say with all the force of the italics at their disposal, that *'quotations are illustrations not proofs'*;[12] yet, given the special difficulties of 'proof' in historical study, this is by no means always so. Quite often the whole burden of a particular phase of a historian's argument depends upon the text of a new document which he or she has discovered, or upon a new significance which he or she has seen in certain sentences in a well-known document. In such cases the quotations must be given a distinctive prominence, usually through indentation and separate type (if the quotation is more than a phrase or two), otherwise by placing them in inverted commas: the last thing the historian wants to do is to merge this vital material with his or her own commentary (of course, the historian has selected the quotation in the first place, but at least by setting it out clearly he or she does enter into a dialogue with the reader – nothing irritates more than those over-confident historians of an earlier generation who wrote their books as, in essence, a paraphrase of what they conceived to be the basic documents for their topic, 'merging' reliable authorities, dubious authorities, and their own errors and prejudices into one undifferentiated whole). Frequently, furthermore, an unadulterated direct quotation from a contemporary source can be a most effective and economical means of conveying a sense of period, a sense of understanding from the inside. Even where the quotation is simply illustrative, its illustrative value will stand out all the more clearly for being properly presented.

Still Barzun and Graff do have a point. Clearly a technique of presentation which is necessary in an academic monograph may be much less suitable for other levels of historical writing; and of course it is open to abuse by the writer of an alleged scholarly monograph. There is all the difference in the world between the deliberate full-dress citation of a long quotation for some definite historical purpose, and the mere stringing together of a miscellaneous collection of such quotations in the hope that the end product will pass for a kind of history. When one comes to the undergraduate essay, or the work of historical popularisation drawing exclusively upon secondary authorities, there will usually be little justification for the indented quotation, save perhaps in the case of a particularly striking and important passage with which the writer does not agree but around which he or she wishes to build up an argument, or in the case of a crucial piece of primary material (even if actually procured from a secondary source). On the whole, quotations should be kept to an absolute minimum in both popularisations and undergraduate essays. The opinion that a case is somehow clinched by citing the direct speech of one or two authorities is as erroneous as it seems to be widespread: a silly un-historical judgement is no less silly because it happens to have been once uttered by a once-eminent authority. The writer who embarks upon that dialogue with the reader which I have several times stressed as integral to historical writing must be sure that it is his side of the dialogue that he is expressing and not an assortment of ill-digested and misunderstood items culled from other people. 'Scissors-and-paste' is the contemptuous phrase we rightly apply to a piece of would-be historical writing which in practice amounts to little more than such an assortment.

Undoubtedly one of the most common errors beginning Ph.D students fall into is the over-use of over-long direct quotations. Partly this is because inexperienced researchers, having, perhaps with some effort, discovered some apparently juicy sources, are desperately keen to show them off; partly it is because, quite frankly, it is simpler to copy out and reproduce large chunks of material than to think very carefully about which particular phrases one needs to quote and why. On the whole, while I maintain my general defence of the importance, for clearly identified purposes, of direct quotation, I would agree with Barzun and Graff that what one wants is the shortest piece of quotation compatible with making the point the historian wishes to make – the provisos always being that the quotations are not so brief, so 'out of context' as to be misleading, and that they are sufficiently clearly identified that readers can, if they wish, check the full original. Here in a brief passage about the Jacobite Rebellion of 1715, taken from *Eighteenth-Century England* by Dorothy Marshall, is an excellent example of the incorporation of two brief quotations, one from a song, the other from a diary, into the general argument:

> *There's some say that we wan; and some say that they wan,*
> *And some say that nane wan at a', man:*

> At all events the stalemate continued, so that the Pretender [The Jacobite claimant to the throne] when he finally reached Scotland at the end of the year wrote to Bolingbroke, 'I find things in a prosperous way.' It was wishful thinking based on inadequate knowledge, for by then English preparations had been made for the kill.

G. R. Elton's textbook *England Under the Tudors*, offers a good example of the use of quotation to illustrate and drive home a specific point about what he calls the 'Tudor Revolution in Government'. Elton doesn't simply leave the quotation lying, as it were, inert, but picks up and discusses a key word in it:

> The essential ingredient of the Tudor revolution was the concept of national sovereignty. The philosophy underlying Cromwell's [Thomas Cromwell, the powerful Secretary of State] work was summarised brilliantly in his preamble to the Act of Appeals (1533), the operative clause of which reads as follows:

> 'This realm of England is an Empire, and so hath been accepted in the world, governed by one Supreme Head and King having the dignity and royal estate of the Imperial Crown of the same, unto whom a body politic, compact of all sorts and degrees of people divided in terms and by names of Spirituality and Temporalty, be bounden and owe to bear next to God a natural and humble obedience.'

> The critical term is 'empire', Kings of England had before this claimed to be emperors – the title occurs in Anglo-Saxon times and was taken

by Edward I, Richard II, and Henry V – but the meaning here is
different. Those earlier 'emperors' had so called themselves because
they ruled, or claimed to rule, more than one kingdom, as Edward I
claimed Scotland and Henry V France. In the Act of Appeals, on the
other hand, England by herself is described as an empire, and it is
clear both from the passage cited and from what follows that the word
here denoted a political unit, a self-governing state free from (as they
put it) 'the authority of any foreign potentates'. We call this sort of
thing a sovereign national state.

When readers pick up a book they usually note the name of
the author: even if they don't they have only, should they be
outraged by something in the book, to turn back to the title-page
to detect the perpetrator. When apprised by quotation marks or
indentation that a certain passage is a quotation from some
different source, the reader has an equal right to have that source
identified. Above all where the entire thesis of a scholarly work
is built up on primary materials, these materials, and the sources
for any specific pieces of information whether contained in direct
quotation or referred to indirectly, must be fully identified for
readers so that they have some check on the reliability of what is
being said. The easiest way to provide this necessary identification
of both primary and secondary sources is a note at the foot of the
page, or, less desirably, at the end of the chapter or of the book.
Only fools scoff at the historian's footnotes and references.
Significantly it was the planners of the old *Cambridge Modern
History* (those 'over-confident historians of an earlier generation')
who thought they could do without footnotes – nobody could
doubt *their* experts. We are wiser today: no work which claims
serious scholarly attention deserves that attention unless it is
equipped with the full apparatus of references, provided to enable
readers, if they wish, to participate to the full in their side of the
dialogue, and as a guide to future researchers in the same field.

And here we have the only true rationale for the rules governing
this technical branch of scholarship: references are for use, not
show; and they must be furnished in such a way that they are
genuinely useful. Almost always there is some good reason for
the finicky styles of presentation evolved by scholars: for example,
if it has come to be accepted that a certain source is cited in a
certain way, it is obviously sensible for all researchers to follow
the same practice rather than introduce possibly confusing styles
or abbreviations of their own. From the point of view of detailed

scholarship it is often important to know whether a particular document cited is published or unpublished (that is, manuscript, or perhaps typescript): scholars therefore have adopted the convention of italicising (or underscoring) titles of published materials, while printing titles or citations of unpublished ones in ordinary roman. Agreed conventions enable economies of space in setting out references (hence the various Latin abbreviations, loc. cit., ibid., and so on, which we need not bother with here); but what is essential is that enough information be provided for another researcher without undue difficulty to track down the same reference. It is a *sine qua non* of the scholarly reference that it be honest. This is why some historians insist upon a golden rule that before any work is published all references must be checked. But there is, of course, a difference between the inaccuracy which is human, and wilful dishonesty (also, alas, all too human). If I confess that I do not myself go in for the systematic checking of all my own references, I can add that I have had occasion to regret my own carelessness when endeavouring to follow up and take further some of my own previous researches, finding certain materials much harder to retrace than my own footnotes would suggest. The historian does well to remember that his most dedicated reader may turn out to be himself.

Earlier in this section I mentioned the case of the undergraduate essayist or popular writer citing a piece of primary material which he has in fact taken from a secondary authority; this is a practice which sometimes is forced upon even the most rigorous scholars. What is called for in the appropriate footnote is a statement both of the primary source involved, and of the secondary source where in fact it was found. If the remarks quoted are those of a Foreign Secretary or Ambassador there is little point in citing as the reference: say. 'W. L. Langer, *The Franco-Russian Alliance 1890–1894* (1929), p. 277' – the reader wants to know *which* Foreign Secretary or Ambassador made the remark, and, of course, *where* and *when*; 1929, needed in the full reference, is *not* the *critical* date. But, on the other hand, to blandly give as the reference 'Aerenthal, Austrian First Secretary in St Petersburg to Kàlnoky of the Russian Foreign Office, 10 November 1892' would be to give the dishonest and misleading impression that the dispatch itself (as distinct from Langer's quotation of it) had been studied. The reference required by honesty and common sense would be something along the lines of 'Aerenthal's dispatch . . . etc. . . . as quoted by W. L. Langer . . . etc.'[13] The need for a footnote reference arises in cases other than where a direct quotation has been made. Most of the time historians take from their sources, primary and secondary, not whole phrases for quotation, but single ideas, or single pieces of information, such as a wage rate, a price increase, or a decision made in some court or council; again, obviously, an appropriate reference is called for.

Valuable historical works have been written with much less in the way of scholarly apparatus than the foregoing paragraphs would seem to call for; they remain good books, but to the extent that they irritate the serious reader who asks (as serious readers of any historical work must constantly ask) 'how does he know *that?*' they are less good than they might be. Since scholarly apparatus is there for use, in the end only common sense can determine how elaborate an apparatus any particular piece of writing requires. Where absurdity marches in is when secondary authorities without pretence to original scholarship attempt to masquerade behind the trappings of scholarship. Whatever the level of the book the duty remains upon the author to identify, at the minimum, his direct quotations; but where the full scholarly apparatus is manifestly inappropriate, as for example in this book where I can make no pretence to having thoroughly studied all the works of Ranke, Gibbon, etc., all the issues of *Annales* etc., or every item that pertains to the philosophy of history, it is possible to provide the necessary information within the text and in a few brief references.

From there let us move logically to the question of bibliographies. In the preface to volume three of his *Economic History of Modern Britain* J. H. Clapham went on record against 'What in my heart I regard as the rather pedantic and ostentatious tradition of the formal bibliography in a book which contains footnotes.' Nothing could be more disingenuous: the compilation of a bibliography is certainly a tedious chore and one which, a book finally finished, any author can be excused for shrinking from; but often, sad though the thought may be, it is the single most useful service the author performs. Clapham and his generation rode high in the supreme confidence that if they wrote a book, that book would be read. They were probably wrong even then: Clapham's *magnum opus* is now much more used as a work of reference than read cover to cover. Increasingly in a busy age one 'savours' books, even good ones – reads carefully passages directly relevant to one's own immediate interest, skiffs through the rest. But what one certainly does want is a bibliography (not as a sign of the author's worthiness as a historian, but as an aid to one's own further reading and research), and one does not want to have to scan through the footnotes to compile one – a labour which properly rests with the author. There are few sights more incongruous than the converted Ph.D. dissertation which some publisher has been prevailed upon to bring out with the minimum of alteration save that, in the interests of economy, the one portion that might conceivably be of use to others, the bibliography, has been chopped off. At its best, as with the E. P. Thompson bibliography I discussed at the beginning of the previous chapter, a bibliography is a significant guide to the raw materials on which the work of history is based. I speak here of the scholarly bibliography appended to a work of original scholarship. In a textbook, or general study, it may well be appropriate for the bibliography to take the rather different form of a guide to further reading.

But to get back to the heart of the matter. Any properly conceived piece of historical writing, in its text as well as in its notes, should make possible the genuine engagement of the interested reader, who should always be able to ask, 'how does the author know *that*?', and should always have a basis on which to disagree with the interpretations and conclusions being presented by the author. Good history should be authoritative, but it should never be authoritarian.

4. Monographs, General Histories, Textbooks and Worse

All who endeavour to write history encounter some of the same problems, but obviously there are differences in the level of activity and intellect upon which different writers are operating. Elton has drawn a rigid distinction between 'amateur' historians and 'professional' historians, including in the former category many who undoubtedly make a professional living out of history.[14] Oakeshott has distinguished between 'practical' and 'pure' history,[15] a distinction which, in all conscience, I find quite meaningless (*all* serious history meets a social need; the use of history in the analysis of contemporary problems is not history, though it may, I have suggested, be thought of as 'applied history'). My distinctions apply not to the man or woman, but to their products; I allow for the obvious fact that one historian will often operate in many different ways, sometimes writing a monograph, sometimes a textbook, sometimes appearing on television, sometimes going fishing and merely cogitating on his subject, sometimes going to a football match and boring his companions with irrelevant pseudo-historical comments; sometimes, in short, he is more practical than pure, sometimes most professional in his amateurism, or vice versa. Not that I can claim any special validity for my own categories. 'Dissertation', 'learned article', and 'monograph' are terms with fairly clear and precise meanings. 'General history', however is rather vague. To some people 'textbook' is a term of praise, to others one of scalding abuse: it has no universally accepted meaning as a descriptive category. 'Pop history' is written by historians of impeccable academic distinction, and by journalists of none: sometimes the work of the latter comes much closer to meeting the minimum standards of 'good' history than does the work of the former. The scale I shall work through here is not primarily one of excellence (though, as I have already made clear, the properly structured monograph or the general history incorporating original research seem to me the highest forms of historical achievement), but rather of numbers. I begin with what commands the smallest audience and work outwards.

The first major piece of serious historical research which most would-be members of the historical profession (those who both teach *and* research in history) undertake is in the form of a dissertation directed in the U.K. and the U.S.A. towards the degree of Doctor of Philosophy (curious name, but let it pass), or for one of the major European distinctions (often carrying entitlement to a particular job within the profession), or for some other research degree such as (in the U.K.) the M.Phil. or B.Phil. Within academic circles there is some uncertainty as to whether postgraduate work of this sort is mainly intended as an apprenticeship exercise in the nature and techniques of historical research whose value in that sense may stand high irrespective of the importance of the end product as a 'contribution to knowledge'; or whether it must, in its own right, stand as a genuine and distinctive contribution to knowledge. Over the last thirty years or so opinion has swung strongly towards the latter position with, in the U.K. at least, the tendency being to award the lesser degrees to mere apprenticeship exercises. On the continent of Europe some of the most distinguished work produced in the twentieth century came in the form of the academic dissertation (one thinks at once of Braudel). For a long time there was no special emphasis in Great Britain upon the doctoral degree: many students who embarked upon it preferred to present their early conclusions in the form of learned articles, and their more rounded ones in the form of books, without ever going through the formality of submitting a doctoral dissertation (there is, usually in later life, the possibility of the Doctor of Letters, awarded for *published* work considered to be a significant scholarly contribution to a particular area of studies). Now even in the U.K. the Ph.D. has taken on the status of a union card for the academic profession which it has always had in the U.S.A. (save that, alas, in these terrible times prospects of entry into the academic profession are dismal). The principle in itself, though, is not a bad one: all historians should, at an early stage, wrestle with the problems of producing a substantial, sustained, well-structured piece of work. Dissertations vary enormously, of course; but in general it is expected of candidates that their research be conducted in depth over a very narrow and specific field so that the bulk of their work will be in primary sources, preferably ones that have not been too thoroughly exploited by others. It is expected that they will provide to a full, even exaggerated, degree all the apparatus of scholarship. In Britain it is widely accepted that such criteria necessarily mean that a successful Ph.D. thesis will not automatically be suitable for publication: even though it will be an important contribution to a specific area of knowledge, it will still be too narrow and too technical to interest anyone beyond the narrow band of specialists (perhaps three or four each year) who will wish to consult it in the university library where it rests, or even purchase it on micro-film. In America, however, such is the pressure on the young academic to publish at all costs, and such is the desire of minor university presses to have something to publish, that quite often the narrowest and most unilluminating of dissertations are immediately reborn as books. It is an American scholar who has spoken of 'converted dissertations . . . with their Germanic earnestness and bulk footnotes magnified in book length format'.[16]

When wiser counsels prevail the dissertation will either serve as the basis for one or more learned articles, or its scope will be extended (more research, wider reading) and it will be published as a reputable academic monograph; or both. Many monographs and many articles, of course, originate elsewhere than in a post-graduate dissertation. Sometimes a historian has an idea which he reckons if followed up will yield an interesting article; as his research proceeds he finds he has a full-length monograph on his hands. Sometimes he or she writes a monograph and finds there are certain fragments left over, interesting in themselves, but of a nature to disrupt the thematic unity of the monograph: so these are worked up into learned articles. The essence at any rate of both the learned article and the monograph is that they deal with one single, clearly defined topic, and they are based on all the relevant primary source materials: their contribution to know-ledge, at the least, is that they make available hitherto unknown, or little-studied, pieces of primary source material.

Occasionally a monograph will capture the attention of a wider audience than that normally expected (students and specialists). Most monographs simply add a little more knowledge along lines not inconsistent with those established by previous workers. But from time to time the new material presented in a monograph totally challenges existing knowledge. Scholars who find them-selves in this position may well break through the bounds of the monograph narrowly conceived and write something of more general significance. This is one clue to the form of historical communication which, most imprecisely, I am going to term the 'general history', an academic work, in short, which is neither monograph (because of the width of its range, and the incorpor-ation and synthesis of the work of others) nor textbook (because both more original and less general). Such books will usually have some highly original central idea or organising principles (as distinct from the ordinary textbook which, essentially, will set out to 'cover the ground'). I can't really make sharp distinctions between such books and the ambitious monograph, but most of the works singled out for attention in Chapter 3 fall into this category (the works of Braudel, Thompson, Fischer). The key will usually be one or more central concepts, themselves contri-butions to knowledge as well as organising principles, as, say, in J. H. Plumb's *Growth of Political Stability in England* (1969),

G. R. Elton's *The Tudor Revolution in Government* or R. R. Palmer's *Age of the Democratic Revolution* (two volumes, 1959 and 1964) a work which opened up a new perspective on the events of the late eighteenth century by making a comparative study of the 'democratical' (a contemporary term) revolutions on both sides of the Atlantic seaboard, in the smaller countries as well as the larger. (A similar concept, it should be noted, was put forward by Jacques Godechot in his *Les Révolutions 1770–1779* (Paris, 1963) published in the United States as *France and the Atlantic Revolutions of the Eighteenth Century 1770–1779* (New York, 1963); historians usually speak of the Palmer–Godechot thesis, somewhat under suspicion nowadays it should be admitted, as further research on the French Revolution has cast doubt on broad class categories). Palmer suggested that the 'original concept' for a historical work of this sort 'does and should come from two altogether different kinds of sources – (1) the knowledge that workable bodies of information exist and (2) some general idea'. Palmer's general idea 'held in advance, was that there had been a "revolutionary era" in all these countries, not adequately perceived as a "culture-wide" phenomenon'.[17]

Truly memorable 'general histories' are few and far between; textbooks are legion. The textbook writer is not, in the first instance, set to work by the combination of 'some general idea' and 'the knowledge that workable bodies of information exist', but rather by the belief that there is need among students and those outside immediate professional circles for a clear and relatively simple exposition of the basic elements of some historical period or topic. The book may indeed be commissioned by a publisher who perceives a gap in the market (the inspiration for the true general history will come solely from the historian). Much more overtly than the monograph or general history, the textbook will be geared towards immediate utility. Though laymen may read it, the prime intention will be that it should live out its life within the confines of the educational system, serving children or students at various levels (it is here distinguished from the work of popularisation, which is aimed at the lay audience). Often textbooks are written by expert professional historians of the calibre of a Palmer or an Elton; but some of the most expert textbook writers have written little else (though one might approach them rather cautiously if they had *never* had experience of working in the raw materials of history). Textbook writing is not to be shrugged off as an undemanding occupation: in fact it poses most of the basic problems to be found in all forms of historical writing – selection, form, the balance of narrative and description against analysis. Furthermore, in interpreting works of scholarship to a relatively unsophisticated audience, special skills are required. Much of the dialogue between writer and reader may go into suspension since what the reader is seeking is authoritative guidance. In highly controversial areas the aim should be a balanced view of competing hypotheses. Unfortunately, the balance can deteriorate into a kind of meaningless neutrality: 'President Roosevelt did much to restore confidence, though many were worried by the increase in federal powers.' Thus elements of interpretation and personal synthesis will be required (taking the best textbooks back towards the general history).

One might summarise the criteria by which a history textbook ought to be judged, in the following manner. First, it should be informed by an understanding of what the major authorities have said; where there is unresolved controversy, something of this should be reflected in the book. Secondly, it should be informed by the latest major discoveries by contemporary researchers. Some scholarly matters, obviously, are too technical or too detailed to command space in a textbook; but no textbook should present interpretations which run contrary to the considered opinions of the recognised experts. Finally, even a textbook should carry with it some of the stuff and excitement of history: history, we all know, is not a mere succession of dates, of kings and presidents; nor does it divide neatly into three-paragraph sections, each of equal length and each amenable to some encapsulating title, such as 'The New Monarchy', 'The Age of Transition', 'normalcy', 'Appeasement'.

Textbooks aimed at more junior audiences are something of a different case; their writing involves much greater understanding of educational psychology than most professional historians can pretend to. All one can ask is that school textbooks, still being the main contact which the majority of people have with history, should not do more violence than is absolutely necessary to historical reality as revealed by the best recent academic writers.

Ordinary readers who survive their school textbooks and allow themselves in later life to succumb to the intrinsic fascination of history will probably seek works of more popular character than those discussed so far. But the category 'popular work', or even 'pop history', though distinctive enough, is not absolute. In the past, works of the best-known historians received a wide sale; in the 1960s publishers again became increasingly aware of the marketable quality of history, and certain books of the most unimpeachable academic pedigree have reached best-seller class (one thinks, for instance, of Robert Blake's *Disraeli*, E. P. Thompson's *The Making of the English Working Class* or Leroy Ladurie's *Montaillou*). This is as it should be: one of the historian's functions is that of *communication*, however much embittered academics may scowl upon colleagues whose books sell too well. Most of the old-style pop history, written by journalists or other professional writers, was pretty dreadful; over-dramatised; over-personalised; given to little circumstantial accounts of how a certain person thought at a certain juncture, or how a certain room was decorated, or what conversation took place, when clearly there is not a whit of evidence on which to base such conjectures. Worse, such 'histories' were frequently conceived in the most shapeless of narrative styles, the authors clearly hoping that the absence of anything verging on historical analysis would pass undetected in the colourful accounts of courtships, massacres, murder trials, sexual morals, and the idiosyncrasies of kings and politicians, enlivened by occasional witticisms. Now that academics are increasingly writing for the wider market, the standard of pop history has risen greatly. In a class of her own stands Barbara Tuchman. Although I expressed (p. 94) a professional criticism of the opening of her *The Proud Tower* (1964), which successfully followed the *Zimmerman Telegram* (1959) and *August 1914* (1962), one cannot but praise very highly the way in which she has brought history of a high quality to a wide audience. *A Distant Mirror: The Calamitous Fourteenth Century* (1978) really is a major achievement and the foreword itself, even if it occasionally irritates, is full of interesting thoughts on the problems and purposes of historical enquiry. One of the great pioneers in breaking down the barriers which grew up in the early twentieth century between the professional historian and the lay audience was Alan Nevins, a journalist who rose to the heights of the American academic profession. Such journals as *American Heritage* (in the U.S.A.), *Historia* (in Italy), *L'Histoire* (in France) and *History Today* (in Britain) have been successful in combining popular appeal with a preservation of high academic standards.

The simple point I am making in this section is that a work of history should be judged by what it is setting out to do, by the level it is aiming to operate on. It is as pointless to criticise a Ph.D. thesis for being narrow as it is to expect a work of pop history to present the last word in sophisticated scholarly analysis. One should be suspicious of mere book-making: book-making arises when someone feels that it would be nice to write a book, without having any ideas about, or commitment to, any particular subject, or simply takes on the task as a mechanical job of work; the book in fact might be about anything, and will usually turn out to be the mindless plunder of the labours of others. One would rightly tend to distrust the work of someone who writes a book about the twentieth-century novel one year, and a book about Magna Carta the next. Worst of all are books which have been written purely to entertain or to make money, but which then make pretentious claims to originality and scholarship. Good history can be written by non-academics (that is by journalists, businessmen, etc.), many of whom may at an earlier stage have had a historical training, and many of whom too are happy to turn to the hard slog of historical research. The biggest advantage, probably, that professional historians have comes from living with their subject day in and day out, from teaching it, and from presenting seminar papers to colleagues: they are constantly forced to examine their thoughts, to organise them coherently, to face the pitfalls of historical explanation, to iron out inconsistencies, to eradicate non-explanations, and to appreciate the difference between flowery rhetoric and genuine historical analysis. But as pop history moves from the printed book to the television screen, the professional historians find that their professional expertise must dovetail with that of cameramen, editors and directors. The very plethora (in all countries) of historical programmes on television again demonstrates the social necessity for history. As with the older forms of pop history, such programmes will go on being made whatever the academic historians think of them: on the whole it would seem best for them to accept that they too are a form of history – and an important one – and that it falls well within their province to do what they can to ensure that they are as historical as possible. This is a topic I shall take up again at the end of the next chapter.

5. The Platitudes and Clichés of History: Historical Semantics and Periodisation

In the main, opinion within the historical profession favours the use of everyday language in historical writing. But historians are at all times involved in the use of proper names and classificatory generalisations which are often minefields of confused or hidden meanings. Louis Gottschalk once referred to the ambiguities and implied assumptions contained in such an apparently simple phrase as 'Columbus discovered America on October 12 1492'. A more refined version, which highlights some of the problems, though it does not overcome all of them, is suggested by Gottschalk: 'on a day conveniently labelled "October 12 1492" a group of sailors captained by a man known in English as "Christopher Columbus" landed on an island which was apparently the one [today] called "Watling Island".' The historian's problem, again to quote Gottschalk, is seldom 'the paucity of ready-made labels . . . but rather the accuracy and fittingness of the available ones'.[18] Most of this section will be devoted to 'historical semantics', to the problems of the use and abuse of the labels which the historian does not always know what to do with, but which he knows he cannot do without; abused, as they so often are, these labels become the platitudes and clichés of history.

One of the most usual causes of the historian's difficulties is the manner in which down the ages men go on using the same word for something which is in fact constantly shifting in meaning and significance. 'Revolution' is a classic and well-worn instance. In origin the word apparently derives from the ancient conviction that the revolving spheres of the heavens directly affected the actions of men. According to some authorities, the critical moment when radical political change achieved recognition as a self-conscious political process occurred in fourteenth-century Italy, where frequent upheavals in the towns gave currency to the term *rivoluzione*. This usage, however, was slow in spreading; it appears in English only at the beginning of the seventeenth century, just in time, as it happened, for the 'revolution' of the

1640s. Yet the word could still be used in its literal sense of a return to a previous state of affairs (the wheel coming full circle): the restoration of the monarchy in 1660 was deemed by Clarendon a 'revolution'. Only in the eighteenth century did the word become established, in both Britain and France, in its modern usage.[19] Yet what truly is its modern usage? A significant change in political structure carried through within a fairly short space of time; that might be an acceptable brief definition in that it covers what are universally agreed to be revolutions: the French ones of 1789, 1830 and 1848; the Russian one of 1917; the Mexican one of 1906. But historians, no doubt because of their very proper preoccupation with change through time, are very free in their use of the word, detecting educational revolutions, scientific revolutions, social revolutions, and even historical revolutions. We come to a second problem in the use of classificatory generalisations: most are heavily loaded emotionally. When the historian wishes to make a point forcefully he brings in the word 'revolution'. In this inexact, emotionally loaded usage, of course, historians are only copying the practice of the common man. Marc Bloch ruefully remarked that while the 'reactionaries of 1815 hid their faces in horror at the very name of revolution . . . those of 1940 used it to camouflage their *coup d'état*'.[20] The word had become respectable, even praiseworthy; however, for historians, the best rule is to be as sparing in their use of it as possible.

Much that might otherwise be sadly misunderstood about our ancestors is clarified if it is remembered that 'liberty' once meant privilege; the wealthy supporters of 'Wilkes and Liberty' were much more concerned for their own rights as solid citizens than for 'liberty', in the modern sense, for the masses. 'Democracy' is another word which has gone through many shades of significance. We like now to give it a rather precise meaning: political and social rights for *everyone*. But as used from Greek times onwards it represented a trend, a tendency towards broader-based government, rather than any kind of mathematical formula. To the Greeks, as to Queen Victoria, who once expressed the fear that the country might 'sink down into a democracy', the word had a pejorative quality. A more modern phrase which gives rise to a good deal of historical controversy, much of it essentially centred on the problem of definition, is 'welfare state'. As usual it was the Germans who had a word for it: *Wohlfahrtsstaat* – used to describe the Bismarckian social insurance system of the 1880s. But although the term 'welfare budget' was sometimes applied in Britain to the Lloyd George budget of 1909 (more frequently and more aptly called 'the people's budget'), the phrase 'welfare state' was not used at all in English till the 1930s, when the classical scholar and historian Alfred Zimmern used it to point a contrast with the Nazi Power State. Its first appearance in print came during the Second World War in Archbishop William Temple's *Citizen and Churchman* (1941), and it was in fact the interest in social reform engendered by war which gave the term wide currency. In Britain the term tended to be associated with the 'universalist' principle in social legislation (welfare to everyone, whether rich or poor); on the European continent it was associated with the centralised direction of social policies. However when the word reached the United States in the late 1940s it assumed a much less thoroughgoing connotation (though still used as a term of abuse by the American Right). Some historians, mostly American, have attempted universal definitions for the phrase, but the social historian of the contemporary period, while, as always, interested in interrelations and comparisons, must accept that in practice it means different things in different countries.

The trouble with 'welfare state' is that it is a recent coinage which is still very much on the lips of politicians and publicists, and of many others who have no very clear idea what it means, save that they feel rather strongly about it. At the opposite pole there are labelling-words like 'sake and soke' or 'hide' (a quantity of land) that have gone altogether out of usage. Medieval historians have a good deal of difficulty with words which not only have gone out of existence but, in the process, have moved from one language to another – from, often, dog-Latin to medieval French. How to find a suitable rendering in modern English for a word in medieval French which is really a bad rendering of something originally in Latin is a fine problem. Translation, indeed, is another great source of imprecision in the handling of labelling generalisations. The Latin word *servus* became *serf* in West European usage, and *serf* is the word historians use to describe the unfree peasantry of medieval Europe; since the condition of the Roman *servus* was much different, historians reserve for him the term *slave*, though, as Marc Bloch pointed out, the term which is thereby transplanted into a Roman environment did not come into existence until about the year 1000, when it was used to describe the markets of human flesh where captive Slavs seemed to provide an example of a complete subjection by that time unknown in the West. 'The device', said Bloch, 'is useful, as long as we confine ourselves to extremes. In the intervening gap, where must the slave give way to the serf?' *Serf* is also widely used as a translation of the Russian *krepostnoi*, though 'the so-called Russian serfdom had almost nothing in common with our medieval serfdom'.[21]

A curious double difficulty is embedded in the French word *ouvrier* (which today means workman) and its eighteenth-century English equivalent, manufacturer. At the time of the French Revolution *ouvrier* included what we would now call manufacturers, and manufacturers included what we would now call *ouvriers*: 'The English term has gone up in the world and the French one down.' The same historian[22] points out that '*Sans-culottes* is a political not an economic description: it could include a wealthy brewer . . . and exclude a valet or a footman.' Similar and even more difficult problems arise with the English term *radical*. By derivation the word ought to mean someone who wishes to carry through a reform 'from the roots'; in practice in nineteenth-century Britain it was a description adopted by men who sought reform in the direction of economic liberalism, but who stopped well short of anything which smacked of socialism. However defined, and the definition must vary with the period and groups studied, the term must always refer to a political attitude; it does not define a social group.

'Geographical abstractions' can be a peculiarly confusing type of label. It is hard sometimes to appreciate that the political map which we know, the labels we use, and the boundaries we recognise, had no meaning throughout many centuries in the past. 'Great Britain', the entire island which includes the three separate countries of England, Scotland and Wales, is a term which still gives difficulty, many English nationalists and many foreigners preferring simply to say England; and the adjective 'Great', quite wrongly, is often taken as having imperialistic implications. Coined by the Romans from a native word, 'Britannia' was used throughout the Anglo-Saxon period, the 'Major' ('Great') coming in to point up the distinction from Lesser Britain – Brittany in northern France. The term entered into (more or less) regular modern usage with the proclamation in 1603 of James VI of Scotland as James I of Great Britain. Trickier terms are 'Europe' and 'Christendom': 'There is no doubt', wrote the medieval and Renaissance scholar, Denys Hay, 'that we have had too much *Europe* about our history, too little *Christendom*.' It is true that Christendom as a unifying idea was long in emerging; but prior to its general currency in the tenth century its alternative was not Europe, which did not receive acceptance as the only framework for politics and culture until the seventeenth century. Hay admitted that it might be necessary to talk of 'the history of Europe' in an earlier period:

> A series of books, or a series of lectures has to have a general title, and it is legitimate . . . 'to trace the medieval ancestry of Europe'. But that is what one must do – not treat the modern grouping of countries as the basis of the past. In the eleventh century even fewer men than today concerned themselves about the larger unities; but those who did thought in religious terms, and if we wish to penetrate their world we must do something similar – that it was not religion as we now know it makes the problem all the more difficult and exciting.[23]

The modern mind seeks to impose not only 'geographical abstractions' on the past but abstractions covering entire social systems and entire eras of human activity. 'Feudal' and 'feudalism' are words historians cannot do without; but they were unknown to those who lived under the so-called 'feudal system'. As Bloch explains in *The Historian's Craft*, the words 'were originally legal jargon, taken over from the courts of the eighteenth century by Boulainvilliers, and then by Montesquieu, to become the rather awkward labels for a type of social structure which was itself rather ill-defined'.[24] Labels like 'the Middle Ages' and 'the Renaissance' take us into the confused world of historical periodisation. The idea of a 'Middle Age' between the splendours of classical antiquity and the modern revival of the classical and humanist outlook was actually developed in the period of the Renaissance itself,[25] and was popularised by the historians of the Enlightenment, though it is usually accepted that the terms *ancient, medieval* and *modern* were invented by Pousin of Friège in his book *Feodium*, published in 1639, and advocated by Christopher Cellarius or Keller (1634–1701) of the University of Halle. We need to periodise, that is to say divide the past up into periods defined by some convenient label, because otherwise history would simply be an undifferentiated flow of time, and because (this is very important) over time societies *do* begin to manifest significantly distinctive characteristics. But this convenient habit of historians has many dangers. The past is really continuous; you do not fall asleep in a period called 'the Middle Ages' and wake up the following day to find that you are in 'the Modern World', nor even do you begin your Christmas holiday in mid-Victorian Britain and celebrate New Year's eve in late-Victorian Britain. We must never lull ourselves into thinking of historical periods as having some inherent God-given truth of their own, or of having sharply defined beginnings and endings. Elementary history text-books are often characterised by a very simplistic notion of sharp breaks between different historical periods. A further important consideration is that the classification into ancient, medieval, and modern is valid only for Western civilisation. It takes no account whatsoever of developments in Nigeria, say, or China, or South America; that is to say, it ignores vast and important areas of human experience.

Medieval historians like to point out that the concept of a 'century' as signifying one hundred years has no meaning till after the Renaissance. How far it is justifiable to talk of the 'century of Pericles', 'the art of the thirteenth century' or 'the twelfth-century Renaissance' must therefore be a cause for thought: as with all of these problems one must be explicit and self-aware; labelling concepts are aids to analysis, not inherent truths. The use of centuries to achieve a rough periodisation of the modern era has more solid foundations since the modern mind is itself receptive to the idea that with a new century new ideas and new aspirations are in order. Ideas obviously do not clock forward on a kind of chronometer geared to the changing centuries, and interesting new perspectives have been opened up by historians deliberately seeking to break through long-accepted chronological frames. Yet it would be a rare pedant indeed who would wish to deny all meaning to such a phrase as 'the trouble with British politicians in the 1920s was that they looked at twentieth-century problems through nineteenth-century eyes'. The phrase is a neat summary, of some value provided the historian does not make it an excuse to shirk his proper duties in the matter of elucidation and explanation.

And that is the text for some important reflections. 'The hallmark of the historically minded person', to quote Denys Hay once more, 'is an itch for the concrete, a desire to get behind generalisations to the facts upon which they are based and to establish an almost physical relationship with the texture of earlier times.' Many of the well-worn labels and generalisations, unhappily, stand as barriers between historians and their readers on one side and the past as it actually was on the other. Despite the wit which has been lavished on the demolition of such hoary old standards as 'the rise of the middle classes', it is too soon to say that this locution has now disappeared from the vocabulary of historians and their students. The trick to be used here, and whenever such phrases come to hand, is to switch on the mental television set, to endeavour to visualise the concrete realities entailed in the phrase. Is it an entire class which is 'rising' (becoming wealthier? more influential?) or just certain members of it? Is the result that what was once a 'middle class' now becomes a 'ruling class', or just that it now asserts a right to have more influence than it previously exerted? Middling men in any given age and social structure are of course always going up in the world (and often down), whether as single spies or in battalions. It will not be *the* middle class which is 'rising' (if that *is* what it is doing) throughout the centuries, but *different* middle classes in different centuries. In a brilliant exposure of 'The Vocabulary of Social History' Alfred Cobban cited the example of Langeois, Intendant of Montauban at the beginning of the eighteenth century, who was the son of a Farmer-General and the grandson of a second-hand clothes-dealer of Paris: 'Is this', asked Cobban, 'the rise of the old rag and bone merchants?'[26]

Two other dangers to good historical writing should be mentioned: the high-falutin' phrase, and the non-quantity. The first covers such familiar friends as 'the workers wanted *economic* as well as *political* freedom'; 'there was greater *toleration* of Catholics and dissenters'; 'women achieved *emancipation*'. Old friends certainly, but what do we really know about them? What is an economic freedom, or, for that matter, a political freedom? The phrase may be valid as a heading, but isn't it better to go on and explain in concrete terms (wages, living conditions, etc.) what exactly the workers wanted? If known, that is; if not known, then: historian, beware! What was it like to be a tolerated Catholic? Could one live a completely normal life? or a reasonably contented life if one kept strictly to oneself? or was one in danger of having one's windows broken at regular intervals? What did it mean for a woman to be 'emancipated'? did this condition apply to all women, or only to some of the more conspicuous ones? did it mean having the vote? getting equal pay? going alone into pubs? These are matters of the concrete realities of life which the historian must get at, and should not conceal behind the fine-sounding phrase which is often far feebler as historical communication than the elaborate and even cumbersome explanation which deals in exact facts ('historical facts' most certainly, but a long long way from Carr's 'select club').

The non-quantity occurs when labour unrest is explained to us through the information that the price of corn has gone up to 180s a quarter, but we have no idea how much corn there is in a quarter, what the 'normal' price was, and what this rise meant in terms of the amount of bread which a working-class family could purchase. Scattered throughout our histories we have assessments of the influence of certain books based on the number of copies sold, descriptions of how the population of a town grew to a certain size, estimates of the total number of men involved in a certain riot. Such statistics are meaningless unless we are given something to measure them against: how many copies did such books normally sell? how many people could read, anyway? and so on. The historical writer must encompass the concrete reality: the isolated statistic, the fine-sounding verb, the hackneyed label, and the sweeping generalisation all run through historical prose like the proverbial dose of salts, emptying it of all true sustenance.

Such is the importance of historical semantics (or historical hot potatoes as I sometimes like to call them), and so critical is the question of semantics ('the study of the meaning of words') in all serious discussion, that I want to provide here a summary of the main categories, and a further discussion of some of them. The fundamental point to make is that in all use of language we encounter changes and shifts in meaning. Only the stupid and the bigoted insist that each word must have one meaning and one meaning only, that is the meaning defined by them. What we have to do in serious study is to understand how words shift in meaning, and always be clear which particular meaning is being used at which particular time. Now let me summarise the seven main types of hot potato:

1. Words that did actually exist in the periods of the past about which the historian wishes to write, but which, down through the ages, have changed in meaning. Example: 'radical'.

2. Words that have been invented to describe something in a past age, but *which were actually unknown to the people of the time*. Example 'feudalism'.

3. Words that we use loosely in everyday speech, which, because of their vagueness, can be confusing when used in a historical context. Example: 'the people'.

4. Words used to suggest a form of periodisation. Example: 'the Renaissance'.

5. Geographical abstractions. Example: 'Europe'.

6. Words that in the hands of some (but by no means all) historians have acquired a particular technical sense. Example: 'class', 'ideology'.

7. Most troublesome of all; words that combine a number of these problems. Examples: 'capitalism', 'imperialism', 'culture'.

From type 6, 'ideology', and from type 7, 'culture', particularly merit further special discussion. 'Ideology' in common usage, means 'body of ideas', so that 'Nazi ideology' would be the body of ideas, attitudes and beliefs espoused by the Nazis. We might speak of 'public-school ideology' or of 'feminist ideology', and so on. In my own approach to historical explanation I tend to make a distinction between 'structural' and 'ideological' trends. However, in the various forms of Marxist and Marxist-derived discourse, ideology is used in a more specific way, directly related to Marxist theory about class. Each class is said to have its own ideology, related, though not necessarily in a simple and direct way, to its basic economic interests. In a period in which the bourgeois class dominates, the 'dominant ideology' is bourgeois ideology, falsely represented as a national ideology. Ideology is then seen as something false, the mask which conceals the reality of bourgeois dominance and repression. Often within the space of pages writers seem to shift between the two meanings, the everyday one, and the technical one. Thus it is important always to try to be clear which usage is intended.

Perhaps most difficult and dangerous of all is the word 'culture'. Essentially, 'culture' is used in two different ways, in a wide anthropological sense and in a more limited ('aesthetic') sense, entailing literary, artistic, intellectual and leisure activities and products. Used anthropologically the word means the total network of human activities in a given society, including economic and social structure, religious beliefs, customs and habits, and even political practices. When books or paintings or sexual behaviour are said to be 'culturally determined' or 'culturally constructed' 'culturally' is being used in this anthropological sense. The word 'culture' almost becomes synonymous with 'society'. Usually historians are interested in culture in the more limited sense as when they study the relationships between culture and society, as Peter Burke does in his brilliant *The Italian Renaissance: Culture and Society in Italy* (1986). 'Culture' in the more limited sense can then usefully be sub-divided into 'high' or 'élite' culture on the one hand (which is usually taken to include such things as 'high' art, classical music and opera, 'serious' literature, and so on); and 'popular' culture, which includes all the leisure and entertainment activities of the vast majority in any given society. Again, within the space even of a page, authors can slide from one meaning to another. There is not necessarily anything illegitimate about this; the necessity, as already stressed, is to be aware of which meaning is being employed at any particular moment.

6. Brief Analysis of A Monograph/General History

Here I choose a very characteristic kind of historical work which, more wide-ranging than the normal monograph, falls into that broad category I have referred to as the general history. James J. Sheehan's *German Liberalism in the Nineteenth Century* (Chicago 1978) would be widely regarded as a standard work on its subject; it is certainly a work of fine professional craftsmanship. It is a model of how by structuring narrative, analysis, and description, a historian both gives a sense of change through time and does justice to important topics. It engages with major issues of three rather different types. First it deals with such concepts as 'liberalism' and 'modernisation', inevitably becoming involved in the problems of historical semantics. Second, it is concerned to stress how longer-term historical forces, particular to Germany, constrained political choices. Third, the book is involved with the whole question of illiberal tendencies in German society and, in particular, with the historical context for the advent of Nazism. Sheehan gives a fine insight into how he got started on a major enterprise of this sort, and also into his awareness of the limits of historical interpretation. He explains that when he began work on the German liberals as his original postgraduate project, he did not plan to define his subject so broadly.

> But every time I tried to study a piece of the movement, a single party or a specific point, I became convinced that it would not be understood without reference to another. Finally, I decided that the best way to contribute to the historiography of German liberalism would be to attempt a synthesis which would describe how German liberalism looked when all of its components were seen together.[27]

In the end, Sheehan adds, 'the price of synthesis has often been uncertainty.'

On his general view of historical causation Sheehan writes:

> Unlike a great deal of recent scholarship on German liberalism . . . my book does not attempt to explain the liberals' failure in terms of their moral deficiencies . . . Obviously, a number of liberals were shortsighted and selfish; many more showed bad judgment and political ineptitude. I do not wish to apologise for these failures of intellect and will. But I am not convinced that these failures sealed liberalism's fate. I wish I did think so, if only because it would make a better story . . . I am much more impressed by the way in which the historical situation narrowed liberals' choices and often precluded alternatives that might have enabled them to save themselves and their ideals. Certainly one reason for this point of view is that I have been concerned with the apparently necessary evolution of long-range trends rather than the potential for change which seems to exist at specific historical moments.

Sheehan then goes on to give another reason which readers should evaluate for themselves. 'I suspect,' he writes:

> another reason is the fact that I worked on this book during the late 1960s and early 1970s, a time when there was little in my own political experience to suggest that reality was malleable and that individual action could change the direction of events. Those historians who studied German liberals during a more promising stage in the evolution of American political life may have found it easier to blame them for not doing more and doing it better.

This is a fashionable kind of explanation among American historians; personally I think the matter of it is that historical studies had actually advanced, and that Sheehan was a better historian than his predecessors (it may be noted that Gutmann and Genovese, older certainly, but developing in the same period, produced a rather different kind of history). While I am being critical, I might comment that, essentially to meet the limitations of American publication, Sheehan's bibliography does not meet the specifications I have set out in this book; archive materials, an important basis for it, are omitted altogether, and printed primary and secondary sources are simply run together in one undifferentiated bibliography.

However, what I propose to do now in the remainder of this section is to summarise the main parts of Sheehan's introduction, illuminatingly entitled 'Liberalism in an Illiberal Society', then to discuss the organisation or structure of his book, then come to his most significant conclusions. Sheehan sees liberalism as an attempt to understand and react to 'modernisation'. Liberalism was to be found everywhere, but German liberals had particular problems of their own to contend with (this point is central to Sheehan's book). While such concepts as Staat ('state'), Volk ('people'), Mittelstand ('middle estate', what, in English would be 'middle class'), Partei ('party') and Bewegung ('movement') all seem to be part of a common European vocabulary, 'in fact the meaning of these German terms was affected by a complete web of traditions, assumptions, and national preoccupations.' German developments were 'profoundly affected by historical traditions and existing structures'. Sheehan then explains that the purpose of his book is to 'examine the relationship between liberalism and German society'. Chronologically, the main emphasis is on the nineteenth century, but there are brief discussions of the years before 1815 and after 1914. There was, of course, no unified Germany till 1871, so Sheehan explains that geographically 'the analysis covers those parts of German-speaking central Europe that were eventually united in the Kaiserreich of 1871.' Should political studies deal with leaders or the led? Sheehan explains that his focus 'includes liberal leaders and, wherever possible, the sources of the movement's popular support.'

The book is divided into six chronological parts, within which three, or in one case two, individual chapters take up analytical topics of special significance in that particular sub-period, or, sometimes, specific political crises. Sheehan adopts the useful device of providing brief overviews at the beginning of each part. Part one 'The Origins of German Liberalism 1770–1847' sets up three important themes, the emergence of liberal institutions, their social composition, and the politics of liberalism:

1. *Partei* and *Bewegung*
2. Social Change and the *Mittelstand*
3. The *Staat* and the *Volk*

Part two, 'Revolutionary Overture 1848–49', esssentially concentrates on a specific political crisis, with, however, one chapter devoted to the context of the revolution, and the other to its actual course. Part three 'Old Problems and New Realities 1850–66', discusses three critical aspects of the real advances made by liberalism after the disappointment of 1848–9:

6. The Search for a Liberal Society
7. The Search for a Liberal *Volk*
8. The Search for a Liberal *Staat*

Part four, 'The "Liberal Era" 1866–77' marks the climax of liberal achievement, but also points to old and new weaknesses:

9. 'Turning the Corner': Liberalism and the Bismarckian State
10. The Challenge of Democratization
11. The Liberal Constituency and the Rise of Interest Politics

Part five echoes part two in being essentially grounded in a particular political crisis, in this case the one provoked by Bismarck when he threatened total withdrawal from politics in order to force through changes (the 'second *Reichsgrundung*') which made it impossible for liberals to contemplate the possibility of continued cooperation with the state, and which in fact provoked a split:

12. The Second *Reichsgrundung*
13. National Liberalism Moves to the Right
14. The Liberal Left and the Burdens of Opposition

The final part 'The Wilhelmine Age 1890–1914' delineates the conditions and expression of liberal weakness:

15. From Movement to Minority
16. The Fragmentation of the Middle Strata
17. The Liberal Parties Between Right and Left

There follows the Conclusion, 'Liberalism, Nationalism and the

German Question', which in length and title nicely balances the
Introduction. Sheehan discusses Hitler and his powerful emphasis
on nationalism: since nationalism had played such a central role
in liberal rhetoric before 1914 Hitler's appeal to it 'provided the
most important and powerful link between established values and
Nazism's success.' While explicitly denying that the Nazi seizure
of power was a necessary culmination of German history, Sheehan
concludes that

> after all the necessary qualifications have been recorded, the fact
> remains that the liberal constituency proved to be especially susceptible
> to Nazism after 1930. This is, I think, the clearest indication of German
> liberalism's bankruptcy and the most consequential effect of liberal-
> ism's failure to provide the ideas and institutions with which the
> Germans could understand and master the problems posed by their
> nation's long journey to modernity.[28]

Notes

1. Jacques Barzun and Henry F. Graff, *The Modern Researcher* (1957,
paperback ed. 1962) pp. 229–30 (my references are to this edition). The
same important points are made in the revised edition, p. 197.
2. The passage is quoted by Barzun and Graff, p. 231. The revised
edition chooses a different passage, from a different book, but again by
poor old E. K. Chambers!
3. G. Kitson Clark, *Guide for Research Students Working in Historical
Subjects* (1960), p. 31.
4. Barzun and Graff, p. 233.
5. Richard Pares, *The Historian's Business and Other Essays* (Oxford,
1961), p. 6.
6. *The Historian's Business*, p. 9.
7. Michael Stanford, *The Nature of Historical Knowledge* (Oxford,
1986), p. 7.
8. Margaret Randolph Higonnet et al., *Behind the Lines: Gender and
the Two World Wars* (1987), Chap. I.
9. Frank Freidel, *America in the Twentieth Century* (1960), p. 218.
10. Gordon Wright, *History of Modern France* (1959) p. 529. This, it
should be added, is a Homeric nod: Professor Wright's book is a brilliant
piece of historical synthesis.
11. Barzun and Graff, p. 290.
12. Ibid.
13. W. L. Langer, *The Franco-Russian Alliance 1890–1894* (1929)
p. 277. Professor Langer was a distinguished American historian in the
mainstream tradition.
14. *The Practice of History*, pp. 16–17.

15. In *Rationalism in Politics* (1962), p. 153.

16. Leonard Krieger, in *History*, ed. John Higham (1965) p. 288.

17. R. R. Palmer, in Gottschalk (ed.), *Generalization in the Writing of History*, p. 66.

18. Louis Gottschalk, *Understanding History* (1956 edn), p. 17.

19. See Denys Hay, 'Geographical Abstraction and the Historian', *Historical Studies*, II (1959) pp. 1 ff., and sources there cited.

20. *The Historian's Craft*, p. 172.

21. Ibid., pp. 159–60, 163.

22. Alfred Cobban, 'The Vocabulary of Social History', *Political Science Quarterly*, LXXI (March 1956), p. 14.

23. *Historical Studies*, II 13.

24. Pp. 169–70.

25. This is the general tenor of, for example, Vasari's Prefaces to his *Lives of the Artists* (2nd edn, 1568). See selection (1965), translated by George Bull, pp. 25–47, 83–93, 249–54.

26. *Political Science Quarterly*, LXXI 8.

27. James J. Sheehan, *German Liberalism in the Nineteenth Century* (Chicago, 1978). This and the next few quotations are taken from the Introduction, pp. 1–3.

28. Sheehan p. 283. Sheehan's own footnote reference at this point is to other secondary sources exploring the relationship between liberalism and Nazism.

Chapter 7 History, Philosophy and Interdisciplinary Studies

1. Philosophy and History

Many people, picking up a book entitled 'The Nature of History' would expect that book to be about the deeper philosophical questions involved in history, considered as the past or as process such as the question of laws and patterns in historical development, the debate over free will and determinism in human activities, and the role of 'great men' (what a rebarbative, anachronistic phrase!), or, at the very least, to be concerned with problems of historical causation and historical explanation, rather than with, as of course this book is, an account of the actual activities of the working historian (actually, I hope that my analysis in the previous chapter *did* offer some help on these very problems). To some people the phrase 'philosophy of history' perhaps still means, as it certainly did in the nineteenth century, the sort of large-scale theorising about the pattern and structure of history conceived of as process practised by such writers as Oswald Spengler (1880–1936) and Arnold Joseph Toynbee (1899–1975), and before them by Georg Wilhelm Friedrich Hegel (1770–1831) who occupies a lofty place in the history of intellectual endeavour, though as a philosopher, not as a historian. This section repeats points already touched on, developing them as part of an interdisciplinary essay on the relationships between philosophy and history. Hegel, as we have seen, took from Plato the notion of 'the dialectic', that is, of argument being followed by counter-argument to produce a new synthesis, and applied it to historical study. Thus, in Hegel's view, each age would be characterised by dominant ideas of a certain type – the 'thesis'. But the same age must also contain within it exactly contradictory ideas – the 'antithesis'. 'Antithesis' working against 'thesis' would ultimately produce a 'synthesis' – the predominating ideas of the new age.

In seeking the fundamental meaning of the historical process, Hegel found it in 'the development of the consciousness of freedom' (since Hegel was an extreme Conservative, and an employee of the autocratic Prussian state it should be noted that his idea of freedom was scarcely ours). Hegel claimed to detect a progression from the despotism and slavery of the oriental world, to the citizenship rights of the Greek or Roman world, to the individual liberties of the Germanic nations of the Europe of his day. The motor of this progression was the dialectic, the process of 'thesis', 'antithesis' and 'synthesis'. History (the past) thus appeared as a grand design unfolding in four states: Oriental, Greek, Roman, and Germanic. Hegel believed he could establish the special characteristics of the people or nation dominating each state in his historical development; furthermore, he saw such 'great men' as Caesar or Alexander as chosen instruments in bringing about the unfolding of this grand design.[1]

The dialectic was taken over by Marx, though, as we noted, 'turned up-side-down' so as to apply to material developments not ideas. The dialectic, which for Marx embodied the opposition between the dominant class of one age and the class below rising up to challenge it, formed the motor in the unfolding of Marx's grand design: from Asiatic, to antique, to feudal, to bourgeois, to the dictatorship of the proletariat leading into the ultimate classless society. The Marxist view of history is sometimes described as 'the materialist interpretation of history', since it places a fundamental emphasis on economics, on the modes of production. Thus, in discussing history as the past, there is scope for a grand-scale philosophical debate (in the nineteenth-century sense of that phrase) over materialism versus idealism, over the weight to be given to material factors as against the weight to be given to ideas. Many practising historians may have a predisposition towards one or other of these over-arching interpretations, but working historians do not usually address themselves to that question as such; most, indeed, would feel that in some circumstances material factors carry most weight, while in other circumstances ideas are crucial. Most often there is a fine mix; and it is not always so easy anyway, when dealing with prejudice and tradition as well as with economic interests and disinterested ideals, to distinguish a material factor from an ideal one. Consider the British Labour Party, and what a strange amalgam of forces lies behind it. Of course one should always be analytic, but at the same time cautious in sponsoring one-horse races. Marxists in general, as we have seen, have abandoned the crude dependence on materialist explanations. But they still hold to the dialectic, which, though it has a more venerable ancestry than the Holy Ghost, has no more solid empirical foundation.

Once upon a time Toynbee would have been called a philosopher of history: the material of his philosophising is the past itself. Toynbee wanted simply to be called a historian: but the word which best encompasses the immense scope and lofty aims of his work is 'metahistory'.[2] Toynbee's precursor in the twentieth century was Oswald Spengler, whose *Decline of the West* (1918) was a comparative study of the rise and fall of whole civilisations which claimed to have the key to historical development in an analogy with a living organism, which is born, matures, ages and dies. When Toynbee became preoccupied with the problem of the genesis of civilisations (the civilisation, he has often said, is the smallest unit which the historian should consider), he sought guidance first from Spengler: but he found Spengler's rigid, Germanic a priori system of little value; he himself would try 'English empiricism' instead.

Toynbee described how he became preoccupied with the comparative study of civilisations:

> The general war of 1914 overtook me expounding Thucydides to Balliol undergraduates reading for *Literae Humaniores*, and then suddenly my understanding was illumined. The experience that we were having in our world now had been experienced by Thucydides in his world already.

There is nothing reprehensible or necessarily 'unscholarly' about such flashes of illumination, which most working historians (and, for that matter, many working scientists) have experienced from time to time. Toynbee never, indeed, concealed the intuitive nature of his historical vision, having described vividly his feeling of having the tide of history flowing in his veins. Toynbee's own specialised expertise lay in the world of Greek history and literature: from 1919 to 1924 he held the Chair of Byzantine and Modern Greek Language, Literature and History at London University. For thirty years thereafter he was Director of Studies at the Royal Institute of International Affairs in London and throughout the interwar years he was responsible for the year-by-year *Survey of International Affairs* published by the Institute: these annual surveys are standard works, both for the information they contain and as models of the writing of contemporary history.

After a number of false starts, Toynbee made his first jottings for the famous *A Study of History* (vols I–III, 1934; vols IV–VI, 1939; VII–X, 1954) while on a train in Egypt:

> This time I had not deliberately set myself to make the plan. I had spent the day looking out of the railway carriage window, and the plan that I had jotted down at the end of the day had seemed to come of itself.

From the Californian philosopher F. J. Tegart, Toynbee got the idea that the best entry into a comparative study of history was to decipher the local differences in the cultures of living societies, and to work back into the past from there. At this stage Toynbee was not familiar with Jungian psychology, though many of his later generalisations about social behaviour were in keeping with the basic tenets of that school. But from the encounter between God and Mephistopheles in Goethe's *Faust* he took a central idea: 'an encounter between two personalities in the form of challenge and response: have we not here the flint and steel by whose mutual impact the creative spark is kindled?'

The Second World War bulldozed a gap in the sequence of publication between the first six volumes and the last four; in the meantime Toynbee's own opinions changed slightly, and the final volumes are marked by a kind of messianic revivalism which was absent in the early volumes, and which undermined Toynbee's constantly reiterated claim that his methods were exclusively empirical and inductive.

Toynbee identified twenty-one civilisations, which he claimed, have passed through similar stages of growth, breakdown (including a 'time of troubles') and eventual dissolution, the final phase in each case being characterised by the formation of a 'universal state'. Certain 'laws' are advanced to account for certain critical developments, for example, the famous challenge and response mentioned above;

> Briefly stated, the regular pattern of social disintegration is a schism of the disintegrating society into a recalcitrant proletariat and a less and less effective dominant minority. The process of disintegration does not proceed evenly, it jolts along in alternating spasms of rout,

rally, and rout. In the last rally but one, the dominant minority succeeds in temporarily arresting the society's lethal self-laceration by imposing on it the peace of a universal state. Within the framework of the dominant minority's universal state the proletariat creates a universal church, and after the next rout, in which the disintegrating civilisation finally dissolves, the universal church may live on to become the chrysalis from which a new civilisation eventually emerges.

The first six volumes of the book are pervaded by the deep pessimism of a man who knows that his own civilisation is in decay: but the revivalist Toynbee shines through in the four published after the Second World War:

> . . . if a vehicle is to move forward on a course which its driver has set, it must be borne along on wheels that turn monotonously round and round. When civilisations rise and fall and, in falling, give rise to others, some purposeful enterprise, higher than theirs, may all the time be making headway, and, in a divine plan, the learning that comes through the suffering caused by the failures of civilisations may be the sovereign means of progress.

Whatever one may feel about this as objective history, Toynbee's own pronouncements about his objectives in writing *A Study of History* do make good sense, and fit well into many of the preoccupations we have detected among historians reacting against the nineteenth-century legacy. Remarking that *A Study of History* had been written side by side with the *Survey of International Affairs*, Toynbee argued that he could not have done either piece of work if he had not been doing the other at the same time. There is here a distinct element of that 'present-mindedness' we have seen in other twentieth-century historians:

> A survey of current affairs on a world-wide scale can be made only against a background of world-history; and a study of world-history would have no life in it if it left out the history of the writer's own lifetime, for one's contemporaries are the only people whom one can ever catch alive. An historian in our generation must study Gandhi and Lenin and Ataturk and F. D. Roosevelt if he is to have any hope of bringing Hammuraki and Ikhanataon and Amos and the Buddha back to life for himself and for his readers.

Secondly, Toynbee stressed the way in which his comparative study of twenty-one civilisations had broken with the tradition of Western-orientated history, increasingly outmoded as formerly 'underdeveloped' parts of the world rise to power, and as archaeological discoveries bring further ancient civilisations to light.

Toynbee, thirdly referred to the division between history and the social sciences:

> In the study of human affairs the first thing now to be done is to explore how far we can carry, in this field, the scientific method of investigating 'laws', regularities, uniformities, recurrences.

While claiming to recognise the value of specialised studies (though he also poured much scorn on some of the activities of professional historians), Toynbee saw his own work as a counterpoise to excessive specialisation. He aimed, he said, at giving a synoptic view of the new knowledge which had recently come to light on different civilisations. Finally Toynbee, in an astonishing echo of some remarks of Langlois and Seignobos, who would have deplored his entire approach to history, gave himself a definite social purpose:

> The historian can help his fellow men of different civilizations to become more familiar with one another, and, in consequence, less afraid of one another and less hostile to one another, by helping them to understand and appreciate one another's histories and to see in these local and partial stories a common achievement and common possession of the whole human family.

Toynbee was received enthusiastically by lay readers, less so by professional historians. In general there is a professional agreement that whatever Toynbee wrote in *A Study of History*, it is not history. Basically the arguments are that far from arguing inductively as he claimed, he first established an a priori system, then made the facts fit. Many of the 'facts' indeed are not in accord with the latest researches in the fields into which he so boldly trod.

Now is the moment to come back to Wilhelm Dilthey (1833–1911). In the first edition of this book I ignored Dilthey altogether. In the second edition I identified him as a rather important figure in the evolution of historical studies. My more mature reflection on Dilthey is that while he focussed attention on an absolutely crucial issue, the manner in which he attempted to resolve this issue did not have entirely beneficial consequences. In his *Introduction to Historical Knowledge* (1883), and subsequent essays, Dilthey established what he saw as the fundamental distinction between scientific knowledge on the one side, and cultural knowledge on the other; his task was to validate the second branch of knowledge. He laid down three basic differences between the two branches (we went over this ground in Chapter 4); scientific knowledge and cultural (or historical) knowledge differ in their fields of research, in the forms of experience they embody, and in the attitudes of the researcher (this I find debatable; I see the pursuit of knowledge, the solving of problems, as common aims). The first difference is obvious; in elaborating the second and third Dilthey developed arguments which were to be seized on by Benedetto Croce (1866–1952) and R. G. Collingwood (1889–1943). Dilthey argued that historical knowledge was derived through some kind of *internal* process, that is to say through living experience and understanding, rather than being merely apprehended *externally* as in the natural sciences. Meaning in history, therefore, was not fixed but changed with the period and culture of the historian himself. Over-emphasis on this line of argument is, in my view, disastrous for historical studies; when everything has been said (and, as I have consistently shown, there *is* much to be said) about how historians are affected by their own historical context, history *is* a cumulative body of knowledge *not* mere relativist fancy.

While some historians took heart that they, in the words of H. Stuart Hughes, 'no longer needed to apologise for the "unscientific" character of their discipline: they understood why its methods could never be the same as those of natural science,'[3] there was really a more challenging aspect to Dilthey's labours. His answer to the problem that he identified of historians themselves being subjectively involved in the material they studied was that this did not matter, since history was different from science. But the issue was a troubling one. As Breisach puts it:

> Dilthey and his successors had discovered how difficult historical explanation became once the traditional method of 'subject observes a clearly defined reality' was abandoned in favor of 'subject observes a reality at least partially constructed in the process of observing.' Now that the traditional view of reality with its transcendent order had been rejected, historical scholars found that with the object of their study having become unclear their methods of understanding and reconstructing the past had been put in question, too.[4]

Many accepted Dilthey's diagnosis (who could deny it), but rejected his prescription. Hence the efforts to assimilate historical study completely to the approaches to the natural sciences, through the formulation of general laws, the application of Marxist theory, etc., etc. This attempt to make history 'respectable', as I have said, I understand, though I believe it ultimately to be misconceived. However, the alternatives are not confined to theory-based 'scientific' history on the one side, and relativism on the other: the previous two chapters, I sincerely trust, have revealed history as a thoroughly systematic subject, akin in aims to the natural sciences, though different in many points of importance.

Let us explore further the dual, and contradictory, legacy of Dilthey. The extreme relativists (Chapter 3) have long since collapsed into their own dustbins, but the two philosophers of history I have already mentioned, Croce and Collingwood, continue to command further attention. Croce served as Minister of Education in the Italian Government of 1920-1. He was a distinguished opponent of fascism and he wrote a fair amount of 'orthodox' history, which was penetrating and liberal-minded in character. But he also produced a number of philosophical essays on the nature of history. In that (in my view, slightly artificial) polarity between the Ideal and the Material which is sometimes posed in the study of historical change, Croce was firmly and unreservedly attracted to the Ideal. Following Dilthey he insisted that there was a fundamental distinction between historical and scientific knowledge, and seemed to see the former as essentially a kind of intellectual intuition. Finally, Croce was one of those who took the view (highly dubious, I suggested in Chapter 1) that the past has no existence, which leads to the conclusion (which I have consistently contested) that history has reality only in the mind of historians: 'all history', then, in one of Croce's famous phrases, 'is contemporary history'[5] – that is, it has existence only in the minds of contemporaries. Probably my understanding is defective, but to me the phrase reeks of relativism run berserk. Croce was convinced that historical thinking was superior to all other kinds of thinking (*I* think historians should settle for parity of status with philosophers and physicists): the relativity of history was not a confession of weakness but an assertion of intellectual and imaginative power.

Croce's ideas were refined and expounded in lucid and persuasive style by R. G. Collingwood, who, it is important to note, was primarily a philosopher rather than a historian, though he was also a practising archaeologist and historian of Roman Britain and he held an Oxford lectureship in history along with his Chair of Philosophy. Based on lectures given in 1935 and 1936, *The Idea of History* was put together and published after Collingwood's death in 1944. Beautifully written and directly appealing in so many ways, it is for me a puzzling and unsatisfactory book. Fourteen years earlier he published for the Historical Association (of Great Britain) a pamphlet on the *Philosophy of History*. Though clearly much inferior to *The Idea of History*, this pamphlet does make an easy point of entry into some aspects of Collingwood's thought. After a somewhat elaborate argument justifying the concept of historical relativism, Collingwood then attempted to refute the criticism that the historian is essentially selective in his approach to evidence. History, being the creation of the historian (that is, it is not synonymous with 'the past', nor even with 'the past as it is known through the activities of historians'), only begins when the historian asks a question. 'History' is the answering of this question: 'the historian does not select, because no past facts are "there" before him, to select from, until he has put them there by sheer historical thinking.' This was a neat twist; critics in the past had so often said that history was all in the mind of the historian: Collingwood was proud of it. Collingwood ended his pamphlet with a fine exposition of the Crocean notion that all history is contemporary history. All history, he said, brings its narrative down to the present day, 'not necessarily as history, but as the history of history'. (By this remark Collingwood seems to mean that the book standing on the shelf is not history, it only becomes history when taken down and read by the contemporary seeker after historical knowledge: rephrased less dogmatically, this recalls the point that *included in* history – though not the fundamental *essence* of history, as Collingwood seems to argue – is the dialogue between historian and reader.) Thus, Collingwood continues in familiar fashion, 'every age must write history afresh':

> Everyone brings his own mind to the study of history, and approaches it from the point of view which is characteristic of himself and his generation; naturally, therefore, one age, one man, sees in a particular historical event things which another does not, and vice versa. The attempt to eliminate this 'subjective element' from history is always insincere – it means keeping your own point of view while asking other

people to give up theirs – and always unsuccessful. If it succeeded, history itself would vanish.

But history does not thereby become something arbitrary and capricious, as the layman would be only too justified in suspecting. Collingwood is excellent in his efforts to meet the doubts of the layman: 'if my thoughts about Julius Caesar differ from Mommsen's . . . must not one of us', he asks, 'be wrong?' The answer is 'no' because, he says, 'the object differs':

> My historical thought is about my own past, not about Mommsen's past. Mommsen and I share in a great many things, and in many respects we share a common past; but in so far as we are different people and representatives of different cultures and different generations we have behind us different pasts, and everything in his past has to undergo a slight alteration before it can enter into mine . . .
> Finally, since the past in itself is nothing, the knowledge of the past in itself is not, and cannot be, the historian's goal. His goal, as the goal of a thinking being, is knowledge of the present; to that everything must return, round that everything must revolve. But, as historian, he is concerned with one special aspect of the present – how it came to be what it is. In this sense, the past is an aspect or function of the present; and that is how it must always appear to the historian who reflects intelligently on his own work, or, in other words, attempts a philosophy of history.

Everyone interested in history should know something about Collingwood's ideas. But it must be stressed again that he does not stand in the mainstream of the development of historical studies: full of deep insights, he is no sure guide to what historians actually do or how they think. *But, perhaps to how they should.*

The most interesting account of Collingwood's thinking occurs in his *Autobiography*, written unhappily when he was already seriously ill. Collingwood reckoned that until the end of the nineteenth century history had been very much a 'scissors-and-paste' matter, and the historian's main business was to know his 'authorities' (there is a much fuller discussion of 'scissors-and-paste' in *The Idea of History*):

> to his authorities' statements he was tied by the leg, however long the rope and however flowery the turf over which it allowed him to circle. If his interest led him towards a subject on which there were no authorities, it led him into a desert where nothing was except the sands of ignorance and the mirage of imagination.

This statement was accurate perhaps for the current state of history in the ancient English universities rather than for historical studies as a whole: however, what Collingwood now went on to say about the effects on his conception of history of his experience on his father's archaeological digs echoed the broadening of historical thinking everywhere. He learned that

> scissors and paste were not the only foundation of historical method. All you wanted, I could see, was a sufficiently extensive and sufficiently scientific development of such work, and it would teach you, not indeed everything, but a great deal, about subjects whose very existence must remain permanently unknown to historians who believed in authorities. I could see, too, that the same methods might be used to correct the authorities themselves, when they had been mistaken or untruthful. In either case, the idea of an historian depending on what the authorities tell him was exploded.

In all this Collingwood was at one with Bloch, Febvre and the *Annales* school. However, immediately after this common-sense appraisal came the rather silly argument taken from Croce which not only insisted that historical thinking was different from scientific thinking, but that somehow historical thinking was supreme because there is always a 'historical element' in scientific method. On examination this appears to mean no more than that when a scientist frames a theory he uses 'certain historical knowledge in his possession as to what experiments had been tried and what their results had been.'

With Croce, Collingwood believed that 'all history is the history of thought' and in this, of course, he was in key with the new emphasis on intellectual history developing in the twenties and thirties. To demonstrate his point Collingwood drew a distinction between history and such 'pseudo-histories' as geology, palaeontology and astronomy:

> History and pseudo-history alike consisted of narratives; but in history these were narratives of purposive activity, and the evidence for them consisted of relics they had left behind (books or potsherds, the principle was the same) which became evidence precisely to the extent to which the historian conceived them in terms of purpose, that is, understood what they were for; in pseudo-history there is no conception of purpose, there are only relics of various kinds, differing among themselves in such ways that they have to be interpreted as relics of different pasts which can be arranged on a time-scale.

This in itself is an illuminating commentary on one part of the historian's method. But Collingwood's contention was that there

[handwritten marginal note:] Marwick is limited to what he sees in this examination. a limitation which confirms Collingwood's position.

'is nothing else except thought that can be the object of historical knowledge':

> Political history is the history of political thought: not 'political theory', but the thought which occupies the mind of a man engaged in political work . . . Military history, again, is not a description of weary marches in heat or cold, or the thrills and chills of battle or the long agony of wounded men. It is a description of plans and counter-plans; of thinking about strategy and thinking about tactics, and in the last resort of what the men in the ranks thought about the battle.

The reader may well share my conviction that this last passage is absolute rubbish, well illustrating what can happen when a highly refined mind pushes a pet theory too far (in fairness, Colling-wood's illness must also be recalled). All that needs to be said is that history can very well be 'a description of weary marches . . . the long agony of wounded men'. Why on earth not?[6] Collingwood surmised in 1939 that we might well be standing on the 'threshold of an age in which history would be as important for the world as natural science had been between 1600 and 1900'.[7] At least he was convinced of the importance of history, and in his writings he expressed the dignity of the subject; for these services all historians must be grateful. But the odd mystical outbursts simply provided material for history's enemies: those who, rightly, derided a history which turned out to depend solely on the historian's intuition.

For the past half century or so, if not longer, the central debate in philosophy of history has been over whether history can be made to conform to the model of explanation exemplified in the physical sciences, or whether it is completely autonomous with perfectly respectable explanatory methods of its own. Croce and Collingwood, obviously, fall very heavily in the latter camp. The debate took off into active life with the formulation of what has usually been referred to as 'the Popper–Hempel thesis' or 'the covering law thesis'. Carl G. Hempel first published his famous and much quoted article 'The Function of General Laws in History' in 1942: he argued that there were indeed general laws in historical study and that therefore history did conform to the scientific model. Some of his arguments had been anticipated by K. R. (Sir Karl) Popper who had argued that an event in history is to be explained when it is subsumed under a covering or general law. However, Popper thought that such laws were usually

[handwritten margin note: or what can happen when a critic takes an idea out of context]

extremely trivial and that frequently historians' 'explanations' were in fact circular in nature: history, therefore, was a poor and inadequate relation in the family of knowledge. Croce and Collingwood had offered one defence of the autonomy of historical method. A rather different one was presented by Michael Oakeshott, for many years a prominent political philosopher at the London School of Economics. Oakeshott simply denied that it was possible (or necessary?) to establish historical explanation as explanation in terms of cause and effect. Oakeshott likened the historian's activities to those of the novelist, arguing that narrative in history, as in a novel, provides all the explanation required.[8]

Broadly speaking there are, with much overlap, and many subtle differences, two important intermediate positions. First, a number of distinguished philosophers have developed much more profound, and much less extreme, analyses of historical explanation, which do differentiate it from scientific or 'covering law' explanations. Raymond Aron's *Introduction to the Philosophy of History* was first published in French in 1938, republished in revised form in 1948, and finally published in English translation in 1961. Its sub-title was all-important – *An Essay on the Limits of Historical Objectivity*. By 'objectivity', Aron explained, he meant 'universality', in the sense in which scientific laws have universality. 'At a certain stage of our experimental knowledge, a physical law compels universal recognition. Can the same validity, at a certain stage of scholarship, be attributed to an historical reconstruction?' Finally, in a very complex and closely textured book, Aron suggested that there were indeed limits upon the applicability of universal laws to historical study: 'all history is both objective and subjective according to the laws of logic and probability, but prejudiced in favour of an individual or a period which for that very reason could not demand universal agreement.'[9] Much of the most important work along these lines in the Anglo-Saxon world has emerged from North America. One leading figure is the Canadian William H. Dray, whose Oxford monograph *Laws and Explanation in History* was published in 1951. Others who have attempted to analyse, and give validity to, the special nature of historical explanation are A. C. Danto, W. B. Gallie and Alan Donagan, yet to my taste, in attempting to bury the covering law thesis these philosophers have gone too

far in banishing the scientific element from historical study;
W. B. Gallie seems not really to have gone much beyond Oakeshott's unsatisfactory view that the telling of the story itself contains the historical explanation.[10]

So we come to the second intermediate position which does
coincide more nearly with what many professional historians
themselves believe. The standard work, now almost forty years
old, remains Patrick Gardiner's *The Nature of Historical Explanation* (1952) whose object was 'to indicate the relationship
between historical explanations and other forms of explanation,
bringing out the differences, it is true, but trying not to forget
that there may be points in common.'[11] While demonstrating that
the 'regularity' explanation of natural science is not the only valid
form of explanation, Gardiner strongly criticised the arguments
for the autonomy of history presented by Collingwood and Oakeshott, and indeed concluded with a view of historical explanation
as different from, yet sharing important points in common with,
scientific explanation. Gardiner also declared forcefully that 'the
conflict supposed to exist between materialistic and idealistic
interpretations of history is an illusory one.'[12] Much the same
viewpoint is presented by W. H. Walsh's *An Introduction to the
Philosophy of History* (1951 and 1967), a rather easier book for
the beginning student, which concludes:

> Our general view can be summarised by saying that history is, in our
> view, a form of knowledge with features peculiar to itself, though it is
> not so different from natural science or even commonsense as it has
> sometimes been thought to be.

Similar views, presented in more trenchant fashion, had been
developed by the American philosopher Maurice Maudelbaum,
from his pioneering *The Problem of Historical Knowledge* (1938)
to his powerful and persuasive *The Anatomy of Historical Knowledge* (Boston, 1977). More recently, a very subtle and sensitive
analysis has been presented by R. F. Atkinson in *Knowledge
and Explanation in History: An Introduction to the Philosophy of
History* (1978). Atkinson distinguishes between 'law' explanation
(that of the positivists, the Marxists, and the Popper–Hempel
thesis), 'rational' explanation (that of those who stress the importance of ideas and individual motivation) and 'narrative' explanation (as stressed by Oakeshott and Gallie). Atkinson argues

②a

②b

[handwritten note:] Some historians (?) blat on about laws in the hope of sounding scientific. But they haven't found a single law. They have identified processes which recur (challenge hypothesis) but not necessary outcomes.

that historians' explanations can cover all three of these types; most critically he insists that history is explanatory, in the ordinary, common-sense, but very rich, meaning of that term, as distinct from a narrowly scientific conception of it.

> What is needed, in order to do justice to history, is somehow to recover the richness of the full ordinary concept, but without obscurantism; without either repudiating the possibility of precise, scientific sorts of explanation, or attempting to confine them to safe areas; and without attaching undue importance to a more old-fashioned sort of history than professionals are nowadays prepared to own.[13]

Few practising historians have actually engaged in dialogue with the philosophers of history. One of the most outstanding exceptions is G. R. Elton. Elton makes himself out to be firm believer in the autonomy of historical study. The arguments of the 'Popper–Hempel School and of those who fall back on symbolic logic' he sees as 'quite mistaken'. Yet Elton in his key work, *The Practice of History* (1967), has no time for Collingwood either:

> The unreal and unrealistic notion that the historian understands history by re-enacting it in his mind, backed up by the fatal suggestion that ideas are the only realities in history, has had some very disturbing consequences, from the conviction that no history is worth writing except intellectual history to the opinion that history is just what the historian dreams up.[14]

Elton is keen to establish that just because historical explanation does not depend upon universal laws, that does not mean that it is not governed by very strict rules (which is, of course, exactly what I am trying to establish in this book). Elton argues that philosophers of history have too often based their conclusions on rather brief excerpts from historical writing (and often not very good examples at that); he maintains that the philosophers need to study much more thoroughly all the activities that go into the production of a piece of historical writing. In dealing with the idea that the telling of the story itself contains the historical explanation, Elton declares that this 'underestimates the difficult complexity of explaining by narrating. In order to explain, narrative needs to contain a great deal of explicit analysis and argument, difficult to write.'[15] Elton sums up the nature of historical causation and the historian's explanation as follows: 'Direct causes explain why the event actually happened; situational causes explain why direct causes proved effective and why the event occupies a particular place in the historical picture and story, both as an effect and as a cause of further effect.'

Elton's arguments do not seem to support his rather conservative dogma that history is completely autonomous. But insofar as he is arguing that there are 'rules', though not 'laws', underlying historical explanation, he represents the views of most working professional historians today. An even more conservative line was taken by the somewhat idiosyncratic *The History Primer* (1971) by the distinguished American historian of seventeenth-century England, J. H. Hexter. This sets out to refute Hempel and, by examples of what the historian actually does, returns to a position of full autonomy for historical explanation. The work is highly amusing but seems to me unfortunate in denying that which history does share with all other branches of knowledge, including science, and in the end, in overstating the significance of 'common-sense' and 'intuition';

Gordon Leff's *History and Social Theory* (1969) is a comprehensive and elegant study by a historian whose specialism, significantly, is the history of thought. Leff puts great stress, as I have done in Chapter 5, on the fragmentary and imperfect nature of historical sources. Unlike Elton he does not believe that the historian can establish distinct 'direct' and 'situational' causes. He puts a stress above all upon contingency in history, leading him to the conclusion that there cannot possibly be any general laws. Leff brings out a point too often ignored by philosophers of history, that the fundamental conceptualising activity of the historian is periodisation.

Many of the difficulties in regard to philosophical attempts to explain what historians are doing arise, first (as Leff has stressed) from the fragmentary nature of historical sources, and second, from the very complexity of the problems which historians set themselves. The term 'Reformation' is relatively straightforward when compared with say 'Humanism' or the 'Counter-Reformation' and, most certainly, when compared with the concept of 'the Renaissance'. When dealing with the Renaissance it is very difficult indeed to devise a clear cause-and-effect model because that which has to be explained, the Renaissance, is in itself a very difficult and complex 'effect' to pin down. Similarly if one is discussing the social consequences of the First World War. It is not enough to say, as Elton does, that this simply involves moving the cause-and-effect model further forward, that the effect is now the social consequences, and the cause is the war. In fact the question of whether there were any substantial social consequences of the First World War is a matter of considerable debate among historians (see Chapter 8): so the problem is not just one of showing an acceptable cause-and-effect relationship, but of demonstrating that the effect exists in the first place (the 'cause', on the other hand, indisputably does exist!).

The critical philosophy of history of today, naturally, involves the study of other problems than that of historical explanation. W. H. Dray's standard short textbook *Philosophy of History* (1964), in the 'Foundations of Philosophy' series, after making the distinction between critical philosophy of history (that which studies the historians' activities) and speculative philosophy of history (the sort of stuff written by Hegel, Spengler and Toynbee – what I have termed 'metahistory') devoted separate chapters to each of the following topics: 'historical understanding', 'historical objectivity', 'causal judgement in history', 'philosophers of history', 'a metaphysical approach' (by which he meant such 'philosophies of history' as those of Hegel and so on), 'an empirical approach' (by which he meant the 'philosophy of history' of Toynbee), and 'a religious approach'. These last four chapter headings really take us into the major area of *meaning* in history, a question, in fact, which many British professional historians would regard as being without meaning. The influential *Annales* school, on the other hand, would maintain that there are underlying structures which give meaning to history (though, frankly, they haven't been overwhelmingly successful in showing just exactly what these are); Marxists believe that the meaning of history lies in the unfolding of Marxist prophecy. The outstanding protagonist of the religious approach was the American theologian and historian Reinhold Niebuhr (1892–1971), the best short statement of whose views is to be found in his *Faith and History* (1949). 'It is Niebuhr's contention,' Dray summarises, 'that nothing less than divine revelation, as elaborated in Christian theology, affords an 'adequate' basis for discerning the meaning of historical events.'[16] A committed Christian, however, could legitimately disagree. Herbert Butterfield (1900–86) believed that if a person had not acquired religious belief from his experience of everyday life, he would be unlikely to find it in the study of history. The concluding words of his *Christianity in History* (1949) were: 'Hold to Christ, and for the rest be totally uncommitted.' Karl Popper's polemical works, *The Poverty of Historicism* and *The Open Society and Its Enemies*, were powerful, and often highly emotional, attacks on the notion of there being meaning in history – in this case *meaning* meant Marxism. An elegant attempt to take issue with Popper in restoring a belief in regularities, and therefore meaning, in history is *Has History Any Meaning?* (1978) by the American philosopher of history Burleigh Taylor-Wilkins. As I have suggested, this is a debate in which few working historians directly intervene.

Of the other major issues identified by Dray, the one which most needs further discussion is that of objectivity and subjectivity in historical study. The contribution of a philosopher would be to try to pin down exactly what is meant by 'subjective'. Most would agree that science subjects as much as history involve an element of human intervention in that, in the end, the scientist does have to interpret his data or show the interrelationships between different phenomena. But if that is all that is meant by subjective then there would appear to be no significant difference between historical and scientific study. Many philosophers, therefore, have put primary stress on the question of 'moral' judgement in history. Although I have already argued that historians should not see it as a major duty to pass value judgements on past personalities and events, I also made it clear that involved in the very terminology of history there are assumed moral judgements, and that these cannot be avoided. Accordingly, some philosophers have argued that what most distinctively separates history from science is not any alleged subjectivity in history, but the moral element ever-present in history but absent from science. As so often, this analysis (in my view trivial and irrelevant) seems to be based on the reading of a few general histories rather than an intensive study of the actual activities of working historians. What I come back to – a major theme throughout this book – is the intractable and fragmentary nature of historical source material. It is here, in my view, that we have a much more fundamental distinction between history and science. Because the historian's evidence is much less satisfactory than the scientist's there is, inevitably, much more scope for the historian's interpretative powers. It is in that sense, primarily, that history is 'subjective'. Historians are not by nature more biased or prejudiced than scientists: simply, they are forced into a greater deployment of personal interpretation by the imperfections of their evidence. To concentrate on the moral elements in history is to evade that fundamental fact. The 'subjective' quality to be found in historical writing actually arises from two circumstances: first, that historians deal with human and social issues; but, second, the point just stressed, that they also have to work with highly imperfect evidence.

As was indicated at the beginning of this book the area of discussion which interests *me* most concerns the value and purposes of historical study. Is history really a social necessity? If it is, how far does that entail an element of present-mindedness in the historian? My argument, just to repeat briefly, is that history does indeed serve present society, but it serves it the better the more it seeks to understand the past on the past's own terms. Only, for example, by truly understanding periods of change in the past as they were understood by contemporaries, can we make legitimate and fruitful contrasts with change in our own time.

2. History and the Other Humanities

Interdisciplinary studies (usually bringing together the arts or humanities subjects and sometimes some social science ones) have been increasingly in fashion over the last decade or so. In part, this has been to history's disadvantage insofar as the separate identity and methods of historical study have been swamped in the general teaching of social studies or liberal arts; on the other hand, interdisciplinary study almost inevitably brings out the central role of history. Many historians have long stressed the relationships between history and literature and the arts. The latter, as was indicated in Chapter 6, can be drawn upon as source materials, though great care must be taken not to presume that such sources are either representative or factual. Almost inevitably the great Victorian novelists have been hungrily cannibalised by historians of the period. Here is Geoffrey Best, discussing the continuing dominance of the aristocracy in the 1850s and 1860s and its *'ancien régime*-like engrossment of political positions':

> Dickens, who felt so strongly about it that he let it provoke one of his rare forays into politics (the Administrative Reform Association of 1855), characteristically digested the outsiders' point of view into his

highly-coloured picture, in *Little Dorrit* (1858), of the Tite Barnacle 'clan, or clique, or family, or connection' (as one of its more cynical members called it); a member of which you could find 'wherever there was a square yard of ground in British occupation under the sun or moon, with a public post upon it . . .'. A shoal of the Barnacles condescendingly attended their relation Henry Gowan's marriage to middle-class Mr Meagles's daughter. Some were established, famous and great; some: '. . . who had not as yet got anything . . . were going through their probation to prove their worthiness . . . And there was not a list, in all the Circumlocution Office, of places that might fall vacant anywhere within half a century, from a Lord of the Treasury to a Chinese Consul, and up again to a Governor-general of India, but, as applicants for such places, the names of some or every one of these hungry and adhesive Barnacles were down.'

All this was intolerable, normally, to Mr Meagles, and he certainly did not enjoy the snubbing and condescension to which these sponges and leeches subjected him; yet – so well did his creator know the bourgeois heart! – after the grisly ceremony was over, and his daughter had gone off with the well-connected wastrel whom the Meagleses (quite correctly) seriously distrusted, Mr Meagles got some consolation from reflecting on the rank of those who thus humiliated him. 'It's very gratifying', he said, often repeating the remark in the course of the evening, 'Such high company!' One recalls Cobden's allegation, about the same year 1857, that 'The more contempt a man like Palmerston . . . heaped upon them the more they [the middle class] cheered him,' Dickens and Cobden were increasingly on the losing side of this debate about the merits of the aristocracy as a political and administrative ruling class. By the time Matthew Arnold presented his highly-coloured picture of them (a picture at least as much of a caricature as Dickens's), his was a cultured voice crying in a cultivated wilderness . . . .[17]

Best sails close to the wind here, as he and other historians have done from time to time, almost seeming to accept a fictional character such as Mr Meagles as a real person. Yet, here, the fictional quotations are woven together beautifully with more 'factual' quotations, and Dickens's position as an occasional participant in organised politics, as well as a creator of fiction, is brought out. Above all, Best cautions us that Dickens's fictional account is 'highly-coloured' and he recognises that Matthew Arnold's 'highly-coloured picture' (in the polemical treatise *Culture and Anarchy*) was 'at least as much of a caricature as Dickens's'.

But apart from the use of literature and the arts as sources, historians have nearly always been anxious to assert history's significance in providing the *context* for the study of cultural artefacts (using cultural in the limited, 'aesthetic' sense). All works of thought, religion, art, music and literature are products of a particular age and a particular society. Their most important features may have little to do with the historical context; nonetheless if any work of philosophy, art, or literature is to be *completely* understood then there will have to be understanding also of the society and community within which the philosopher, composer or poet operated. History's function may be twofold: it can help explain *how* particular works of art come to be produced in the precise form in which they actually appeared; and it can help in the elucidation of what may be called referential elements in cultural artefacts, elements, which refer to real historical circumstances, as when Renaissance painters render the rich and powerful historical figures of their day, or Balzac alludes to the changes of regime and shifts in the class structure of France at the end of the eighteenth century and in the early nineteenth century. It may appear that philosophical ideas genuinely are autonomous since the major issues over which philosophers argue transcend time, and since philosophical enquiry essentially progresses through philosophers arguing with, developing from, and reacting against each other, often over very long periods of time, stretching, say, from the age of Aristotle to the present. Yet, in some respects at least, the agenda of philosophers does change as the historical context changes; thus connections can be made between the great social and economic upheavals in the seventeenth century, involving the break up of many of the remaining elements of the feudal order, and the turning of philosophers to questions of humanity's freedom of choice – something earlier philosophers had not preoccupied themselves with; as also between industrialisation, the growth of towns and the emergence of new social problems in the early nineteenth century, and the turning of philosophers to questions of social organisation and social morality. And the direction taken by the thought of Wittgenstein can hardly be totally explained without some consideration of the great upheavals of the twentieth century, and the final loss of any sense of a stable universe. At a more banal level philosophical works which seek to enter into contemporary political debate may well contain references which historians can help to explain. Later editions of John Stuart Mill's *Principles of Political Economy* (first published in 1848) for instance made reference to 'the consistent good sense and forbearance' of the

Lancashire cotton workers during the cotton famine occasioned by the American Civil War. With regard to literature, art, and music, one does not have to labour the point that certain obvious differences between the poems of Chaucer and those of Robert Burns, between the novels of Jane Austen and those of Thomas Hardy, between the paintings of the pre-Raphaelites and those of Picasso, and between the symphonies of Mozart and those of Beethoven, bear some relationship to the changes in the social environments in which they were created.

Yet very loud warnings have to be sounded against any simplistic reading of cultural artefacts as 'a mirror of their times' or as expressing 'the spirit of the age'. Apart from the fact that these phrases are mindless metaphors, it is always important to give attention to what may best be termed the *relative autonomy* of art, that is to say internal artistic, formal, aesthetic, or conceptual influences, as well also as the factors of personal genius, personal predilection, personal idiosyncrasy, and perhaps even personal circumstances, which can shape the final form of a particular work of art. Furthermore, a proper emphasis on the importance of the historical context should not lead to the assumption that there must be peculiar and different characteristics in each age and society which will, as it were, produce automatic responses in art: artists may react to revolutions, or to, say, industrialisation, but in a deeper way their work is shaped by the whole complex of values evolved over a period of time in a particular society, values which, in Western society, may well have their origins in classical Greece. The individual arts affect, and react upon each other also: for example, nineteenth-century romantic music, as well as being influenced by autonomous developments within music (the great innovations of Beethoven, for instance) and by the larger historical and technological changes (affecting, for example, patronage, audiences, the image of the artist, musical instruments, and accepted modes of expression) was also influenced by the examples set by contemporary literature and painting.

Establishing the social context, it should be stressed, is not always as easy as musicologists or literary critics believe. In studying the works of England's greatest playwright, it is possible to establish with some clarity the major cultural upheavals which impinged upon all thinking people in Renaissance England, though the Renaissance in itself is a complex phenomenon. But when it comes to establishing in detail and with absolute certainty exactly when Shakespeare wrote a particular play, and why, we often simply do not have the evidence. *A Midsummer Night's Dream*, as A. L. Rowse brought out in his biography *William Shakespeare* (1963) is particularly difficult to pin down in this way. Yet there are questions about the play towards which historians can help to give answers. Clearly it is a Renaissance play, directly in the humanist tradition, with Shakespeare drawing upon English translations of Ovid, Plutarch's *Lives*, and Apuleius's *Golden Ass*. Where the play is of central interest to the historian is in the handling of the village artisans and craftsmen, and of their beliefs and superstitions. Here we have both a reflection of, and a source for, the village life, and beliefs, of Elizabethan England, though, of course, much care is needed since Shakespeare might well have been deliberately propagating the myth of 'merry England'.

On the one hand historians use cultural artefacts as sources; on the other they help to establish the context for the full understanding and appreciation of such artefacts. In these two areas the relationships are essentially with the creative artists themselves and their products, with literature and art as what is produced by writers and artists. In the concerted attempt to understand the full richness and cultural experience in the past and of cultural change historians have to relate also to art historians, professors of literature, etc. (those who *study* art and literature rather than produce it) and *their* products (works of art history, literary criticism, etc.). Anyway the important issue is that the achievements of a society, after all, are its works of art, as well as its political and social organisation and its technological innovations. The classic nineteenth-century work looking at the full cultural achievements of a society and their implications, was Burckhardt's *Civilization of the Renaissance in Italy*. Great richness is to be found in such more recent works as *The Age of Humanism and Reformation* (1972) by A. G. Dickens, with its carefully chosen and carefully placed visual illustrations, and its quotations from contemporary poems and writings. Dickens is a historian, and the political narrative and sense of change through time are strong, but in a very practical way he had to be a practitioner of interdisciplinary study, as when, for example, he discussed the relationship between the Counter-Reformation and artistic developments:

Thus within two decades of his death, history falsified the prediction of Martin Luther that a moribund Papacy would swiftly vanish from the scene. Its victory had perhaps been won at a heavy price, yet although the Inquisition and the Index hampered some thinkers, this price did not include the atrophy of intellectual life, much less that of great art and music, within the Catholic countries. Despite such episodes as the persecution of Galileo, southern Europe continued its contribution to most branches of scientific enquiry, while the worlds of Palestrina, of Rubens and Bernini, were far from being cast into the shade by those of Rembrandt, Newton, and Bach. Yet concerning one related theme beloved by many histories of civilization, the present writer must admit to scepticism: the notion that the Baroque art and architecture of the seventeenth century was the child of the Catholic Reformation, a 'Jesuit-style,' 'a hymn of joy raised by the triumphant Church.' The style of the middle and later decades of the sixteenth century was not of course Baroque: it was what we now call Mannerism, that somewhat cold and stilted derivative from that *maniera* of Michelangelo. The full-blooded Baroque had its origins around 1600 but did not reach its climax until a full century after the formation of the Society of Jesus. On this reckoning it seems to have taken the Church a long time to decide whether it was enjoying the Counter Reformation! In actual fact, when it did at last arrive, Baroque soon became a multipurpose style contributing as much to the glorification of monarchs and aristocrats as to the triumph of the Church. Even in Rome, the building and decoration of the great Baroque churches came far less from the religious Orders than from the aristocracy and cardinalate, rich patrons allowed once more to rival the splendors of the High Renaissance – but in return for an adherence to dogmatic and moral purity. The great spirits of the Catholic Reformation had strangely little in common with the Baroque age: they were surely among the least pompous and flamboyant characters in the history of the Church.[18]

One also thinks of Paul Fussel's deservedly praised *The Great War and Modern Memory* (1978) which (Fussel is an American Professor of English) employs literature to illuminate the impact of the Great War, and the Great War to illuminate transformations in literary modes.

The links between history and the other humanities, then, have not been newly forged. It was in fact literature, and in lesser degree art history and musicology, which for long remained rather aloof from history. The new developments which have led to the enunciation of 'cultural theory' and the study of the social relations of the arts were in part a reaction against isolationism, and what was held to be an overly élitist aesthetic approach. The new movement has been broadly Marxist in inspiration, taking up in particular the refinements of Gramsci and Lukacs. Since my criticisms of Marxism have been made known several times in the course of this book, it is important to acknowledge how much of the pioneering work in interdisciplinary cultural studies has been carried out by those with a Marxist orientation: one of the great strengths of Marxism was its emphasis on the interconnectedness of human activities; inspiration also came from a Marxist-inspired desire to understand how the values of a society are maintained and transmitted. The best work, associated for instance with such figures in the world of literary studies as Raymond Williams and Terry Eagleton, has greatly enhanced understanding of art and literature as social phenomena. My reservations are the ones already stated: that much work in this genre is based on assumptions (often unstated) about the nature of class structure, class conflict, and the operation of dialectical processes. But the stress on the need to study the conditions of cultural production and cultural consumption, and to define and explain the status which different cultural artefacts achieved, both in the society in which they were created, and subsequently, is a valuable one, and in fact very congruent with historians' long-held belief in the significance of the social and historical context. Difficulties arise when the vision of historical stages inevitably succeeding each other is invoked, together with rigid definitions of capitalist and bourgeois society, longer-term cultural influences and the phenomena of relative autonomy being ignored. I have said something already of the new jargon which the new approach has brought: from the point of view of the pragmatic historian the fanciful metaphor of processes of negotiation taking place in the formation of cultural hegemony carries too heavy a freight of untested assumptions about dialectical conflict. It is difficult to believe in alternative and emergent ideologies which never actually emerge. To me such assertions as that Carol Reed's film *The Stars Look Down* (1958) 'proved that cinema was maturing as a hegemonic instrument, becoming more clearly an area of exchange and negotiation rather than a patronising instrument of ideological coercion'[19] simply re-states a predetermined position without saying anything of real interest about this fascinating film. Discourse theory, which envis-ages all texts in terms of the discourses they embody is indissolubly linked to the Marxist notion of ideology, which it never seeks to question. Language is seen as a central medium of power.[20]

Somehow I cannot see discourse theory, trapped as it is in its preoccupation with dominance, ever making major contributions to historical knowledge – so far its areas of investigation have been extremely circumscribed.

However it would be ungracious, and indeed downright unfair, not to acknowledge the immense stimulus provided by both cultural and linguistic theory, not least in their raising of the question of whether art really exists, or whether the canonised art forms (high or élite culture) deserve the superior status they are given over popular culture. The argument is made that since interdisciplinary studies are so limitless there must be the control and discipline of theory.[21] I understand the argument, but can't avoid the feeling that if the theory is in fact wrong, there is little point in applying it. Perhaps theoreticians and pragmatics can come together in agreeing some kind of list of issues which might be explicitly raised in any form of interdisciplinary cultural studies. Here are my suggestions:

1. *Methodology*. In what ways do the methodological approaches followed in the various arts, or in literature, differ from those employed in history; are there, for instance, different ways of approaching 'texts', or is there perhaps some common ground? Or is there simply one methodology applicable in 'cultural studies'?

2. *Theory*. What is the place of theory when studying the relationship between the arts, literature and the historical and social context? Is it necessary in each individual case to establish the precise nature of social structure and social relationships, or can one accept some prior theory about the nature of class structure, class conflict, dominant and oppositional ideologies, etc?

3. *Style, Period, Taste*. How valid are any, or all, of these concepts, and how useful are they in bringing together cultural artefacts and the social context?

4. *National culture and foreign influences*. Is the notion of a national culture a useful one? Is it possible to detect influences from one culture affecting another? (British art is often said to be parochial, Dickens to be 'very English'. The influences of Italian Renaissance architecture have, on the other hand, been widely detected in other societies; it is sometimes said that in his later years Verdi absorbed influences from French opera; the notion

that America has influenced twentieth-century popular culture is widespread.)

5. *Autonomy versus Social Construction.* In discussing cultural products what weight is to be placed on such concepts as autonomy (or relative autonomy), individual genius, the particular traditions, preoccupations or 'logic' of a particular art form? Can it be successfully argued that all art is socially constructed?

6. *Cultural production, consumption, and status.* Is it helpful, and if so in what ways, to analyse the conditions of cultural production and consumption, and to evaluate the status awarded to particular cultural artefacts, at the time of their production and subsequently?

7. *The Existence of Art.* Does something called Art (or Literature) exist, separate from, say, the traditional documents of the historian? Or is what has traditionally been canonised as art simply one product, or interpretation, of society to be placed against countless others?

Personally, I do believe that high art exists, and that it is possible to make at least relative value judgements about art. (Those who deny this might honestly consider what they are prepared to pay for certain cultural experiences as against others – really the same for a James Bond movie as for an opera?; literary scholars tell me that poems, and certain novels, have to be read carefully several times – a mark surely of high art? – one does not usually read Agatha Christie or *The Beano* several times.) The extent to which one agrees or disagrees that art exists may colour one's approach to the first of my questions, concerning methodology, which is the only one which I am going to develop here. It seems to me that the critical methodology which I have described in this book has many parallels in the other humanities: at the central core, one directly studies *texts*, whether these be historical documents, poems, pieces of music, buildings, paintings, or philosophical treatises. In studying (or *reading*, in the jargon of today) these texts, one has to:

1. decide what category they fall into (act of parliament or private diary, novel or poem, symphony or sonata);
2. *understand* what is in them;
3. apply principles of *criticism* (these vary from discipline to

discipline; I have been concerned with the principles of historical source criticism);

4. follow up references and allusions in the text (for history, this formed part of the list of questions I gave in connection with the principles of historical source criticism).

Of course there are important differences between studying history and studying the other humanities. However much art historians or musicologists, for example, may be concerned with the way in which art or music is produced and consumed, and with its relationship to the surrounding culture, there must be questions (unless one denies altogether the existence of art) about whether a particular composer is 'great' or not, or whether a particular painting is a 'masterpiece' or not, even if it is insisted that these terms in the end are 'culturally constructed'. No one would ever claim that the sort of documents historians mainly deal with are 'great' or 'masterpieces'. Domesday book is a phenomenal achievement; one has great respect for those who drafted the American Declaration of Independence; and one may find enjoyment in the literary style of Ficino's letter which I quoted earlier: but one would not compare any of these documents with a poem by a major poet or a painting by a major artist. In fact, in the other arts subjects there is much value in studying one single painting or listening to one piece of music, or analysing one short piece of philosophical exposition. But one cannot usually learn much history from one document (Domesday Book is exceptional in its size as in other things – but much in Domesday Book, taken in isolation, has little meaning). The whole essence of historical study lies in the putting together of a large number of documents to build up a complete interpretation. History is concerned with a vast range of human activities within society. It is concerned with public events, relationships between groups and society, changes in these relationships, and with questions of causes, consequences and interrelationships over a wide field of social activities. Yet this subject matter invites our admiration and moves our emotions, as do great art, great music and great literature. There is indeed much to admire in the creation of political and social institutions, in the building of cities and transport systems, as in the creation of cathedrals and palaces; and as also in the struggle of the underprivileged against oppression, and of individuals and groups in all walks of society against man's inhumanity to man. History joins with the other humanities in being both the celebration, and the rigorous analysis and criticism of, human activities and human achievements.

Thus, history and the other humanities come together because, in the last analysis, *they are concerned with the same objective*: expanding and developing our perceptions and understanding of the world and the place of humanity within it. Barbara Hardy in her lively introduction to Thomas Hardy's *The Trumpet Major*, speaks of that 'essential part of history, the part that had to be written not by historians proper but by the novelists'.[22] What Barbara Hardy is here thinking of, is the history of ordinary people, to which the novelist can give life and intensity by creating fictional characters; but a warning again – no novel, however perceptive, can ever have the status of a secondary source (and it is only a primary source, and a problematic one, for the period in which it is written). Today many historians would feel that they have a great duty to record the history of ordinary people, though debarred of course from creating fictional personages. Here certainly is a realm for fruitful cross-disciplinary discussion between historians and literary critics. All of Thomas Hardy's novels have a sense of period and a sense of history, though *The Trumpet Major* is the only one consciously set as far back in time as the beginning of the nineteenth century within a deliberate historical frame created by Napoleon's threatened invasion of England. Hardy himself stressed the amount of research which had gone into the making of *The Trumpet Major* and, indeed, regarded himself as in a real sense 'a historian'; though in the end, of course, his purposes, the illumination of the mundane, irrational, and underlying tragedy of ordinary human affairs, are not the *particular* ones of the historian – though *in general*, as suggested above, historian and novelist combine to illuminate the nature of human experience. I speak here – as a basis for discussion – of ultimate objectives. I do not in any way dilute my insistence that in method and approach the writing of history has little more in common with the writing of a novel than it has with composing a symphony or cooking a three-course meal.

Two other of the great nineteenth-century English novelists each consciously wrote one deliberately historical novel: *A Tale of Two Cities* (Dickens) and *Middlemarch* (George Eliot). The apocalyptic vision of the French Revolution presented by Dickens owed too much (he fully admitted his debt) to Thomas Carlyle to pass without criticism by professional historians; its true origins, anyway, lay not in a desire to portray revolution, but in the theme, as again Dickens acknowledged, presented in a play by his friend Wilkie Collins in which Dickens himself acted, the theme of two suitors for the same woman, one of whom sacrifices himself for his rival.[23] George Eliot's *Middlemarch*, however, does do rich justice to the crisis of the great Reform Bill and its effects on a group of relatively ordinary people. The novels of Balzac illuminate significant social developments in early nineteenth century France, but are concerned also with matters of moral choice and the exposure of human frailty. Such works enhance human understanding, offer important topics on which historians and literary scholars can work together; but they are not history. Co-operation is much to be desired, confusion to be avoided like the plague. The historian who aspires to the imaginative insights and the narrative style of Honoré de Balzac or George Eliot had better give up writing history.

3. Making Films, T.V. and Videos

Film, television tapes, and the many kinds of visual source have already been mentioned in connection with the great variety of primary sources available to historians. In general, they call for the range of critical techniques which has already been discussed, requiring in addition, particular technical skills. To analyse a film, it is necessary to break it down into sequences, and sometimes into scenes, and shots. It is necessary to recognise the different types of shot and the use of different lenses, understand the language of dissolves, fades, and cuts, and to be sensitive to the way a sound track is dubbed and to the deployment of music.[24] With cartoons it is necessary to understand, among other things, the idiom within which they are conceived. With paintings it is necessary to understand the objectives of the artist (artistic and historical), the conventions within which he is operating, and the reception accorded his paintings by his patrons and his audiences. But in the two final sections of this chapter I am concerned with film, video and other visual materials, not as sources, but as modes of historical communication, or components of such modes. I have already stressed that the fourth of the historian's tasks is one of the most important and most difficult. I have also consistently argued that history must involve dialogue, must invite the participation of readers or audience. Everything comes together. If historians have used film or other visual material as basic pieces of evidence, then they will need to show these pieces of evidence in support of whatever interpretation they are putting forward. Let us consider film, television, and video programmes of various sorts. In the real world, as governed by the prevailing conditions of production, consumption and status, there will be a distinction between historical documentaries made on a broadly commercial basis for transmission to relatively large audiences, and videos specially made by historians for their own educational purposes. But wherever professional historians are involved they should, I strongly believe, endeavour to impose their own standards.

The British Broadcasting Corporation has a high reputation for producing serious historical documentaries: it is not overridingly governed by commercial considerations, though it does feel a necessity to put on programmes which will, as conventionally understood, have audience appeal. High standards have also been achieved by the independent television networks in Britain. On BBC the regular series *Timewatch* shows genuine concern to bring to an intelligent general audience insights into new research areas being opened up by professional historians. Yet, the difference between what conventional broadcasters think audiences should be offered, and the potential for the serious exploitation of the medium by historians is sometimes enormous.

In May 1984 the *Timewatch* series presented a programme on the Norman Conquest. Though praised by the T.V. critics, this programme was a classic example of how not to do history on television. Exactly what the programme was trying to do was never made clear, though various devices were used to try to make the viewer feel that there was some exciting controversy over which historians were in passionate conflict and that, in particular, from the application of computer techniques to Domesday Book, breathtaking discoveries were on the way. History *is* an exciting subject but the excitement must, as it were, be allowed to emerge from within, particularly on television where tricks and clichés, unless forcibly restrained, just tumble out one after the other. John Tusa, the presenter, hammed up the fictitious drama, pausing, drawing a deep breath, turning across the camera like a latter-day Kenneth Clark (presenter of the famous art history series *Civilisation*). There were excerpts from interviews with famous and less famous historians edited to convey donnish dedication to a particular cause, but so brief, and so lacking in context, as to be practically incoherent. At the end the various dons were brought together in a kind of brains trust, a highly stereotyped way of ending a T.V. documentary of any description. Professor J. C. Holt was asked if he thought the Norman Conquest had any real impact on Britain. Yes, of course, he said, one had simply to compare pre-Norman Romanesque churches with post-Conquest churches. What a perfect opportunity for a genuine televisual exploration of a point totally grounded on visual evidence. But, whereas earlier the programme had lost no opportunity to unload the usual old wallpaper (an actor reading from Domesday Book mentions cows, so grazing cows come up on the screen), this time the point passed as a purely verbal one without the viewer being given any opportunity to assess the validity of the evidence upon which it was based. The entire programme had been planned as a series of television clichés, not built outwards from the richness of the available visual evidence.

There have of course been some good *Timewatch* programmes, careful reports on current research rather than attempts to blitz viewers into bemused acquiescence, and in the early seventies Thames Television's *World at War*, directed by Jeremy Isaacs, set new standards for prodigious research and integrity of presentation. Even that series, however, did in the end follow the old formula of settling first on an interpretation or storyline, then illustrating it with archive film material and edited 'eye-witness' interviews, rather than working outwards critically from the visual material. The general theme was that all war is dreadful, expressed in the opening sequence of the opening programme where, after the hideous civilian massacre carried out by the Germans at Oradour, the commentator (plummy and sententious Sir Laurence Olivier) remarks that shortly the young German soldiers too will be killed. That a more open approach might have been preferable was driven home strikingly in May 1988 when Isaacs, in a T.V.

lecture on the series, without batting an eyelid, expressed a different view; the war *had* been necessary.

The essential consideration in my view is as follows: theses, articles, monographs, general histories, and textbooks are made up of paragraphs and sentences and are, despite the enormous variety of non-traditional sources that exist, drawn mainly from written sources, primary and secondary. Film and television programmes are made up of visual images, though they will also contain other elements such as spoken commentary and perhaps even music (just as a book may contain illustrations or diagrams); they should be largely drawn from visual evidence. That contrast is the key to the whole discussion over the value and use of film. However, the opinion is controversial. Some historians and certainly many film makers and television producers would argue that a film or television programme can be used to put over exactly the same topic as a book or article might be used for; only, they argue, film, having greater immediacy and emotional potency, particularly in a world when we are all used to the visual media, will put over whatever particular historical interpretation is agreed on with much more force and appeal than a mere book or lecture would. Here, then, is the great divide: the divide between those who wish to use the visual media and all their allied resources to put over a particular interpretation with the greatest possible force, and those who believe in using film and television to explore the complexities of visual evidence. The battle was joined at a meeting of the American Film Historians' Committee in 1972 when Rolf Schuursma from the Netherlands argued for an approach to film-making based on patient reconstruction from primary visual documents, while the Americans spoke of the deeper insights into historical processes provided by the imaginative skills of the professional film maker.[25] The 'American' approach is exemplified in R. C. Raack's compilation film *Storm of Fire: World War II and the Destruction of Dresden* which many European academics have criticised as simply attempting to bludgeon students into accepting one interpretation without any attempt to give serious consideration to the evidence, visual or otherwise. A slightly different approach has been followed by certain French academics, including Marc Ferro and Pierre Sorlin. They too have taken complete historical episodes, rather than topics basically arising from, and delimited by, the available visual evidence, but have followed a much more open approach in that by presenting interesting contrasts and juxtapositions (including in Sorlin's case, the use of music) they hope to raise in their students' minds questions about underlying structures and relationships within the episodes they are analysing. Yet again, it can be argued that such films impose too much of the maker's cleverness on the student and do not leave enough opportunity for students themselves to analyse the visual material they are being presented with. Sorlin has recently been concentrating on filmed histories of urban areas (in Paris and in Italy), ideal subjects for exposition on film. The method of patient reconstruction, combined with the most detailed scholarly analysis of film as source material and exploration of the uses of film for educational purposes, is exemplified in the work of the Institut für den Wissen-schaftlichen Film at Göttingen, of Stichting Film in Wetenschap at Utrecht, of Karsten Fledelius and his compatriots in Denmark, and of the British Universities' Film Consortium in Britain. Further developments, always to the highest academic standards, have been fostered by the International Association for Audio Visual Material in Historical Research and Education (IAMHIST).[26]

The argument, then, is that if history film or television programmes are to be made (and they definitely should be made) they should concentrate on those topics where visual evidence is genuinely of significance. It follows that no major historical topic could be exhaustively covered in a film or television programme; and that no complete history course could be given through the medium of television alone. For many major topics, and for most of the conceptual arguments, it will be necessary to have resort to the traditional printed or spoken word. No doubt, the various general broadcasting services will go on presenting historical programmes which attempt to give a comprehensive coverage of their subject. Obviously the major television stations cannot expect their viewers to undertake a heavy course of supplementary reading before viewing such programmes, which, at their best, may be regarded as the equivalent of the very highest quality coffee-table history books. However they will be better as history, for general audiences as well as students to the extent to which they adhere to the basic principle that visual programmes should essentially deal with visual evidence, and should not unload vast amounts of conceptual analysis or even factual narrative which can only be presented over either (a) irrelevant 'wallpaper', or (b) interesting unidentified visual material which will, in fact, run in competition with the commentary, making it difficult to concentrate on one or the other.

One stock-in-trade of the conventional film maker is the 'eye-witness interview', too often used without any apparent awareness of the fallibility of eye-witness accounts, particularly of events which may have taken place a generation before. It is always intriguing to see and hear the veterans of old wars or old trade-union battles; but whether what they say is actually much of a contribution to historical knowledge is another matter. Usually what they say either fits in with the predetermined interpretation of the film maker, or simply provides a little light relief. Both criticisms apply, for instance, to the interviews with trade-union veterans featured in the immensely moving and skilful film *The Wobblies* (U.S.A., 1979) directed by Stuart Bird and Deborah Schaffer. This film presents a highly sympathetic account of the International Workers of the World, while being scathing about the American Federation of Labor and American society generally. The message is insistent; there in no analysis of the visual evidence nor of the enormous issues being raised.

Thus I come to the fundamental principle that anyone making a historical film or television programme should be as familiar with the visual materials which will provide the basis of that programme as they would be with the written materials which would form the basis of an article or book. They will also have to have a belief in the value of visual evidence, whether it be archaeology, history on the ground, paintings, cartoons, advertisements, or newsreel, documentary, or feature film: I take it that this book has already made out the case for the immense value of all such sources, but shall here say a little bit more about film as primary source (as distinct from my main purpose in this section of discussing film and television as secondary sources or teaching aids). Broadly, one can list the following uses of film evidence in academic research: film in common with most other forms of visual evidence, such as photographs or paintings, shows the reality of life-styles – newsreel of the 1930s, for example, shows just how absurd it is to claim that all social classes dressed alike and looked alike; film shows concretely, as perhaps no other source can, the reality of particular situations, activities, or processes – for example Second World War footage brings home sharply the inequality in terms of combat between highly mobile fighter planes and ponderous, heavily laden bombers; film can be a particularly effective form of portraiture of particular individuals – wild Lloyd George, waffling Ramsay MacDonald, dynamic Franklin D. Roosevelt; film, in common with all other sorts of creative artefacts, is a particularly rich source for the perceptions and assumptions held within particular groups and societies; and film, finally, is obviously a central source for the study of film itself, and for the way in which it is exploited, consciously or unconsciously, by governments and private individuals to put over particular assumptions about society, or propagandist messages. Here I have been speaking of existing archive film, whether newsreel, documentary, or feature film. When one comes to the actual making of a film or television programme one can, of course, specially create film of one's own: this can be particularly useful for conveying life-styles or physical appearances in regions not readily accessible to one's students or viewers; it can also be particularly useful for conveying the realities of certain processes, such as printing, or the different sorts of manufacture.

But the film or television maker is not confined to film sources alone. It is possible to do much with photography, paintings, advertisements, cartoons, provided always that these are treated with respect as documents, just as written documents should be treated respectfully by the serious historian. I say 'just as' but in fact a specially deliberate care has to be taken with visual evidence. One can interleave quotations, direct or indirect, from many written sources into one paragraph. Sleight of hand has been such a regular device of film makers for so long, and anyway visual evidence is not easy to identify separately unless a special effort is made, that it is important to be particularly self-conscious in this respect when putting together a film. It should at all times be clear to the viewer exactly what it is he or she is seeing and where it came from. This of course runs entirely contrary to the basic film maker's craft of montage, of editing tiny clips from here and there into one beautiful smooth compilation. But such very smoothness does violence to the complex problems of historical study.

It is easier, of course, to enunciate such principles than to realise

them successfully in practice. Much will depend upon the exact
context within which the completed film or television programme
is to be used. But the principle that the programme will not in
itself be self-contained remains true. Either it will have to be
supplemented with the printed word, or it will have to be set
within a classroom context in which the lecturer can provide the
necessary verbal and conceptual information. Still, there can be
no doubt that every programme, however rooted in, and confined
to visual evidence, will need to contain a certain amount of verbal
analysis and explanation. How to deal with this is one of the
fundamental problems. Is it best simply to have the academic
whose analysis and explanation is being conveyed speak directly
to camera? If not, there is inevitably going to be something of a
wallpaper effect as the analysis and explanation are presented
over some visual material which cannot possibly be directly and
continuously relevant. Perhaps the words themselves should come
up on the screen. But such devices become self-defeating if the
programme, as programme, begins to break down.

No one has yet found all the answers; all that can be offered
are a few guidelines. One can also suggest the sorts of areas in
which television and film programmes are likely to be particularly
successful. John Ramsden, working with the British Inter-Universities Film Consortium produced an excellent film, drawn from
Conservative party films and newsreels, on Stanley Baldwin: the
essential thrust of the programme was the changing way in which,
in parallel with his fluctuating political fortunes, Baldwin was
presented on the screen. This is a limited and scholarly purpose,
arising naturally from the material, which nonetheless results in
genuine additional illumination of Baldwin and his place in British
political life.

Propaganda is obviously an especially fruitful subject: the Open
University history programme *German and Russian Propaganda
Film* is a perfect example of a piece of historical analysis which
could not be presented any other way than in the form of a film
programme. An example of a film programme basically aiming to
take students into an unfamiliar environment, both in period and
in place, is another one from the same Open University history
series, *Paris the Imperial City*, which of course had to use contemporary prints and paintings, blended with specially shot film of
surviving buildings. Without rhetoric or artifice this programme

really does project one back into the nineteenth century. At one point, while we are scrutinising a contemporary painting of the Place de la Concorde, our attention is drawn to a couple of hunters appearing in this urban square, unwitting testimony to the continuing closeness at that time of country and town.

But, for my money, the most fertile area of all is that of assumptions and perceptions. Dan Leab has shown how film can be used to illuminate the attitudes in American society towards the Black American. Kenneth Short has done rather similar work on British attitudes towards Jews, though as yet he has not had the opportunity to turn this basic research into a compilation film. The comparative study of feature film from different countries can illuminate the different perceptions of social structure held in the different countries; feature film can be important evidence of, and perhaps even an agent in, changes in attitudes to class, and in sexual attitudes and behaviour. Film can also be valuable evidence for material conditions, and I want here to give some detail on the Open University programme *Film as Historical Evidence: Poverty in the 1930s*, which is a comparative study of Britain and America.

After a brief to-camera introduction the programme shows, interspersed with more to-camera commentary and analysis: (1) a British Paramount news item from November 1936, *King Visits South Wales; says 'I will help;'* (this clip is repeated so that students can follow up points and questions which I put to them); (2) a long extract from the American documentary of 1940, *Men and Dust*; (3) excerpts from Robert Flaherty's documentary, *The Land*, begun in 1939 and released in 1941; (4) an excerpt from the feature film *Love on the Dole* of 1941; (5) an excerpt from King Vidor's feature film *Our Daily Bread* of 1933. Here are some excerpts from the script:

... First a British newsreel item of 1936 during the very brief reign of King Edward VIII. As you watch it try to respond to certain specific points. What aspect of poverty does the film illuminate? What exactly does it tell us, wittingly and unwittingly? What do you feel about the tone of the commentary? Do you notice any characteristically British clichés?

Well, it's about unemployment and we – and of course, the large cinema audiences of the time – are given the hard figures – one in three out of work in South Wales; Dowlais shut down since 1928. But a further important witting message is that King Edward cares and that his concern will produce results. Unlike politicians, we are told, he's not self-interested – actually, as you probably know, even if he hadn't been forced to abdicate there's not really a lot a King could have done. Still unwittingly, the film tells us a lot about the reverence for this particular King. The phoney urgency of the commentary is typical of newsreels of the time. Essentially they were made as part of the entertainment industry with the definite intention of never presenting anything too disturbing. The overall tone is one of threadbare optimism. Let's take another look . . .

The historical significance is twofold: we see what contemporaries were being told, and we ourselves get a unique sense of the way things looked in depressed South Wales and of the complacent treatment offered by newsreels . . .

. . . we also see film evidence at its best, with very potent and accurate images of specifically American types of poverty. We see the special influence of geography, of climate. *Men and Dust* tells us about the 'belly' of America – did a compact little country like Britain have a 'belly' in any similar sense? Note above all the enormous pride in America as 'the richest country in the world' – this is a recurrent and crucial contrast with the threadbare optimism of British films . . .

I'm sure you were struck by the need to bring in water at ten cents a barrel, but there were other powerful images of deprivation. The trick is to filter out the emotive music, the biblical cadences of the commentary, and to concentrate on the very powerful factual evidence which *is* undoubtedly there . . .

The story of unemployment and deprivation in industrial Lancashire is recognisable and real enough. *Our Daily Bread* of 1933 concerns a middle-class couple who run a farming commune in the Mid-West employing a miscellaneous gang of migrants – a significant group, as we have seen, in America of the 30s. It's not soil erosion this time, but drought which threatens disaster. I suggested the mood of *Love on the Dole* was impotent resignation – now decide how you would describe the mood of *Our Daily Bread* . . .

I know, you'd rather go on watching the film than listen to me again. Feature film can be particularly seductive, even hypnotic. Using feature film as evidence, you have to be particularly on guard: there's a lot of unwitting testimony about totally different geography and climates: and about different fundamental assumptions – did you pick up the point that all the migrants had cars while Sally's taxi was an almost unimaginable extravagance? With all historical evidence, be on guard: but look carefully and you will learn a lot.

The essence of this programme is (and I believe this should be the essence of all video programmes) that visual documents are the starting point, analysis and commentary from other sources then being brought in as appropriate; this is the opposite procedure from starting off with the verbal argument, then looking around for visual sources to provide mere illustration. A further refinement is to drop all presentation and commentary and simply provide students with video cassettes of archive film material, on which they are set exercises to carry out themselves.

There is another, rather different, sphere in which the film or television programme can be of great use. This is in putting over basic methodology. For example the British Inter-Universities Film Consortium have a programme on palaeography. Three introductory programmes in the Open University Arts Foundation Course bring out, in a way which only film can, the many different processes and activities that historians go through in producing works of history.

4. Incorporating Visual Sources into Written History

Film is glamorous, but one should never forget the importance of woodcuts, etchings, cartoons, photographs and paintings. For too long these have simply been used as decoration, added to books by publishers, often quite independently of the author or his written text. Braudel and many French scholars have tried to emphasise the importance of visuals of many sorts in helping one to understand a past society, though usually they have not been very successful in integrating the illustrations with the text (typically French books print a collection of illustrations at the *end* as a kind of appendix). The American expert on film, television and photography, David Culbert has written acutely and wittily about the consistent misuse of visuals in textbooks, where often the illustration bears little relationship to what the author is actually saying.[27] In a historical book using illustrations one should in fact aim to realise the same principles as I have enunciated with regard to television and video programmes. The visual should be a genuine source which makes points of its own. It should then be placed in the text at the point where it is actually being discussed so that readers can be examining the visual in conjunction with the critical analysis which the author makes of it.[28]

A truly pioneering venture, and one of the most impressive demonstrations of the value of visual sources is R. W. Scribner's 'attempt to combine print and picture' in 'a study of visual

propaganda, and of its role in the dissemination of the evangelical
movement during the first half-century of the Reformation in
Germany',[29] entitled *For the Sake of Simple Folk* (Cambridge,
1981). Scribner triumphantly vindicates his argument 'that through
a study of visual propaganda we may gain a wider understanding
of how the Reformation appealed to common folk than by concentrating attention more narrowly on printed propaganda alone.'
The logistic difficulties of presenting illustration at exactly the
point in the text where it is discussed are considerable, as anyone
who has tried will know. Scribner admits that, partly for commercial reasons, some of his illustrations are smaller than he would
desire. However, the integration of print and picture really does
command admiration. There is space here for only one exemplifi-
cation of the Scribner method, taken from the two facing pages
60 and 61 (with footnotes omitted) on the lower quarter of each
of which is to be found a reproduction of a woodcut (illustrations
43 and 44 respectively in the book). At this stage in his analysis,
Scribner is making the point that within the popular culture of
the day the 'uses of play for a propagandist are numerous'.

A good example can be found in the title page to the pamphlet *The
Lutheran Strebkatz* (ill. 43). The Strebkatz was a popular game in
which two opponents engaged in a tug-of-war by gripping between
their teeth two rods, which were connected by cords. This contraption
was itself called the *Strebkatz* and the players contended for its sole
possession. In this version, the cords pass around the contestants'
necks. The original form of the game is depicted in the title page of a
1522 pamphlet (ill. 44), where two monks contend for the prize, a
wreath held by a watching damsel. In the first instance, the contestants
are Luther and the pope, who is helped by a crowd of supporters
representing some of Luther's main opponents – Eck, Emser,
Cockleus, Murner, Hochstraten, Lemp and Alfeld. Although the
contest seems unequal, Luther has dragged the pope to his knees so
violently that his tiara has fallen off and his money purse has burst.
Luther's victory is aided only by the crucified Christ, signified by the
small crucifix he holds aloft in the faces of his opponents . . .

The scene at the top of illustration 44 uses a similar technique, based
on another typical contest of the time, the tournament. Christ is shown
jousting with the pope, who wears armour and is seated on a war-steed
attended by a footsoldier-devil . . . The pope carries in his left hand a
letter hung with seals, signifying a papal bull, the weapon of the pope.
It is from this hand that the lance has fallen, connoting that Christ is
more powerful than papal condemnations.

In the very last sentences of his book, Scribner effectively quotes from Luther himself:

> 'without images we can neither think nor understand anything.' Here he called attention to a first principle of the study of popular mentalities; in this book we have but followed his sound advice.

Perhaps the most splendid example yet to appear of the integration of visual sources (and in this case not simply woodcuts, but the full richness of Dutch painting at its height) with an analytical text, is Simon Schama's *The Embarrassment of Riches: An Interpretation of Dutch Culture in the Golden Age* (New York, 1987). I can give only one sample here, taken from pages 204–5, where the commentary runs beside and underneath the Jan Steen painting, *Tavern Scene* on page 205 (footnote omitted):

> As a source of bawdy innuendo, the pipe seems to have been inexhaustibly ribald. Jan Steen made the most relentless use of the device in genre scenes where coarse mirth is prudentially qualified by faint flushes of embarrassment, perhaps even shame. One of the many tavern paintings to include a guffawing self-portrait is virtually an anthology of Dutch smut. No lewd reference to the condition of the girl or to the act which brought it about has been omitted. Broken egg shells, mussels, an open *flapkan* tankard, a gaping bunghole, a scrutinized chamberpot and no fewer than three pointing handles and stems provide rib-nudging visual counterparts for the cruel prurience of the cacophonous laughter. There is eloquent visual communication between the girl and her seducer, a study in rancid dissipation extraordinary even for Steen, whose second occupation as innkeeper enabled him to observe tavern behaviour at first hand. Even their body language is telling, reinforcing the distinction between victim and malefactor. While the girl places a hand on the maternal bosom, her wrong-doer pokes a little finger into the bowl of his pipe, re-enacting by the obscene gesture the cause of her distress.

A final word. It is all too easy to be bewitched by the attractions of visual sources of all sorts, and particularly with film. Both are difficult to handle, yet with a little thought, can be used in the serious communication of research discoveries, and in teaching. But the areas which visual and film sources illuminate are relatively limited. For the vast part of our knowledge about the past, we will continue to depend very heavily on written sources. Let us then use both in the best and most appropriate ways.

Notes

1. For a discussion of Hegel see: B. Taylor Wilkins, *Hegel's Philosophy of History* (1974).

2. For what follows, see M. F. Ashley Montague (ed.), *Toynbee and History* (1956).

3. H. Stuart Hughes, *Consciousness and Society* (1958), 1977 pb edn, pp. 199–200.

4. Breisach, p. 323.

5. Benedetto Croce, *History as the Story of Liberty* (1955), p. 43.

6. Colleagues whose wisdom I respect have tried to explain to me why not. But I still don't understand.

7. R. G. Collingwood, *An Autobiography* (1939), pp. 87–8.

8. Central passages from the writers cited in this section can be found in the useful collections edited by Patrick Gardiner, *Theories of History* (1959), William H. Dray, *Philosophical Analysis and History* (1966), and Sydney Hook, *Philosophy and History: A Symposium* (1963).

9. Raymond Aron, *Introduction to the Philosophy of History* (1961), pp. 9, 277.

10. See the source books cited in note 8.

11. Patrick Gardiner, *The Nature of Historical Explanation* (1952), p. 27.

12. Ibid., p. 136.

13. R. F. Atkinson, *Knowledge and Explanation in History* (1978), p. 138.

14. G. R. Elton, *The Practice of History* (1967), p. 138.

15. Ibid., p. 136.

16. W. H. Dray, *Philosophy of History* (1964), p. 98.

17. Geoffrey Best, *Mid-Victorian Britain* (1971), pp. 263–4.

18. A. G. Dickens, *The Age of Humanism and Reformation* (Englewood Cliffs, 1972), pp. 190–2.

19. Peter Miles and Malcolm Smith, *Cinema, Literature and Society: Elite and Mass Culture in Inter-War Britain* (1987), p. 98.

20. See John B. Thompson, *Studies in the Theory of Ideology* (Cambridge, 1984), pp. 1–12, 131, 257. Thompson comments on p. 8 that 'the various forms of discourse analysis have yielded results which are disappointing in many ways.'

21. See, e.g., Roderick Floud in *History*, LXIX (1984), pp. 57–8 (Floud was writing specifically on the subject of industrialisation).

22. Barbara Hardy, Introduction to *The Trumpet Major* (New Wessex edition, 1974), p. 29.

23. Introduction by George Woodcock to *A Tale of Two Cities* (Penguin edition 1970), p. 9.

24. See Pierre Sorlin, *The Film in History; Restaging the Past* (Oxford, 1980), Part I, 'Principles and Methods'.

25. Reported in *University Vision* no. 10, June 1973, pp. 48–50.

26. See the section 'Film et Histoire' in Comité International des

Sciences historiques, *XVIe Congress International des Sciences Historiques: Rapports* I (Stuttgart, 1985), pp. 180–239, papers by Fledelius, Dolezel and Bodensieck, and Sorlin and Marwick.

27. David Culbert, 'Visual History: The Use of Media in Teaching American History in the United States.' Proceedings of the Xth International Conference on History of the Audio-Visual Media, Imola, Italy, September 1983, pp. 60–86 Microfiche; Copenhagen: Eventus, 1985.

28. I have tried to practise what I preach in my *The Home Front: the British and the Second World War* (1976), *Britain in our Century: Images and Controversies* (1984), and *Beauty in History: Society, Politics and Personal Appearance, c. 1500 to the Present* (1988).

29. R. W. Scribner, *For the Sake of Simple Folk* (Cambridge 1981), pp. 1–2.

Chapter 8 Controversy in History

1. The Significance of Controversy in History

Because historical sources are fragmentary and imperfect there is much scope for differences in the interpretations produced by historians. There are many famous controversies in history. 'Why did the American colonists rebel against the British government?' 'What exactly was the Renaissance and when did it take place?' 'Did the Industrial Revolution raise or lower the standard of living of the majority of the British people?' 'What exactly was the impact of colonisation on Africa?' 'What was the precise nature of the manorial economy in the Middle Ages?'. 'What, over the centuries, have been the main changes in the institution of the family?' 'What were the causes of the English Civil War in the seventeenth century?' 'What were the causes of the Second World War in the twentieth century?' 'What was the relationship between the French Revolution and the social structure of France?' 'Who killed the princes in the tower?'

In my view it is unfortunate when history is simply presented as a series of grand debates on such issues. There is a form of historiographical discourse (particularly prevalent in the United States) where the historical writing on any issue is divided up into different schools ('conservative', 'progressive', 'revisionist', etc.) each said to present a distinctive view on the issue. To concentrate on the differences of interpretation which historians present is to miss the main purpose of historical study: deepened understanding of the past. Sometimes historians themselves have a vested interest in exaggerating the novelty, or 'revisionist' nature of their own interpretation; yet often it becomes apparent that much-vaunted differences amount to little more than differences of detail and emphasis. The real function of historical controversy is that by identifying the genuine areas of disagreement, by bringing competing hypotheses into open confrontation with each other, by forcing re-examination of methodology and sources, by forcing authors to consider new approaches and new evidence, it ultimately advances the cause of historical understanding. However, it would be an incomplete account of the nature of history which did not give some indication of the *ways* in which historians disagree over some of the major topics which concern them.

The sections which follow are cursory and abbreviated in their treatment and do not claim to be fully inclusive or fully up-to-date summaries of the topics with which they deal; on all of them, expert textbooks have been, and continue to be, produced – with these I do not seek to compete. The purpose is solely to give the general reader some idea of the sorts of things historians argue over and why, to illuminate some of the main technical and conceptual matters discussed in this book, and above all that development of historical studies which I see as far more significant than the dilettante delights of pursuing to the nth degree why one historian emphasised certain approaches and concerns, another others; there is, in fact, some deliberate overlap with Chapter 3. New preoccupations with the underprivileged, with, earlier this century, working-class movements, and, much more recently, with everday 'non-political' life, with the losers in history, and, perhaps most important of all, with the roles and achievements of women in history have opened new perspectives. Nevertheless that form of historiographical discourse which presents different schools of history as if they are competing football teams has tended to exaggerate the extent to which the wave of feminist studies beginning in the early 1970s brought a complete transformation, and ignore the extent to which previous historians, both male and female, had studied the place of women in society. That is not to downplay the important achievements in broadening and extending historical study, in raising issues and aspects of life which had simply been ignored previously. The exaggeration lies in singling out 'feminist history' as somehow a different kind of (and, it seemed to be assumed, better) history. The basic assumptions and values which historians hold will (as, for example, we shall see in studying the controversies over the two World Wars) play a part in shaping their conclusions and the emphases they give to them, but as I said at the beginning of this book, the final and really meaningful distinction is not between feminist and non-feminist, or Marxist and non-Marxist, but between competent historians and incompetent ones. Those who

put political programmes and slogans before the much more difficult task of patient analysis of the evidence are among the incompetent ones: they may be in fashion, they may briefly provoke
useful controversy, but in the slow accumulation of knowledge
their work is unlikely to have great significance.

For years now students of history have been furnished with
different series of textbooks on 'problems in history'. My highly
encapsulated summaries cannot possibly seek to compete with
these, though they do depend heavily upon them. The issues I
have chosen are: the significance of Magna Carta – sometimes
held to be the foundation stone of liberty throughout the English-
speaking world (there is an excellent edition with an introduction
(revised 1982) by G. R. C. Davis, published in paperback by the
British Museum, which can be studied in conjunction with J. C.
Holt's volume in the Major Issues in History series, *Magna Carta
and the Idea of Liberty* (1972)); the causes and consequences
of the English Civil War (Lawrence Stone's *Social Change and
Revolution in England 1540–1640* (1965) can be supplemented by
R. C. Richardson's *The Debate on the English Revolution* (1977),
together with Conrad Russell's, *The Causes of the English Civil
War* (1972), and John Morrill's *Reactions to the English Civil War
1642–1649* (1982)); the history of the family (Michael Anderson,
Approaches to the History of the Western Family 1500–1914 (1980)
is the best guide); the causes and significance of the American
Revolution (there is a volume entitled *The Causes of the American
Revolution*, (revised edition 1962), edited by John C. Wahlke,
which can be studied along with Chapter 4 of the more up-to-date
Interpretations of American History, volume I (1972), edited by
Gerald N. Grob and George A. Billias and the useful 'General
History' by E. James Ferguson, *The American Revolution* (revised
edition, 1979) and the recent collection of readings *The American
Revolution: Whose Revolution?* (1977) by J. K. Martin and K. R.
Stubaus); several of the controversies surrounding the industrial
revolution (of many selections three of the most illuminating are
M. W. Flinn's *Origins of the Industrial Revolution* (1966) in the
'Problems and Perspectives' series, Philip A. Taylor's *The Indus-
trial Revolution: Triumph or Disaster?* (1970), and A. J. Taylor's
The Standard of Living in Britain in the Industrial Revolution
(1975); a good general history is Phyllis Deane, *The First Industrial
Revolution* (second edition 1979)); imperialism, which involves us

in problems of historical semantics as well as of fact and causation (three excellent collections here are: George H. Nadel and Perry Curtis, *Imperialism and Colonialism* (1964) in the 'Main Themes of European History' series, Robin W. Winks, *British Imperialism: Gold, God, Glory* (1964) in the 'European Problems' series, and Wm. Roger Louis, *Imperialism* (New York, 1976)); and the origins, consequences, and significance of the two World Wars (the choice here is large: Taylor's famous *Origins* has already been mentioned, and can be read in conjunction with Alan Bullock's Raleigh Lecture, *Hitler and the Origins of the Second World War* (1969), published by the British Academy; two good collections of readings are *The Origins of the First World War* (1972) and *The Origins of the Second World War* (1971) edited respectively by H. W. Koch and Esmonde M. Robertson, to which now must be added *The Origins of the First World War* (1984) by James Joll and *The Origins of the Second World War Reconsidered: The A. J. P. Taylor debate after twenty-five years* (ed. G. Martel) (1986)).

Equally vigorous and important controversies exist over the pace and extent of settlement and colonisation in early medieval Europe, the nature of the manorial economy, over the characteristics of feudalism, over the significance of medieval parliaments, over the relations between science and industrial development, over the role of women in history, and so on. A final caution: although every student of history should understand the scope and significance of historical controversy, the excitement of battle should not obscure the main task of the historian, primary research directed towards greater understanding of the past. The true concern of the historian is history, not historiography.

2. Magna Carta

Stated in its most extreme form, the question raised by Magna Carta is this: is it the fundamental constitutional defence of English liberties, or is it merely a 'feudal document', reactionary in tone, by which a baronial clique extracted certain concessions beneficial only to themselves? Because the source material is so patchy historians have not been able to establish an exact account of the events leading to the drawing up and sealing of Magna Carta in June 1215. The charter itself is in medieval Latin: much of the debate centres upon the particular shade of meaning the scholar attaches to certain difficult passages. The bare outline of events is not, however, in dispute. As a king, John does not seem to have been much more arbitrary than his two immediate predecessors, but his manner was such as to make him always seem even shabbier than he was. What counted anyway was the series of disasters which bedevilled his reign. Philip of France waged successful war against the once-great English Empire in France while John became embroiled in a dangerous quarrel with the Pope. In 1214 John made his last desperate bid to recover Normandy: he failed, and in doing so bankrupted himself completely.

As a feudal ruler John was entitled to certain 'incidents', which could be a valuable source of income, due to him on certain occasions: when a tenant-in-chief died the king could exact a substantial 'relief' from the succeeding heir; if the heir was under age, the king had right of 'wardship' of his lands, which meant that he could himself pocket all the revenues they yielded; the king had the right to dispose of heirs and heiresses in marriage; the king was also entitled to certain 'aids' due on specified occasions, as for example, when his eldest daughter got married. This system of rights and dues extended through the social structure: tenants-in-chief (the great feudal barons) exacting similar payments from their tenants (the knights) and so on. By 1215 the older obligation of barons and knights to furnish the king with military service had been commuted to yet another financial payment, scutage. John certainly squeezed the last drop and more out of these customary rights, raising the cry that he was in fact going far beyond what was customary and right; the dismal failure of his policies greatly strengthened the position of the protesters. As early as 1213 the barons began to discuss proposals for exacting some guarantee from John that he would rule in conformity with the customs of the kingdom. In the past, kings had often made promises of this sort on their coronation: the barons lighted upon the comparatively elaborate Coronation Charter of Henry I (1100) which itemised the abuses which Henry swore to renounce; this the barons took as their model.

The collapse of 1214 opened the way to the baronial revolt of 1215: John quickly conceded defeat (suggesting that the barons had managed to secure wide support) and in June 1215, on the

Thames-side meadow of Runnymead, he agreed to put his seal to Magna Carta. The essential shape of Magna Carta derives directly from the demands known as the 'Articles of the Barons', modified and rephrased by the officials of the great royal office of Chancery. The two great men who stood somewhat apart from the conflict, William, the Earl Marshal, and Stephen Langton, Archbishop of Canterbury, may or may not have played an important part in formulating the final draft. This is one of the minor controversies associated with Magna Carta, which in turn is bound up with the major controversy. Many of the historians who have argued that Magna Carta does indeed have significance in the wider story of English liberties have attributed this element to the good offices of the saintly Langton, who is said to have transmuted the purely selfish claims of the barons into a statement of universal significance. Circumstantial evidence and the known facts about the character of Stephen Langton make this argument entirely reasonable, but it does not rest on any sufficient direct evidence.

The sealing of Magna Carta did not restore civil peace. Having little faith in John's word, the barons wrote into the Charter (clause 61) an elaborate provision whereby a special committee of twenty-five barons would be responsible for seeing that the other provisions were in fact carried out. John however proceeded at once to try to overthrow the charter, now enlisting the support of the Pope, who declared it to be null and void; open rebellion broke out again, and Louis, son of the French king Philip Augustus, came over from France in the hope of profiting from English divisions. It may well be that at this point Magna Carta would have sunk without trace had not John suddenly died in October 1216 at the age of forty-nine. The supporters of John's nine-year-old son Henry seem to have seen at once that Magna Carta could be used as a rallying call for unity behind the young king. On 12 November 1216 a pruned and revised version was issued on behalf of the newly crowned Henry III. By the autumn of 1217 Louis had been defeated, and Magna Carta, further revised, was again reissued (that is, copies, or 'exemplifications', were sent out to various parts of the country, there to be publicly announced). In 1225 Magna Carta was issued once more in what proved to be its final form, the king securing in return the right to levy a special tax on movable goods. This version was confirmed three times by Henry III (1237, 1253, 1265), once by Edward I

(1297), and on various occasions by later kings. It was Edward I's confirmation which was placed on the newly established Great Roll of Statutes.

Magna Carta was appealed to by seventeenth-century lawyers at the time of the gathering conflict with the Stuarts: in it they found the legal basis for such fundamental rights as parliamentary control of taxation, trial by jury, habeas corpus, equality before the law and freedom from arbitrary arrest. 'The Great Commoner', William Pitt, Earl of Chatham, in 1770 included Magna Carta with the Bill of Rights (the statement of 1689 which embodied the permanent results of the Civil War) as the 'Bible of the English constitution'. References to Magna Carta figured prominently in the claims of the American colonists, and it has continued ever since to play an important role in American concepts of basic justice.

As with many big issues in history, it is very difficult to disentangle the history from the myth. It should however be possible to make distinctions between the significance of Magna Carta in 1215; its significance throughout the thirteenth century; and its significance in the subsequent development of constitutional theory and practice. Seventeenth-century lawyers, American colonists or William Pitt were no more making objective historical judgements than is an American Democrat when he invokes the memory of F.D.R. or a British Prime Minister when he appeals to 'the spirit of Dunkirk'. The trouble came when nineteenth-century 'Whig' historians combined their zealous researches among the primary sources with a too ready acceptance of the mythology of Magna Carta. A minor, but typical, legal historian, Sir Edward Creasy, expressed a common view in 1853 when he described Magna Carta as 'a solemn instrument deliberately agreed on by the King, the prelates, the great barons, the gentry, the burghers, the yeomanry, and all the freemen of the realm'. Creasy had few doubts about the import of the famous clause 39 which, in Davis's translation, reads:

> No free man shall be seized or imprisoned, or stripped of his rights or possessions, or outlawed or exiled, or deprived of his standing in any other way, nor will we proceed with force against him or send others to do so, except by the lawful judgement of his equals or by the law of the land.

'I believe', said Creasy, 'that the trial by peers here spoken of means trial by jury.' Nineteenth-century historians put great weight, too, on clause 61 mentioned above, seeing it as a sign of wide acceptance of the *representative* principle, and on clause 12 which stated that 'no "scutage" or "aid" [apart from the customary 'incidents'] may be levied in our kingdom without its general consent.' Even the meticulous Bishop Stubbs could not free himself of the romanticised, Whig view of Magna Carta: the 'scientific' onslaught had to await the arrival of a younger Scottish contemporary of J. B. Bury, W. S. McKechnie. In his *Magna Carta* (1905), which is still a standard authority, McKechnie presented the forceful definition, and delimitation, of the Great Charter as 'a feudal document'. Clause by clause McKechnie elucidated the technicalities and explained the demands of the barons by reference to the early thirteenth-century feudal context. As he clearly demonstrated, a great part of the Charter is indeed concerned to set firm limits upon the demands which the king can make of the barons. Clauses 17 and 18 simply attempt to stabilise the legal procedures which had been developed in the reign of Henry II. Not only are clauses 12 and 61 (the 'general consent' and the 'representative' ones) vague and ambiguous, but in any case they are omitted from all subsequent reissues. Whatever the intentions of clause 39, trial by jury did not, as a matter of actual fact, become firmly established in the immediately succeeding years.

   McKechnie's scrupulous work establishes very clearly the significance of Magna Carta in its immediate temporal context, though, as a lawyer, McKechnie was primarily concerned with its implications for the history of law. For historians today Magna Carta is of greatest interest as a priceless revelation of the preoccupations and prejudices of the leaders of early thirteenth-century English society: J. C. Holt's *Magna Carta* (1965) aimed at presenting 'the Charter in the context of the politics, administration and political thought of England and Europe in the twelfth and thirteenth centuries'. Since McKechnie, too, historians have stressed the *symbolic* importance that Magna Carta came to have for later generations; and they have emphasised that the reissues of the thirteenth century imply a recognition that good government depends upon co-operation between the king and his principal subjects. Historians have also examined those parts of the Charter which relate to men of lesser social status than the great barons. Clause 60 calls upon all men (albeit somewhat vaguely) to behave towards their own tenants as the king is undertaking to behave towards his; the rights of the city of London (clause 13), the free movement of merchants (clause 41), and the interests of consumers (clause 35) are to be protected. More important is the basic theme which seems to underlie the somewhat diffuse phraseology of the whole document: that there *is* a body of law covering political and personal relationships throughout the kingdom, and that there are accepted and acceptable processes for implementing this law: the last few words of clause 39, referring to 'the law of the land', now emerge as the important ones. To have orderly rather than arbitrary government was, historians have maintained, in the interests of the entire community. Rather than attribute this generalising of the Charter to the vision of Stephen Langton or William Marshal, some historians, in the more cynical style of a Namier, have attributed it simply to the need of the barons to win allies from all walks of life.

Much about Magna Carta necessarily remains obscure. Perhaps an agreed version would run like this: Magna Carta in 1215 was a political bargain struck between a desperate king and his rebellious magnates; the men who put their seals to it lived in a type of society which later generations have termed 'feudal' – clearly these men could no more escape from the accepted concepts of that society than we can escape from the accepted concepts of twentieth-century society; yet Magna Carta does contain clauses which suggest that it went beyond mere service of the self-interests of a selfish clique. But for the accident of John's early death little more might have become of it; but in the minority of Henry III Magna Carta became established as an earnest of the community of interests between king and subjects, and a guarantee that the king would not violate that community of interests. In much later centuries Magna Carta became a potent symbol for radicals and revolutionaries. Without Magna Carta other symbols would doubtless have been found; but historians, at any rate, have learned to place due weight upon the importance in human history of the image and the symbol.

3. The 'Great Rebellion' alias the 'Great Civil War' alias the 'Puritan Revolution' alias the English 'Bourgeois Revolution'

In the later years of the reign (1558–1603) of Queen Elizabeth there were rumblings of discontent from some members of parliament over the Queen's insistence that certain topics, such as foreign policy and the religious settlement, were matters for royal decision alone and inappropriate for parliamentary discussion. Careful management of parliament had clearly become necessary; Elizabeth was not so successful in this in her last years as she had been in her earlier and middle years. Under James I (1603–20) there were signs that the discontent was intenisfying. His successor, Charles I, was autocratic by nature and totally incapable of comprehending parliamentary demands: in 1629, after the boldest statement so far of such demands, the Petition of Right, Charles dispensed altogether with parliament. The so-called eleven years' tyranny ended when in 1640 Charles had become so embroiled in financial and religious difficulties that he sought escape in the summoning of parliament. The demands made by the 'Long Parliament' in 1640, and the events attending them, are usually taken as marking the beginning of the revolutionary crisis. In 1642 open civil war broke out; in 1648 after the King had been captured, had escaped and had been captured again, a group usually known to history as the 'Independents' (and distinguished from the politically more moderate 'Presbyterians') seized power. In 1649 Charles I was executed. From then till the Restoration of 1660 England had no king: Oliver Cromwell, leader of the 'Independents', ruled as Lord protector from 1653 to 1658.

Without doubt great social, economic and cultural changes took place in the century 1540 to 1640. The inflationary trend, caused in part by population growth and by repeated debasement of the coinage, had a highly disruptive effect on existing social and economic relations; in certain spheres important advances were being made in trade and industry; scholars and intellectuals were developing a new faith in empirical science and the possibilities of human reason; the Elizabethan church settlement did not please the more extreme Protestants, the 'Puritans', whose successors were to find themselves in sharp conflict with Charles I, whom they suspected of undue tenderness towards Roman Catholicism; some individuals and groups were growing more prosperous and found that the existing political structure did not give them the power they felt was their due; others were doing badly and developed a dangerous sense of insecurity; the central monarchy was growing in prestige – those upon whom the King looked with favour prospered, those out of favour became embittered. The controversy among historians has been over the exact nature of these changes, their relative importance, and their relationship to the political events of the 1640s.

Seventeenth-century commentators on the Civil War – men who lived through it – came out remarkably strongly for an interpretation based on a simple clash of economic and social interests; Winstanley, Harrington, Hobbes, Baxter and Clarendon can all be read in this sense. Richard Baxter (1615–91), a Presbyterian minister, listed on the King's side lords, knights, gentlemen 'and most of the tenants of these gentlemen, and also most of the poorest of the people'. On Parliament's side were

> the smaller part (as some thought) of the gentry in most of the counties, and the greatest part of the tradesmen and freeholders and the middle sort of men, especially in those corporations and counties which depend on clothing and such manufactures . . .[1]

Edward Hyde, Earl of Clarendon (1609–74), the Royalist historian, presented a similar view: support for Parliament in 1642 was to be found 'in those corporations and by those inferior people who were notorious for faction and schism in religion'. In the county of Somerset Parliamentary leaders were

> for the most part clothiers, and men who, though they were rich, had not been before a power or reputation there . . . Though the gentlemen of ancient families and estates in that country were for the most part well affected to the King . . . yet there were a people of an inferior degree who by good husbandry, clothing and other thriving arts had gotten very great fortunes, and by degrees getting themselves into the gentlemen's estates, were angry that they found not themselves in the same esteem and reputation with those whose estates they had . . . These from the beginning were fast friends to parliament . . . .[2]

In crude essentials these analyses were strikingly like the materialist interpretation put forward in the nineteenth century by Karl Marx and his disciples. Friedrich Engels, Marx's celebrated collaborator, explained that Calvinism (or Puritanism) was the doctrine of the 'bourgeoisie', and maintained that it was the bourgeoisie which 'brought Charles I to the scaffold'.[3]

However. as we have noted, Marxism played little part in the nineteenth-century revolution in British historical studies. That monument of detailed scholarship, S. R. Gardiner's eighteen-volume *History* covering the years 1603 to 1656, presented the Civil War quite distinctly as 'the Puritan Revolution', a war fought to secure religious and constitutional liberty. This interpretation triumphantly held the field till the First World War: as R. G. Usher noted in 1913, the enigma of the Civil War was to be solved 'by repeating the Grand Remonstrance' – the Long Parliament's statement of its political and religious grievances. Then came the new interest in economic history. R. H. Tawney had already explored *The Agrarian Problem of the Sixteenth Century* (1912), and his studies were taken further by Joan Thirsk; A. P. Newton showed, in his *Colonizing Activities of the Early Puritans* (1914), that Pym and other Long Parliament leaders had important trading connections; the detailed researches of John U. Nef, Peter Ramsey, Maurice Dobb, W. H. Court and others suggested, as Christopher Hill put it in his summary of the state of research in the mid-fifties, that there had been 'something like an industrial revolution in the century before 1640'.[4] There was in the interwar years no satisfactory synthesis of these valuable contributions towards an economic rather than a religious and constitutional interpretation of the Civil War. But R. H. Tawney added a further important element when in *Religion and the Rise of Capitalism* (1922) he elaborated the various subtle interconnections between Puritanism and capitalism. For historians to go on speaking simply of a 'Puritan Revolution' seemed to beg the question of the great variety of other interests which Puritanism might mask.

From Tawney, too, came the first attempt at synthesis: a learned article entitled 'The Rise of the Gentry, 1558–1640' published in the *Economic History Review* in 1941. Tawney postulated a changing social and economic balance resulting from a decline in the wealth and influence of the old-fashioned landowners and a rise in a new class of gentry made up primarily of 'agricultural capitalists', but also including merchants and industrialists. These men fought the Civil War in order to establish a political position commensurate with their economic and social one. In keeping with the growing fashion of the time, Tawney provided impressive-looking statistical evidence which seemed to show first, that the number of manors held by the aristocracy was declining compared with those held by the gentry, and second, that the number of large holdings was declining, while the number of medium-sized ones was increasing. Support for this thesis came from another statistic-laden article which took further the idea of a declining Elizabethan aristocracy, published in 1948 by Lawrence Stone. It was now that H. R. Trevor-Roper launched his devastating counter-attack, exposing the grave deficiencies in the statistical methods adopted by Tawney and Stone. In 1953 Trevor-Roper presented his own synthesis, *The Gentry 1540–1640*, published as an *Economic History Review Supplement*. The 'mere gentry' – those who had no access to the gifts and patronage of the Court or to the spoils of law and trade – were in fact declining: they were the 'Country' who finally rose in anger against the corrupt, centralising 'Court'. The gentry could not in any event be regarded as an entirely separate social class from the 'aristocracy': thus the Civil War, essentially, was fought by two factions of the same ruling class, the luxurious, free-spending courtiers on the one side, and the jealous, puritanical country party on the other. There are shades of Namier in this essentially Tory conception of the mighty struggling over immediate material interests. And the applications to *Members of the Long Parliament* (1954) of overtly Namierite 'multiple biography' methods by D. Brunton and D. H. Pennington seemed to bolster the view that no broad social classification of the contestants in the Civil War into aristocracy on one side, and the gentry or bourgeoisie on the other, was feasible: gentlemen, lawyers and merchants were to be found among M.P.s on both sides.

In the late fifties important criticisms were made of the Trevor-Roper–Namierite synthesis. First of all new sources – always of critical moment in the development of historical inquiry – had been studied, since the taxation policies of the postwar Labour Government had provoked the release of a whole flood of private family papers. Furthermore a number of historians had got down to the necessary task of fundamental research at the local level, resulting in such important publications as *The Committee at Stafford 1643–5* (1957), edited by D. H. Pennington and I. A. Roots, *The County Committee of Kent in the Civil War* by A. M. Everitt, and *Essays in Leicestershire History* by W. G. Hoskins. Just as the new material was becoming available, further general theses were enunciated. J. H. Hexter drew attention away from the 'gentry', whether 'rising' or 'declining', to the aristocracy, whose critical weaknesses, he argued, could be seen in the collapse of their military power. The result was

> a power vacuum in England during the very years when a concurrence of fiscal, constitutional, political and religious grievances evoked widespread opposition to the Crown and made it necessary for that opposition to achieve some measure of co-ordinated action. Into that vacuum created by the temporary incapacity of the magnates poured the country gentry – not the brisk hard-bitten small gentry of Professor Tawney, nor yet the mouldy flea-bitten mere gentry of Professor Trevor-Roper – but the rich, well-educated knights and squires who sat in the Parliaments of James I and Charles I . . . .[1]

This particular theory was developed and put on a solid base by the extensive researches in the family archives, backed by an updated and sophisticated statistical expertise, which issued in Lawrence Stone's *Crisis of the Aristocracy* (1965). Perez Zagorin meanwhile pointed out that the Revolution must be considered in two stages: the first, 1640–2, was indeed a mere struggle between different factions within the ruling class; thereafter, however there developed a true social revolution, aiming at the establishment of a democratic republic.

Meantime the basic Marxist position that the English bourgeois revolution had taken place in the seventeenth century was being developed and elaborated by Christopher Hill (*Puritanism and Revolution: Studies in the Interpretation of the English Revolution of the 17th Century* (1958), *The Century of Revolution 1603–1714* (1961)). He saw this as a revolution which affected all aspects of life 'clearing the decks for capitalism'. With regard to the origins of this 'revolution' Hill stressed the geographical aspects of the socio-economic conflicts as he saw them:

> The Parliamentary areas were the South and the East, both economically advanced, while the strength of the royalists lay in the still half-feudal North and West. All the big towns were parliamentarian; though often (as in London) their ruling oligarchies were for the King . . . Only one or two cathedral towns, such as Oxford and Chester, were royalist. The ports were all for Parliament.[6]

Having reasserted the need to give due attention to the broader socio-economic conflicts underlying the Civil War, Hill, then, as we have noted, reaffirmed the importance of ideas, religious and non-religious, in shaping the Revolution. Our understanding of the intellectual roots of the Revolution, too, has been greatly furthered by C. H. and K. George's study of *The Protestant Mind of the English Reformation 1570–1640* (1961).

Much of the most recent work has aimed to see events 'from below', as in Christopher Hill's own *The World Turned Upside Down: Radical Ideas During the English Revolution* (1972) and Brian Manning's *The English People and the English Revolution* (1976). The upshot of further detailed work (the younger generation of historians includes Conrad Russell, Derek Hirst, David Underdown, Blair Worden, and John Morrill) is that Hill's geographical classification has been seriously undermined and that among the present generation of historians nothing remains of the notion of a bourgeois revolution. Almost all writers now accept that civil war was not expected, that but for Charles's stupidity and stubbornness if could have been avoided, and that certainly it was not determined by a clear-cut conflict of social classes. But once the war had actually broken out it did stimulate changes (Antonia Fraser *The Weaker Vessel: Women in Seventeenth Century England* (1984) brings out some of the effects on women). The idea of there being a second stage towards the end of the civil war (as proposed by Zagorin) has been developed, though the notion of this involving a 'true social revolution' has been largely rejected. Charles was executed because he could not be trusted; religion remained a more important force than class; the 'revolutionaries' were a small active minority. For full understanding the events of the 1640s have to be placed in the perspective of developments later in the century: the restoration of monarchy in 1660 and the 'Glorious Revolution' of 1688 which definitively established a monarchy responsive to the major interests in the community. The establishment of limited, constitutional, monarchy can be considered a revolution, but essentially a *political* one. At the same time there *were* great cultural changes across the century (in science, music, and architecture, for instance): here Christopher Hill is clearly right.

One attempt to express that resolution which, I have stressed, is the ultimate function of historical controversy, was made by Lawrence Stone himself in the November 1985 issue of *Past and Present*:

Hill and I are thus now in agreement that the English Revolution was not caused by a clear conflict between feudal and bourgeois ideologies and classes; that the alignment of forces among the rural élites did not correlate with attitudes towards ruthless enclosure; that the Parliamentarian gentry had no conscious intention of destroying feudalism; but that the end result, first of the royal defeat and second of the consolidation of that defeat in the Glorious Revolution forty years later was decisive. Together they made possible the seizure of political power by landed, mercantile and banking élites, which in turn opened the way to England's advance into the age of the Bank of England, the stock-market, aggressive economic liberalism, economic and affective individualism, and an agricultural entrepreneurship among the landed élite to whose unique characteristics Bremner [in an earlier article in *Past and Present*] has recently drawn attention. But, as I have argued elsewhere [in Stone's, *An Open Elite? England 1540–1880* (Oxford, 1984)], even the bustling world of Daniel Defoe can hardly be described as a bourgeois society, because of the continued dominance of an admittedly entrepreneurial landed élite.

4. The Family

In 1972 *Annales* published a special double issue on 'Family and Society'; in the same year there appeared in Britain *Household and Family in Past Time*, edited by Peter Laslett, and in America *The Family in History*, edited by T. K. Rabb and R. I. Rotberg, and also the English translation of the seminal French work *L'enfant et la vie familiale sous l'ancien régime* (1960) by Philippe Ariès. Published as *Centuries of Childhood* this book had a characteristic preoccupation with the balance between the *longue durée* and identifiable change: Ariès suggested that pre-industrial society did not make any critical distinction between adults and children, whereas our own society's perception of the distinction is brought out in our obsession with the education of children. By the later seventies the proliferation of articles, collections of papers, and full-length general studies on the family indicated that this topic had become a major historical fashion, much as had urban history a decade or so previously. As well as demonstrating the changing concerns of historians and, especially, the emphasis on a particular type of social history, the controversies over the history of the family bring out well some of the more enduring features of the nature of historical study. In the last analysis, as with every other historical 'problem', historians disagree over the structure, characteristics, and significance of the family in past times because the evidence available to them is so fragmentary, uncertain, and intractable. As always, of course, different approaches count too: some are more willing to generalise and speculate than others; some believe in the fruitful employment of theory; some prefer to accept only that for which they have what they believe to be sound testimony. Broadly speaking, as in most aspects of social history, there are three main approaches: that of those who give an over-riding primacy to numbers and quantitative methods; that of those who insist that historians must make the best use they can, and 'squeeze the last drop out' of whatever sources they can lay hands on, however imperfect, and then endeavour to produce coherent interpretations and generalisations; and that of those who set great store by theories developed within the social sciences. The major difference of interpretation which has emerged is that between those who see a fundamental change in the modern period to 'affective individualism', involving the primacy of love over more prosaic considerations in marriage, and those who stress continuity.

Some of the important achievements of Peter Laslett and his associates have already been mentioned. In the collections of papers he edited and above all, in his own introductions to them, (*Household and Family in Past Time* (1972); *Family Life and Illicit Love in Earlier Generations* (1977)), the emphasis was on getting the size and composition of the household right, and on debunking the traditional view that in earlier times there was a large, complex, extended family becoming by the early modern period a 'stem' family in which one son and his descendants co-resided with the family patriarch. In criticising writers who relied on literary sources rather than numbers, Laslett had other targets too:

> Perhaps the most conspicuous, and unfortunate, effect of reliance on such sources is the support it seems to give to the very habit of attaching the name of a nation, or of a religious outlook, or of a social class, to a particular form of the family – the American family, the Puritan family, the bourgeois family and so on. This tendency is related to an even deeper seated expectation that change in matters of this kind will necessarily be related to change in other spheres, again usually in religion and politics.[7]

Laslett hoped above all to see 'the abandonment of the rise of individualism as the universal explainer of familial change.'

However, it has to be recognised that primacy in the field remained with the French. Jean-Louis Flandrin has given particular attention to sexuality as in, for instance, *Familles: parenté, maison, sexualité dans l'ancienne société* (1976). But he has also brought out the material constraints upon marriage: 'in a society where the overwhelming majority of families drew their subsistence from assets, small or large, which bore fruit or not, depending on their own labour, it was criminal with respect to children yet to be born to marry without having the capital necessary to maintain a family'.[8] The distinguished medievalist Georges Duby has concentrated on the institution of marriage, its nature and forms, suggesting that there were two models in the early medieval period, the rather predatory one of the knights, the moral one of the priests, and that together these produced 'the new structures of conjugality'.[9] Duby concludes his *Le Chevalier, la femme et les prêtres: le Mariage dans la France Féodale* (1981) with the comment that for his period we know little of the woman's view. Fortunately, one result of the feminist impulse for later periods has been a cluster of studies, often stressing the important managerial role of women within marriage (e.g. J. Kirshner and S. F. Wemple, *Women of the Medieval World* (1985), M. W. Labarge, *Women in Medieval Life* (1986), M. Segalen, *Love and Power in the Seventeenth Century* (1984), M. Slater, *Family Life in the Seventeenth-Century* (1984)).

The two single works which have attracted most attention in the English-speaking world are Edward Shorter's *The Making of the Modern Family* (1977) and Lawrence Stone's *The Family, Sex and Marriage in England from 1500–1800* (1977). As his title suggests Shorter's book is integrated into the grand generalising concept of 'modernisation'. His concern, too, is very much with 'mentalities', with Shorter explaining what he perceived as the dislodgment of the traditional family by 'a surge of sentiment in three different areas': the rise of romantic love; the emergence of maternal love as a primary concern; and the separating off of the family as more and more a private emotional unit from the community with which, traditionally, it had had close functional ties. Shorter admitted to a major unanswered (but, the implication was, unanswerable) question:

Did the terrible shocks of 'modernization' shatter the stable community structure within which the traditional family was nestled? Or did these massive social changes first affect the mentalities of individual family members, causing them to embrace one another and block off as an annoying disruption the stream of traffic through the household: In the exchange of peer-group allegiance for emotional intimacy, which came first the chicken or the egg?[10]

Shorter's book, therefore, apart from a brief introduction, and two brief concluding chapters, consists of two chapters on 'Traditional Society', that is to say society as it was up till the end of the eighteenth century, followed by chapters defining the relevant changes in the period of 'modernisation': 'The Two Revolutions', 'Romance'. 'Mothers and Infants', and 'The Rise of the Nuclear Family'. Shorter continues his story into the 1960s: thus the first sexual revolution, which came at the end of the eighteenth century, when emotional attachment and sexual feeling replaced economic convenience or necessity, was followed in our own day by the second sexual revolution, that of 'permissiveness'. The book ranges over many societies and presents fascinating pieces of evidence from many different sources.

Stone's book, on the other hand, while also drawing upon an immense range of source material, confined itself to one society and a precisely defined period. But he too was concerned with fundamental change; and his definition of this change was such as to put him into flat confrontation with Laslett: 'The critical change under consideration is that from distance, deference and patriarchy to what I have chosen to call Affective Individualism. I believe this to have been perhaps the most important change in *mentalités* to have occurred in the Early Modern period, indeed possibly in the last thousand years of Western history.'[11] Stone postulated three stages in the development of the family: the Open Lineage Family existing up to the sixteenth century; the Restricted Patriarchial Nuclear Family existing roughly between 1580 and 1640; and the Closed Domesticated Nuclear Family coming into existence thereafter. Of the Open Lineage Family the two most striking features were permeability by outside influences, and its members' sense of loyalty to ancestors and to living kin. It was

an open-ended, low-keyed, emotional, authoritarian institution which served certain essential political, economic, sexual, procreative and nurtural purposes. It was also very short-lived, being frequently dissolved by the death of husband or wife, or the death or early departure from the home of the children. So far as the individual members were concerned, it was neither very durable, nor emotionally or sexually very demanding. The closest analogy to a sixteenth-century home is a bird's nest (p. 7).

The 'decisive shift' comes with the development of the Closed Domesticated Nuclear Family after 1640. This suffered setbacks in the nineteenth century but then became widely diffused throughout society:

the four key features of the modern family – intensified affective bonding of the nuclear core at the expense of neighbours and kin; a strong sense of individual autonomy and the right to personal freedom in the pursuit of happiness; a slackening of the association of sexual pleasure with sin and guilt; and a growing desire for physical privacy – were all well established by 1750 in the key middle and upper sectors of English society. The nineteenth and twentieth centuries merely saw their much wider social diffusion (pp. 8–9).

Stone's book was in large measure an affirmation of the significance of the social context and of historical change as against the assumptions of Freudian psychology about the unchanging nature of the sex drive. The sexual drive, writes Stone (going, in my view absurdly far towards a 'sociology of knowledge' approach), is 'stimulated or controlled by cultural norms and learned experience.'

Despite appearance, human sex takes place mostly in the head. Thus in the history of the West, infantile sexuality has sometimes been condoned and sometimes repressed; adolescent masturbation has sometimes been ignored and sometimes fanatically repressed; bisexual and homosexual instincts among men have usually been strongly condemned by the masses, but often tolerated by the élite; homosexual relations between women have usually been ignored; premarital sexual experiments have sometimes been tacitly tolerated and sometimes strictly forbidden; the double standard of sexual behaviour for men and women has usually, but not always, been deeply embedded in customary morality and in legal codes; incest taboos have everywhere existed, but have varied widely in scope, and in the zeal with which they have been enforced; the female sexual libido has usually been regarded as dangerously powerful, but in the Victorian middle class was virtually non-existent; women have sometimes been expected to achieve orgasmic fulfilment and sometimes to be passive and inert recipients of the semen of the male. The Freudian assumption that sex is an unchanging infrastructure, and that there has been no change in the strength of the libido over time has therefore no basis in reality, so deeply is it overlaid by cultural norms (pp. 483–4).

Among the more squarely social science approaches to the history of the family, that developing from psychology has not, indeed, proved very fruitful. The truly creative employment of the social sciences heritage has been entirely in keeping with that central obsession of much of the most advanced work in the humanities and social sciences in recent years, the 'structures' which (allegedly) underlie all aspects of human and social activity. As would be expected, the contributions from this direction (largely from those with a background in economics or sociology) are in the form of articles rather than books. As Michael Anderson, who, revealingly, began his academic career as a sociologist but then became Professor of Economic History at Edinburgh University, has explained

> the questions they raise are inspired not by sources or by observations of the present-day family, but by social-science-inspired theories about the patterning of social relationships and of change in relationships. The main thrust of these theories involves attempts to isolate 'structural' constraints, arising from pressures often quite outside the consciousness of the individuals involved. Central among these factors are those which arise in economic or other exchange relationships within the family and between family members and others. The main emphases are on the ways in which, and the conditions under which, resources (including human resources) become available to the family and to its members, on strategies which can be employed to generate and exploit resources, and on the power relationships which arise as by-products of these activities. The particular forms taken by family behaviour are seen, very largely, not as free-floating independent variables, but as a corollary of these structural constraints.[12]

Thus there has been detailed investigation of inheritance, of the relationship of the family to the productive process, of family consumption patterns, and of what in general can be called 'the family economy'. Key studies have been Hans Medick's 'The Proto-Industrial Family Economy: The Structural Function of Household and Family during the Transition from Peasant to Industrial Capitalism' (in *Social History*, 1976). J. Scott and L. Tilley, 'Women's Work and the Family in Nineteenth Century Europe' (in *Comparative Studies in Society and History*, 1975), and the collection of papers edited by J. Goody and others, *Family and Inheritance: Rural Society in Western Europe 1200–1800*

(1976). Alan Macfarlane has brought a social anthropological background to his controversial *Marriage and Love in England: Modes of Reproduction 1300–1840* (Oxford, 1986), one of several challenging works in a form of social history he has made his own. In conflict with the notion of a *change* to 'affective individualism' and choice in marriage, Macfarlane argues that personal choice was an important factor throughout the period he studies:

> Ideally 'love' would convincingly resolve the complex equations whereby individuals tried to balance a whole set of criteria – wealth, beauty, temperament, status – against which they would measure the prospective partner. The wedding and subsequent married life reflected the premises on which the system was based, showing that the heart of the matter was the deep attachment of one man to one woman. (p. 322).

In such writings (not, however, Macfarlane's) the 'theory' is sometimes no more than what a less ambitious person might call 'assumptions', the jargon oppressive, and the use of such notions as 'strategies' unsatisfactory; but often, too, these writings have a time-specificity and a use of documentation to delight any historian. There can be no doubt that they are adding an important dimension to the historical study of the family, without so far yielding any comprehensive theory. On that score, Shorter's volume remains stimulating and suggestive. Professional preference would probably be given to Stone's tome since the limits of his study are more precise: Shorter's habit of bringing in pieces of evidence from here there and everywhere and his assumption that there is one single historical pattern does not always persuade. Of course, both Stone and Shorter have been severely criticised for making generalisations which their evidence does not support. Peter Laslett and his school have throughout waged a vital battle against rash generalisation. As with the study of all historical phenomena it is essential to sort out what society (continent, country, region or community), what social group, and what point in time one is talking about. But Laslett's statistics, culled from records whose compilers had purposes and standards of accuracy very far from Laslett's own, are, as so often when quantitative methods are used in historical study, not necessarily totally reliable; and his answers miss many of the most important features of the family, the nature of relationships within it, and its social function and significance.

It is from within the historical profession that the lead has come in the great reassessment and re-evaluation of the family in the last two decades. The family, whatever changes it is undergoing, remains a central institution in contemporary society. That historians today should be studying it so assiduously is a tribute to the resilience and the relevance of history.

5. The American Revolution

Two interrelated problems are involved in the study of the American Revolution: what caused it? and what sort of revolution was it anyway? In a curious way the historiography of the American Revolution echoes that of the English one. The first commentators, writing with the live experience still throbbing in their minds, put forward a common-sense proto-sociological explanation, involving social, economic and cultural factors. *The History of the American Revolution* (Philadelphia, 1789) by David Ramsay is in many respects worthy of being ranked with the leading works by the contemporary Scottish historical school (Ramsay, who lived from 1749 to 1815, was born in Pennsylvania of Scottish Presbyterian parents). Ramsay stressed such circumstances as 'the distance of America from Great Britain', which, combined with the essentially tolerant policies of the mother country, encouraged both the growth of attitudes favourable to liberty and the establishment of local legislatures which implemented these ideas. Liberal ideas were in any case promoted by the Puritan ideology of a large number of the colonists. The social composition of the colonies, Ramsay argued, fostered egalitarianism and democracy – the vast majority of the colonists being independent farmers. At the same time he accepted that the handful of rich colonial merchants were motivated by their own special economic interests when in the later stages of the crisis they gave a lead to the agitation against Britain. To Ramsay the specific event which converted background preconditions into an immediate state of crisis was the British Government's imposition upon the colonies of the Stamp Act (the attempt made in 1765, two years after the ending of the Seven Years War, to recoup some of the expenses of that war, which had once and for all provided the colonists with security from the French). Although the Stamp Act was immediately repealed, the vigorous cry of 'No taxation without representation' had already gone up: this constitutional principle, derived of course from socio-economic and cultural circumstances, was, Ramsay contended, 'the very hinge of the controversy'. Ramsay was moderate in his assessment of the responsibilities of British ministers; he could see that in an extraordinarily complex situation there were indeed two points of view:

> From the unity of empire it was necessary, that some acts should extend over the whole. From the local situation of the Colonies it was equally reasonable that their legislatures should at least in some matters be independent. Where the supremacy of the first ended and the independency of the last began, was to the best informed a puzzling question.

Finally Ramsay stated quite clearly that the colonists were far from united in their opposition to Britain: but he explained that because of 'the resentment of the people' the opponents of revolutionary action tended to hold their peace.

The balanced sociological account of Ramsay and his contemporaries (the others are listed by Professor Page Smith in his brilliant article 'David Ramsay and the Causes of the American Revolution' in the collection of readings edited by John C. Wahlke, from which I have borrowed extensively) quickly gave place to the wildly Whig (or 'democratic' as Ranke termed it) account of George Bancroft, which conjured up the twin images of the wicked tyranny of George III and the selfish evil of 'mercantilism' as basic causes of the Revolution: images which proved extraordinarily durable. This interpretation, born in the period of strong American nationalism and Jacksonian democracy, is of course almost an exact counterpart of the Whiggish interpretation of Magna Carta noted above, or of the 'Puritan Revolution' interpretation of events in seventeenth-century England.

American historiographers are generally agreed that in the period of the Rankean revolution and the 'new history' reaction, that is, from around 1890 to the Second World War, two broad schools of historical inquiry can be identified (which indeed coincide roughly with the Rankean, mainstream professional approach on the one hand, and the 'new' approach on the other). Grob and Billias describe these respectively as the 'imperial' school and the 'progressive' school, the former school stressing 'constitutional' issues, the latter social and economic ones; Wahlke, with all necessary qualifications and reservations, suggests a distinction between those historians who, *in the last analysis*, hold to a political interpretation and those who, in similar case, hold to an economic one. Actually, so subtle and intricate are the arguments in the leading books in both schools that the result was not, save in the minds of inferior polemicists, to produce a sharp polarisation of views, but rather to produce a broad consensus which directed attention away from the alleged villainies and heroisms of individuals towards examination of broader forces and circumstances. This movement was reinforced, appropriately enough given Namier's own original bent towards the American Revolution, by the Namierite revision of British eighteenth-century political studies. The 'imperial' school – headed by George L. Beer, Charles M. Andrews and Lawrence H. Gipson – brought new light to bear on the question by setting it within the wider perspective of the problems of the British Empire. All presented sympathetic portrayals of Britain's imperial and economic policies towards the colonies. Andrews stressed that at the heart of the Revolution lay the fact that a new nation had grown up in North America, a fact which simply could not be accommodated to existing imperial ideas (this, it may be noted, has been very much the line taken by British historians such as Vincent Harlow and Esmond Wright). Gipson stressed the strategic dificulties which faced the British Empire and argued that it was reasonable for the British Government to expect the colonists to contribute to the costs of their own defence. These historians emphasise constitutional and political issues only in the sense of seeing such issues as the offspring of much deeper conflicts of interest. Leaders in the other school were Charles A. Beard, Arthur Schlesinger Sr and Louis M. Hacker. Arguably, these historians fell into the error later repeated in Britain by the violent protagonists in the Tawney–Trevor-Roper controversy, an exaggeration of the dominance and autonomy of economic motivation.

As in the controversy over the English Revolution, the freshest work accomplished since the Second World War has been in the direction of restressing the importance of ideas: it is not, I think, fanciful to note a parallel between Bernard Bailyn's *Ideological Origins of the American Revolution* (1967), and the book by

Christopher Hill which bears a remarkably similar title. Earlier Edmund S. and Helen M. Morgan in their *The Stamp Act Crisis: prologue to Revolution* (1953) had redirected attention to the wave of popular resistance, based apparently on constitutional principle, aroused by the Stamp Act. Here we have a reminder (which again can be compared with the re-emphasis in British historiography upon the character and actions of Charles I) that amid all the talk of broader forces the historian should not neglect the specific, unique event. One final historiographical parallel: to set beside the 'general crisis of the seventeenth century' hypothesis, we have of course Palmer's thesis of the Atlantic-wide 'Democratic Revolution'.

What sort of Revolution was it anyway? As early as 1910 Carl M. Becker identified two revolutions: the colonial rebellion, and the internal socio-economic clash over who should rule in independent America. There was, as Becker put it with characteristic elegance, the 'question of home rule' and the 'question . . . of who should rule at home'. Schlesinger reckoned that in the struggle for power which followed the colonial rebellion the rich merchants finally reasssserted control, whereas J. Franklin Jameson in *The American Revolution Considered as a Social Movement* (1926) argued that during the war sweeping reforms in the direction of economic and social democracy did in fact take place. Historians writing after the Second World War, following through on the sociological-cultural interpretation which stresses the growing sense of identity of an American *nation*, have seen the Revolution as essentially a conservative one, fought to maintain the existing liberal-democratic *status quo* against the threatened encroachments of British imperial power: such have been the arguments of Robert E. Brown in *Middle-Class Democracy and the Revolution in Massachusetts 1691–1780* (1955), a depth study of social structure in one colony (again comparison is invited with the recent local studies of the English Revolution) and of Daniel J. Boorstin in his sparkling work of original synthesis *The Genius of American Politics* (1953). These interpretations, needless to say, have not stood unchallenged.

As was to be expected much of the freshest work in the sixties and seventies turned towards the role of the crowd, the place of women (for example Carol R. Berkin, *Within the Conjuror's Circle: Women in Colonial America* (1974) and Joan Hoff Wilson,

'The Illusion of Change: Women and the American Revolution', in *The American Revolution* (1976) ed. A. F. Young), and the involvement of blacks (for example Duncan J. MacLeod, *Slavery, Race, and the American Revolution* (1974)) and of American Indians (for example, Barbara Graymont, *The Iroquois in the American Revolution* (1977)). No clear view has emerged as to whether either women or blacks were better off after the revolution or before (almost certainly the Indians were worse off) though there is some agreement that, in the longer term, the potential for the emancipation of both was enhanced. Let me quote three sentences from a letter written by Abigail Adams in the spring of 1776 to her husband, the revolutionary leader John Adams, a rousing, and justly celebrated primary document:

> I desire you would remember the Ladies, and be more generous and favorable to them than your ancestors. Do not put such unlimited power into the hands of the Husbands. Remember all Men would be tyrants if they could, if particular care and attention is not paid to the ladies we are determined to foment a Rebellion, and will not hold ourselves bound by any Laws in which we have no voice, or Representation.[13]

The most recent work has tended to challenge the notion of the Revolution as essentially conservative and to stress the way in which the new nation's rulers had to accommodate to the demands of the popular movement; in Ferguson's words, 'the Revolution was not only the first modern revolution; it was also the first *popular* revolution of modern times that succeeded.'[14]

6. The Industrial Revolution

The Industrial Revolution will be treated here as essentially a problem in British history; the fact that other countries subsequently went through similar revolutions and that some countries are at present going through such a revolution, in any case, gives the topic a wider significance to both historians and social scientists. Of all the wide variety of controversies this simple two-word phrase conjures up, perhaps the least important is that of whether there was an Industrial Revolution at all (though the argument that there was not is much in fashion at the moment). We shall simply glance briefly at that one in passing. Accepting that there was a 'revolution' (significant, wide-ranging, irreversible change) the question then arises, when did it begin? – involved here are all sorts of sub-controversies over population growth, the 'stages of economic growth', the relationship of technology to economic demand and to intellectual progress, and so on. But before we turn to that and these, we shall take what for many historians and laymen is *the* issue, involving the entire nature of the Industrial Revolution and the changes which it brought to the whole of society: were these changes for better or for worse?

As with the seventeenth-century English Revolution and the American Revolution, there was no shortage of contemporary comment on the Industrial Revolution. Much of this was summarised and given his own peculiar gloss by Friedrich Engels in the opening chapter of his *Condition of the Working Class in England* (1845): here in its pristine freshness is the tale of the sturdy independent yeomen driven off their land into a squalid existence in the industrial slums, a tale with which many of us were regaled at school. A sense of outrage over the social evils attending upon the process of industrialisation, too, lay at the core of Arnold Toynbee's *Lectures on the Industrial Revolution* (1884), the book which did more than any other to popularise the concept of an Industrial Revolution. Toynbee's concern for the exploited poor was developed further by the Hammonds in their studies of *The Village Labourer* (1911) and *The Town Labourer* (1919). Until the recent book by Hobsbawm and Rudé, the Hammonds were the last historians to study the peasant risings of 1830. Then, as we saw in Chapter 3, came the tough-minded school of economic historians led by Sir John Clapham, who declared that their statistics controverted earlier soft-hearted accounts of the declining living standards of the poor, and that, anyway, the greater good of general economic growth far outweighed any temporary sufferings on the part of the poor. Recent work by Peter Laslett and others has certainly demonstrated very conclusively that the story of idyllic pre-industrial conditions shattered by industrialisation is quite without foundation: children performed sweated labour within the confines of their own homes; women worked in primitive mines; whole families trembled year in year out on the verge of starvation; rural slums were just as noxious as those later to be found in the industrial towns.

The question of whether or not the British standard of living was rising or falling in the early nineteenth century became embodied in one of the most strident of all controversies in British economic history. Eric Hobsbawm reopened the issue in 1957 in an article on 'The British Standard of Living 1790–1850' in the *Economic History Review*. Many of his arguments had to be indirect, including the one that since meat sales at Smithfield Market were not increasing, while population clearly was, living standards must be falling. A vigorous reply came from R. M. Hartwell in 'The Rising Standard of Living in England, 1800–50' in the *Economic History Review* for 1961. Hobsbawm's article was 'marred', he said (admittedly in a footnote) 'by carelessness in the use of evidence, argument and language'. Among other points, he referred to sales of fish and to meat sales outside of Smithfield. What, perhaps, came out most strongly was the unsatisfactory nature of the statistical evidence. It may be that, for many, living standards did go down in the early decades of the nineteenth century; for them the fact that subsequently their children and grandchildren enjoyed some of the fruits of economic growth cannot have been any consolation. In recent years the area of dispute has moved away from the quantitative aspects (which in fact have not been successfully quantified) to the qualitative changes brought about in the lives of the many by the Industrial Revolution. E. P. Thompson has been to the fore in stressing how the new factory discipline, the new omnipresent sense of time, the new master-operative relationship affected the quality of life. In the end few historians today would deny the long-term boons of the Industrial Revolution; it is scarcely to be argued anyway that the Revolution could somehow have been 'stopped'. But within that wider, slightly complacent framework historians are now, with the help of modern social psychology, looking more closely at the human implications of industrialisation. As Thompson has put it:

> What needs to be said is not that one way of life is better than the other, but that this is a place of the most far-reaching conflict; that the historical record is not a simple one of neutral and inevitable technological change, but is also one of exploitation and of resistance to exploitation; and that values stood to be lost as well as gained.[15]

Toynbee, naturally, was clear that there had been an Industrial Revolution: the social implications which he saw all around him were too great to be ignored. Yet the economic historians of the interwar years came close to denying any validity to the term: they were in fact the victims of tunnel history (and indeed perhaps of ball-of-string history as well); examining only economic development in the narrowest sense, they saw steady evolution stretching far into the past, and missed the really important phenomena: the rapid (though uneven) urbanisation and the social and cultural upheavals of the late eighteenth and early nineteenth centuries. Toynbee had thought the Revolution began somewhere around 1760; curiously the cataclysmic view (which still holds the field in many textbooks) was given its most forceful expression by the young Charles A. Beard, who saw it as coming to what was 'virtually a medieval England . . . almost like a thunderbolt from a clear sky'. As early as 1908 an important study postulated that the Revolution had a much broader chronological base in the eighteenth century; but that book was in French, and did not become generally available to the insular British till 1928 (E. Mantoux, *The Industrial Revolution of the Eighteenth Century*). Historians are now inclined, thanks in particular to the quantitative (in the Marczewski sense) studies by Phyllis Deane and W. A. Cole, to distinguish two phases in the Industrial Revolution: a slight intensification of economic activity from the 1740s, followed by a more 'revolutionary' upturn in the 1780s; the traditional attribution of the 'beginning' of the Revolution in 1760 (accession of George III) has been thoroughly discredited. The most important contribution of recent studies has been to stress (what was already apparent, but often ignored) that industrialisation in Britain proceeded patchily and unevenly, and that many parts of the contry remained remarkably unchanged until well into the second half of the nineteenth century (this is the basis on which it is argued that there was no *revolution*).

Now to the question of the 'causes' of the Industrial Revolution. Toynbee and his generation produced a somewhat simple list which again has embedded itself deeply in the textbooks: the list included the alleged replacement of mercantilism by *laissez-faire*, the growth of population, enclosures, a collection of inventions, and the substitution of the factory for the domestic system. The great achievement of the interwar economic historians was, through thorough investigation of individual industries, to lay the basis for a more complex analysis. However, the really important advances towards a convincing synthesis only came after the Second World War: partly this derived from more efficient detailed studies into particular areas long dominated by specious generalisation, such as historical demography, the sources of finance for industrialisation, the availability of new markets, and the complicated relationship between culture, education and the willingness to innovate, as seen in technological inventiveness or (something recent historians have greatly stressed) entrepreneurship; partly it derived from the enlistment not just of the more refined statistical methods, but also of the modes of analytical conceptualisation more usually found in the social sciences. These developments are admirably summarised in M. W. Flinn's *Origins of the Industrial Revolution* (1966).

The first important general advance after the Second World War was made by T. S. Ashton's deceptively textbookish *The Industrial Revolution 1760–1830* (1948). Ashton laid particular stress on the lowering of interest rates in the early eighteenth century as a reason for the quickening pace of economic development. Scarcely less important, Flinn argued, was his emphasis on the connection between nonconformity and business enterprise, which Ashton thought could be most readily explained through reference to the high level of education nonconformists received in their own academies. In 1960 W. W. Rostow published a full version of his famous theory of *The Stages of Economic Growth*. Rostow's five stages are: the traditional society, the preconditions for take-off, the take-off into self-sustained growth, the drive to maturity, and the age of high mass consumption. Relevant to the study of the Industrial Revolution, obviously, are the 'preconditions for take-off', and, of course, the 'take-off', which at one level are extremely precise and at another are totally vague. They have been subjected in detail to some devastating criticism. Nonetheless this model has proved an appealing one. In his concluding chapter Flinn offered an interesting and flexible three-tier model. First he placed 'the accumulation of a set of necessary prerequisites', which he listed (in a much more elaborate fashion than can be represented in this blunt summary) as 'improvement in agriculture', efficient means of transport, a 'sophisticated monetary system', making in particular for 'increased availability of capital', and an 'educational system suitable for the new orientation of society'. On the second tier Flinn placed the emergence of 'a group of sectors of steady expansion' – industrial and regional. These sectors, as it were, set the pace, making for the diffusion of a 'growth mentality' among businessmen, and for technological innovation. Flinn's third element, the one which is 'concerned with the timing of the beginning of rapid economic development', is the least satisfactory. In it he runs together, in ascending order of importance, 'population growth', 'the expansion of home and overseas markets' and 'technology'. Yet one cannot leave this topic without commenting on how well Flinn's balanced yet immensely stimulating textbook summed up the advances that had been made by the mid-sixties in twentieth-century historical study: compare it with works of similar scale by Toynbee or Ashton, and the point is made.

7. Imperialism

With imperialism we encounter again the problem of historical semantics. Beyond that we have problems of motivation: what makes men and nations imperialistic? We have problems of periodisation: was there a particular era when, say, Great Britain pursued imperialist policies, which can be contrasted with other periods when she did nothing of the sort? What, finally, were the consequences of imperialism? We shall see that as in other controversies we have studied, historians have gradually abandoned monocausal, instrumental explanations for more complicated ones which take account of the irrational in man and of the appeal to him of apparently abstract ideals.

Richard Koebner showed that the word 'imperialism' first came into general use in Britain to describe the aggressive policies pursued by Napoleon III in the 1850s. It remained a term of abuse when Radicals and Liberals used it of Disraeli's policies in the 1870s.[16] However, by a not unfamiliar process ('Whig' and 'Tory' both began life as terms of abuse) the word became respectable in the 1880s and a number of politicians and publicists were proud to announce themselves as imperialists. But the South African War at the turn of the century again knocked most of the burnish off the word. The epoch-making study *Imperialism*, published in 1902 by the self-styled 'economic heretic' J. A. Hobson, presented a most disenchanted view which attributed imperialism to the

pressure of selfish economic and financial interests, unable to find
profitable outlets for investment at home. Lenin's *Imperialism,
The Highest Stage of Capitalism* (1916) borrowed heavily from
Hobson. Marxists and others denounced the First World War as
an imperialist war, the final and logical outcome of the struggle
of rival capitalisms for world markets. If one could go by the
history of the word alone, one might deduce that British imperialism as a historical phenomenon lasted only from the 1880s to
the early twentieth century. In fact the activities and relationships ·
which the word was coined to describe have a much longer history.
(The fact that Hobson and Lenin *thought* the phenomenon they
were describing was intimately bound up with economic causes
does not mean that it necessarily was so.) Nadel and Curtis, in
the introduction to their valuable collection of readings, offer a
useful definition: imperialism is 'the extension of sovereignty or
control, whether direct or indirect, political or economic, by one
government, nation or society over another together with the
ideas justifying or opposing this process. Imperialism is essentially
about power both as end and means.'[17] Behind the slogans and
the symbols of the imperial power, they continue, lies the reality
of its superior military, economic, political and moral power. In
fact the imperial power always has a conscious sense of its own
superiority. Imperialism involves the collision of two or more
cultures and a subsequent relationship of 'unequal exchange'.

Hobson believed that a new age of imperialism began in the
1870s – and it is indeed fairly usual for the history textbooks to
describe the last decades of the nineteenth century as the age of
the 'new imperialism'. At heart Hobson was really concerned with
domestic social problems: he saw 'underconsumption' as the basic
evil – the masses were not paid high enough wages so they could
not afford to buy the goods they themselves were helping to
manufacture, which in turn meant that the manufacturers in
Britain and elsewhere were in effect overproducing:

> Overproduction in the sense of an excessive manufacturing plant, and
> surplus capital which could not find sound investments within the
> country, forced Great Britain, Germany, Holland, France to place
> larger and larger portions of their economic resources outside the
> area of their present political domain, and then stimulate a political
> expansion so as to take in the new areas.[18]

Lenin specifically associated imperialism with the growth of large-scale monopoly capitalism, which again, he argued, cut down investment opportunities at home.

The Hobson–Leninist thesis has been subject to attack from four angles. First of all it has been criticised for its epochal, discontinuous view of events; it implies that since imperialism only began in the 1870s, the period from the end of the Napoleonic Wars (1815) till then had been a time of peace and hostility to imperial ventures. In the pages of the *American Historical Review*[19] J. H. Galbraith attacked what he called 'The Myths of the Little England Era', arguing that at no time did the vociferous Manchester school of 'anti-imperialists' in practice influence government policy. This was the view also of J. Gallagher, R. Robinson and Alice Denny, who in a famous book, *Africa and the Victorians: The Official Mind of Imperialism* (1961), introduced the term 'informal empire' to cover British overseas activities and attitudes in the mid-Victorian period. The argument here then is that there was no such sharp break in the 1870s as Hobson maintained, or indeed as other utterly non-Leninist historians maintained through taking Disraeli's speeches of that decade at their face value. Secondly, overseas trade statistics have been cited to confute Hobson. Without any doubt the figures quoted by Hobson do not prove his case; but there has been a certain amount of confusion on the other side as well – although it can be shown that Britain *as a whole* did not make much of a profit out of the Empire that does not necessarily mean that certain influential individuals were not doing well and so might still be strong protagonists of imperial expansion. A very important work by D. C. M. Platt, *Finance, Trade and Politics in British Foreign Policy 1815–1914* (Oxford, 1968) brought out that with respect to the motives of the British government towards imperialism the importance of preserving existing markets and not missing any opportunities with respect to prospective ones was an extremely important consideration. Thirdly, a single glance at the record demonstrates that the great burst of imperial activity, on the part of all European countries, not just Britain, came in the 1880s, not the 1870s. Finally, accepting that there was indeed a 'scramble for Africa' in the 1880s, though generally arguing that no sharp break with the past could be posited, historians have offered various alternative explanations to the Hobson–Leninist 'economic' one.

Some of these possibilities are expressed pungently in the

subtitle to Winks's collection of readings, *British Imperialism; Gold, God, Glory* (1963). Hobson had admitted the important part played by missionary idealists, but dismissed them as the tools of economic interests. Historians nowadays are less happy about this kind of facile dismissal, and Galbraith has been one among several to stress the reality of the missionary motive in the period of informal empire. The new factor provoking the great burst of formal expansion is no longer thought to lie exclusively (if at all) in the development of large-scale capitalism in the European countries (such a development is not, for instance, very apparent in Italy, which nonetheless had her imperial adventures). Robinson and Gallagher find the starting-point in a series of nationalist crises *within* Africa (this emphasis is in itself very much in the modern idiom) which provoked the aggressive and insecure powers of Europe into violent response. Ultimately, then, we are back to a question of European power politics (which, of course, could still be determined by economic rivalries). Certain historians, including D. K. Fieldhouse, have identified the new factor as the sudden entry in 1884–5 of Germany into the 'bid for colonies'. Such experts on Bismarckian Germany as Erich Eyck, or on German colonialism as Mary E. Townsend (writing in 1921) explained Bismarck's switch in policy as due to pressure from, or a desire to win the support of, German commercial interests. A. J. P. Taylor, as we noted, provided an important link in the 'power politics' argument by suggesting that Bismarck's main motive was to stir up rivalry between France and Britain. The *immediate* impelling motive for the new imperialist expansion, then, is the exigencies of the European diplomatic scene; imperialism is the projection into the wider world of the power struggle in Europe.

This helps to explain specific events. But it does not satisfactorily explain the wider phenomenon which affected Italy and the United States as well as France, Britain and Germany, which affected entire peoples as well as statesmen. Hence the search for 'sociological' explanations. Joseph A. Schumpeter (1883–1950), one of the great 'sociological' economic historians in the tradition of Sombart, had suggested, in an essay on the Sociology of Imperialism, published in English translation in '*Imperialism' and 'Social Classes*' (1951), that the new imperialism involved a kind of atavism among the masses, a throwback to ancient glories. Research on the psychology of imperialism has not yet got very far (see O. Mannoni's case study of Madagascar, *Prospero and Caliban: The Psychology of Colonization* (1950), and Bruce Mazlish's discussion of it in the *Journal of Contemporary History*)[20] but some thought has been given to such Freudian suggestions as that dominion over another society reconciles Western man to the disciplines of his own society, especially if he can be reassured that the subject peoples are inferior to himself; or perhaps the great colonisers have simply re-enacted their childhood fantasies and fears in the colonial environment. The latter notion will probably not prove helpful in explaining the responses of whole sectors of society to the imperial idea. The post-1945 state of professional opinion can best be summed up in two quotations, one from D. K. Fieldhouse, one from Nadel and Curtis. 'It is clear', said Fieldhouse,

> that imperialism cannot be explained in simple terms of economic theory and the nature of finance capitalism. In its mature form it can best be described as a sociological phenomenon with roots in political facts: it can properly be understood only in terms of the same social hysteria which has since given birth to other and more disastrous forms of aggressive nationalism.[21]

Nadel and Curtis pointed out that 'anyone who believes in the diversity of human behavior and who rejects cosmic solutions or single causes in history will not hesitate to point out the inconsistencies, mysteries, and even absurdities of imperialism'.

To assess the effects of imperialism one must take the wider context and the universal meaning. Karl Marx, who was of course on the side of the 'march of history', noted the modernising effects, as well as the evident exploitation, inherent in imperial rule. Many of the English Fabian Socialists also approved of imperialism as a civilising influence. As with the study of the Industrial Revolution, it is important not to make blanket assertions one way or the other: again to echo E. P. Thompson, there is no record of neutral and inevitable change, but of exploitation and resistance, values lost and values gained. Herbert Luethy, the distinguished Swiss scholar (the Swiss incidentally were never colonisers), has seen imperial and colonial expansion as part of the development of civilisation: 'the history of colonisation is the history of humanity itself'.[22] Victor Kiernan, a leading Marxist in the contemporary school, has shown in scholarly style just how evil in practice this 'history of humanity' could be.[23]

Much of the most interesting work now (a good deal of it from inside black Africa) is being done with respect to the significance of African nationalist and resistance movements, a subject which can be broached in *Historians and Africanist History: A Critique. Post Colonial Historiography Examined* (1981) by Arnold Temu and Bonaventure Swai.

Yet, a book which has achieved wide acclaim, is in many senses traditional. This is the magnificently wide-ranging *The Rise and Fall of the Great Powers* (1988) by Paul Kennedy, which in looking at the fate of past empires, draws out lessons for America today – a fine and explicit tribute to the relevance of history.

8. The Two World Wars

Not long ago mention in historical circles of the First World War immediately concentrated attention on the controversies over the 'causes' of that war. There has, too, been an extensive literature on the origins of the Second World War. But for many years now a great deal of effort has gone into studying the conduct, significance, and consequences of these two cataclysmic wars. The study of their origins raises basic issues about the nature of historical causation and the relationship (if, that is, one accepts the distinction in the first place) between 'situational' causes and 'immediate' causes, while questions about the nature and conse- quences of war involve controversies over the approaches appro- priate to historical study.

But apart from such professional issues the causation of these two twentieth-century wars brings up very live political issues; particularly that of the extent of German responsibility for both wars. By the time the first generation of debate, which broke out with the war itself in August 1914, had run its course, the consensus (controverted, of course, in many individual cases) was that no one individual power could be blamed (unless, perhaps, it were the Austro-Hungarian Empire, which, after 1918, no longer existed). The great event disturbing this calm was the publication in Germany in 1961 of Fritz Fischer's *Griff nach der Weltmacht* (English translation published as *Germany's Aims in the First World War* in 1967). Fischer stressed both the technological– industrial developments in Wilhelmine Germany which, he argued, made her naturally an aggressive expansionist power, and the detailed annexationist policies set out very clearly in an indisputably authentic document written by the Chancellor Bethmann-Hollweg, once regarded as a relatively liberal and pacifist politician whose true gentle nature was subverted by the belligerent Kaiser and his generals. Fischer's thesis which, in effect, revivified the idea of Germany's prime responsibility for the war, aroused violent hostility in Germany. It was also pointed out that the Bethmann-Hollweg document, being written during, not before the war, was scarcely evidence of German pre-war plans; if similar expressions of war aims from the other powers were to be studied they too might well appear aggressive and annexationist. However, whatever comments in detail might be made on Fischer's epochal work, it became impossible thereafter to wish away all notions of a special responsibility attaching to Germany as Europe's trouble-maker in the first part of the twentieth century. Within the 'Fischer school' one can number Imanuel Geiss, who, already in 1960, had published a book on German war aims in Holland, Hertmut Kaelble, and Volker Berghahn, (*Der Tirpitz Plan* (Dusseldorf, 1971), and *Germany and the Approach of War in 1914* (1973)). The emphasis was very much on structural and sociological factors within Germany, disposing powerful interest groups towards war-like policies.

Less politically controversial yet just as prone to the arousal of strong emotions, is the question of the First World War as a 'great divide', or not, in modern history. How does one answer a question like that? It is instructive to look for a moment at the case of Great Britain. Two very careful historians of twentieth-century Britain, Charles Loch Mowat (in *Britain Between the Wars*, 1955) and Alfred Havighurst (in *Twentieth Century Britain*, 1962, and subsequent editions) argued from the evidence of the continuities in politics and political institutions and in social life that on balance the First World War had changed little. In my own book *The Deluge: British Society and the First World War* (first published in 1965) and in other publications I, on the contrary, maintained that important aspects of British society had been changed by the war; A. J. P. Taylor in his *English History 1914–1945* (1965) also stressed the new role assumed by the state and the social upheavals of war. While my concern was with a whole constellation of social change affecting workers, women, social geography, application of technology, and social customs, I suggested (in an article of January 1968 in the *Journal of Contemporary History*) that it was 'instructive to make two comparisons: the post–1918 Labour Party with the pre-1914 Labour Party, and the post-1918 Franchise with the pre-1914 one.' In his justly praised, and immensely thorough *The Evolution of the Labour Party 1910–1924* (1974), Ross McKibbin set up the contrary view (p. 239).

> It is a question how obvious or how true these apparently obvious truths are . . . In any case, had the structure of Britain changed so much as a result of the war? The towns were no larger than they had been; there were few new industries; there was no increase in the mobility of the population; despite fashionable forms of social dissent there was little of the political disorientation so noticeable on the Continent. Though the staple industries were soon to be in difficulties, they had also been in some before 1914, and the labour disturbances of 1917–1919 were no worse than those of 1911–13. The war had clearly extended the role of the state, but so had the most important social legislation of the Campbell-Bannerman and Asquith governments. As to those two 'instructive' comparisons made by Marwick: the post-war Labour Party was, of course, not nearly so different from its predecessor as he believes. Of the franchise reform it is worth noting that suffrage bills had been before parliament in 1912 and 1913, and, despite the dilly-dallying of the Liberal government, some kind of legislation would have been passed before long. The 1918 Act, for its part, was the most conservative that could have been devised in the circumstances. The vote for all men over twenty-one was irresistible, but for women the suffrage was limited by age and property qualifications, a franchise widely admitted to be illegitimate even before 1914.

Another thorough study, based on all the relevant political archives, *Electoral Reform in War and Peace 1906–18* (1978) by Martin Pugh explicitly disagreed with those (particularly myself) who argued that the war had significance in bringing votes for women. Pugh's arguments are based on political sources; McKibbin, in the passage quoted, implicitly brought in quantities: towns no larger than they had been; few new industries. Yet it could be argued that the new war-based industries, though tiny in size, were crucial in their social impact: electrical, internal combustion engine, radio valves. One could argue that the population disruptions in, say, remote Welsh villages (again scarcely showing up in the statistics) had a considerable effect on social mores – the decline in traditional religion in particular. It is perfectly true that the statistics for women's employment are most unimpressive: only a handful more in employment in 1920 than there had been in 1914. But, it might be argued, it is not in this case any more a matter of quantities than it is of political documentation: it is a question of 'mentalities', of the changing experience and changing attitudes of women.

As is usually the case, historical controversy brought new discoveries, generally agreed by all participants in the debates. In fact, as so often, disagreement often boiled down to the way in which questions were posed, or the way in which such concepts as 'change' were defined. A younger generation of feminist historians, in particular, tended to argue against the war's having had any effect on the 'emancipation' of women. Largely this was because they defined 'emancipation' (in 1918, it simply meant winning the vote) in such a sweeping way that such changes as did take place inevitably seemed very trivial; in part, also, it was because feminists prefer only to identify change brought about by conscious militant action, and are unhappy with the suggestion that change might come about irrespective of such action.[24] Marxist writers, with their own views about how social change ought to come about, have also recently tended to play down the significance of war. Gerd Hardach's *The First World War* (1973), being firmly Marxist in orientation, sees only continuities in the western countries, and the only significant result as the Russian Revolution, a judgement echoed by Marc Ferro (see below). Jurgen Kocka, taking an explicitly Marxist approach, found that the First World War in Germany brought about a polarisation of classes, thrusting the lower middle class down into the proletariat – a rather astonishing conclusion given the expansion that has actually taken place subsequently in the lower middle class.[25] The most thorough economic studies, covering various European countries, have been carried through by A. S. Milward, whose impressively total approach has led him to conclude that war did induce important changes in social psychology.[26]

The point here is not to argue this particular case one way or the other. The function of historical controversy, anyway, is to bring out the many-sidedness of events and to emphasise the absurdity of riding any one hobby horse too hard. No, the purpose here is to show the manner in which historical study of war has broadened out in the last fifteen years. The gains made by labour

and the new style of 'social contract' established in Germany
despite the disasters of the war were stressed in Gerald Feldman's
Army, Industry and Labor, (1966). The most wide-ranging study
of all, stressing, as one would expect, the war's effect on attitudes
and perceptions, was Marc Ferro's *The Great War* (published in
France in 1967; English translation 1973). For France itself there
has been the collection of essays edited by Patrick Fridenson,
L'Autre Front (1977) and for the United States *From Progress-
ivism to Prosperity: World War I and American Society* (1987) by
Neil A. Wynn. Fascinating new directions have been opened up
by Eric J. Leed in his *No Man's Land* (1979), a study of the
psychological repercussions of the war for the soldiers who fought
in it, Paul Fussel in his exploration of the literary imagination
already mentioned, and John Fuller in his (as yet unpublished)
exploration of British popular culture in the trenches. There has
been a similar shift in emphasis with regard to the Second World
War – *The People's War* by Angus Calder (1969), *War and Society:
America 1941–1945* (1972) by Richard Polenberg, and *Valley of
Darkness: The Japanese People and World War II* (1979) by
Thomas R. H. Havens – and similar controversies. As always in
historical controversy differences are exaggerated and positions
are presented as harder than they really are. It is, above all, as
the various writings taken together bring out, important not to
speak in any simple-minded way of the war causing this, or the
war stopping that, nor to get into some naïve calculation of 'gains'
and 'losses'. Whatever war's immediate effects, long-term trends
clearly are also very important.

If we turn back now to the causation of the Second World War
there is a link between the present section and the previous one
in Professor W. N. Medlicott's heart-felt but hopeless cry of 1963
that 'Appeasement should now be added to Imperialism on the
list of words no scholar uses.' The mention of appeasement is a
reminder that really there are two major controversies over the
origins of the Second World War – interrelated certainly, but not
necessarily interdependent: the big question, presumably, is 'Was
it *Hitler's* war?' but a much larger amount of ink, blood, and
synthetic emotion has been lavished over the 'appeasement' policies of British governments in the thirties which failed to 'stop'
Hitler when they could and should have done so – thus the
'appeasers' were said to hold a particular responsibility for the

war. In an indispensable article Donald Cameron Watt maintained that the condemnation of the appeasers rests upon the acceptance of the 'Hitler's war' thesis.[27] This is not absolutely true: it is possible to attribute more diffuse and less clear-cut ambitions to Hitler, to accept that there are deeper economic, social and ideological causes of war, and yet still to maintain that appeasement had the unfortunate effect of encouraging rather than deterring Hitler's aggressive impulses. Still it is true that until the publication of Taylor's *Origins* in 1961 the accepted versions of events conflated the idea of a war carefully planned in advance by Hitler with a blind and craven policy on the part of the British which failed to prevent this plan from running its course: the fundamental point was repeated again and again that the Second World War was, in Churchill's phrase, an 'unnecessary' war, that by simply following an obvious set of alternative choices the British Government could have averted the war. The breathtaking naïvety of this thesis would be unbelievable were it not for the fact that honest souls (mostly American) go on serving it up to this day.

Taylor's *Origins* cuts across both controversies. In the opening chapter of the first edition he explained his intention of re-examining the simple accepted explanation that Hitler's will alone caused the war; but in the 'Second Thoughts' of the revised edition he explained that the 'vital question' concerned Great Britain and France – the 'appeasing nations'. To me it has always been clear that in planning and writing the *Origins* Taylor was in process of changing his own mind, and that this explains certain unsatisfactory features of his book. At one stage Taylor seems to have wished to defend the appeasers against the wilder denunciations which had been fashionable from the time of the polemical tract *Guilty Men* (1940) through J. W. Wheeler-Bennett's magisterial *Munich: Prologue to Tragedy* (1948) and on to the then unpublished *Appeasers* (1963) by Martin Gilbert and Richard Gott: yet in the end the arguments of the book, while removing from Hitler a peculiar and special responsibility for the war, seem to rivet responsibility all the more heavily on the appeasers; he removed, as again he announced in the first chapter, the basis for the 'claim that appeasement was a wise, and would have been a successful policy if it had not been for the unpredictable fact that Germany was in the grip of a madman'. (This argument, with refinements, lies at the base of what might be called the contemporary 'pacifist' defence of appeasement.)

The importance of Taylor's book was that it threw open again what had seemed likely to become a closed subject – though it should not be forgotten that in a number of earlier scholarly works Medlicott and Watt had already pointed the road towards revisionism. An important study, already completed though at that time not yet published, Esmonde Robertson's *Hitler's Pre-War Policy and Military Plans* (1964), brought out forcefully that from 1937 onwards Hitler simply rushed from one hasty improvisation to another, and that when war came in 1939 it was two or three years earlier than expected. Two general works took matters rather further through a deliberate renunciation of old-style narrative diplomatic history. An important essay in F. H. Hinsley's *Power and the Pursuit of Peace* (1963) argued that the root cause of war in 1939 was an imbalance in the European power structure: apparently defeated in 1918, Germany was in fact potentially in a relatively more overwhelmingly strong position than ever before – for the time being the Russian Empire was out, and the Austrian Empire was gone for good, and France, though nominally a victor, had been gravely weakened by the long war of attrition fought largely on her own soil. Hinsley clearly saw himself as an opponent of the Taylor thesis, but the differences are more apparent than real; Taylor, in less abstract fashion, had covered much the same ground in his second and third chapters. In 1966 F. S. Northedge published his masterly *The Troubled Giant: Great Britain Among the Powers 1916–1939*. Northedge's title was carefully chosen: his theme was that of a Great Power, still ruling over a nineteenth-century Empire yet, through political sluggishness and economic weakness brought on by the sacrifices of the previous war, unable to come to terms with the problems and the new ideologies of the twentieth century. Northedge suggested that British policies in the later thirties were not uniquely immoral or uniquely craven. Britain's rulers then, as in the nineteenth century, really wanted nothing more than to be allowed to carry on peaceful trading policies: Britain in the nineteenth century had cut no very noble figure over the Schleswig-Holstein crisis; but when serious jeopardy threatened, Britain always had in reserve the possibility of intervention with overwhelming effect, as in 1914. In the thirties,

Northedge argued, Britain had neither the power nor the *will* for such intervention (though in the end she did just that).

Historians have steadily mopped up the various myths surrounding the appeasement issue. It used to be argued that Hitler could have been 'stopped' at the time of the invasion of the Rhineland in 1936 for he would have 'climbed down': Watt has shown that this is by no means certain. There was much talk about how the Czechs ought to have been 'saved' in 1938; given the geographical and strategic factors involved, it is hard to visualise this 'saving' – unless again Hitler was expected to 'back down'. Northedge singled out the British Foreign Secretary's clear-sighted appraisal of the situation at the time of Munich:

> To fight a European war for something that you could not in fact protect and did not expect to restore was a course which must deserve serious consideration before it was undertaken.

To sum up: on balance the appeasers still do not come out very well, but they are now seen in the wider context of the deeper weaknesses of the British political structure in the interwar years; their mistakes were the counterpart of the economic miscalculations which brought depression and unemployment – unhappily the stakes in modern war are immeasurably higher. To return to the Hitler controversy: Taylor does not in this case carry the day, though he has rendered the old simple formulations completely obsolete. The clearest and most convincing short analysis is to be found in Alan Bullock's Raleigh Lecture. Bullock points out that Hitler was neither crazy fanatic (the traditional view) nor cynical opportunist (the Taylor view): he was each in turn; his foreign policy 'combined consistency of aim with complete opportunism in method and tactics'. Hitler's consistency of aim, Bullock continues, with obvious reference to Taylor:

> has been confused with a time-table, blueprint, or plan of action fixed in advance, as if it were pinned up on the wall of the General Staff Offices and ticked off as one item succeeded another. Nothing of the sort. Hitler frequently improvised, kept his options open to the last possible moment, and was never sure until he got there which of several courses of action he would choose. But this does not alter the fact that his moves followed a logical (though not a predetermined) course . . .

But in restoring the traditional, and surely correct, interpretation of Hitler, Bullock is not accepting the thesis of the 'unnecessary war'. After summarising Hitler's consistency of purpose, as shown in his aims – restoration of German military power and a new German Empire in the east – his full recognition from the first that such aims would involve war, and the strength of will which enabled him to run ever more dangerous risks, Bullock concludes:

> Given such an attitude on the part of a man who controlled one of the most powerful nations in the world, the majority of whose people were prepared to believe what he told them about their racial superiority and to greet his satisfaction of their nationalist ambitions with enthusiasm – given this, I cannot see how a clash between Germany and the other Powers could have been avoided. Except on the assumption that Britain and France were prepared to disinterest themselves in what happened east of the Rhine and accept the risk of seeing him create a German hegemony over the rest of Europe. . . .
>
> If the Western Powers had recognised the threat earlier and shown greater resolution in resisting Hitler's (and Mussolini's) demands, it is possible that the clash might not have led to war, or at any rate not to a war on the scale on which it had finally to be fought. The longer they hesitated, the higher the price of resistance. This is their share of the responsibility for the war: that they were reluctant to recognise what was happening, reluctant to give a lead in opposing it, reluctant to act in time. Hitler understood their state of mind perfectly and played on it with skill. None of the Great Powers comes well out of the history of the 1930s, but this sort of responsibility even when it runs to appeasement, as in the case of Britain and France, or complicity as in the case of Russia, is still recognisably different from that of government which deliberately creates the threat of war and sets out to exploit it.

This is a gloomy view, perhaps too gloomy. But then history, in many ways, is a gloomy subject. History teaches that there are no easy solutions. At best, some historians would argue, different policies from Versailles onwards would have put Europe in the 1930s in less dangerous straits – there will always be danger.

But is it perhaps too parochially European to concentrate on Britain and Germany, on appeasement and Hitler? So would argue, among others, the German historian Eberhard Jäckel who has pointed out that the Second World War only genuinely became a world war with the entry of Japan and America in December 1941. Jäckel has developed a wider perspective suggesting (to put it at its simplest) that this truly world war ranged on one side the satisfied powers, Britain and the United States, and on the other the dissatisfied powers, Japan and

Germany. The continued refinement of, and advance in, analysis, the persistence of A. J. P. Taylor's *Origins* as a point of reference, and the manner in which highly significant work can still often be presented in that sometimes stupidly despised mode of historical communication, the learned article, is brought out in two recent pieces to which interested readers are recommended to refer: Richard Overy, 'Germany, "Domestic Crisis" and War in 1939' in *Past and Present*, (July 1987) and G. Martel (ed.) *The Origins of the Second World War Reconsidered. The A. J. P. Taylor Debate after 25 years* (1986). At the opposite extreme to these two highly concentrated specimens of the historian's traditional craft, stand the twenty-six volumes of the official history of the Netherlands in the Second World War (1967–87) by Louis de Jong. This incredible work is one of the most substantial monuments there is to the power the past exercises over the present, for, so eager are the Dutch to engage with what was for them sometimes a murky past, each volume has been a best-seller. It is also, when so many other governments fall over themselves to falsify the past, or to preserve their 'official secrets', a tribute to the Dutch government's recognition that in the study of history, itself a social necessity, nothing but the persistent pursuit of the truth will do.

Notes

1. Quoted in Lawrence Stone, *Social Change and Revolution in England* (1965) p. 164.
2. Quoted in Stone, p. 166.
3. Ibid., p. 4.
4. *History* (1956).
5. Quoted in Stone, *Social Change and Revolution in England*, p. 43.
6. Ibid., p. 61.
7. P. Laslett (ed.), *Household and Family in Past Time* (1971), p. 12.
8. Jean-Louis Flandrin, *Familles: parenté, maison, sexualité dans l'ancienne société*, pp. 80–81.
9. Georges Duby, *Le Chevalier, la femme et les prêtres: le Mariage dans la France Féodale* (Paris, 1981), p. 303.
10. E. Shorter, *The Making of the Modern Family* (1975; pb edn, 1977), p. 15.
11. L. Stone, *The Family, Sex and Marriage in England from 1500–1800* (1977), p. 4.

12. Michael Anderson, *Approaches to the History of the Western Family 1500–1914* (1980), pp. 65–6.

13. Quoted in the Introduction to the excellent collection of readings already mentioned, *The American Revolution: Whose Revolution?* (New York, 1977), edited by James Kerby Martin and Karen R. Stubaus).

14. E. James Ferguson, *The American Revolution* (revised edition, Homeward, Illinois, 1979), p. viii.

15. E. P. Thompson, 'Time and Work-Discipline' in *Past and Present* (Dec. 1967), pp. 93–4.

16. Richard Koebner, articles in *Economic History Review* (1949) and *Cambridge Journal* (1952) discussed in G. H. Nadel and Perry Curtis, *Imperialism and Colonialism* (New York, 1964), pp. 1–2.

17. Ibid., p. 1.

18. J. A. Hobson, *Imperialism: A Study* (1902), quoted in Robin W. Winks, *British Imperialism: Gold, God, Glory* (New York, 1963), p. 25.

19. LXVIII (Oct. 1961).

20. III 2 (1968) 174–5.

21. D. K. Fieldhouse, 'Imperialism', *Economic History Review*, second series, XIV (1961), p. 209.

22. Quoted in Nadel and Curtis, p. 29.

23. V. G. Kiernan, *The Lords of Human Kind* (1969).

24. See e.g. Gail Braybon, *Women Workers in the First World War* (Beckenham, 1981).

25. Jurgen Kocka, *Facing Total War* (Leamington Spa, 1984).

26. A. S. Milward, *War, Economy and Society, 1939–1945* (1977).

27. D. C. Watt, 'Appeasement: the rise of a revisionist school' in *Political Quarterly* (1965). See also W. N. Medlicott's Historical Association pamphlet *The Coming of War in 1939* (1963).

Chapter 9 Conclusion: The Nature and Profession of History

From time to time there come impassioned pleas from within the profession for historians to mend their ways, to form up in ranks for the march into the promised land of a truly scientific, or a truly relevant, history. Marc Bloch's *The Historian's Craft*, E. H. Carr's *What is History?*, and Philip Abrams's *Historical Sociology* are all compelling personal statements about how, in the author's views, history ought to be written. Gordon Connell-Smith and Howell A. Lloyd demanded a history more relevant to the needs of a changing society, and Geoffrey Barraclough has spoken passionately of history's opportunity to break into a new scientific dimension, incidentally criticising my own apparent conservatism and complacency in defending the modest advances which historical study has made over the years.[1] History has relevance, but that relevance must not be a forced relevance. The appearance in 1980 of a Public History Association in America to press for the practical applications of history was to be welcomed: but there will always have to be a distinction between public, or 'applied' history and truly scholarly history, without which all history, at all levels, will ultimately decay. I believe deeply in the importance of history, but I cannot share in the messianic fervour of writers like Carr and Barraclough. In fact, those who confuse analysis of the objectives, methods, and achievements of history, with the enunciation of a political programme, tend, with the passage of time, to look rather silly. Given our well-founded sensitivity now to the destruction wrought on the natural environment, and to the ever-present menace in contemporary societies of persuasion and indoctrination, Carr's faith in his own superior objectivity and understanding of the progressive direction of history seems not only naïve, but downright crass:

> . . . man has begun, through the conscious exercise of reason, not only

to transform his environment but to transform himself . . . the control of population has become a matter of rational and conscious social policy. We have seen in our time the lengthening by human effort of the span of human life and the altering of the balance between the generations in our population. We have heard of drugs consciously used to influence human behaviour, and surgical operations designed to alter human character. Both man and society have changed, and have been changed by conscious human effort, before our eyes. But the most significant of these changes have probably been those brought about by the development and use of modern methods of persuasion and indoctrination. Educators at all levels are nowadays more and more consciously concerned to make their contribution to the shaping of society in a particular mould, and to inculcate in the rising generation the attitudes, loyalties, and opinions appropriate to that type of society; educational policy is an integral part of any rationally planned social policy.[2]

The thesis of this book is that to understand the nature of history one should look at the real objectives of historical study, its very real achievements, and at what working historians, upon whose labours these achievements are based, actually do. I shall shortly summarise the main arguments in support of that thesis, but first I want to draw out the implications of what I have been saying for the teaching of history at universities. Whatever is taught in the way of period or geographical area, a history degree, or the history component of a wider degree, ought to contain four elements. First, the nature and methodology of history, its relation to other disciplines, the relevance of quantification and other techniques drawn from the social sciences: in other words, 'historiography' in the broad sense in which I have tried to present it in this book. Secondly, the writing of essays, which are invaluable as exercises both in marshalling evidence and in *communication*: in modest fashion they exemplify the historian at work. The crucial point is that the essay should be properly written up and should be carefully read and annotated by the tutor: it is only by the constant correction and discussion of written work that students learn to produce written history which avoides cliché and empty rhetoric, and is securely founded in evidence. The third element is the study of primary sources of all types. Here students learn the basic techniques and methodology of the subject, learn how historians develop that special gift of 'squeezing the last drop' out of the text in front of them. Detailed work on sources is best examined, not through short gobbets, or 'context questions', but by setting whole passages, paragraph-length or more, and asking for a full commentary which will be as long as the traditional essay answer (the formula I recommend is: 'Comment on one of the following extracts, saying what the document is, setting it in its historical context, commenting on specific points in the text, and summing up the extract's historical significance for the study of European history 1500–1800 [or whatever the topic of the course happens to be]'). Finally, any decent history degree should involve a piece of private research on topics chosen by individual students: given that the other elements have been mastered, it is only here that students can develop true originality, develop that talent for asking the right questions which must appertain to any good historian (not to mention 'public' or 'applied' historians).

David Lodge's wickedly witty novel of university life in the 1960s, *Changing Places* (1975) has some delicious words on Philip Swallow's supreme talents in the setting of exam papers. Yet there are well set exam questions designed to test the knowledge and skills a particular course sets out to teach, as well as sloppy ones. Two deplorable types of sloppiness are questions which contain an in-built assumption ('What factors contributed to the making of the English working class in the early nineteenth century?') and ones which contain a decorative quotation which bears little relationship to the question actually being asked. Example:

> The whole map of Europe has been changed . . . The mode and thought of men, the whole outlook on affairs, the grouping of parties, all have encountered violent and tremendous changes in the deluge of the world, but as the deluge subsides and the waters fall we see the dreary steeples of Fermanagh and Tyrone emerging once again; The intensity of their quarrel is one of the few institutions that has been left unaltered in the cataclysm which has swept the world.' (W. S. Churchill, *The World Crisis*).
>
> What was the effect on British politics of successive failures to 'solve' the Irish question between 1900 and 1922?

Remedy: cut the quotation, or rephrase the question to:

> What is Churchill saying here about the Irish Question? Did he understand its significance?

One way in which university teaching could be improved at all levels is by the conscious enunciation of aims (that is to say, a broad statement of what each individual course of lectures, tutorials, etc. is endeavouring to achieve) and objectives (that is to say, a detailed spelling out of what it is students will be expected to be able to do after each section of the course that they could not do before embarking on that section). Of course, the spelling out of aims and objectives can become a tedious, formalistic ritual, and sometimes they are a mere apologia preceding a formless, amateurish, unstructured mass of aimless information. Probably the spelling out of aims and objectives is a more useful exercise for the teacher than for the taught. If the teacher already knows, however sub-consciously, what it is he or she is trying to do, there may well be no need to articulate this. But generally when a course has a clearly enunciated set of aims and objectives, and when the entire course, including essays, examinations, and all the rest, really works towards achieving these aims and objectives, then the probabilities are that the course will be a good course, well taught, and that students will benefit correspondingly. Aims and objectives need not be dreary and restrictive: if one aim is to encourage students a little bit along the way of thinking like a historian, of understanding the complexities of the subject, of realising the dangers of jumping to rapid conclusions, then no harm in spelling that aim out. Better to spell it out than to have a constant implied mismatch between what the tutor really believes history to be and what, cynically, he believes to be the limits of his students' understanding. (For some specimen aims and objectives, see Appendix A.)

On the question of content, I will say little more than it is not absurd to start off with the society in which students themselves are placed, though the more that society can be set in the context of wider relationships (Britain within Europe, Europe within the world, for example) the better. If the expertise and resources are there, obviously courses in non-Western history seen from a non-Western point of view are much to be desired. To concentrate exclusively on the contemporary period (perhaps in the name of some kind of 'relevance') would, in my view, be not to teach history at all. The significance of the past goes far beyond the immediate past. At the same time I do want to knock on the head the weary cliché (trotted out again I see in a recently translated *History of Italy*)[3] that because of 'lack of perspective' contemporary history cannot be studied at all. *All* history is difficult; perspectives do change anyway. Contemporary history (in common with every aspect of history) has its special problems, but the principles set out in this book can as well be applied to contemporary history as to any other branch. The rule is *never* to rely on personal experience or memory, *always* to have supporting evidence of the type which would be required in every other sphere of investigation.

How should courses be designed and titled? Should one, for instance, have a course simply, and relatively neutrally, labelled 'European History, 1789 to the Present', or should one, say, have a course labelled 'Legitimacy and Dissidence in Europe, 1789 to the Present'? There is much to be said for endeavouring, aggressively as it were, to introduce concepts and themes into history courses; at the same time care has to be taken to avoid introducing unstated assumptions and a priori reasoning. It may be that striking titles, which indicate some principles of structural organisation, are best reserved for the books which historians write, and that university courses should pay heed to the need which can never be glossed over for the presentation and discussion of certain fundamental information.

The nature of history, I have said, emerges from the purposes, achievements, and general practices of the subject. That argument I shall now, by way of a conclusion, summarise under six headings.

1 *Purposes and Achievements*. The purpose of history is the understanding of the past, a social necessity since the past is such a dominating influence on our lives. We cannot escape from history. Our lives are governed by what happened in the past, our decisions by what we believe to have happened. Without a knowledge of history, humanity and society would run adrift, rudderless craft on the uncharted sea of time. The achievement of history is that we do in fact know a great deal about past societies, and are constantly learning more: we are in a strong position to challenge myths and the self-serving exploitation of history which obtains in many societies throughout the world.

2. *Definitions*. The words 'history' and 'historical' are, quite properly, used with a variety of shades of meaning. To say that 'history' *must* be what Marx, or Carr, or Braudel, or for that matter, Marwick, says it is, is absurd. The best single brief definition of history, as it is used in such well-known phrases as 'the revolution changed the course of history', or as I have

just used it, in 'we cannot escape from history', is 'the past as
we know it through the systematic studies of historians'.
History, though there are many critical differences, is to the
human past, as science is to the natural world. Once it was
believed that science revealed God's handiwork, as it was
believed that history revealed God's will. History, like science,
does not, in that sense, have meaning. The relationships
studied by history, unlike relationships in many of the sciences,
are not fundamentally mathematical. Thus, there are no
general laws, is no overarching theory, in history.

3. *Theory.* The desire to impose such theory upon history arises
either from a romantic faith that there must be a positive
direction in history, or from a personal fascination with the
intellectual excitements of theoretical speculation and a public
desire to make history 'respectable'. It would be not inaccurate
(as I hope it would not be offensive) to say that, desiring a
better world, and desiring clear rules for getting there, even
brilliant minds become 'intoxicated' on Marxism. In historical
study there are generalisations, concepts, interrelationships,
theories (plural), but no theory (singular). Marxist theory does
not in fact work in practice, and all the subsequent refinements,
emerging, in particular, in 'cultural theory' are simply attempts
to explain why what ought to have happened, didn't happen,
when the sensible course would be to abandon the notion of
what ought to happen. Marx made immense contributions to
mainstream historical study; Marxist-inspired interest in the
underdog has had many beneficial results; some of the most
distinguished historians of today still call themselves Marxists.
But the greater part of the very real achievements of historical
study (this is my central point) has been made by those who
are not Marxists and have no over-arching theory.

4. *Facts.* A preoccupation with the nature of facts is largely irrelevant to understanding the nature of history. Facts are of many
orders, and what is crucial to historical study is the nature of
evidence.

5. *Sources.* This evidence is to be found in the sources, relics and
traces left by the past. The fundamental historical skills lie in
the analysis, criticism, and interpretation of these sources,
which exist in an enormous variety, though also, alas, are
almost always fragmentary, imperfect, and intractable. The

sources used, and the methods followed (though basically informed by the same principles) depend upon the questions being addressed: there is no golden rule that statistical sources, or the methods of the *Annales* school, are *always* better than other alternatives.

6. *Writing History.* Due emphasis (as Marxists have always insisted) must be given to longer-term forces, which may conveniently be defined as structural and ideological, it always being remembered, however, that these 'forces' are in fact created by the activities of multitudes of human beings; these forces both help to create, and also interact with, 'events' (wars, revolutions, etc.), and individual actions and political decisions (though these are always circumscribed by the social context as it has emerged from the past), and with 'accidents' (though few accidents, when closely examined, turn out to be pure accidents). Getting it right, amid this complex of interactions, is the difficult task of the historian. A sustained piece of historical analysis will require a complex structure, the production of which depends not upon intoxicants, but upon dedicated problem-solving and craftsmanship. History should always be written in such a way that the informed reader can enter into a dialogue over the sources used and the conclusions drawn out from them.

The world is much in need of changing. But it can only be changed if it is understood as it really is, not as one would wish it to be, or as some a priori theory proclaims it to be. History is in its nature a deeply involving, and a deeply relevant subject. It does indeed belong to every man and every woman: that is a strength, not a weakness.

Notes

1. Gordon Connell-Smith and Howard A. Lloyd, *The Relevance of History* (1972); Geoffrey Barraclough, *Main Trends in History* (1979), esp. pp. 209 ff.

2. Carr, p. 142.

3. Giuliano Procacci, *History of the Italian People* (1973), p. 458.

Appendix A: Examples of Aims and Objectives

I Aims of Open University Course, War, Peace and Social Change: Europe c. 1900–c. 1955*

I To enable students to argue in an informed way over the nature, extent and causes of social change within and across the main European countries c. 1900–1955, which are defined for the purposes of this course as Russia, Austria-Hungary (up to the aftermath of the First World War only), France, Germany, Italy and the United Kingdom; Turkey and the Balkans, and Central European Countries as relevant. (There will also be references to Scandinavian and other European countries.)

II To help students to understand the nature of total war and the differences between different kinds of war, including internal and civil war, and to help them to discuss in an informed way the relationship between war and revolution in the twentieth century.

III To enable students to discuss the causes of the two total wars, evaluating 'structural' (that is to say 'concerning economic and industrial imperatives') forces against other forces such as those of geopolitics, ideology, nationalism and contingency.

IV To enable students to argue in an informed way about the causes of twentieth-century social change, and in particular to evaluate the significance of the two total wars with respect to this change relative to 'structural' (see aim 3), political, and ideological forces, and to enable them also to discuss the relationship of the wars to the major geopolitical changes.

* Introduction to the Course: Copyright the Open University 1989.

V To assist students to develop further the skills learned at Foundation and Second Level in:

(a) the critical analysis and interpretation of primary source materials, including written documents, as well as literary and artistic materials, film, radio and manifestations of popular culture;

(b) understanding some of the different approaches to historical study, in particular Marxist/sociological/linguistic approaches on the one side, and 'liberal humanist' ones on the other, and also quantitative and qualitative approaches;

(c) dealing with such problems as periodisation and historical semantics; and

(d) writing essays of Honours History standard.

VI To take further students' understanding of the nature of historiographical controversy (a matter first raised in the Foundation course, dealt with further at second level) and to enable them to arrive at informed judgements on the issues and debates presented within the framework of the course.

2 Examples of Objectives from Open University Course, Conflict and Stability in Development of Modern Europe: 1789–1970*

(A) Social Conflict and Social Integration in Britain and France 1918–1931

(Section 1)

1 You should be able to discuss in general how far economic trends in the inter-war period were making for conflict or stability in France and Britain.

2 You should be able to indicate briefly some of the other major factors which might have made conflict more likely.

3 You should be able to make a preliminary assessment of the effectiveness of the main forces of social control.

* Block III, part 3: Copyright the Open University 1980.

(Section 2)
4 You should be able to discuss how near to (or far from) revolution Britain and France were in the postwar period.

(Section 3)
5 You should be able to compare and contrast the degree of political stability in the British and French parliamentary systems in the 1920s. You should also be able to analyse the extent of the success (or failure) of the political leadership in the two countries in dealing with fundamental social and economic problems.

(Section 4)
6 You should be able to discuss what (a) the General Strike of 1926, and (b) the political crises of 1931 reveal about social conflict and social integration in Great Britain.

(B) Britain and France in the 1930s

(Section 1)
1 You should be able to assess the seriousness of the events of February 1934, with particular reference to the question of how near France was to a fascist *coup d'état*.

2 You should be able to discuss the Popular Front in France and its relationship to the existence of conflict and/or stability in France.

(Sections 2 and 3)
3 You should be able to discuss how far there was serious social conflict in Britain in the 1930s and be able to compare the situation in Britain with that in France.

Appendix B: Some Aphorisms

Not to know what took place before you were born is to remain forever a child (Cicero).

All men are born and live and die in the same way and therefore resemble each other (Machiavelli).

In reading history each man may have a glass to behold the beauty of virtue and deformity of vice (Thomas Norton).

When one is too curious about the practices of past centuries, one ordinarily remains very ignorant of the practices of this one (Descartes).

To future ages may thy dulness last,
As thou preserv'st the dulness of the past.
(Pope, addressing historians).

History is but a pack of tricks we play on the dead (Voltaire).

History is the most popular species of writing, since it can adapt itself to the highest or lowest capacity (Gibbon).

History is little more than the crimes, follies and misfortunes of mankind (Gibbon).

The proper, unique and profound theme of the history of the world, the theme to which all other themes are subordinated, consists of the conflict between belief and disbelief (Goethe).

The mutual relations between the two sexes seem to us to be at least as important as the mutual relations of any two governments in the world (Macaulay).

History is as much an art as a science (Renan).

The dignity of an historical epoch depends not upon what proceeds there-from, but is contained in its very existence . . . each epoch has its own dignity in itself (Ranke).

General tendencies do not decide alone; great personalities are always necessary to make them effective (Ranke).

Men make their own history, but they do not know that they are making it (Marx).

There will always be a connection between the way in which men contemplate the past and the way in which they contemplate the present (Buckle).

We get our ethics from our history and judge our history by our ethics (Troeltsch).

It is a reproach of historians that they have too often turned history into a mere record of the butchery of men by their fellow men (Green).

Such is the unity of history that anyone who endeavours to tell a piece must feel that his first sentence tears a seamless web (Maitland).

In its amplest meaning history includes every trace and every vestige of everything that man has done or thought since he first appeared on the earth (J. Harvey Robinson).

History is the story of the deeds and achievements of men living in societies (Pirenne).

The quickest and the surest way of finding the present in the past, but hardly the soundest, is to put it there first (McIlwain).

History is the sextant and compass of states, which, tossed by wind and current, would be lost in confusion if they could not fix their position (Nevins).

The historians are the guardians of tradition, the priests of the cult of nationality, the prophets of social reform, the exponents and upholders of national virtue and glory (Bagby).

The study of history is a personal matter, in which the activity is generally more valuable than the result (V. H. Galbraith).

A society sure of its values had needed history only to celebrate the glories of the past, but a society of changing values and consequent confusions also needed history as a utilitarian guide (Cochran).

Man generally is entangled in insoluble problems; history is consequently a tragedy in which we are all involved, whose keynote is anxiety and frustration, not progress and fulfilment (Arthur Schlesinger Jr.).

The study of the past with one eye, so to speak, upon the present is the source of all sins and sophistries in history (Butterfield).

The task of the historian is to understand the peoples of the past better than they understood themselves (Butterfield).

History fulfils a social need, and that is its essential function (Renier).

Political and social history are in my view two aspects of the same process. Social life loses half its interest and political movements lose most of their meaning if they are considered separately (Powicke).

What better preparation for a history which seeks to bring societies to life and to understand that life than to have really lived, commanded men, suffered with them and shared their joys (Febvre on Marc Bloch).

A document is a witness, and like most witnesses it rarely speaks until one begins to question it (Marc Bloch).

The conflict supposed to exist between materialistic and idealistic interpretations of history is an illusory one (Patrick Gardiner).

A mere collector of supposed facts is as useful as a collector of matchboxes (Febvre).

Consciousness of the past alone can make us understand the present (Herbert Luethy).

The aim of the historian, like that of the artist, is to enlarge our picture of the world, to give us a new way of looking at things (James Joll).

History free of all values cannot be written. Indeed, it is a concept almost impossible to understand, for men will scarcely take the trouble to inquire laboriously into something which they set no value upon (W. H. B. Court).

The justification of all historical study must ultimately be that it enhances our self-consciousness, enables us to see ourselves in perspective, and helps us towards that greater freedom which comes from self-knowledge (Keith Thomas).

History is not a succession of events, it is the links between them (Evans-Pritchard).

It is a mark of *civilised* man that he seeks to understand his traditions, and to criticise them, not to swallow them whole (M. I. Finley).

Sociology is history with the hard work left out; history is sociology with the brains left out (D. G. MacRae).

Periodization is indispensable to historical understanding of any kind (Gordon Leff).

A general history always requires an overall model, good or bad, against which events can be interpreted (Braudel).

No one any longer supposes that all that is required of the historian is the practical application of common sense (Geoffrey Barraclough).

To those who know no history, life seems a series of revolutions (Charles Wilson).

One of the most important obligations of the historian is to keep good faith with the dead and not score cheap points off them (John Cannon).

British historiography in the last 100 years provides a spectacular case of arrested intellectual development, and conceptual poverty (Gareth Stedman Jones).

Better hindsight deepens insight and makes for a less imperfect foresight (W. H. McNeill).

Dilthey and his successors had discovered how difficult historical explanation became once the traditional method of 'subject observes a clearly defined reality' was abandoned in favor of 'subject observes a reality at least partially constructed in the process of observing' (Ernst Breisach).

As can be seen, by its structures alone, without recourse to its content, historical discourse is essentially a product of ideology, or rather of imagination (Barthes).

The theory of ideology invites us to see that language is not simply a structure which can be employed for communication or entertainment, but a social–historical phenomenon which is embroiled in human conflict (John B. Thompson).

History as a discipline is not a form of art, and what each historian accomplishes he does not accomplish alone, as an individual: The significance of any historical inquiry, like the research of any scientist, depends directly upon what others have already done or will be enabled to do because of his work (Maurice Mandelbaum).

There is no such thing as 'innocent' historical explanation, and written history is itself located in history, indeed *is* history, the product of an inherently unstable relationship between the present and the past, a merging of the particular mind with the vast field of its potential topics of study in the past (François Furet).

The prudent historian does well to pause before translating the proverbial wisdom of the poets into the assumed behaviour of society (Neil McKendrick).

Appendix C: An Example of Myth and an Exercise in Source Criticism

Samuel Smiles was a highly popular Victorian writer; 250,000 copies of his *Self-Help* (first published 1859) were sold within his own lifetime. In these paragraphs from Chapter XIII of *Self-Help*, Smiles is appealing to actual historical occurrences in order to exemplify the Victorian concept of the gentleman. Smiles almost certainly believed in the truth of what he was writing, as would the overwhelming majority of his Victorian readers. In fact, these paragraphs form a classic instance of myth, founded in events which actually happened, but distorted and exaggerated to support a particular propagandist message. This kind of 'history' was, indeed, taught in British schools till well into the twentieth century. Readers are invited to note for themselves the extremely dubious nature of the testimony upon which the account of the wreck of the *Birkenhead* is based. I'll make my own comment at the end.

Samuel Smiles, *Self-Help* (Second Edition, 1860), pp. 351–3.

Above all, the Gentleman is truthful. He feels that truth is the 'summit of being,' and the soul of rectitude in human affairs. Lord Chesterfield, with all his French leanings, when he came to define a gentleman, declared that Truth made his success; and nothing that he ever said commanded the more hearty suffrage of his nation. The Duke of Wellington, who had an inflexible horror of falsehood, writing to Kellerman, when that general was opposed to him in the Peninsula, told him that, if there was one thing on which an English officer prided himself more than another, excepting his courage, it was his truthfulness. 'When English officers,' said he, 'have given their parole of honour not to escape, be sure they will not break it. Believe me – trust to their word; the word of an English officer is a surer guarantee than the vigilance of sentinels.'

True courage and gentleness go hand in hand. The brave man is generous and forbearant, never unforgiving and cruel. It was finely said of Sir John Franklin by his friend Parry, that 'he was a man who never turned his back upon a danger, yet of that tenderness that he would not brush away a musquito.' A fine trait of character – truly gentle, and worthy of the spirit of Bayard – was displayed by a French officer in the cavalry combat of El Bodon in Spain. He had raised his sword to strike Sir Felton Harvey, but perceiving his antagonist had only one arm, he instantly stopped, brought down his sword before Sir Felton in the usual salute, and rode past.

Notwithstanding the wail which we occasionally hear for the chivalry that is gone, our own age has witnessed deeds of bravery and gentleness – of heroic self-denial and manly tenderness – which are unsurpassed in history. The events of the last few years have shown that our countrymen are as yet an undegenerate race. On the bleak plateau of Sebastopol, in the dripping perilous trenches of that twelvemonths' leaguer, men of all classes proved themselves worthy of the noble inheritance of character which their forefathers have bequeathed to them. But it was in the hour of the greatest trial in India that the qualities of our countrymen shone forth the brightest. The march of Neill on Cawnpore, of Havelock on Lucknow – officers and men alike urged on by the hope of rescuing the women and the children – are events which the whole history of chivalry cannot equal. Outram's conduct to Havelock, in resigning to him, though his inferior officer, the honour of leading the attack on Lucknow, was a trait worthy of Syndey, and alone justifies the title which had been awarded to him of 'the Bayard of India.' The death of Henry Lawrence – that brave and gentle spirit – his last words before dying, 'Let there be no fuss about me; let me be buried *with the men*,' – the anxious solicitude of Sir Colin Campbell to rescue the beleaguered of Lucknow, and to conduct his long train of women and children by night from thence to Cawnpore, which he reached amidst the all but overpowering assault of the enemy, – the care with which he led them across the perilous bridge, never ceasing his charge over them until he had seen the precious convoy safe on the road to Allahabad, and then burst upon the Gwalior contingent like a thunderclap; – such things make us feel proud of our countrymen, and inspire the conviction that the best and purest glow of chivalry is not dead, but vigorously lives among us yet.

Even the common soldiers proved themselves gentlemen under their trials. At Agra, where so many poor fellows had been scorched and wounded in their encounter with the enemy, they were brought into the fort, and tenderly nursed by the ladies; and the rough, gallant fellows proved gentle as any children. During the weeks that the ladies watched over their charge, never a word was said by any soldier that could shock the ear of the gentlest. And when all was over – when the mortally-wounded had died, and the sick and maimed who survived were able to demonstrate their gratitude – they invited their nurses and the chief people of Agra to an entertainment in the beautiful gardens of the Taj, where, amidst flowers and music, the rough veterans, all scarred and mutilated as they were, stood up to thank their gentle countrywomen who had clothed and fed them, and ministered to their wants during their time of sore distress. In the hospitals at Scutari, too, many wounded and sick blessed the kind English ladies who nursed them; and nothing can be finer than the thought of the poor sufferers, unable to rest through pain, blessing the shadow of Florence Nightingale as it fell upon their pillow in the night watches.

The wreck of the *Birkenhead* off the coast of Africa on the 27th of February, 1852, affords another memorable illustration of the chivalrous spirit of common men acting in this nineteenth century, of which any age might be proud. The vessel was steaming along the African coast with 472 men and 166 women and children on board. The men belonged to several regiments then serving at the Cape, and consisted principally of recruits, who had been only a short time in the service. At two o'clock in the morning, while all were asleep below, the ship struck with violence upon a hidden rock which penetrated her bottom; and it was at once felt that she must go down. The roll of the drums called the soldiers to arms on the upper deck, and the men mustered as if on parade. The word was passed to *save the women and children*; and the helpless creatures were brought from below, mostly undressed, and handed silently into the boats. When they had all left the ship's side, the commander of the vessel thoughtlessly called out, 'All those that can swim, jump overboard and make for the boats.' But Captain Wright, of the 91st Highlanders, said, 'No! if you do that, *the boats with the women must be swamped*;' and the brave men stood motionless. There was no boat remaining, and no hope of safety; but not a heart quailed; no one flinched from his duty in that trying moment. 'There was not a murmur nor a cry amongst them,' said Captain Wright, a survivor, 'until the vessel made her final plunge.' Down went the ship, and down went the heroic band, firing a *feu de joie* as they sank beneath the waves. Glory and honour to the gentle and the brave! The examples of such men never die, but, like their memories, are immortal.

The evidence of Captain Wright's noble declaration and the bravery of the men, rests entirely on the testimony of Captain Wright himself who, rather peculiarly in the circumstances, was a survivor. One can only presume that Samuel Smiles and his readers were so intoxicated by this tale of heroism that they failed to apply those critical standards which it has been a major purpose of this book to advance.

Appendix D: Glossary

ANNALES, ANNALES 'SCHOOL': *Annales* is the historical journal founded in 1929 by Lucien Febvre and Marc Bloch, and given a new lease of life after 1945 when it was associated with the prestigious École des hautes Études en Sciences Sociales (to give the institution its most recent name). *Annales*, the journal, and the 'school' loosely associated with it and the École, are characterised above all by an insistence that history should make use of the discoveries of the social sciences and follow social science approaches. The approach (which in fact is far more diverse than usually assumed) has been described as structural-functionalist, and certainly *Annales* historians, greatly influenced by structuralism in anthroplogy, place great emphasis on what they perceive to be the underlying structures in history.

ARTS: in British universities a Faculty of Arts usually includes such subjects as English (or Literature), Philosophy, Art History, and also History. Sometimes 'The Arts' connnotes these various disciplines; on other occasions it means the 'creative arts' – that is to say painting, poetry, sculpture, etc.

ASSIMILATIONIST: the view that history should be assimilated to the methods of the natural sciences.

AUTONOMOUS: when applied to history it means the view that history has no relationship to the sciences, but has an autonomous, or independent methodology of its own.

CAPITALISM: used in a general way by historians to describe the kind of economic system that has existed for at least the last hundred or two hundred years in the 'western' countries, very definitely from the time of industrialisation, and with respect to important elements, since the commercial developments of the sixteenth, seventeenth, and eighteenth centuries: In Marxist discourse there is a more precise meaning, Marxism postulating that capitalism is the social order which succeeded feudalism, having overthrown it, and is now, in the contemporary period, subject to overthrow by working-class or socialist revolution.

CHARISMA: a term coined by the famous German socialist Max Weber meaning the almost magical qualities of attractiveness possessed by certain political leaders.

CLASS: as generally used by historians it means the broad aggregations of families and individuals into which modern societies divide, these aggregations falling into a rough hierarchy according to the wealth, influence, power, etc. possessed by individuals within each aggregation, and generally characterised by common life-styles, patterns of behaviour, etc. Such historians would see classes as coming into existence only in, say, the later eighteenth century, under the impetus of industrialisation and the political upheavals of the time. Marxists, however, apply the term to all periods of history, and in a precise technical way. According to Marxism a person's class is determined by their relationship to the dominant mode of production, and in every 'stage' of history one class will dominate – for example the bourgeois, or capitalist class, in the age of capitalism.

CLASS AWARENESS: an awareness of belonging to a particular class without necessarily feeling that this involves conflict or a need to take action.

CLASS CONSCIOUSNESS: this is a specifically Marxist term and occurs, or is alleged to occur, when members of a class become aware of the way in which their interests are in conflict with those of another class and are prepared to take action in pursuit of their interests.

COMPARATIVE HISTORY: history which, by fixing on like or analogous institutions or practices in different countries, produces comparisons and contrasts between these countries.

CONDITIONS OF CULTURAL CONSUMPTION: the market conditions within which novels are purchased and read, paintings are bought and exhibited, plays are watched, music listened to, etc.

CONDITIONS OF CULTURAL PRODUCTION: the social, economic, political, and ideological context within which cultural artefacts are produced.

CONJONCTURE: favoured term of *Annales* historians – trend or cycle (e.g. of prices), seen as operating within the constraints of structure and the *longue durée*.

CONTINGENCY: unexpected event or circumstance.

CULTURAL THEORY: an approach to the study of the arts which stresses the importance of the social and historical context and is based on Marxist assumptions about class, ideology, and the dialectic.

CULTURALLY CONSTRUCTED: (as in, say, sexual practices or notions of beauty) created by the society to which they belong – as distinct from having any natural or universal existence.

CULTURE: (a) ('Anthropological' meaning) the entire network of activities, practices and institutions within a given society; (b) ('aesthetic' meaning) the artistic and leisure activities and products of a given society.

DEVELOPMENTAL HISTORY: history which sees each age as developing out of the previous age.

DIALECTIC: originating with Plato, developed by Hegel and then by Marx, a concept postulating that within every society there is thesis and antithesis, dominant idea and countervailing idea, existing mode of production, and emerging mode of production, dominant ideology and alternative ideology. This concept lies at the heart of even the most sophisticated contemporary Marxist thinking though it has no basis in empirical observation.

DIPLOMATICS: the science of the study of charters, decrees, etc., and of the style and language in which they are written.

DISCOURSE THEORY: an approach which posits language as the central (and in some cases only) subject for academic study. All primary sources, it is alleged, embody one or more *discourses* (originally simply a unit of writing or speech longer than a sentence) which are seen as expressing the structure of power in a particular society; rather than divide sources into different categories, the crucial task is to identify different discourses. Heavily dependent on Marxist assumptions about dominance and ideology.

DISENCHANTMENT: the usual sociological, though rather inaccurate, translation of Max Weber's German word *Entzauberung*. A better translation would be 'demagification'. Weber, and many historians following him, have seen this as a characteristic of modernisation, the rejection of old authorities, superstitions, etc.

DISSERTATION: the typed, book-length product, which a scholar submits for a degree (for example Ph.D.) or other academic honour or status. In English sometimes also described as a 'thesis'.

ENTZAUBERUNG: see DISENCHANTMENT.

EXEMPLAR HISTORY: history designed to teach potential members of the ruling élite how to govern.

FEUDALISM (adjective FEUDAL): the term was invented in the seventeenth century to describe the legal and social order prevailing in most European countries in the Middle Ages: originally, its essential feature was that men held land from their superior by virtue of performing for him some designated service (for example, military service). In Marxist discourse the term has a more precise connotation as defining the 'stage' in the unfolding of history which preceded capitalism.

GENERAL HISTORY, A: obviously such a term could mean almost anything, but as used in *this* book it refers to a work which is more wide ranging than a monograph, but which contains far more original research than a textbook.

GLOBAL HISTORY: could mean world history, but as used by recent members of the *Annales* school it means history which integrates together all aspects, cultural, social, economic, and perhaps political.

HEGEMONY: in traditional history this simply meant the power or influence exercised over several countries by one country: for instance, in pre-1914 European history, one might talk of German hegemony over eastern Europe. However, in contemporary Marxist cultural theory (developed from the work of Gramsci) hegemony refers to the cultural monopoly allegedly exercised by the dominant class: thus it is alleged that working-class cultural practices (such as reading books by right-wing authors) are not really 'genuinely' working-class at all, but simply a part of bourgeois hegemony.

HERMENEUTIC: pertaining to the understanding of texts.

HERMENEUTICS: the study of the understanding of texts (however a special Marxist version has developed in the last 20 years, associated in particular with the German Marxist scholar Jurgen Habermas).

HISTORICISM (adjective HISTORICIST): an approach which sees history as an absolutely central discipline because it postulates that everything is explained by its past development, while at the same time insisting that each age has unique characteristics, and a unique value of its own (however, the word has more recently been taken over by Karl Popper to refer to grand scale theorising about history – metahistory I call it – particularly Marxism).

HISTORIOGRAPHY: the systematic study of historians' interpretations of (or writings about) the past.

HISTORY: in the course of this book I suggest six different ways in which the word can be used. Probably the three most important uses are:
1. the past as we know it through the activities of historians (i.e. the *subject area* or *body of knowledge*);
2. the systematic study of the past (i.e. the *discipline*);

3. the interpretations produced by historians (i.e. *historical writing*).

HOLISTIC (when applied to history): a view which sees the whole of history (in the sense of process or 'the past') as a self-contained unity as, say, in a religious view of history, or even a Marxist one.

HUMANITIES: sometimes an alternative for 'Arts' as in the first definition given above; sometimes taken to include both the arts in that sense and the social sciences.

IBID. (as used in footnote references): means that the source is exactly the same as the one given in the previous footnote.

IDEAL TYPE: another concept coined by Max Weber meaning an abstract, average, or 'model' type, not something that actually exists, but a composite of all the basic characteristics: for instance, one could create the 'ideal type' of the medieval peasant, which would have all the characteristics agreed upon by historians, but would not be any actual peasant who really lived (note that 'ideal' means 'pertaining to an idea', or 'in the mind', it does not mean 'perfect').

IDEOGRAPHIC: represented entirely visually (as in a picture) and without the use of words: for example as in an inn sign.

IDEOLOGY:
1. Cluster or system of ideas, values and beliefs (of e.g., an entire society, a social group, a political party);
2. (In Marxism, Cultural Theory, and Discourse Theory) the system of ideas, values and beliefs through which the ruling class preserves its dominance.

IDIOGRAPHIC: the approach to history which argues that history is entirely different from the sciences and should follow purely pragmatic approaches of its own.

IMPERIALISM: the attitude of mind pertaining to the support of the idea of empire, that is to say one country ruling over, and exploiting, others. In Marxist thought imperialism is seen as an advanced stage of capitalism, and as belonging specifically to the period after 1880. Other historians would argue that imperialism can happen in many different ages.

INTEGRAL HISTORY: history which integrates together cultural, social, economic and political aspects.

LOC. CIT.: technical term used in footnotes, meaning the same place (page, etc.) as has already been cited.

LONGUE DURÉE: basic term of *Annales* school: the almost unchanging long-term structures of everyday life which act as a constraint upon shorter-term trends (*conjonctures*).

MARXISM: the approach to history developed by Karl Marx and refined by his followers, stressing that history, conceived of as process, unfolds in a series of stages which, after the current phase of bourgeois capitalism, will lead to the triumph of the proletariat and the classless society, that the dialectic (the existing mode of production coming into conflict with an emergent mode of production) is central to this process of unfolding, and that class conflict is the motor of history, classes being determined by their relationship to the dominant mode of production (see also CLASS CONSCIOUSNESS and IDEOLOGY).

MENTALITIES: the mental sets, attitudes and outlook, of particular groups or even of whole societies.

METAHISTORY: grand-scale theorising in history as in Marxism, or the writings of Spengler or Toynbee.

MIDDLE AGES: the term originates in the Renaissance and applies to the period of history between classical times and the Renaissance: it is important to note that the phrase can only be applied to European history, and has no meaning for most of the rest of the world.

MODERNISATION: used to describe the whole complex network of developments which are held to be characteristic of the modern world, e.g. exploitation of technology, economic growth, mass society, etc., etc.

MONOGRAPH: published scholarly work which goes in great depth into one topic, usually wider than a Ph.D. dissertation, but narrower than a 'general history'.

MYTH: a version of the past which usually has some element of truth in it, but which distorts what actually happened in support of some vested interest.

NEGOTIATION: has an obvious and straightforward meaning in political history, but as used in Marxist cultural theory refers to the way in which, allegedly, the dominant ideology 'negotiates' with alternative ideologies in order to maintain the hegemony of the ruling class.

NOMINALISM: originally the doctrine that concepts have no realities corresponding to them, used in historical study to apply to an approach to history which denies any value to conceptual approaches or generalisation.

NOMOTHETIC: the approach to history which tries to assimilate it to the natural sciences by postulating general laws and the need for theory.

OP. CIT.: technical term used in footnotes, meaning the work already cited.

PALAEOBOTANY: the scientific study of the traces of old vegetation making it possible, for instance, to trace older patterns of cultivation in, say, medieval society.

PALAEOGRAPHY: the science of studying archaic forms of handwriting.

PARADIGM (in historiography): the (alleged) dominant approach to historical study in any particular period or society, hence for example, the exemplar paradigm, the developmental paradigm, and the functional-structural or *Annales* paradigm, or, say, the progressive paradigm, the new left paradigm, etc., etc.

PASSIM: technical term in footnotes meaning that the point being cited can be found in many places throughout the book being referred to.

PAST, THE: what has actually happened, what has actually existed: always, at any point in time, gone for good, it is the basic subject area of the historian (or, more acurately, the *human* past is the basic subject area of the historian).

PHILOLOGY: the science of language.

POSITIVISM: the approach to history developed by Auguste Comte which tried to make history a science with regularities and general laws. However, Marxists often use the word to criticise what I have termed 'mainstream' history, that is to say, history which above all stresses the importance of the systematic criticism of primary sources. Though confusing, this usage can be legitimated because of the phrase used by the French scholar Fustel de Coulanges 'positivism of the document', which in effect was an extreme statement of the mainstream position.

PROCESS: series of continuous and interlinked developments; when one speaks of 'history as process' one has in mind that these developments are in some sense predetermined, or at least conform to a certain theory as to how they should develop (for example, Marxism).

PROSOPOGRAPHY: multiple biography, the building up of an interpretation of the past by detailed biographical studies of individuals.

PROTESTANT ETHIC: the attitude of hard work and saving associated (by Weber in the first place) with the Protestant religion.

PUBLIC HISTORY: the phrase was invented in America to apply to the public, and usually commercial use, of history, as in journalism, or in tracing family trees, or providing histories for business corporations.

RADICAL: literally 'from the roots': i.e. an extreme reformer; but the word has taken on various inflections of meaning, and in late nineteenth century usage, for example, really meant a rather moderate liberal reformer.

REGRESSION: a method of studying the past by starting with phenomena in the present which may in one way or another be survivals from the past.

RENAISSANCE: literally 'rebirth'; usually applied to the period of change (perhaps lasting several centuries) in which, to express matters in a rather unsatisfactory cliché, the medieval or feudal world in Europe came to an end. The essential original characteristic was the revival or rebirth of classical learning.

REVOLUTION: overthrow of existing system or set of ideas: in political history means more than a simple *coup d'état* or change of ruler, and always implies some change affecting more groups in society than simply the ruling family.

SEMIOLOGY: the science of the signs by which human beings communicate.

SEMIOTICS: the study of patterns of human behaviour in communication in all its modes.

SERIAL HISTORY: history based on the premise that statistical series (of landholding, prices, etc., etc.) provide a firm structural base to which other social phenomena can be related.

SEROLOGY: the study of blood groups; can be useful for tracing population movements in the past for societies for which there is little other evidence.

SOCIAL CONTROL: used by right-wing sociologists to explain the way in which stability is maintained in societies, and by left-wing sociologists and historians to explain the way in which the dominant class, allegedly, maintains its hegemony.

SOCIOLOGY OF KNOWLEDGE: an approach to academic study which maintains that everything is socially constructed.

SOURCE, PRIMARY: a relic of a past age (document, artefact, etc.) which originated in that age.

SOURCE, SECONDARY: an interpretation written up later, using (if a serious historical work) primary sources.

STATUS: Weber made a distinction between an individual's class, which he held to be an entirely economic category and their status group, which referred to their position on the prestige hierarchy. Historians often use the word class to include prestige as well as economic elements.

STRUCTURAL: when applied to a 'force' or 'factor' in history, it means relating to economic, industrial, and technological developments. When used generally of an approach to history, it means an approach which stresses such factors.

STRUCTURALISM: An approach to academic study which originated in linguistics, but which was also developed in social anthropology. It is the structuralism of social anthropology which has affected some historical writing, particularly that associated with *Annales*. Structuralism seeks to find basic structures in human behaviour and human societies and stresses that a principle of communication lies behind many human customs. Structuralism becomes readily linked to Marxism and Cultural and Linguistic theory insofar as it 'seeks its structures not on the surface, at the level of the observed, but below or behind empirical reality' (Michael Lane, 1970).

STRUCTURE: usually, in historical discourse, used in the sense of a basic relationship or framework which explains other phenomena in the same society; the best dictionary definition I know is: 'the mutual relation of the constituent parts or elements of a whole as determining its particular nature or character.' As used by *Annales* school means fundamental characteristics of society which change only slowly, and which constrain shorter term economic trends, *conjonctures*.

THESIS: can be used in two very different ways: (1) the hypothesis, or theory, of interpretation put forward by a particular historian, as in Turner's 'Frontier Thesis'; (2) as a synonym for dissertation (for a Ph.D., etc.).

TOTAL HISTORY: history which endeavours to integrate together all aspects of human society, aesthetic and cultural, as well as social economic and political, private as well as public.

WHIG INTERPRETATION OF HISTORY: the view, prevalent in nineteenth-century Britain, that history was steady progress towards liberal ideas and institutions.

Bibliography

There is an excellent classified bibliography by Martin Klein in Louis Gottschalk (ed.), *Generalization in the Writing of History* (Chicago, 1963) pp. 231–47. The present bibliography is more selective, but includes the main works published since 1963. It does not include the historical (as distinct from historiographical) works mentioned in the text or notes. A splendid bibliography ranging across many continents can be found in Geoffrey Barraclough, *Main Trends in History* (New York, 1979). There is also a useful bibliography in Ernst Breisach, *Historiography: Ancient, Medieval and Modern* (Chicago, 1983).

A. History of History

Antonio, Carlo, *From History to Sociology: the Transition in German Historical Thought* (Detroit, 1959).

Ausubel, Herman *et al.* (eds.), *Some Modern Historians of Britain* (New York, 1952).

Ausubel, Herman, *Historians and their Craft: a Study of Presidential Addresses to the American Historical Association 1884–1945* (New York, 1950).

Barnes, H. Elmer, *A History of Historical Writing* (Norman, Okla, 1936; revised pb edn, New York, 1962): encyclopaedic; too often reads like an encyclopaedia.

Beasley, W. G. and Pulleybank, Edwin, *Historians of China and Japan* (London and New York, 1961).

Bell, Henry E., *Maitland: a Critical Examination and Assessment* (London, 1965).

Bellot, H. Hale, *American History and American Historians* (Norman, Okla, and London, 1952).

Bendix, Reinhard, *Max Weber: an Intellectual Portrait* (Garden City, N.Y., and London, 1960).

Black, J. B., *The Art of History* (London, 1926): a study of the Enlightenment historians.

Breisach, Ernst, *Historiography: Ancient, Medieval, and Modern* (Chicago, 1983): comprehensive and authoritative.

Brumfitt, J. H., *Voltaire: Historian* (London, 1958).

Burke, Peter (ed.), *Economy and Society in Early Modern Europe* (London, 1972): essays from *Annales*, brilliantly introduced – the best starting point.

Butterfield, Herbert, *Man on his Past: The Study of the History of Historical Writing* (Cambridge, 1955; Boston, Mass., 1966).

Butterfield, Herbert, *The Whig Interpretation of History* (London, 1931).

Cannon, John (ed.), *The Historian at Work* (1980): authoritative essays on individual historians with an excellent editor's introduction.

Clark, G. N., *Sir John Harold Clapham, 1873–1946* (London, 1947).

Drion de Chapois, François, *Henri Pirenne* (Brussels, 1964).

Finley, M. I., *The Greek Historians: the Essence of Herodotus, Thucydides, Xenophon, Polybius* (New York, 1959; London, 1960).

Fisher, H. A. L., *Frederick William Maitland* (London, 1910): interesting for what it tells about Fisher and his generation, as well as for what it says about Maitland.

Fitzsimons, M. A., Pundt, A. C. and Nowell, C. E., *The Development of Historiography* (Harrisburg, Pa, 1954): brief, useful, dull.

Galbraith, V. H., *Historical Research in Medieval England* (London, 1951).

Gooch, G. P., *History and Historians of the Nineteenth Century* (New York, 1949; London, 1952).

Hale, J. R., *The Evolution of British Historiography: From Bacon to Namier* (London and New York, 1967).

Halperin, S. William, *Some 20th Century Historians* (Chicago, 1961): contains illuminating essays by James L. Cate on Pirenne, Henry R. Winkler on Trevelyan, Gordon H. McNeil on Lefebvre, S. William Halperin on Renouvin, and Palmer A. Throop on Febvre.

Hay, Denys, *Annalists and Historians: Western Historiography from the VIIIth to the XVIIIth Century* (1977).

Higham, John with Krieger, Leonard and Gilbert, Felix, *History* (Englewood Cliffs, N.J., 1965): a classic account covering American and some leading European historians.

Higham, John, *History: Professional Scholarship in America* (new edition, Baltimore, 1983): authoritative for American developments in the twentieth century.

Hofstadter, Richard, *The Progressive Historians: Turner, Beard, Parrington* (New York, 1968; London, 1969).

Hughes, H. Stuart, *Consciousness and Society: the Reorientation of European Social Thought 1890–1930* (New York, 1958; London 1959): intellectual history at its finest, specially relevant here for chapter 6 on Dilthey, Croce and Meinecke.

Iggers, George, *New Directions in European Historiography* (revised edition, 1985): absolutely indispensable.

Iggers, George, *The German Conception of History* (1968).

Kenyon, John, *The History Men: The Historical Profession in England since the Renaissance* (1983): very strong on the earlier periods, very brief on the twentieth century.

Kohn, Hans (ed.), *German History: Some new German Views* (Boston, Mass., and London, 1954).

Knowles, M. David, *Great Historical Enterprises: Problems in Monastic History* (Cambridge, 1963).

Lambie, Joseph T. (ed.), *Architects and Craftsmen in History* (Tübingen, 1956): includes valuable essays by F. C. Lane (on Schmoller, Sombart and Schumpeter), Edgar Salin (on Sombart), C. B. Welles (on Rostovtzeff), Lucien Febvre (on Bloch) and Charles Verlinden (on Pirenne), with a stimulating introduction by W. N. Parker.

Momigliano, A. D., *Studies in Historiography* (London, 1966): mainly concentrates on ancient history, with a particularly valuable study of Rostovtzeff (whom, unfortunately, I have had to leave out of this edition).

Powicke, F. M., *Historical Study in Oxford* (London, 1929).

Schlesinger, Arthur Sr, *In Retrospect: the History of an Historian* (New York, 1963).

Schuyler, R. L. (ed.), *Frederick William Maitland, Historian: Selections from his writings . . . with an introduction . . .* (Berkeley, Calif., 1960).

Shafer, Boyd C., François, Michel, Mommsen, W. J., and Milne, A. T., *Historical Study in the West* (1968).

Smith, Page, *The Historian and History* (New York, 1966).

Smith Fussner, F., *The Historical Revolution: English Historical Writing and Thought, 1580–1640* (London and New York, 1962).

Snyder, P. L. (ed.). *Carl L. Becker: Detachment and the Writing of History* (New York, 1958).

Stedman Jones, Gareth, 'History: the Poverty of Empiricism', in R. Blackburn (ed.), *Ideology in Social Science* (1972) pp. 96–115: fine knockabout attack on the 'conceptual poverty' of British history.

Stern, Friz (ed.), *The Varieties of History: Voltaire to the Present* (Cleveland, Ohio, 1956; 2nd edn London, 1971): the justly famous and indispensable collection of readings.

Syme, Ronald, *Tacitus* (Oxford, 1958).

Thompson, G. M., *Gibbon* (London, 1948).

Thompson, James Westfall, *A History of Historical Writing*, 2 vols (New York, 1942): still an important work of reference, though there are many inaccuracies, and the judgements are trite.

Tomlin, E. W. F., *R. G. Collingwood* (London and New York, 1953).

Wish, Harvey, *American Historians* (New York, 1962).

Wish, Harvey, *The American Historian* (New York, 1960).

Woodman, A. J., *Rhetoric in Classical Historiography* (1988).

B. Theory, Method and Philosophy of History.

Abrams, Philip, *Historical Sociology* (Shepton Mallet, 1982): pleads for a merging of history and sociology, but on Marxist terms.

Aron, Raymond, *Introduction to the Philosophy of History* (London, 1961).

Ashley, M. P., *Is History Bunk?* (London, 1958).

Ashley-Montague, M. F. (ed.), *Toynbee and History* (Boston, Mass., 1956).

Atkinson, R. E., *Knowledge and Explanation in History* (London, 1978): a philosopher who really understands historians.

Bagby, Philip, *Culture and History* (London, 1958; Berkeley, Calif., 1959).

Ballard, Martin, (ed.), *New Movements in the Study and Teaching of History* (1970).

Barraclough, Geoffrey, *History in a Changing World* (Oxford, 1955; Norman, Okla, 1956).

✓ Barraclough, Geoffrey, *Main Trends in History* (1979): indispensable and wide-ranging study.

✓ Barzun, Jacques and Graff, Henry F., *The Modern Researcher* (New York, 1957; revised edn 1977): wise advice on how to go about writing history at all levels.

Barzun, Jacques, *Clio and the Doctors* (Chicago, 1974): ultraconservative.

Beale, Howard K., 'The Professional Historian: his Theory and his Practice' in *Pacific History Review*, XXII (1953).

Bebbington, D., *Patterns in History* (Leicester, 1979).

Bedarida, François, 'The Modern Historians' Dilemma: Conflicting Pressures from Science and Society', *Economic History Review*, XL (1987).

Bennett, Tony, *et al.* (eds.). *Culture, Ideology and Social Process* (London, 1981): useful samplings of approaches of which I have been critical.

Benson, Susan Porter, Brier, Stephen and Rosenzweig, Roy, *Presenting the Past: Essays on history and the public* (New York, 1980): essays in support of public history.

Beresford, M. W. and St Joseph, J. K. S., *Medieval England: an Aerial Survey* (Cambridge, 1958).

Berlin, Isaiah, *Historical Inevitability* (London, 1954; New York, 1955).

Berlin, Isaiah, *The Hedgehog and the Fox* (London and New York, 1953): a study of Tolstoy, but containing material of wider general importance.

Best, G. F. A., 'History, Politics, and Universities', in *Philosophical Journal*, VI (July, 1969).

Bloch, Marc, *The Historian's Craft* (Manchester and New York, 1954): classic by one of the two founders of the first generation of the *Annales* school.

Bottomore, T. B. and Rubel, M., *Karl Marx: Selected Writings in Sociology and Social Philosophy* (London, 1956; pb edn 1967).

✓ Braudel, Fernand, *On History* (London, 1980): collection of

writings by the historian regarded by many as the greatest of
his generation.

British Universities Film Council, *Film and the Historian* (1968).
✓Brooke, C. N. L., *The Dullness of the Past* (Liverpool, 1957).
Burke, Peter, *History and Sociology* (1980).
Burston, W. H. and Thompson, D. (eds), *Studies in the Nature
and Teaching of History* (London, 1967): contains some very
important articles by S. W. F. Holloway, W. H. Walsh and
others.
Bury, J. B., *Selected Essays* (London, 1930).
Butterfield, Herbert, *History and Human Relations* (London,
1951).
Cahnman, Werner J. and Boskoff, A. (eds), *Sociology and
History: Theory and Research* (New York, 1964).
✓Canary, Robert H., and Kozicki, Henry, *The Writing of History:
literary form and historical understanding* (Madison, Wis.,
1978).
Cantor, Norman and Schneider, R., *How to Study History* (New
York, 1967).
Carr, E. H., *What is History?* (London, 1961; New York, 1962;
pb edn, 1964): still stimulating in many ways, but ought to have
been titled *What E. H. Carr Thought History Ought to Be*;
contains some misconceptions.
Centre for Contemporary Cultural Studies, *Making Histories:
studies in history-writing and politics* (1982): taxing introduction
to sophisticated Marxism; intellectually exciting but has the feel
of a self-contained game detached from history as one actually
knows it.
Childe, V. Gordon, *What is History?* (New York, 1953): a brief
study, first published in England as *History* (London, 1947).
Clark, G. Kitson, *The Critical Historian* (London, 1967).
Clark, G. Kitson, *Guide for Research Students working in
Historical Subjects* (Cambridge, 1960).
Cochran, Thomas C., *The Inner Revolution: Essays on the Social
Sciences in American History* (New York, 1964).
Collingwood, R. G., *An Autobiography* (London, 1939).
Collingwood, R. G., *The Idea of History* (London, 1964).
Collingwood, R. G., *The Philosophy of History* (London, 1930):
much less subtle than *The Idea of History*, this last pamphlet
forms a useful introduction to Collingwood's thought.

Commager, H. S., *The Nature and the Study of History* (Columbus, Ohio, 1965).

Connell-Smith, Gordon and Lloyd, Howell, A., *The Relevance of History* (London, 1972).

Conway, David, *A Farewell to Marx: an outline and appraisal of his theories* (1987).

Crombie, A. C. (ed.), *Scientific Change* (New York, 1963): contains important essays on history of science by A. C. Crombie and M. A. Hoskin, and by Henry Guerlac.

Crump, C. G., *History and Historical Research* (London, 1928): useful for British professional orthodoxy in the 1920s.

Daniels, Robert V., *Studying History: How and Why* (Englewood Cliffs, N.J., 1966): useful, but rather elementary.

Davis, Ralph, *History and the Social Sciences* (1965).

Denley, Peter, and Hopkin, Deian (eds), *History and Computing*, (Manchester University Press, 1987).

Dickinson, A. K., Lee, P. J. and Rogers, P. J., *Learning History* (1984): useful essays.

Donagan, Alan and Barbara, *Philosophy of History* (New York, 1965): brief excerpts from Augustine, Vico, Hegel, Dilthey, and so on.

Dovring, Folke, *History as a Social Science* (The Hague, 1960);

Dray, W. H., *Philosophy of History* (Englewood Cliffs, N.J., 1964): ideal encapsulation of the topics which, to a professional philosopher, make up 'philosophy of history'.

✓ Dunne, Tom (ed.), *The Writer as Witness: literature as historical evidence* (Irish Historical Studies XVI, Cork, 1987): collection of solid essays with excitable introduction which cites the usual authorities in asserting, unpersuasively, that history 'is a statement as personal in its way as that of the poet or novelist.'

Dyos, H. J. (ed.), *The Study of Urban History* (London, 1968).

Elton, G. R., *Political History: Principles and Practice* (London, 1970).

Elton, G. R., *The Practice of History* (London, 1967): clear statement of the mainstream professional position.

Esposito, Joseph L., *The Transcendence of History: essays on the evolution of historical consciousness* (Athens, Ohio, 1984): of little relevance to practising historians.

Evans-Pritchard, E. E., *Anthropology and History* (Manchester, 1961).

Ferro, Marc, *L'histoire sous surveillance* (Paris, 1985): stimulating, naturally, but rather assertive on behalf of the *Annales* school.

✓ Ferro, Marc, *The Use and Abuse of History: or how the past is taught* (1984): fabulously informative, provides the essential justification for the systematic study of history.

Film et Histoire, in *XVIe Congrès Internationale de Science Historique: Rapport*, vol. 1, pp. 180–239: with essays by Fledelius, two Germans, a Russian, Sorlin and Marwick, this is probably the best guide within a short space to both methods and literature.

Finberg, H. P. R. (ed.), *Approaches to History* (London and Toronto, 1962): contains important essays by S. T. Bindoff, David Talbot Rice, Harold Perkin and many others.

Fischer, David H., *Historians' Fallacies* (1970).

Fleischer, Helmut, *Marxism and History* (1969).

Floud, Roderick, *An Introduction to Quantitative Methods for Historians* (1973).

Furet, François, *In the Workshop of History* (Chicago, 1984): almost jingoistic assertion of the case for the *Annales* approach.

Galbraith, V. H., *An Introduction to the Study of History* (London, 1964).

Galbraith, V. H., *The Historian at Work* (London, 1962).

Gardiner, Patrick (ed.), *Theories of History* (Glencoe, III., 1959): a useful collection of readings.

Gardiner, Patrick, *The Nature of Historical Explanation* (1952): historical explanation as most historians themselves understand it (if and when they think about it at all).

Gay, Peter, *Style in History* (New York, 1974): studies Gibbon, Ranke, Macaulay and Burckhardt; says history is art and science.

Gay, Peter, *Art and Act: on causes in history – Manet, Gropius, Mondrian* (New York, 1976): studies three artists; says causation is complex.

Gay, Peter, *Freud for Historians* (New York, 1985): since Gay has magnificently practised what he preaches in *The Bourgeois Experience: Victoria to Freud* this guide is fully worthy of attention.

Gerth, H. H. and Wright Mills, C., (eds), *From Max Weber: Essays in Sociology* (London, 1948).

Geyl, Pieter, *Debates with Historians* (Cleveland, Ohio, 1958).

Glass, D. V. and Eversley, D. E. C., *Population in History* (London, 1965).

✓ Gottschalk, Louis (ed.), *Generalization in the Writing of History* (Chicago, 1963).

Gottschalk, Louis, *Understanding History: A Primer of Historical Method* (New York, 1951).

Guerlac, Henry, 'Some historical assumptions of the history of science' in A. C. Crombie (ed.), *Scientific Change* (New York, 1963), pp. 797–812: re-reading this essay I was struck by how much wisdom is condensed into so little space.

Gustavson, Carl G., *A Preface to History* (New York, 1955): rather elementary.

Hamerow, Theodore S., *Reflections on History and Historians* (Madison, Wis., 1987): original study of the nature of the historical profession.

Hancock, W. K., *Country and Calling* (1954): interesting testimony of a mainstream professional of his generation.

Hancock, W. K., *Professing History* (Sidney, 1974).

Handlin, Oscar, *Truth in History* (London, 1979).

Handlin, Oscar, *et al.*, *The Harvard Guide to American History* (Cambridge, Mass., 1954): part I is an admirable introduction to the Nature and Methods of History.

Hexter, J. H., *Reappraisals in History* (Evanston, Ill., and London, 1961).

Hexter, J. H., *The History Primer* (1971): very idiosyncratic.

Hexter, J. H., *On Historians: Reappraisals of Some of the Makers of Modern History* (1979).

History and Social Science, in *International Social Science Journal*, XVII 4 (1965).

Hockett, Homer C., *The Critical Method in Historical Research and Writing* (New York, 1955).

Hoskins, W. G., *Field Work in Local History* (London, 1967).

Howard, Michael, *The Lessons of History: An Inaugural Lecture* (Oxford, 1981).

Hughes, H. Stuart, *History as Art and as Science* (New York, 1964).

Hughes, H. Stuart, 'The Historian and the Social Scientist' in *American Historical Review*, LXVI (Oct 1960).

Iggers, George, 'The Image of Ranke in American and German Historical Thought' in *History and Theory*, II (1962).

Irish Committee of Historical Sciences, *Historical Studies*, I, II and III (1958–60): important papers by Alfred Cobban, Denys Hays, W. H. Walsh and others.

Knowles, M. D., *The Historian and Character* (Cambridge, 1963).

Koebner, Richard, 'Semantics and Historiography' in *Cambridge Journal*, VII (1953).

Komarovsky, Mirra, *Common Frontiers of the Social Sciences* (Glencoe, Ill., 1957).

Krieger, J. B., 'The Historical Value of Motion Pictures' in *The American Archivist*, XXXI, 4 (Oct. 1968).

Ladurie, E. Leroy, *The Territory of the Historian* (London, 1979).

Lambert, Sir Henry C. M., *The Nature of History* (London, 1933): a rather slim essay.

Landes, David and Tilly, Charles (eds.), *History as a Social Science* (1971).

Lane, Michael (ed.), *Structuralism: A Reader* (1970): an excellent introduction; includes an essay on 'Historical Discourse' by Roland Barthes himself.

Langlois, C. V. and Seignobos, C., *Introduction to the Study of History* (London, 1898; new edn; London and New York, 1966).

Lee, Dwight E. and Beck, Robert N., 'The Meaning of "Historicism" ' in *American Historical Review*, LIX, 3 (April 1954).

Leff, Gordon, *History and Social Theory* (London, 1969): particularly strong on 'contingency', on the fragmentary nature of sources, and on the significance of periodisation.

Lewis, I. M. (ed.), *History and Social Anthropology* (London, 1968).

Lloyd, Christopher, *Explanation in Social History* (Oxford, 1986): comprehensive survey of almost everybody (Marx, Hempel, Habermas, Foucault, etc.) except those who actually write history, concluding, as it starts out, in favour of a theory-based, unified, sociological history.

Lowenthal, David, *The Past is a Foreign Country* (Cambridge, 1985): rich evocation of the potency of the past, embracing conservation, restoration, etc., etc. which quite fails to understand the activity and achievements of professional historians.

MacKisack, May, *History as Education* (London, 1958).

MacLennan, Gregor, *Marxism and the Methodologies of History*

(1981): insists that those who place great emphasis on the methodology of empirical history (as I do) are as ideologically motivated as any Marxist, but, interestingly, nowhere engages with
any of my own arguments on the matter.

Mandelbaum, Maurice, *The Anatomy of Historical Knowledge*
(Baltimore, 1977): pioneering philosopher in the field gives
mature reflections on what constitutes explanation in history
and whether historical knowledge is as reliable as other forms
of knowledge, and concludes (I agree) that historical explanations are adequate and historical knowledge securely-based.

Marho, *Visions of History* (Manchester, 1983): radical historians
speak, with some illuminating confessions from Eric
Hobsbawm.

Mazlish, Bruce, *The Riddle of History* (New York, 1966).

Merton, Robert K., *Social Theory and Social Structure* (Glencoe,
Ill., 1961).

Meyerhoff, Hans (ed.), *The Philosophy of History in Our Time*
(New York, 1959): useful collection of readings.

Morison, S. E., *Vistas of History* (New York, 1964).

Namier, L. B., *Avenues of History* (London, 1952): includes in
the essay on 'History' a condensed statement of Namier's views
on historical writing.

Neff, Emery, *The Poetry of History* (London, 1947).

Nevins, Allan, *The Gateway to History* (New York, 1938; revised
pb edn, 1962).

New Ways in History, *Times Literary Supplement*, 7 April, 28 July
and 8 September 1966: stimulating articles by Keith Thomas,
M. I. Finley, Peter Temin, Bruce Mazlish and many others.

Oakeshott, M. J., *Rationalism in Politics* (London, 1962).

Pares, Richard, *The Historian's Business* (Oxford, 1961).

Perkin, Harold, *History: A Guide for the Beginning Student*
(1970): introductions to the different 'sub-histories', with a
stimulating opening essay by Harold Perkin.

Plumb, J. H. (ed.), *Crisis in the Humanities* (London, 1964).

Plumb, J. H., *The Death of the Past* (London, 1969): a characteristically rich and life-enhancing affirmation of purpose in
history, though Plumb uses 'the past' almost in the sense of
'myth'.

Pointon, Marcia, *History of Art: A Students' Handbook* (1986): a revised edition, still fair to traditional approaches, which introduces the newer approaches.

Poster, Mark, *Foucault, Marxism and History: mode of production vs mode of information* (Cambridge, 1984): lucid and helpful.

Rabb, Theodore K. and Rotberg, Robert I., *The New History, the 1980s and Beyond: Studies in Interdisciplinary History*: interesting essays of variable quality,

Reappraisals: A New Look At History; The Social Sciences and History, *Journal of Contemporary History*, III, 2 (1968): papers by Herbert Luethy, Charles Morazé, C. Vann Woodward, Jean Marczewski and others.

Reddy, William M., *Money and Liberty in Modern Europe: a critique of historical understanding* (New York, 1986): shows where Marxist analysis of the various allegedly bourgeois revolutions has gone wrong, and strong on the misuse of metaphor in history.

Renier, Gustav J., *History: Its Purpose and Method* (London, 1950).

Ricoeur, Paul, *The Contribution of French Historiography to the Theory of History* (Oxford, 1980).

Roads, C. H., 'Film as Historical Evidence' in *Journal of Society of Archivists*, III (1966).

Rowse, A. L., *The Use of History* (London, 1946; New York, 1963).

Schmitt, Bernadotte, *The Fashion and Future of History* (Cleveland, Ohio, 1960).

Shorter, Edward, *The Historian and the Computer: a practical guide* (Englewood Cliffs, 1971).

Smith, Paul (ed.), *The Historian and Film* (Cambridge, 1976): a sound introduction.

Snell, John and Perkins, Dexter, *The Education of Historians in the United States* (New York, 1962).

Sorlin, Pierre, *The Film in History: restaging the past*: the opening section on methodology is particularly useful.

Southern, R. W., *The Shape and Substance of Academic History* (Oxford, 1961).

Stanford, Michael, *The Nature of Historical Knowledge* (Oxford, 1986): lucid study of the use of structures in history.

Stoianovich, Traian, *French Historical Method: the* Annales

Paradigm (Ithaca, N.Y., 1976): very thorough study of the *Annales* school.

Stone, Lawrence, *The Past and the Present* (Boston 1981): reprint of essays published between 1962 and 1980; chapter three 'The Revival of Narrative: Reflections on a new old history' is from *Past and Present*, 1979.

The Uses and Abuses of History, *Encounter*, XXXIII 4 (October 1969): essays by Max Beloff, Asa Briggs, Denis Brogan and others.

Tholfsen, Trygve, *Historical Thinking: an introduction* (New York, 1967).

Thomas, Keith, 'History and Anthropology' in *Past and Present*, no. 24 (April 1963).

Thompson, E. P., *The Poverty of Theory and Other Essays* (1978): the main essay is indispensable reading, with the defence of sound historical method coming over at least as strongly as the Marxist inflections.

Thomson, David, *The Aims of History* (London, 1969), a personal statement, stressing history as liberal education.

Thrupp, Sylvia, 'History and Sociology: New Opportunities for Cooperation', in *American Journal of Sociology*, LXIII I (July 1959).

Tosh, John, *The Pursuit of History: Aims, methods and new directions in the study of modern history* (1984): admirably achieves the objectives set out in the sub-title; strongly Marxist and therefore a useful antidote to my own book.

Toynbee, A. J., *The New Opportunity for Historians* (London, 1956).

Trevor-Roper, H. R., *History, Professional and Lay* (Oxford, 1957).

Trevor-Roper, H. R., *Men and Events* (London, 1957).

United States Social Science Research Council, *Bulletin 54: Theory and Practice in Historical Study* (Washington, 1946); *Bulletin 64: The Social Sciences in Historical Study* (Washington, 1954).

Veyne, Paul, *Writing History: essay on epistemology* (Manchester, 1984): latter-day defence of historical writing being analogous to novel-writing.

Walsh, W. H., *Introduction to the Philosophy of History* (London and New York, 1951; revised pb edn 1967): clear and unpretentious.

White, Hayden, *Metahistory: The Historical Imagination in Nineteenth-Century Europe* (Baltimore, 1973): declares *all* history to be rhetorical, poetic, philosophical.

White, Hayden, *Tropics of Discourse* (Baltimore, 1978): collection of essays with the same basic refrain.

Widgery, Alban Gregory, *Interpretations of History: Confucius to Toynbee* (London, 1950); *The Meanings in History* (London, 1967): both of these books are philosophical rather than historiographical in character.

Wilkins, Burleigh Taylor, *Has History any Meaning? A critique of Popper's philosophy of history* (Ithaca, N.Y., 1978).

Wilson, Edmund, *To the Finland Station: A Study in the Writing and Acting of History* (London, 1940; pb edn 1960).

Wolff, Janet, *The Social Production of Art* (London, 1981): this is not the place to broach the monstrous literature of cultural theory, but this book is a most sensible starting-point.

Index